Media, Economy and Soci<

This essential guide to the critical study of the media economy in society teaches students how to critically analyse the political economy of communication and the media.

The book introduces a variety of methods and topics, including the political economy of communication in capitalism, the political economy of media concentration, the political economy of advertising, the political economy of global media and transnational media corporations, class relations and working conditions in the capitalist media and communication industry, the political economy of the Internet and digital media, the information society and digital capitalism, the public sphere, Public Service Media, the Public Service Internet, and the political economy of media management.

This will be an ideal textbook for a variety of courses relating to media and communication, including Media Economics; Political Economy of Communication; Media, Culture, and Society; Critical Media and Communication Studies; Media Sociology; Media Management; and Media Business Studies.

Christian Fuchs is Professor of Media Systems and Media Organisation at Paderborn University, Germany. He is a critical theorist of communication and society. He is co-editor of the journal *tripleC: Communication, Capitalism & Critique*. He is author of many publications, including the books *Social Media: A Critical Introduction* (2021, third edition; 2024, fourth edition), *Digital Capitalism* (2022), and *Communication and Capitalism: A Critical Theory* (2020).

Media, Economy and Society
A Critical Introduction

Christian Fuchs

Routledge
Taylor & Francis Group

LONDON AND NEW YORK

Designed cover image: fotosipsak / Getty Images

First published 2024
by Routledge
4 Park Square, Milton Park, Abingdon, Oxon OX14 4RN

and by Routledge
605 Third Avenue, New York, NY 10158

Routledge is an imprint of the Taylor & Francis Group, an informa business

British Library Cataloguing-in-Publication Data
A catalogue record for this book is available from the British Library

ISBN: 978-1-032-48876-9 (hbk)
ISBN: 978-1-032-48875-2 (pbk)
ISBN: 978-1-003-39120-3 (ebk)

DOI: 10.4324/9781003391203

Typeset in Sabon
by codeMantra

Contents

Acknowledgement

I thank Malissa Rastoder for proofreading the English and German version of this book, Natalie Foster and Kelly O'Brien at Routledge for their editorial work, and the students at the University of Westminster and Paderborn University who attended my modules "Political Economy of Communication" and "Grundlagen der Medienökonomie" where the content of this book was developed between 2014 and 2023.

1 Introduction

What You Will Learn in This Chapter

- You will get a basic idea of what this book is about and an overview of its chapters.

1.1 Research Traditions in Media and Communication Studies

This book is an introduction to the critical study of the media and communication in the economy and society. It is focused on how to critically theorise and analyse the relationship between media, communication, the economy, and society. There are different ways, approaches, and traditions of doing so. The tradition and approach introduced in this book are also known as the critical research tradition. It differs from other research traditions.

1.1.1 The Lasswell Formula: A Traditional Research Approach

Media and Communication Studies is an academic field of inquiry that analyses how humans communicate and use media in society. A widely established understanding of Media and Communication Studies' tasks is the Lasswell Formula that was established by Harold Lasswell (1948): Who says what in which channel to whom with what effect? Figure 1.1 visualises the Lasswell Formula and the dimensions of Media and Communication Studies it defines.

Let us consider an example. We want to conduct research about Apple and the iPhone. Guided by the Lasswell Formula, we could therefore ask research questions such as the following ones:

- Who is the typical iPhone user?
- For what purposes do people use the iPhone? How often do they use specific apps?
- How often do they use the iPhone in comparison to other media?
- With whom does the iPhone user typically communicate? And how often?
- What are the effects of the use of the iPhone on users' everyday lives?

DOI: 10.4324/9781003391203-1

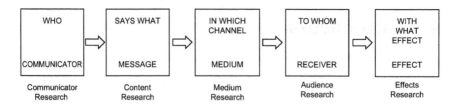

Figure 1.1 The Lasswell Formula.

1.1.2 *The Political Economy of Communication and the Media*

The Political Economy of Communication and the Media (PECM) is an approach and tradition of how to analyse the media and communication in society. It is a subfield of Media and Communication Studies that sees the Lasswell Formula and research questions such as the ones just formulated as insufficient. PECM is situated in what Paul Lazarsfeld (1941/2004) characterised as critical communication research in distinction from traditional communication research and what Max Horkheimer (1937/2002) characterises as critical theory in distinction from traditional theory (see also Smythe and Van Dinh 1983).

PECM asks questions about class, power structures, ethics, society, capitalism, domination, and ideology that are missing in traditional communication research. It uses social theory, empirical social research, and moral philosophy to analyse media and communication in the context of the interaction of the economy and politics. Critical research investigates power structures, inequalities, and injustices in society. PECM is a special type of critical research in that it is focused on media and communication in the context of society and gives particular attention to economic structures and their interaction with politics and society at large. This means that PECM is particularly interested in the analysis of the interaction of communication, class, and capitalism.

Concerning the iPhone and Apple, PECM asks, for example, research questions such as the following ones:

- Who are the owners of transnational communication companies such as Apple?
- What commodities does Apple sell? How have its profits and capital accumulation strategies developed?
- How concentrated is the ownership of the mobile phone market that Apple operates in? What are the implications of a concentrated mobile phone market for society?
- How does Apple present itself in advertisements? What are the problems of these ads for society? What kind of ideologies (sexism, stereotyping, racism, neoliberalism, etc.) can be found in the context of Apple and the iPhone advertising and how do they operate?
- How do transnational media corporations such as Apple operate in global capitalism? Who benefits from this system of globalisation and who has disadvantages?

- Who produces the iPhone under what working conditions? What is the role of class? How does class interact with gender and racism in the context of Apple?
- What are the problems society faces to which Apple contributes? What is the role of Apple in the context of these societal problems?

1.2 This Book

I developed a particular way of teaching the Political Economy of Communication and the Media (PECM) that I want to document in this book. The approach is focused on themes that each form a chapter in this book respectively one or more teaching unit(s) in my module. Each chapter is focused on one particular communication issue that matters to society.

The book has two parts. The first part (Foundations) covers the foundations of how to study the relationship of media, communication, economy, and society critically. Chapters 2–5 belong to Part 1. Part 2 is focused on applications. The "Applications" part of the book contains Chapters 6–14. It applies the critical foundations to concrete media phenomena, including media concentration, advertising, global media, cultural labour, the Internet, the information society, digital capitalism, the public sphere, Public Service Media, the Public Service Internet, and media management.

Each chapter asks one or more fundamental questions that we need to answer to understand how media and communication work in and beyond capitalist society. The following questions are addressed in this book:

- Chapter 2: What is Political Economy?
- Chapter 3: What is Media Economics?
- Chapter 4: What is the Political Economy of Communication and the Media (PECM)?
- Chapter 5: What are the features of the critical analysis of media, communication, the economy, and society?
- Chapter 6: How does the political economy of media concentration work? What are the causes, impacts, and problems of media concentration?
- Chapter 7: What is the role of advertising in capitalism? What are the problems of advertising for society?
- Chapter 8: How do transnational media corporations work and what is their role in capitalism?
- Chapter 9: How do class relations and working conditions look like in the capitalist media and communication industry?
- Chapter 10: How does the political economy of the Internet and digital media look like?
- Chapter 11: What kind of society do we live in? Do we live in an information society or a capitalist society? What is digital capitalism?
- Chapter 12: What does the political economy of the public sphere and the digital public sphere work?

- Chapter 13: How does the political economy of Public Service Media and the Public Service Internet look like?
- Chapter 14: What is media management and what does its political economy look like?

Each chapter includes recommended readings as well as exercises that I have myself used in the classroom and that have therefore been "tested" in actual teaching.

There are two other textbooks on the Political Economy of Communication and the Media, namely Vincent Mosco's (2009) book *The Political Economy of Communication* and Jonathan Hardy's (2014) *Critical Political Economy of the Media: An Introduction.* I have used both books along with other books (including my own book *Marxism: Karl Marx's Fifteen Key Concepts for Cultural and Communication Studies*, Fuchs 2020), chapters, and essays as materials in my teaching.

There is never one perfect textbook, so it is important that for institutionalising a specific field, a range of textbooks is developed. I, therefore, do not see my book as competing with Mosco's and Hardy's textbooks, but as complementing them and enabling teachers, students, and scholars, to access a wide range of materials that they can use in the learning and research process.

References

Fuchs, Christian. 2020. *Marxism: Karl Marx's Fifteen Key Concepts for Cultural and Communication Studies*. New York: Routledge.

Hardy, Jonathan. 2014. *Critical Political Economy of the Media: An Introduction.* Abingdon: Routledge.

Horkheimer, Max. 1937/2002. Traditional and Critical Theory. In *Critical Theory*, 188–252. New York: Continuum.

Lasswell, Harold. 1948. The Structure and Function of Communication in Society. In *The Communication of Ideas*, edited by Lyman Bryson, 32–51. New York: Harper & Row.

Lazarsfeld, Paul F. 1941/2004. Administrative and Critical Communications Research. In *Mass Communication and American Social Thought: Key Texts, 1919–1968*, edited by John Durham, 166–173. Lanham, MD: Rowman & Littlefield.

Mosco, Vincent. 2009. *The Political Economy of Communication*. London: SAGE. Second edition.

Smythe, Dallas W. and Tran Van Dinh. 1983. On Critical and Administrative Research: A New Critical Analysis. *Journal of Communication* 33 (3): 117–127.

Part I
Foundations

2 What is Political Economy?

What You Will Learn in This Chapter

- You will gain an understanding of Political Economy;
- You will read about the differences between various Political Economy approaches: Classical Political Economy, Critique of Political Economy, Neoclassical Political Economy, and Keynesian Political Economy;
- You will encounter further approaches, namely Feminist Political Economy, The Political Economy of Racism, and the Political Economy of the Environment (Political Ecology).

2.1 Introduction

This chapter deals with the question of how the economy can be analysed theoretically. In this context, the notions of Economic Theory, Schools of Economic Thought, and Political Economy are important. It asks the question: What is Political Economy?

Politics and the economy are two realms of society. Traditionally, they are often analysed separately, which is expressed in the existence of the two separate academic disciplines of Economics and Political Science. Today, however, the economy is regulated by the state through laws. In today's economy, there are also often conflicting interests, which are expressed in the form of organised interest representation organisations such as trade unions and business associations and public discussions about wealth distribution and socio-economic (in)justice. The concept of Political Economy emphasises the interconnection of the economy and politics.

Section 2.2 focuses on defining Political Economy. Section 2.3 presents four Political Economy approaches. Section 2.4 discusses some further approaches. Section 2.5 draws conclusions.

2.2 Defining Political Economy

The world's largest digital corporations have come under criticism for many things, including tax avoidance and violating their users' privacy. The European Union has responded by tightening data protection measures with

DOI: 10.4324/9781003391203-3

Exercise 2.1   Brainstorming

Write down up to three keywords that you associate with the term "politics".

Next, write down three keywords you associate with the term "economy".

After you have done that, discuss in class or think individually about what interconnections and relations there are between politics and the economy. Try to find examples that show how politics and the economy are related.

---

its Data Protection Regulation, plans for a digital services tax affecting the digital giants, and anti-monopoly measures in the form of the Digital Markets Act. **The political is economic:** This means that politics regulates the economy in the form of policies and laws. States face the risk of companies outsourcing their activities to other countries. They are confronted with the different interests of companies, citizens, civil society, associations, etc.

A report has shown that tech corporations spend around €100 million annually for lobbying the EU on digital policies (Corporate Europe Observatory and Lobby Control 2021, 6). In terms of the annual money invested, Google, Facebook, and Microsoft are the biggest lobbyists in Brussels, bigger than, for example, the pharmaceutical company Bayer and the oil corporation Shell (Corporate Europe Observatory and Lobby Control 2021, 11). Facebook paid the salary of 14 lobbyists dealing with EU affairs, Google 5 (Corporate Europe Observatory and Lobby Control 2021, 15). **The economy is political:** Corporations try to influence legislation in their interest. Corporations are not only business enterprises, but also political actors that try to influence legislation according to their economic interests. Large companies invest in lobbying for this purpose.

Political Economy deals with both the economic dimension of politics and the political dimension of the economy. It analyses the economy, politics, and these realms' interactions and forms of interlocking.

Political Economy is on the one hand a specific aspect of society. On the other hand, it is also a name of a tradition of analysis in academia. Its focus of analysis is on the intersection of the economy and politics. For providing an answer to the question of what Political Economy is, we need to understand what politics and the economy are.

2.2.1 Politics and the Economy

Figure 2.1 shows Caporaso and Levine's model of conceptions of politics. They argue that concepts of the political have to do with the public (A) and/or government (B) and/or authority (C). The public means everyone in society. "We call events and occasions 'public' when they are open to all, in

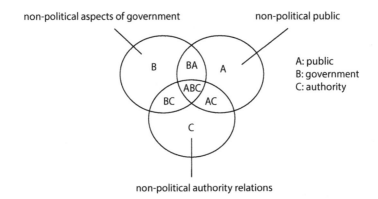

Figure 2.1 Conceptions of politics.
Source: Based on Caporaso and Levine (1992, 20).

contrast to close or exclusive affairs" (Habermas 1991, 1). A government is a system in which humans have the power to make decisions that are collectively binding for all members of the public. Authority is the process and capacity to influence and take collective decisions that apply to all members of society. Different conceptions of politics derive from the combination of these categories. For example, politics as public includes all individuals in a society and their need to make collective decisions.

Caporaso and Levine argue for understanding politics as the intersection of all three categories (ABC). "Politics refers to the activities and institutions that relate to the making of authorative public decisions for society as a whole" (Caporaso and Levine 1992, 20). Politics involves the citizens who form the public (A: public) and create a mechanism of government (B: government) for making collectively binding decisions (C: authority) – laws and policies – that apply to the public.

Political Economy is not just an analysis of politics, but also of the economy. Caporaso and Levine (1992, 31) outline three understandings of the economy:

1 The economy as provision, which means the production of human wants and needs and the satisfaction of these wants and needs with the help of produced goods;
2 The economy as organising something "economically", which involves economic calculation of how to gain access to scarce resources, and how to work efficiently and minimise the effort;
3 The economy as economic system, market institutions, and exchange economy.

The economy is the realm where humans work and produce goods and services that satisfy their needs, are distributed and consumed. Production is on the one hand a specific aspect of the economy, where humans produce goods. On the other hand, the economy can be found in all other social systems and realms of society because humans are socially producing beings. They produce goods, decisions, worldviews, information, meanings, etc. Social production can therefore be seen as the foundation of society (Fuchs 2020, chapters 2 and 3). Communication and production stand in a dialectical relationship.

Politics deals with collective decision-making. The economy deals with the production, distribution, and consumption of goods. Political Economy is focused on the analysis of the intersection, interactions, and interlocking of the economy and politics. It analyses the production, distribution, and consumption of goods and how political interests, conflicts, decisions, and institutions influence the economy and are influenced by the economy.

2.2.2 Foundations of Political Economy

The economy comes from the Greek term "oikos", which is the management of the household (Gibson-Graham 2005; Mosco 2009, 23).

> Political economy referred to the management of the economic affairs of the state. […] In its earliest period, political economy sought to advise the statesman on how he could best manage the economic affairs of the state so that the wants of the citizens would be met. The emergence of political economy brought with it a debate over the responsibilities of the state (or statesman) with regard to the economy. […] Should, for example, housing, medical care, education, welfare be provided by private citizens using the resources they have available to them? Or should they be provided by the state?
>
> (Caporaso and Levine 1992, 1)

Political Economy as a field of study has its origins in the provision of analysis and consultancy on how the state should manage the economy.

2.2.3 Ibn Khaldûn

Political Economy is often presented as a field of study that has purely European origins. Early contributors were Antoine de Montchrétien in France, who in 1615 published his *Traité de L'Economie Politique*, and William Petty, who in England in 1690 published *Political Arithmetick*. Karl Marx points out that by Political Economy, we should understand all those economists and their theories and studies that analyse capitalist relations of production: "Let me point out once and for all that by classical political economy I mean all the economists who, since the time of W. Petty, have investigated the real internal framework of bourgeois relations of production" (Marx 1867, 174–175). Political Economy has not just European foundations: Ibn Khaldûn (1332–1406) was a philosopher, historian, and sociologist. He was born in and lived in Tunis, which was part of Ifriqiya (today

Tunisia and parts of Libya and Algeria) that was ruled by the Hafsid dynasty. He is considered one of the founders of "economics, anthropology, political science and historical geography" (Deen 2010, 157) and "one of the great founders of the modern social sciences" (Santos 2017, 279). Khaldûn's "advances in the direction of a scientific social thought are unequalled before him and unsurpassed until the eighteenth and nineteenth centuries" (Amin 2009, 133). Written in 1377, the *Muqaddimah* ("Introduction", "Prolegomena") is Khaldûn's (2015) main work. It is a foundational work in Political Economy.

2.2.4 Definitions of Political Economy

James Steuart (1712–1780) was a Scottish aristocrat and the author of An *Inquiry Into the Principles of Political Economy*, a book that is by some considered the first economics book published in English. Steuart gives the following characterisation of Political Economy:

> What oeconomy is in a family, political oeconomy is in a state, [...] The principal object of this science is to secure a certain fund of subsistence for all the inhabitants, to obviate every circumstance which may render it precarious; to provide every thing necessary for supplying the wants of the society, and to employ the inhabitants (supposing them to be free-men) in such a manner as naturally to create reciprocal relations and dependencies between them, so as to make their several interests lead them to supply one another with their reciprocal wants. [...] In order to communicate an adequate idea of what I understand by political oeconomy, I have explained the term, by pointing out the object of the art; which is, to provide food, other necessaries, and employment to every one of the society.
>
> (Steuart 1767, 2–3, 15)

Steuart defines Political Economy as the study of what needs to be done in a society and how to organise society in order to supply the wants of humans.

Adam Smith (1723–1790) was a Scottish philosopher and economist. His two main works are *The Theory of Moral Sentiments* and *An Inquiry into the Nature and Causes of the Wealth of Nations*. Smith defines Political Economy as a science that studies how to create society's good of subsistence and how to create funding for public services:

> Political economy, considered as a branch of the science of a statesman or legislator, proposes two distinct objects: first, to provide a plentiful revenue or subsistence for the people, or more properly to enable them to provide such a revenue or subsistence for themselves; and secondly, to supply the state or commonwealth with a revenue sufficient for the public services. It proposes to enrich both the people and the sovereign.
>
> (Smith 1776, Volume 1, 428)

James Mill (1773–1836) was a Scottish historian and economist who was influenced by the economist David Ricardo. Mill argues that there are four dimensions of Political Economy analysis:

> It thus appears, that four inquiries are comprehended in this science.
> 1st. What are the laws, which regulate the production of commodities:
> 2dly. What are the laws according to which the commodities, produced by the labour of the community, are distributed:
> 3dly. What are the laws according to which commodities are exchanged for one another:
> 4thly. What are the laws which regulate consumption.
>
> (Mill 1824, 4)

For James Mill, then, the analysis of the production, distribution, exchange, and consumption of commodities is the task of Political Economy. The economist, philosopher, and Member of the British Parliament (MP) for the Liberal Party, John Stuart Mill, who was James Mill's eldest son, gave the following definition of Political Economy: "Political Economy informs us of the laws which regulate the production, distribution, and consumption of wealth" (Mill 1844, 72). His understanding of Political Economy is thus very similar to that of his father.

John Stuart Mill and James Mill argue that Political Economy analyses the production, distribution, and consumption of goods. David Ricardo (1772–1823) was an English economist and Whig member of the British Parliament. His most well-known book is *On the Principles of Political Economy and Taxation*.

Whereas Steuart, Smith, James Mill, and John Stuart Mill gave general definitions of Political Economy that have in common the definition that Political Economy analyses what society needs to do in order to produce and distribute goods that satisfy human wants and needs, which is true of any society, Ricardo limits Political Economy to the analysis of capitalism:

> The produce of the earth – all that is derived from its surface by the united application of labour, machinery, and capital, is divided among three classes of the community; namely, the proprietor of the land, the owner of the stock or capital necessary for its cultivation, and the labourers by whose industry it is cultivated.
>
> But in different stages of society, the proportions of the whole produce of the earth which will be allotted to each of these classes, under the names of rent, profit, and wages, will be essentially different; depending mainly on the actual fertility of the soil, on the accumulation of capital and population, and on the skill, ingenuity, and instruments employed in agriculture.
>
> To determine the laws which regulate this distribution, is the principal problem in Political Economy.
>
> (Ricardo 1824, v)

Ricardo argues that Political Economy wants to understand how labour, machinery, and capital are used for producing rent, profit, and wages. He thereby says that Political Economy is the analysis of capitalism. In the third volume of Marx's *Capital*, there is a chapter on "The Trinity Formula", in which Marx takes up and reflects on Ricardo's understanding of Political Economy.

> In capitalist society, this surplus-value or surplus product is divided among capitalists as dividends proportionate to the share of the social capital each holds. [...] Capital directly pumps from the workers the surplus labour that is expressed in surplus-value and surplus product. It can be considered in this sense as the producer of surplus-value. Landed property has nothing to do with the actual production process. Its role is limited to transferring a part of the surplus-value produced from capital's pockets into to its own. [...] The worker, finally, as owner and seller of his personal labour-power, receives under the name of wages a part of the product; in this there is expressed the portion of his labour that we call necessary labour, i.e. labour necessary for the maintenance and reproduction of his labour-power [...] Disparate as these relations may now appear, they have one thing in common: capital yields the capitalist profit, year in year out; land yields the landowner ground-rent; and labour-power [...] yields the worker wages.
>
> (Marx 1894, 959)

On the one hand, Marx acknowledges that in setting out the Trinity Formula of rent, profit, and wages, Classical Political Economists outline three important elements of capitalism. On the other hand, he criticises that they often present capital, land, and labour as independent from each other and do not conduct a class analysis. Therefore, capitalism's "inner connection is obliterated" and the Trinity Formula advances the "self-interest of the dominant classes, since it preaches the natural necessity and perpetual justification of their sources of income and erects this into a dogma" (Marx 1894, 969). Marx argues that in capitalism, capital exploits labour, which produces profit, wages, and rent.

2.2.5 The Two Aspects of Political Economy

Marx on the one hand builds on certain insights by Smith, Ricardo, and other Political Economists. On the other hand, he argues that these classical political economists ignore the centrality of class relations that need to be analysed or analyse capitalism as if it were an analysis of society in general. Marx speaks of the Critique of Political Economy, whereby he means an empirical and theoretical critical analysis of capitalism, as well as a Critique of Classical Political Economy.

Marx argues that there is an exoteric and an esoteric aspect of Political Economy (Marx 1861–1863, 391). This sounds complicated, but what he means by it is that one can analyse a concrete political economy from the outside so that one focuses on general aspects that go beyond the specific mode of production. This is the exoteric analysis. The esoteric analysis focuses on the analysis of the inner constitution of the mode of production. Marx argues that Classical Political Economy often analyses capitalism as if it were characteristic of all societies or presents analyses of society in general without connecting it to the analysis of capitalism and class societies.

> One of these conceptions fathoms the inner connection, the physiology, so to speak, of the bourgeois system, whereas the other takes the external phenomena of life process as they seem and appear and merely describes, catalogues, recounts and arranges them under formal definitions.
>
> (Marx 1861–1863, 390)

Marx criticises analyses that declare parts of the inner dynamics of capitalism, that is historical aspects of society, to be eternal natural necessities of all societal formations, thus mixing the esoteric and the exoteric view and neglecting the historical character of capitalism and class societies. In this context, his concept of fetishism plays an important role (Marx 1867, chapter 1.4).

Marx argues for analyses of the dialectic of esoteric and exoteric Political Economy, inner dynamics/outer appearances, particular/universal, specific/general, capitalism/society in general, economy/society, capitalist economy/capitalist and class society, etc. For Marx, Critique of Political Economy is a dialectical analysis of "the inner physiology of bourgeois society" (esoteric analysis) and its "externally apparent forms of life" (Marx 1861–1863, 391) (exoteric analysis) and the relations between both. It analyses the

> basis on which the inner coherence, the actual physiology of bourgeois society rests or the basis which forms its starting-point; and in general, [its task is] to examine how matters stand with the contradiction between the apparent and the actual movement of the system.
>
> (391)

Vincent Mosco mentions two understandings of Political Economy:

1 "study of the social relations, particularly the power relations, that mutually constitute the production distribution, and consumption of resources" (Mosco 2009, 24);
2 "the study of control and survival in social life" (Mosco 2009, 25), where control is a political process and survival the economic process of producing use-values in the economy.

I reformulate these definitions of Political Economy:

1 Critique of Political Economy is the study of class and other power relations in class societies and capitalist societies with a special focus on the
  economic relations' impact on society; and
2 Political Economy is the analysis of the production, distribution and consumption of goods whereby humans reproduce themselves and society and
  so survive.

These two levels are what Marx termed the esoteric and the exoteric levels
of analysis. The analysis of capitalism requires a general theory of society,
but such a general theory needs to be made concrete as an analysis of the
actual societies we live in today, and as an analysis of capitalist society and
the capitalist world system (see Fuchs 2020 as such an example analysis that
is focused on capitalism and communication).

An example of the interaction of the exoteric and the esoteric level of
analysis is Marx's concept of the commodity. He starts his Critique of Political Economy analysis of capitalism – that he outlines in his main work
Capital – with the analysis of the commodity:

> The wealth of societies in which the capitalist mode of production pre-
> vails appears as an 'immense collection of commodities'; the individual
> commodity appears as its elementary form. Our investigation therefore
> begins with the analysis of the commodity.
>
> (Marx 1867, 125)

A commodity is a good that is sold on a market and exchanged for a certain
amount of money for a particular price that is measured by money. The commodity has, according to Marx, a use-value and an exchange-value:

> The commodity is, first of all, an external object, a thing which through
> its qualities satisfies human needs of whatever kind. The nature of these
> needs, whether they arise, for example, from the stomach, or the imagi-
> nation, makes no difference. [....] Every useful thing, for example, iron,
> paper, etc., may be looked at from the two points of view of quality and
> quantity. [...] The usefulness of a thing makes it a use-value. [...] Use-
> values are only realized [*verwirklicht*] *in* use or in consumption. They
> constitute the material content of wealth, whatever its social form may
> be. In the form of society to be considered here they are also the mate-
> rial bearers [*Träger*] of ... exchange-value.
>
> Exchange-value appears first of all as the quantitative relation, the
> proportion, in which use-values of one kind exchange for use-values of
> another kind. This relation changes constantly with time and place. [...]
> The simple expression of the relative value of a single commodity, such

as linen, in a commodity which is already functioning as the money commodity, such as gold, is the price form. The 'price form' of the linen is therefore: 20 yards of linen = 2 ounces of gold, or, if 2 ounces of gold when coined are £2, 20 yards of linen = £2.

(Marx 1867, 125, 126, 163)

Marx stresses in this passage that a commodity has a qualitative and a quantitative side. Like all goods, the commodity satisfies human needs. This is the use-value side. We eat bread because we want to satisfy our need to eat and our want for good food. We watch and read the news because we want to satisfy our need to be informed about what is going on where we live. Use-value is the exoteric aspect of the commodity; it represents the aspect of the commodity that goes beyond the commodity and does not just exist in commodity-producing societies, but in all societies. Goods that are not commodities, such as public education and public health care, are also use-values that satisfy the human needs of learning and staying alive and healthy.

Bread and news are both use-values. Use-values can be either tangible or intangible in character. They arise either from the body or the brain, "from the stomach, or the imagination", as Marx (1867, 125, see the longer quote above) says. The commodity also has an esoteric side, features that are only specific to the commodity. It is exchanged in the relationship x commodity A = y commodity B on a commodity market. For example: one loaf of bread = €3.50; or one month of a newspaper subscription = €50.

The example of commodity analysis shows that Political Economy analyses general, universal features of society, as well as particular, concrete features of social systems, social relations, and formations of society. In the Political Economy of Communication, we need to analyse what needs media commodities satisfy as use-values and how they do so or do not do so and how they are traded as commodities that have exchange-value and yield profit for capital.

2.2.6 A Model of Political Economy

Figure 2.2 shows a model of Political Economy as analysis of society.

Political Economy is different from Business Studies, Organisation Studies, Management Studies, the Sociology of Work, and Industry Studies. It is, however, also focused on the analysis of businesses, organisations, labour, management, and industries, but conducts such research based on the analysis of the interactions of organisations and industries with the broader picture and context of society, that is capitalist society. It focuses on the interaction of the media economy and communication polity in the macrocontext of society, which includes capitalism, class structures, the state, policies, legislation, the public sphere, globalisation, power structures, domination, inequalities.

Political Economy is an approach that analyses society. It utilises social theory, empirical social research, and moral philosophy. It studies how the

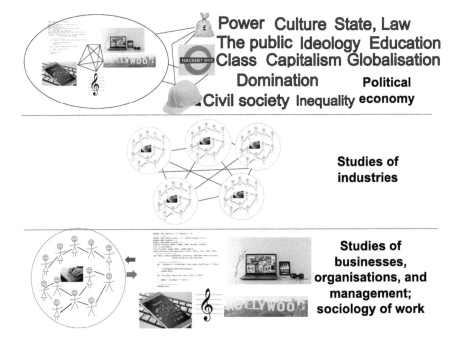

Power Culture State, Law
The public Ideology Education
Class Capitalism Globalisation
Domination   Political
Civil society Inequality economy

Studies of industries

Studies of businesses, organisations, and management; sociology of work

Figure 2.2 A model of Political Economy.

interaction of politics and the economy works and its roles in society. It sees the dialectic relationship between the economy and politics as the most important factor shaping society. An important focus is the analysis of the production, distribution, and consumption of goods and services in the context of society. Political Economy often is a critical analysis of how capitalist society works, is organised, and impacts society and the lives of humans in society. This approach is also termed Critique of the Political Economy.

In 2022, Apple was the world's 7th largest company.[1] It is the world's largest company in the realm of digital technologies, media, communication(s). Apple is infamous for its avoidance of paying taxes, which led the EU to fine Apple to pay €13 billion in back taxes, a decision that was reverted by the European General Court, to which the EU Commission appealed.[2] The EU argued that Apple shifted billions of Euros in profits through its Irish subsidiary and benefited from a tax deal with the Irish government that exempted these profits from taxation.

The example shows that the economy is political: Various groups in society have different interests. Capitalist companies have an interest to make ever more profit. They accumulate capital. It is Apple's political interest to pay low taxes and low wages. They lobby for paying low taxes. Transnational corporations (TNCs) such as Apple are not just companies but also political actors that influence state policies such as tax laws. That the economy is political also means that there are class relations and class struggles. Capital owners and workers have different, antagonistic interests. Many TNCs invest in lobbying, which means they pay for consultants and PR workers and lobbyists who help them develop strategies and practices of how to influence politicians and governments.

The example also shows that **politics is economic and influenced by the economy**: Nation-states are often afraid that companies relocate their headquarters. Nation-states, therefore, compete with each other for an "investment-friendly" climate, including low corporation tax and low wages. This explains why Ireland creates tax havens for transnational corporations. Nation-state politics regulates the economy and is confronted with the interests of companies, citizens, civil society, parties, etc. In 2019, Apple spent US$ 7.4 million on lobbying, and in 2020, US$ 6.6 million.[3] Apple paid the salaries of 46 lobbyists in 2019 and of 48 in 2020.[4] Paying lobbyists is a strategy of how economic actors try to influence political decision-making.

Having dealt with the question of how to define Political Economy, we will in the next section discuss different Political Economy approaches.

2.3 Political Economy Approaches

2.3.1 Ibn Khaldûn

We already mentioned in the previous section that Ibn Khaldûn is one of the founders of Political Economy. His *Muqaddimah* (Prolegomena, Introduction) is an early work in Political Economy.

Khaldûn formulated the assumption that labour is the source of wealth and profit:

> It should further be known that profit results from the effort to acquire (things) and the intention to obtain them. Sustenance requires effort and work. [...] human labour is necessary for every profit and capital accumulation. When (the source of profit) is work as such, as, for instance, (the exercise of) a craft, this is obvious. When the source of gain is animals, plants, or minerals, human labour is still necessary. Without it, no gain will be obtained, and there will be no useful (result). [...] If all this has been established, it should be further known that the capital a person earns and acquires, if resulting from a craft, is the value realized from his labour.
>
> (Khaldûn 2015, 446–447)

The analysis of work as the source of wealth and working time as the measure of wealth is also called the Labour Theory of Value. It argues that the value of a commodity corresponds to the average amount of hours necessary for its production. A good is considered to be more valuable if it is harder to produce and more labour time is needed for its production. In market societies, this results in a tendency for higher prices of more valuable commodities that have a longer production time.

The Labour Theory of Value can be found in Classical and Critical Political Economy, especially in the works of Adam Smith, David Ricardo, and Karl Marx.

Adam Smith formulated the Labour Theory of Value in the following words:

> The real price of every thing, what every thing really costs to the man who wants to acquire it, is the toil and trouble of acquiring it. What every thing is really worth to the man who has acquired it and who wants to dispose of it, or exchange it for something else, is the toil and trouble which it can save to himself, and which it can impose upon other people.
>
> (Smith 1776, Volume 1, 47)

"Toil and trouble" is the formulation that Smith uses for expressing that the value of a good depends on the expended labour time it takes to produce it. David Ricardo too formulated a Labour Theory of Value. He stresses that labour time is the measure of a commodity's value:

> Possessing utility, commodities derive their exchangeable value from two sources: from their scarcity, and from the quantity of labour required to obtain them. [...] If the quantity of labour realized in commodities, regulate their exchangeable value, every increase of the quantity of labour must augment the value of that commodity on which it is exercised, as every diminution must lower it.
>
> (Ricardo 1824, 2, 4)

Karl Marx makes a similar argument: "The basis, the starting-point for the physiology of the bourgeois system – for the understanding of its internal organic coherence and life process – is the determination of *value by labour time*" (Marx 1861–1863, 391).

Marx argues that the socially necessary labour time, which is the average labour time it takes to produce a commodity, determines the commodity's value:

> A use-value, or useful article therefore has value only because abstract human labour is objectified or materialized in it. How, then, is the magnitude of this value to be measured? By means of the quantity of the 'value-forming substance', the labour, contained in the article. This quantity is measured by its duration, and the labour-time is itself measured on the particular scale of hours, days etc. [...] Socially necessary labour-time is the labour-time required to produce any use-value under the conditions of production normal for a given society and with the average degree of skill and intensity of labour prevalent in that society.
>
> (Marx 1867, 129)

Marx differs from Smith and Ricardo in that his approach is a Critique of Political Economy, which includes a critique of value. He stresses that capital exploits labour in class relations where workers are made to produce part of the commodity and the working day without payment. He introduces the notions of surplus labour and surplus value in this context. His theory wants to understand how surplus value is produced and formulates the categorical imperative to socialise surplus value so that the surplus of society is not controlled by individual capitalists but by society.

> We have seen that the worker, during one part of the labour process, produces only the value of his labour-power, i.e. the value of his means of subsistence. [...] I call the portion of the working day during which this reproduction takes place necessary labour-time, and the labour expended during that time necessary labour; necessary for the worker, because independent of the particular social form of his labour; necessary for capital and the capitalist world, because the continued existence of the worker is the basis of that world.
>
> During the second period of the labour process, that in which his labour is no longer necessary labour, the worker does indeed expend labour-power, he does work, but his labour is no longer necessary labour, and he creates no value for himself. He creates surplus-value which, for the capitalist, has all the charms of something created out of nothing. This part of the working day I call surplus labour-time, and to the labour expended during that time I give the name of surplus labour. It is just as important for a correct understanding of surplus-value to conceive it as merely a congealed quantity of surplus labour-time, as nothing but objectified surplus labour, as it is for a proper comprehension of value in general to conceive it as merely a congealed quantity of so many hours of labour, as nothing but objectified labour. What distinguishes the various economic formations of society – the distinction between for example a society based on slave-labour and a society based on wage-labour – is the form in which this surplus labour is in each case extorted from the immediate producer, the worker.
>
> (Marx 1867, 324–325)

For Marx, the socially necessary labour time is the time needed to produce the goods necessary for society. He refers to labour time that is worked in addition to this as surplus labour time. In capitalism, surplus labour time is the material basis of profit, which belongs to the capitalists, is produced by the workers and is achieved through the sale of commodities.

2.3.2 Mainstream Economics and "Heterodox" Economics

Mainstream Economics tends to mostly ignore the Labour Theory of Value. For example, widely used Economics textbooks such as Blanchard's (2017)

Macroeconomics or Williamson's (2018) *Macroeconomics* do not discuss labour, do not mention Marx, define money as the measure of economic value (e.g. Mankiw 2018, 321) and disregard the role of the working class and its labour in capitalism. Although the Labour Theory of Value plays no important role in contemporary mainstream Economics, it continues to be of relevance in the age of digital capitalism. For example, struggles over automation and its impacts on society are struggles over value and labour time (see Fuchs 2019, chapter 4). Capital tries to use digital and nowadays AI-based automation to increase the productivity of labour so that more value can be produced in less time, which requires hiring and paying fewer workers and promises more profit. Representatives of working-class interests in contrast fear and stress that automation in capitalism can increase unemployment, poverty, and inequality.

Since the 2008 world economic crisis, there have been new calls to revise Economics university curricula and attempts to establish alternative, heterodox textbooks in Macroeconomics/Political Economy (see, e.g., De and Thomas 2018; Thomas 2021).

The crisis and increasing criticism of neoliberalism and along with it of Neoclassical Economics has led to some changes in Economic Theory. N. Gregory Mankiw is the author of very widely used Economics textbooks such as *Principles of Economics* (Mankiw 2021, ninth edition) and *Economics* (Mankiw and Taylor 2020, fifth edition). In the third edition of *Economics*, there is no real discussion of critical approaches such as Marxist Economics and Feminist Economics (Mankiw and Taylor 2014). The authors added a discussion of such approaches, including Marxism and Feminism, to the fourth edition, acknowledging that these approaches question the "*neoclassical* approach" that is also called "mainstream Economics" and the neoclassical view that "the market is a central feature in generating well-being" (Mankiw and Taylor 2014, 16).

In the fifth edition of *Economics*, Mankiw and Taylor (2020, 25–26) identify four Schools of Economic Thought: Neoclassical Economics, Feminist Economics, Marxist Economics, and the Austrian School. They also added discussions of Marxism and Feminism to the chapters on the labour market, well-being, unemployment, Heterodox Economics, and inequality (see Mankiw and Taylor 2020, 325–327, 363–364, 422–425, 433–434, 501). The fifth edition introduced a chapter on "Heterodox Theories in Economics" (Mankiw and Taylor 2020, chapter 19: 416–431). By Heterodox Economics, the two authors mean approaches that are "outside the 'mainstream' of economics, where the term 'mainstream' is associated with the neo-classical approach" (Mankiw and Taylor 2020, 418) and that have been "revived as a result of questions asked following the Crisis [of 2007/2008]" (Mankiw and Taylor 2020, 428). The category of Heterodox Economics is extremely broad and often includes very unlike approaches such as Marxism and the Austrian School.

These changes in a major Economics textbook are an indication that while mainstream Economics was for a long time ignoring critical approaches, its representatives now increasingly feel compelled that they at least have to acknowledge the existence of theories and analyses that stress the roles of unpaid labour, class, and inequalities in the contemporary economy.

The distinction between Classical, Neoclassical, Marxian, and Keynesian approaches is a widely used way of classifying Political Economy approaches (Caporaso and Levine 1992; Hunt and Lautzenheiser 2011; Lee 2011; Wolff and Resnick 2012). Marxian and Keynesian Political Economy are often together with further approaches labelled as Heterodox Economics or Heterodox Political Economy.

The concept of "Heterodox Political Economy" is somewhat unclear and confusing because heterodoxy means approaches that differ from the dominant approach. Consequently, Heterodox Political Economy encompasses a broad variety of approaches. For example, Marxist approaches are often included just like the Austrian School of Economics that goes back to the works of Carl Menger who has influenced neoliberal thinkers such as Friedrich Hayek. Marx and Hayek have oppositional analytical and political approaches. Beyond a dynamic concept of the economy, they have little in common. It is therefore better to differentiate Heterodox Political Economy into different approaches.

We will now briefly introduce various Political Economy approaches.

2.3.3 Classical Political Economy

Ibn Khaldûn was, as already discussed, an early non-Western representative of Classical Political Economy. According to Karl Marx, who in his *Theories of Surplus-Value* (Marx 1862/1863) engaged with Classical Political Economists' works, representatives include James Steuart, Adam Smith, Jean Charles Léonard de Sismondi, Germain Garnier, Charles Ganilh, David Ricardo, James Frederick Ferrier, James Maitland (Earl of Lauderdale), Jean-Baptiste Say, Destutt de Tracy, Henri Storch, Nassau Senior, Pellegrino Rossi, Thomas Chalmers, Jacques Necker, François Quesnay, Simon-Nicolas-Henri Linguet, Thomas Hobbes, William Petty, Dudley North, John Locke, David Hume, Joseph Massie, Louis-Gabriel Buat-Nançay, John Gray, Karl Rodbertus, John Barton, Nathaniel Forster, Thomas Hopkins, Henry Charles Carey, Thomas Robert Malthus, James Deacon, Thomas Hodgskin, James Anderson, Robert Torrens, James Mill, Samuel Bailey, John Ramsay McCulloch, Edward Gibbon Wakefield, Patrick James Stirling, John Stuart Mill, Piercy Ravenstone, John Francis Bray, Sir George Ramsay, Antoine-Eliseé Cherbuliez, Richard Jones, Pierre-Joseph Proudhon, and Martin Luther.

The most well-known works of Classical Political Economy are Adam Smith's (1776) *Wealth of Nations*, David Ricardo's (1824, first published in 1817) *Principles of Political Economy and Taxation,* and John Stuart Mill's (1848) *Principles of Political Economy.*

What these thinkers have in common is a relative focus and propagation of what has come to be known as "laissez-faire" Economics. They proclaim that markets can regulate themselves and that the state should not intervene in markets.

Smith and Mill argue that a civilised society is the result of profit-seeking individuals who aim at maximising their profits. Smith has in this context coined the metaphor of the invisible hand. He argues that independently acting, self-interested economic agents (companies, capitalists) who try to maximise their economic profits are led by an invisible hand (the market) so that their private ends of making profit foster the public good. The individual

> intends only his own gain, and he is in this, as in many other cases, led by an invisible hand to promote an end which was no part of his intention. [...] By pursuing his own interest he frequently promotes that of the society more effectually than when he really intends to promote it. I have never known much good done by those who affected to trade for the public good.
>
> (Smith 1776, Volume 1, 456)

The basic assumption is that the public good can best be achieved without the intervention of politics in the economy such as the redistribution of wealth from the rich to the poor and from capital to labour. The role of the state is limited to the defence of the nation-state and capital. Smith discusses as duties of the state (Smith 1776, Volume 2, book 5, chapter 1):

1 Protection from invasion;
2 Protecting citizens; and
3 Public institutions that facilitate commerce (roads, bridges, canals, education, etc.).

Smith (1776, Volume 2, 715) says a major role of the state is to protect "the rich against the poor or of those who have some property against those who have none at all".

Smith's other major work besides the *Wealth of Nations* was *The Theory of Moral Sentiments*, which is a moral philosophy that mainly sees morals as individual human quality and does not much engage with aspects of property, capital and markets. Smith argues that humans sympathise with the feelings of others and care about their well-being. He introduced the idea of the invisible hand first in the *Theory of Moral Sentiments*:

> The rich only select from the heap what is most precious and agreeable. They consume little more than the poor, and in spite of their natural selfishness and capacity, though they mean only their own conveniency, though the sole end which they propose from the labours of all the thousands whom they employ, be the gratification of their own vain and insatiable desires, they divide with the poor the produce of all their improvements. They are led by an invisible hand to make nearly

the same distribution of the necessaries of life, which would have been made, had the earth been divided into equal portions among all its inhabitants, and thus without intending it, without knowing it, advance the interest of the society, and afford means to the multiplication of the species. When Providence divided the earth among a few lordly masters, it neither forgot nor abandoned those who seemed to have been left out in the partition. These last too enjoy their share of all that it produces. In what constitutes the real happiness of human life, they are in no respect inferior to those who would seem so much above them. In ease of body and peace of mind, all the different ranks of life are nearly upon a level, and the beggar, who suns himself by the side of the highway, possesses that security which kings are fighting for.

(Smith 1759, 184–185)

The invisible hand that Smith describes in this quote means the assumption that the market and the selfish pursuit of profit produce a just society and that therefore no state intervention in the market is necessary. Justice has for Smith (1759, 84) to do with the protection of private property:

Breach of property, therefore, theft and robbery, which take from us what we are possessed of, are greater crimes than breach of contract, which only disappoints us of what we expected. The most sacred laws of justice, therefore, those whose violation seems to call loudest for vengeance and punishment, are the laws which guard the life and person of our neighbour; the next are those which guard his property and possessions; and last of all come those which guard what are called his personal rights, or what is due to him from the promises of others.

John Stuart Mill (1859, 37) understood freedom as the individual right of possession: "The only freedom which deserves the name, is that of pursuing our own good in our own way, so long as we do not attempt to deprive others of theirs, or impede their efforts to obtain it". Mill (1848, 16–17) acknowledged that capitalism creates inequality and argued that full individual freedom of property is preferable to equality:

The perfection both of social arrangements and of practical morality would be, to secure to all persons complete independence and freedom of action, subject to no restriction but that of not doing injury to others: and the education which taught or the social institutions which required them to exchange the control of their own actions for any amount of comfort or affluence, or to renounce liberty for the sake of equality, would deprive them of one of the most elevated characteristics of human nature.

For Mill, a society in which a few live in luxury and others die of hunger and overwork is a free society as long as there is a market economy and private property. Mill does not recognise that private property in such a case produces social unfreedom.

2.3.4 Karl Marx: Critique of Political Economy

Karl Marx (1818–1883) was a German philosopher, political economist, sociologist, and socialist. His magnum opus consists of three volumes of *Capital. A Critique of Political Economy*. His relevance for the study of Political Economy becomes evident from the book title. He worked together with Friedrich Engels (1820–1895) with whom he also co-authored works such as the *Manifesto of the Communist Party* (Marx and Engels 1848).

Marx's approach and the whole tradition of thought and research built on his work is also called Critique of Political Economy because (a) he built on and criticised Classical Political Economy and (b) his analysis aimed at advancing a critique of capitalism, namely a so-called immanent critique that shows that the reality of society under capitalism does not correspond to its potentials.

He argues that "political economy is bourgeois" when it "views the capitalist order as the absolute and ultimate form of social production" (Marx 1867, 96). Marx argues that Classical Political Economists naturalise capitalism or certain phenomena of capitalist or class societies. They make these phenomena appear as universal and existing in all societies:

> Economists express the relations of bourgeois production, the division of labour, credit, money, etc., as fixed, immutable, eternal categories. [...] Economists explain how production takes place in the above-mentioned relations, but what they do not explain is how these relations themselves are produced, that is, the historical movement which gave them birth.
>
> (Marx 1847, 162)

> Ricardo, after postulating bourgeois production as necessary for determining rent, applies the conception of rent, nevertheless, to the landed property of all ages and all countries. This is an error common to all the economists, who represent the bourgeois relations of production as eternal categories.
>
> (Marx 1847, 202)

Let us have a look at how Marx criticises Classical Political Economists, namely Adam Smith and David Ricardo.

Adam Smith (1776) argues that the commodity can be found in all societies and is therefore a natural feature of society: There is

> a certain propensity in human nature [...] to truck, barter, and exchange one thing for another. [...] It is common to all men, and to be found in no other race of animals, which seem to know neither this nor any other species of contracts.
>
> (Smith 1776, Volume 1, 25)

Smith argues that the nature of humans as being that trades on markets is "the necessary consequence of the faculties of reason and speech" (Smith 1776, Volume 1, 25).

David Ricardo argues that capital, money, and profit are natural parts of the human economy that can be found in all economies: Capital "is that part of the wealth of a country which is employed in production, and consists of food, clothing, tools, raw materials, machinery, etc. necessary to give effect to labour" (Ricardo 1824, 89). He generalises the concept of capital and speaks, for example, of "the hunter's capital, the weapon" (Ricardo 1824, 16) and sees money as "the general medium of exchange between all civilized countries" (Ricardo 1824, 48). Ricardo presents the striving for profitability as a natural human property.

> Whilst every man is free to employ his capital where he pleases, he will naturally seek for it that employment which is most advantageous; he will naturally be dissatisfied with a profit of 10 per cent, if by removing his capital he can obtain a profit of 15 per cent.
>
> (Ricardo 1824, 81)

Ricardo characterises capital at the same time existing in all societies and as a tool of capital accumulation in capitalism, whereby he naturalises capitalist society, markets, money, commodities, and the logic of accumulation as the natural and ideal state of any society.

Marx argues that capital is a social relationship between the capitalist and the worker that requires the exploitation of labour and enables accumulation and exchange as part of class societies. He criticises that Ricardo sees class relations as a feature of all societies: "Ricardo, ultimately (and consciously) made the antagonism of class interests, of wages and profits, of profits and rent, the starting-point of his investigations, naively taking this antagonism for a social law of nature" (Marx 1867, 96).

In this context, Marx also speaks of the fetish character of the commodity, money, and capital, by which he means that the economy appears as determined by things and the decisive role of labour as a social and societal relation is veiled by things (commodities, money, capital): "It is nothing but the definite social relation between men themselves which assumes here [in the fetishism of the commodity], for them, the fantastic form of a relation between things" (Marx 1867, 165).

Vis-à-vis Ricardo, we can ask: Are all our social relations mediated by money and markets? In the world of the media, think of Wikipedia, which provides encyclopaedic knowledge as a commons and does not sell commodities. What would happen if all of our social relations were based on money, markets and exchange? Wouldn't there be very negative consequences if this were the case? Think of the following example:

Two prospective lovers meet for a candlelight dinner that one of them cooks. They eat a delicious meal and drink wine. At the end of the meeting, the invited person puts a 100 Euro note on the table before they leave and says: "This was such a nice and romantic evening with delicious food, I appreciate it very much and want to express my gratitude in the form of money". How would the other person react? They might be furious and scream:

> Are you crazy? Money can't buy you love. The logic of money does not belong into the setting of a candlelight dinner. I thought we could fall in love and become a couple. Money destroys everything. This makes me sad. I do not want to see you any longer. Please leave!.

The example shows that the logic of money can have quite alienating effects. Marx's argument now is that money and capital are alienating as such and alienate humans from the self-determined control of their lives. They become compelled to work for others and define the world through commodities. Love and solidarity are a counter-logic to exchange and competition.

For Crawford Macpherson (1962), possessive individualism is the "conception of the individual as essentially the proprietor of his own person or capacities, owing nothing to society for them" (Macpherson 1962, 3). According to Macpherson, possessive individualism is the underlying worldview of liberal-democratic theory since John Locke and John Stuart Mill.

Marx was critical of the possessive individualism advanced by Classical Political Economy in three respects:

1 Marx argued that there is no pure individual existence.
    All human existence is socially conditioned. Marx described the position of the relationship between the private and the general in the theories of Classical Political Economists:

> The economists express this as follows: Each pursues his private interest and only his private interest; and thereby serves the private interests of all, the general interest, without willing or knowing it. [...] The point is rather that private interest is itself already a socially determined

---

Exercise 2.2   Alienation and the Logic of Money

Discuss in groups:
Should all our social relations be mediated by money, markets, and exchange? Why respectively why not? If not, what are examples of social relations that are not mediated by money, markets, and exchange? Can you give examples of where the application of the logic of money and commodities has caused harm?

What about the world of the media? Can you think of examples, where the logic of money in the realm of the media has created harm to society?

---

interest, which can be achieved only within the conditions laid down by society and with the means provided by.

(Marx 1857/1858, 156)

Marx argues that the notion of the private in Classical Political Economy is individualistic and neglects that all individual actions take place within and are conditioned by society;

2 Marx argues that the individualism advanced by liberal theories results in egoism that harms the public good.

Marx furthermore stresses that capitalist society is based not only on individualism but also on egoism (Marx 1843b, 153–155, 164–168, 171–174). Liberty in bourgeois society "is the liberty of man viewed as an isolated monad, withdrawn into himself. [...] The practical application of man's right to liberty man's right to private property" (Marx 1843b, 162, 163). Modern society's constitution would be the "constitution of private property" (Marx 1843a, 32). The right of private property in the means of production and to accumulate as much capital as one pleases would harm the community and the social welfare of others who are by this process deprived of wealth: "The right of man to private property is, therefore, the right to enjoy one's property and to dispose of it at one's discretion (à son gré), without regard to other men, independently of society, the right of self-interest" (Marx 1843b, 163).

None of the so-called rights of man, therefore, go beyond egoistic man, beyond man as a member of civil society, that is, an individual withdrawn into himself, into the confines of his private interests and private caprice, and separated from the community.

(Marx 1843b, 164)

Marx further criticises that the accumulation of capital results in the concentration of capital and thereby of wealth: "Accumulation, where private property prevails, is the *concentration* of capital in the hands of a few" (Marx 1844, 251). This means that he says that capital has the tendency to form monopolies;

3 Marx argues that the concepts of private property and individualism are ideological foundations of the modern class structure.

Marx says that capitalism's "principle of individualism" and a constitution of state and society that guarantees the existence of classes is the attempt "to thrust the human being back into the narrowness of his individual sphere" (Marx 1843a, 81) and to thereby make him a *"private individual"* (Marx 1843a, 81). If the private sphere in modern society is connected to the notion of private property, then it is an inherent foundation of the class antagonism between capital and work: "But labour, the subjective essence of private property as exclusion of property, and capital, objective labour as exclusion of labour, constitute *private property* as its developed state of contradiction – hence a dynamic relationship driving towards resolution" (Marx 1844, 294). The capitalist mode of production is based on the "socialization of labour" and "socially exploited and therefore communal means of production" (Marx 1867, 928). This social dimension of capitalism is, according to Marx, circumvented by private ownership of the means of production: "Private property, as the antithesis to social, collective property, exists only where the means of labour and the external conditions of labour belong to private individuals" (Marx 1867, 927). He says that capitalism is based on a "system of producing and appropriating products, that is based on class antagonisms, on the exploitation of the many by the few" (Marx and Engels 1848, 498).

For Marx, the capitalist economy is political because it is shaped by a class conflict between workers and capitalists, two classes that have according to him opposed interests.

Marx challenged the classical view that markets are self-regulating and argued that capitalism is inherently crisis-ridden. For Marx, the capitalist economy is based on the accumulation of capital, which means that there is the imperative that they make ever more profit, which is an increase in the invested money, in order to survive on the market. He speaks of surplus value, surplus labour and surplus product in this context by which he means that workers produce more than they are paid for. In *Capital Volume 1*, he describes the logic of capitalism in the following words:

Accumulate, accumulate! That is Moses and the prophets! 'Industry furnishes the material which saving accumulates'. Therefore save, save, i.e. reconvert the greatest possible portion of surplus-value or surplus product into capital! Accumulation for the sake of accumulation, production for the sake of production: this was the formula in which classical economics expressed the historical mission of the bourgeoisie in the

period of its domination. Not for one instant did it deceive itself over
the nature of wealth's birth-pangs. But what use is it to lament a historical necessity? If, in the eyes of classical economics, the proletarian is
merely a machine for the production of surplus-value, the capitalist too
is merely a machine for the transformation of this surplus-value into
surplus capital. Classical economics takes the historical function of the
capitalist in grim earnest.

(Marx 1867, 742)

Marx argues in this quote that capitalism is based on the accumulation of
money capital and that this makes accumulation an end in itself. He also emphasises that capital exploits the workers who produce surplus value.

Marx characterises commodity sale as x commodity A = y commodity B:
A certain amount of one commodity is exchanged for a particular amount of
another commodity. Money is for Marx the generalised commodity that can
be exchanged for any other commodity so that x commodity A = y commodity B = z amount of money. This is what he calls the money form.

In the three volumes of *Capital*, Marx analyses the cycle of capital accumulation that he characterises as M – C (Mp, L).. P.. C' – M'. This means
that in the capitalist economy, companies invest money M to purchase commodities C, namely means of production (Mp: technologies, resources, buildings) and labour-power (L: workers' capabilities, subjectivities, and skills
they utilise in the production process). In the production process P, workers
utilise their labour-power to use the means of production, which results in
a new commodity C'. The new commodity C' contains a surplus product:
Labour makes it more than the commodities used for its production. The
commodity contains surplus value, which means that the average number of
hours it takes to produce a commodity contains an equivalent of the hours
the workers are paid for plus an unpaid part. The new commodity C' is then
sold on the market. When the sale is successful, an increased sum of money
M' that is larger than the invested sum of money M is created: M' = M +
ΔM. The increase (ΔM) over the invested amount of money M is also termed
profit. Marx says that capital is a dynamic process that undergoes a "meta-
morphosis", which means it takes on the form of money (M, M') and commodities (C, C') in the cycle of capital accumulation. Parts of the capital M'
are used for paying interest to banks, rent to those from whom companies
lease property, dividends to shareholders, and bonuses to managers. The rest
is reinvested. The goal is to produce more in less time in order to make ever
more profit. This is according to Marx the logic of the capitalist economy.

2.3.5 Neoclassical Political Economy

Neoclassical Political Economy is an approach that emerged in the second
half of the 19th century. Among its basic works are William S. Jevons' (1863)

General Mathematical Theory of Political Economy, Carl Menger's (1871) *Principles of Economics*, Léon Walras (1874)'s *Elements of Pure Economics*, and Alfred Marshall's (1890) *Principles of Economics*.

Two things become evident from these book titles: First, many Neoclassical approaches are focused on mathematical models of the economy. And second, many Neoclassical approaches gave up the term "Political Economy" and instead use the term "Economics". Classical Political Economists such as Smith and Ricardo and Marx's Critique of Political Economy differ in their theories but have in common the interest in combining the analysis of the economy with moral philosophy. They were not just economists but also philosophers. "In the drive to become a mathematical and parsimonious science, economics shed most of the fundamental characteristics that characterize political economy" (Mosco 2009, 46). In Neoclassical Political Economy, philosophy plays a subordinate role or no role at all. One can even say that mathematics has in Neoclassical approaches largely replaced Classical and Critical Political Economy's focus on and interest in ethics and philosophy. William Jevons writes that one should substitute "the name Political Economy" for the "single convenient term Economics" (xxxv). Political Economy would be an "old troublesome double-worded name" (xxxv). At the same time, he argues that "Economics, if it is to be a science at all, must be a mathematical science" (3).

For Jeremy Bentham (2000), utility has to do with pain and pleasure (14). Action can "augment or diminish the happiness of the party whose interest is in question" (14). Building on Bentham's concept of utility, many Neoclassical Political Economists argue that in the economy, one tends to act in such a way as to maximise the utility of goods for oneself and individual satisfaction.

> Pleasure and pain are undoubtedly the ultimate objects of the Calculus of Economics. To satisfy our wants to the utmost with the least effort – to procure the greatest amount of what is desirable at the expense of the least that is undesirable – in other words, to *maximise pleasure*, is the problem of Economics.
>
> (Jevons 1871, 37)

The "object of Economics is to maximise happiness by purchasing pleasure, as it were, at the lowest cost of pain" (Jevons 1871, 23)

Neoclassical Economists see prices and value of commodities as determined by subjective utility, which means that they say that value is for them not objectively defined by working hours, but subjectively by what players in the market think a good is worth.

> Repeated reflection and inquiry have led me to the somewhat novel opinion, that *value depends entirely upon utility*. Prevailing opinions

make labour rather than utility the origin of value; and there are even those who distinctly assert that labour is the *cause* of value.

(Jevons 1871, 1)

Neoclassical Economists assume that economic action is based on rational calculations and preference ordering. This is also called rational choice. Such economists argue that individuals choose behaviours that maximise their own welfare and that group welfare results from individual rational choices. They argue that the more competitive markets are, the more choice there is and the more likely is social welfare. They typically oppose regulation of the economy by the state and reduce the role of the state in securing private property.

The Chicago School of Economics is a particular version of Neoclassical Political Economy. Its representatives include, among others, George Stigler (1911–1991), Friedrich Hayek (1899–1992), Milton Friedman (1912–2006) and Gary Becker (1930–2014). Hayek won the Nobel Memorial Prize in Economic Sciences in 1974, Friedman in 1976, Stigler in 1982, and Becker in 1992. The Chicago School is known for its market radicalism, which means that it propagates the market as an organisational principle of large parts of society. It influenced politicians and governments such as the ones of Ronald Reagan and Margaret Thatcher, who came to be known as political pioneers of neoliberalism, a model of society that is largely based on the logic of the market and commodities and that dominated the world from the 1980s until the 2010s.

Hayek advocates Adam Smith's theorem of the invisible hand: "We are led – for example, by the pricing system in market exchange – to do things by circumstances of which we are largely unaware and which produce results that we do not intend" (Hayek 1988, 14). He propagates competition instead of co-operation and individuals' egoistic actions instead of solidarity. Hayek argues that there are two forms of orders: spontaneous, self-forming orders (kosmos) and planned orders (taxis). He says that any attempt by humans and the state to intervene in markets is harmful and creates problems. Only left to itself, the economy would produce good outcomes. For Hayek, it is a "fatal conceit" and the basic foundation of socialism to assume "that man is able to shape the world around him according to his wishes" (Hayek 1988, 27). For Hayek, the market is an information system that spontaneously or-ders the economy and creates wealth. Capitalism would have the "superior capacity to utilise dispersed knowledge" (Hayek 1988, 8).

Milton Friedman argued much like Hayek. He says that the market should not intervene in the distribution of income in society: "The ethical principle that would directly justify the distribution of income in a free market society is, 'To each according to what he and the instruments he owns produces'" (Friedman 2002, 161–162). Both Hayek and Friedman argued that interven-tion of the state in the economy will result in tyranny as in Stalin's Russia and that therefore the state should better not regulate markets. They thereby equalise Social Democrats who want to combine a society that benefits all and democracy with Stalinism which is anti-democratic and supports the creation of a bureaucratically controlled economy.

Friedman propagates Adam Smith's idea of the invisible hand: He argues that good outcomes are "the product of the initiative and drive of individuals co-operating through the free market. Government measures have hampered not helped this development. [...] The invisible hand has been more potent for progress than the visible hand for retrogression" (Friedman 2002, 200). Convinced by the theorem of the invisible hand, Friedman argues that it is the "social responsibility of business is to increase its profits" (Friedman 1970/2015, 110).

Hayek and Friedman have an individualist conception of freedom. Freedom for them means that individuals should be allowed to do whatever they please without constraints. Concepts of social freedom in contrast argue that individual freedom is important as long as it does not harm others and that egoism can harm the public good, which requires policies that regulate the distribution of income and wealth and put limits on egoistic action. Hayek and Friedman conceive social phenomena purely on an individual basis. They argue that egoistic individual action leads to good outcomes at the social level. This approach is also called methodological individualism. Dialectical approaches in contrast argue that the social level of society and the individual level interact and that structures such as the state and individual action in their interaction produce and reproduce society.

The neo-Keynesian economist Thomas Piketty characterises the worldview advocated by Hayek and Friedman as neoproprietarism – the propagation of a radical right to increase individual wealth without state redistribution towards the poor, without considerations of justice and without regard to the suffering of others.

> The conservative revolution of the 1980s, the collapse of Soviet communism, and the development of neo-proprietarian ideology vastly increased the concentration of income and wealth in the first two decades of the twenty-first century. Inequality has in turn heightened social tensions almost everywhere.
>
> (Piketty 2020, 966)

The Critical Political Economist David Harvey argues that Hayek and Friedman, who played a key role in the Mont Pelerin Society, founded neoliberal theory that is "deeply opposed to state interventionist theories, such as those of John Maynard Keynes", adheres to the "free market principles of neoclassical economics" (Harvey 2005, 20), and became very influential in politics when Margaret Thatcher came to power in the UK in 1979 and Ronald Reagan in the USA in 1981.

Harvey characterises neoliberalism in the following way:

> Neoliberalism is in the first instance a theory of political economic practices that proposes that human well-being can best be advanced by liberating individual entrepreneurial freedoms and skills within an institutional framework characterized by strong private property rights, free markets, and free trade. The role of the state is to create and preserve an institutional framework appropriate to such practices. The state has to guarantee, for example, the quality and integrity of money. It must also set up those military, defence, police, and legal structures and functions required to secure private property rights and to guarantee, by force if need be, the proper functioning of markets. Furthermore, if markets do not exist (in areas such as land, water, education, health care, social security, or environmental pollution) then they must be created, by state action if necessary. But beyond these tasks the state should not venture. State interventions in markets (once created) must be kept to a bare minimum because, according to the theory, the state cannot possibly possess enough information to second-guess market signals (prices) and because powerful interest groups will inevitably distort and bias state interventions (particularly in democracies) for their own benefit. There has everywhere been an emphatic turn towards neoliberalism in political-economic practices and thinking since the 1970s.
>
> (Harvey 2005, 2)

For Harvey, neoliberalism is a theory, ideology, and form of politics that calls for the extension of the market economy as an organising principle to many spheres of society, including those that are organised as public services in many societies.

Harvey argues that neoliberalism has increased inequality:

> Redistributive effects and increasing social inequality have in fact been such a persistent feature of neoliberalization as to be regarded as structural to the whole project. Gérard Duménil and Dominique Lévy, after careful reconstruction of the data, have concluded that neoliberalization was from the very beginning a project to achieve the restoration of class power.
>
> (Harvey 2005, 16; see also Duménil and Lévy 2004)

Neoliberal politicians such as Ronald Reagan and Margaret Thatcher have put Hayek and Friedman's doctrine into political action. Their policies were characterised by privatisation, tax giveaways for the wealthy and corporations, the underfunding of public services and the welfare state, the pushing back of trade unions' influence, the deregulation of the economy and the financial markets, and the redistribution of wealth from the wage-earning working population to the rich and the owners of capital. The outcomes were rising inequalities and the emergence of high-risk financial markets that in

Table 2.1 The development of the wage share in selected countries

Country	1975	1980	1990	2000	2008	2024
USA	61.1	61.7	60.8	61.4	58.5	56.7
UK	66.4	59.3	55.4	55.0	57.4	55.5
Germany	64.1	63.7	58.8	59.0	55.2	56.9
France	65.8	65.9	58.3	55.9	55.7	55.9
Italy	66.5	63.4	58.4	50.9	52.7	52.5
Norway	59.9	54.2	52.8	45.7	44.5	41.1
Turkey	N/A		72.6	55.0	42.0	43.6
Japan	N/A	71.0	62.7	61.5	59.2	57.0

Data source: AMECO, adjusted wage share, total economy, GDP at current market prices, accessed on 13 February 2023.

2008 triggered a world economic crisis. The journalist Naomi Klein (2007, 392) argues that "extreme inequality [...] resulted from the generalized triumph of Chicago School economics".

The wage share is the share of wages in the national wealth, the gross domestic product (GDP). Table 2.1 shows how the wage share developed in selected countries during the phase of neoliberal capitalism. The data confirms rising socio-economic inequality. In all selected countries, the wage share was in 2008 when a new world economic crisis started significantly lower than in 1975 or 1980 when neoliberalism started to transform societies around the world. In 2024, more than 15 years later, the situation of the working class had not improved in terms of the wage share. A decline of the wage share means at the same time the increase in the power of capital, as the wealth controlled by capital grows in proportion to the decline of the wage share. Even Scandinavian countries like Norway, which are often praised for their welfare states, are affected by a declining wage share.

2.3.6 Keynesian Political Economy

John Maynard Keynes (1883–1946) was an English economist who challenged Neoclassical Economics and is credited for the idea of the welfare state. His main book is *The General Theory of Employment, Interest and Money* (Keynes 1936).

Keynes' theory distinguishes itself from Classical and Neoclassical Political Economy by the assumption that private capitalist action does not automatically serve the public good. He assumes that there is tension. Marx assumed there is a fundamental incongruence and antagonism.

Keynes argues that markets create problems of aggregate demand. He questions the self-regulatory capacity of the market. "Thus our argument leads towards the conclusion that in contemporary conditions the growth of wealth, so far from being dependent on the abstinence of the rich, as is commonly supposed, is more likely to be impeded by it" (Keynes 1936, 373).

Keynes opposed Neoclassical Political Economy. He argued that if left to itself without state intervention, capitalism results in problems such as inequalities and unemployment: "The outstanding faults of the economic society in which we live are its failure to provide for full employment and its arbitrary and inequitable distribution of wealth and incomes" (Keynes 1936, 372). Keynes says that Neoclassical Economics "cannot solve the economic problems of the actual world" (378). He argues that capitalism's "economic forces" need to be "curbed or guided" (380). Keynes writes that the creation of a welfare state "for the redistribution of incomes" is likely to "raise the propensity to consume" and "may prove favourable to the growth of capital" (373). He says that inequalities can exist, but they should not be extreme. Keynes' goal was to find ways of how to tame capitalism. His idea of the welfare state is based on free public services, "higher taxation of larger incomes and inheritances" (377), job creation by public investments and projects, income redistribution, collective wage bargaining, the state acting as employer, and government borrowing and spending. All of this requires "a large extension of the traditional functions of government" (379). Laissez-faire capitalism would advance the threat of war (381–383).

Keynes also formulated a criticism of financialisation that is still topical today: "When the capital development of a country becomes a by-product of the activities of a casino, the job is likely to be ill-done" (Keynes 1936, 159).

2.4 Further Political Economy Approaches

There are not just these four approaches of Political Economy we discussed, but more. We cannot present all strands here but will give some further examples. Three of them are Feminist Political Economy, the Political Economy of Racism, and the Political Economy of the Environment (Political Ecology). They are partly intersecting with Marxian Political Economy and Keynesian Political Economy.

2.4.1 Feminist Political Economy

Feminist Political Economy gives particular attention to the analysis of gender aspects of capitalism, including the analysis of women's roles in class relations, of gendered divisions of labour, and of reproductive labour, which is labour that helps reproducing labour-power such as work in the household and care labour.

- "Gender, race/ethnicity and regionality/nationality interact with class in various ways with one being more salient than another at different points in time. The problem for socialist feminism is to develop a theoretical account of these different types of oppression and the relations between them with a view to ending them all. To end the subordination of women, we need theory, research and action. Theory guides our research and action, and research and action provide the basis for our theorizing" (Armstrong and Connelly 1989, 5–6);

- "The gendered organization of political economic processes has been insisted upon; issues of biological reproduction and of sexuality have been incorporated; important studies of women's paid work, women in the trade union movement and of the development of state management of women's domestic lives, have been done" (Smith 1989, 48).

Feminist Critical Political Economy is an analysis of the relationship between patriarchy and capitalism. The term capitalist patriarchy emphasises "the mutually reinforcing dialectical relationship between capitalist class structure and hierarchical sexual structuring" (Eisenstein 1979, 5). The concept of capitalist patriarchy is for quite some representatives of Feminist Political Economy the "recognition of housework as productive labour and as an area of exploitation and a source for capital accumulation" (Mies 2014, 32). Sylvia Walby (1990, 13) argues that

housewives and husbands are classes, but that men and women are not. That is, certain aspects of patriarchal relations can be captured by the concept of class, but not all. Further, gender impacts upon class relations within capitalism. This means there are two class systems, one based around patriarchy, the other around capitalism.

2.4.2 The Political Economy of Racism

The Political Economy of Racism studies the relationship of racism and capitalism in the form of racist wage discrimination ("unequal pay for the same work", Leiman 1993, 146), racist employment discrimination ("not hiring blacks because of race, thus generating a higher unemployment rate for blacks than for white", 147), racist occupational discrimination ("hiring more blacks than whites in inferior occupations", 147), and racist access discrimination ("denying blacks opportunities to acquire qualifications", 214). The Political Economy of Racism "helps to illuminate the fundamental realities of racism by its tripartite emphasis on the changing socioeconomic structure, the relationship of class to race, and the political consciousness of the historical agents" (Leiman 1993, 147).

Racial capitalism is a concept that has been established in the Critique of the Political Economy of Racism. Cedric J. Robinson shows that the exploitation of people of colour has been an important aspect of capitalism's Political Economy since that societal formation's start. The racist division of labour of capitalism started with the transatlantic slave trade in the 16th century. Racism emerged as an ideology that justified the "domination, exploitation, and/or extermination of non-'Europeans' (including Slavs and Jews)" (Robinson 2000, 27).

Racial capitalism might be a name for the extraction of additional value from subordinated groups or it might be a name for the racialised expropriation of resources from populations deemed disposable or it might point to processes of expulsion – and it might, most likely, be a name for the world that emerges from these combined processes.

(Bhattacharyya 2018, 181)

Racial capitalism means that racism is utilised in order to enforce capitalist interests (Bhattacharyya 2018, 103).

2.4.3 *The Political Economy of the Environment (Political Ecology)*

The Political Economy of the Environment has tried to integrate Political Economy and Environmental Studies. It analyses

how people control and, periodically, struggle for control over the institutions and organizations that produce and regulate the flows of materials that sustain people (corporations and the state). Scholarship on the political economy of the environment focuses on the environmental effects of these flows and on how regulatory bodies try to shape efforts to amass wealth without threatening vital environmental services such as a safe place to live and safe food and water. Scholarly work on the political economy of the environment also includes efforts of nongovernmental actors – corporations and environmental social movements – to shape environmental policies and behaviour.

(Rudel, Roberts and Carmin 2011, 222)

Clapp (2018) distinguishes between a liberal, an institutional, and a political approach to Environmental Political Economy.

Environmental political economists have extended the focus of political economy. Some scholars focus their analysis on trying to understand the ways in which economic activity affects environmental outcomes, while others concentrate their efforts on the political challenges of designing and implementing economic policy tools to address environmental problems.

(Clapp 2018, 430)

The Critique of the Political Economy of the Environment studies the relationship between capitalism and nature. For example, James O'Connor (1998) argues that there is in capitalism not just a class antagonism and an antagonism between productive forces and relations of production, but also a "second contradiction of capitalism" (O'Connor 1998, 158–177), "the contradiction between capitalist production relations (and productive forces) and the conditions of capitalist production, or 'capitalist relations and forces of social reproduction'" (O'Connor 1998, 160). This means that there is "a potential catastrophic conflict between global capitalism and the global environment" (Foster 2002, 10)

The analysis of gender, racism, and the environment matters for Political Economy. Gender-based discrimination and exploitation, racism, and the destruction of the environment cannot be reduced to capitalism but have played particular roles in the capitalist economy and capitalist society that Political Economy should and does study.

2.5 Conclusion

This chapter asked: What is Political Economy?
We can now summarise the main findings.

Finding 1: Political Economy

Political Economy is focused on the analysis of the intersection of the economy and politics. Political Economy is an approach that analyses society. It utilises social theory, empirical social research, and moral philosophy. It studies how the interaction of politics and the economy works and its roles in society. It sees the dialectical relationship between the economy and politics as the most important factor shaping society. An important focus is the analysis of the production, distribution, and consumption of goods and services in the context of society. Political Economy often is a critical analysis of how capitalist society works, is organised, and impacts society and the lives of humans in society. This approach is termed Critique of Political Economy. Critique of Political Economy is the study of class and other power relations in class societies and capitalist societies with a special focus on the economic relations' impact on society. Political Economy is the analysis of the production, distribution, and consumption of goods whereby humans reproduce themselves and society and so survive.

Finding 2: Ibn Khaldûn

Ibn Khaldûn was an early representative of Political Economy who formulated foundations of the Labour Theory of Value.

Finding 3: Four Political Economy Approaches

Four important approaches to Political Economy are Classical Political Economy, Critique of Political Economy, Neoclassical Political Economy, and Keynesian Political Economy.

Finding 4: Classical Political Economy

Classical Political Economy studies the production, distribution, and consumption of goods in society. Important representatives were Adam Smith, John Stuart Mill, and David Ricardo.

Finding 5: Critique of Political Economy

The Critique of Political Economy is the work of Karl Marx and those who build on it. Marx analyses how the capitalist mode of production and class societies work and gives a particular focus to the study of class relations, labour, and commodification.

Finding 6: Neoclassical Political Economy

Neoclassical Political Economy renamed Political Economy to Economics. It is often building mathematical models of the economy and lacks moral philosophy. Friedrich Hayek and Milton Friedman are representatives of the Chicago School. They have updated Adam Smith's theorem of the invisible hand that argues that markets are self-ordering and self-organising systems into which the state should not intervene. This assumption has influenced the rise of what has often been characterised as neoliberalism, a market fundamentalism that preaches the commodification of everything.

Finding 7: Keynesian Political Economy

Keynesian Political Economy is based on the works of John Maynard Keynes. Keynes argues that capitalism creates inequalities and that a welfare state is needed for taming the capitalist economy and its inequalities.

Finding 8: Further Approaches to Political Economy

Further approaches to Political Economy include, among others, Feminist Political Economy, the Political Economy of Racism, and the Political Economy of the Environment (Political Ecology).

Finding 9: Feminism, Racism, and Environmentalism

Feminist Political Economy studies the interaction of capitalism and patriarchy. The Political Economy of Racism analyses racial capitalism. The Political Economy of the Environment (Political Ecology) investigates the relationship between capitalism and nature. The analysis of gender, racism, and the environment matters for Political Economy. Gender-based discrimination and exploitation, racism, and the destruction of the environment cannot be reduced to capitalism, but have played particular roles in the capitalist economy and capitalist society that Political Economy should and does study.

The main dividing line in contemporary Political Economy is between Neoclassical Political Economy and the Critique of Political Economy. Table 2.2 shows differences between these two strands of Political Economy.

Table 2.2 Differences between Neoclassical Economics and the Critique of Political Economy

Dimension	Neoclassical Economics	Critique of Political Economy
Structuration principle	Markets structure the economy	Class structures the economy
Economic logic	The market self-regulates and is a self-organising system; crisis and monopoly are the exceptions to the rule	Markets do not self-regulate; rather, crisis and monopoly are immanent features of the capitalist economy and its markets
Models and concepts of the economy	Static equilibrium models	Dynamics, history, and dialectics
Scope	Microeconomics	Totality: Macroeconomics, economy, and society
Value	Subjective concept of value	Objective concept of value: Labour Theory of Value
Approach and Methods	Mathematics	Moral philosophy, social theory, and empirical social research
The role of the state	Non-intervention of the state in markets, and redistribution from labour to capital	Regulation of the economy by the state, welfare state, and redistribution from the rich to the poor and capital to labour
Agency	Methodological individualism	Dialectics of structure and agency, and analysis of class and social struggles and contradictions
Concept of freedom	Individual freedom of property that justifies inequality	Social freedom that guarantees a good life for all
Role of ethics	Claim that Economics is a value-neutral science	Explicit use of moral philosophy

Notes

1 Data source: Forbes 2000 List (2022), https://www.forbes.com/global2000/#6c84e024335d, accessed on 12 December 2022.
2 See: https://en.wikipedia.org/wiki/Ireland_v_Commission
3 Data source: https://www.opensecrets.org/federal-lobbying/clients/summary?cycle=2019&id=D000021754, accessed on 26 October 2021.
4 Ibid.

References

Amin, Samir. 2009. *Eurocentrism*. New York: Monthly Review Press.
Armstrong, Pat and M. Patricia Connelly. 1989. Feminist Political Economy: An Introduction. *Studies in Political Economy* 30: 5–12.
Bentham, Jeremy. 2000. *An Introduction to the Principles of Morals and Legislation*. Kitchener: Batoche Books.
Bhattacharyya, Gargi. 2018. *Rethinking Racial Capitalism. Questions of Reproduction and Survival*. London: Rowman & Littlefield.
Blanchard, Oliver. 2017. *Macroeconomics*. Harlow: Pearson.
Caporaso, James A. and David P. Levine. 1992. *Theories of Political Economy*. Cambridge: Cambridge University Press.
Clapp, Jennifer. 2018. Environmental Political Economy. In *Companion to Environmental Studies*, edited by Noel Castree, Mike Hulme, and James D. Proctor, 430–434. London: Routledge.
Corporate Europe Observatory and Lobby Control. 2021. *The Lobby Network: Big Tech's Web of Influence in the EU*. Brussels: CEO & Lobby Control. https://corporateeurope.org/sites/default/files/2021-08/The%20lobby%20network%20-%20Big%20Tech%27s%20web%20of%20influence%20in%20the%20EU.pdf
De, Rahul and Alex M. Thomas. 2018. Rethinking Undergraduate Economics Education. *Economic & Political Weekly* 53 (3): 21–24.
Deen, Sayyed Misbah. 2010. *Science under Islam – Rise, Decline and Revival*. Morrisville, NC: Lulu.
Duménil, Gérard and Dominique Lévy. 2004. *Capital Resurgent: Roots of the Neoliberal Revolution*. Cambridge, MA: Harvard University Press.
Eisenstein, Zillah. 1979. Capitalist Patriarchy and Socialist Feminism. In *Capitalist Patriarchy and the Case for Socialist Feminism*, edited by Zillah R. Eisenstein, 5–40. New York: Monthly Review Press.
Foster, John Bellamy. 2002. *Ecology against Capitalism*. New York: Monthly Review Press.
Friedman, Milton. 2002. *Capitalism and Freedom*. Chicago, IL: The University of Chicago Press.
Friedman, Milton. 1970/2015. The Social Responsibility of Business Is to Increase Its Profits. In *Business Ethics. Case Studies and Selected Readings*, edited by Marianne Moody Jennings, 110–115. Stamford, CT: Cengage Learning. Eighth edition.
Fuchs, Christian. 2020. *Communication and Capitalism. A Critical Theory*. London: University of Westminster Press. DOI: https://doi.org/10.16997/book45
Fuchs, Christian. 2019. *Rereading Marx in the Age of Digital Capitalism*. London: Pluto Press.
Gibson-Graham, J.K. 2005. Economy. In *New Keywords*, edited by Tony Bennett, Lawrence Grossberg, and Meaghan Morris, 94–97. Oxford: Blackwell.

Habermas, Jürgen. 1991. *The Structural Transformation of the Public Sphere. An Inquiry into a Category of Bourgeois Society.* Cambridge, MA: The MIT Press.

Harvey, David. 2005. *A Brief History of Neoliberalism.* Oxford: Oxford University Press.

Hayek, Friedrich A. 1988. *The Fatal Conceit: The Errors of Socialism: Collected Works, Vol. 1.* London: Routledge.

Hunt, E.K. and Mark Lautzenheiser. 2011. *History of Economic Thought. A Critical Perspective.* Armonk, NY: Sharp. Third edition.

Jevons, William S. 1911. *The Theory of Political Economy.* Basingstoke: Palgrave Macmillan. Fourth edition.

Jevons, W. Stanley. 1871. *The Theory of Political Economy.* London: Macmillan. Fifth edition.

Jevons, W. Stanley. 1863. *Notice of a General Mathematical Theory of Political Economy.* London: John Murray.

Keynes, John Maynard. 1936. *General Theory of Employment, Interest and Money.* Cambridge: Cambridge University Press. Third edition.

Khaldûn, Ibn. 2015. *The Muqaddimah: An Introduction to History. The Classic Islamic History of the World.* Princeton, NJ: Princeton University Press.

Klein, Naomi. 2007. *The Shock Doctrine. The Rise of Disaster Capitalism.* New York: Metropolitan Books.

Lee, Frederic. 2011. *A History of Heterodox Economics. Challenging the Mainstream in the Twentieth Century.* Abingdon: Routledge.

Leiman, Melvin M. 1993. *The Political Economy of Racism. A History.* London: Pluto.

Macpherson, Crawford B. 1962. *The Political Theory of Possessive Individualism.* Oxford: Oxford University Press.

Mankiw, N. Gregory. 2021. *Principles of Economics.* Boston, MA: Cengage. Ninth edition.

Mankiw, N. Gregory. 2018. *Principles of Macroeconomics.* Boston, MA: Cengage Learning. Eighth edition.

Mankiw, N. Gregory and Mark P. Taylor. 2020. *Economics.* Andover: Cengage. Fifth edition.

Mankiw, N. Gregory and Mark P. Taylor. 2017. *Economics.* Andover: Cengage. Fourth edition.

Mankiw, N. Gregory and Mark P. Taylor. 2014. *Economics.* Andover: Cengage. Third edition.

Marshall, Alfred. 1890. *Principles of Economics.* New York: Cosimo Books.

Marx, Karl. 1894. *Capital Volume III.* London: Penguin.

Marx, Karl. 1867. *Capital Volume I.* London: Penguin.

Marx, Karl. 1862/1863. *Theories of Surplus Value. Parts 1, 2, 3.* London: Lawrence & Wishart.

Marx, Karl. 1861–1863. *Economic Manuscript of 1861–63.* In *Marx & Engels Collected Works (MECW) Volume 31.* London: Lawrence & Wishart.

Marx, Karl. 1857/1858. *Grundrisse.* London: Penguin.

Marx, Karl. 1847. The Poverty of Philosophy. Answer to the "Philosophy of Poverty" by M. Proudhon. In *Marx & Engels Collected Works (MECW) Volume 6*, 105–212. London: Lawrence & Wishart.

Marx, Karl. 1844. Economic and Philosophic Manuscripts of 1844. In *Marx & Engels Collected Works (MECW) Volume 3*, 229–346. London: Lawrence & Wishart.

Marx, Karl. 1843a. Contribution to the Critique of Hegel's Philosophy of Law. In *Marx & Engels Collected Works (MECW) Volume 3*, 3–129. London: Lawrence & Wishart.

Marx, Karl. 1843b. On the Jewish Question. In *Marx & Engels Collected Works (MECW) Volume 3*, 146–174. London: Lawrence & Wishart.

Marx, Karl and Friedrich Engels. 1848. The Manifesto of the Communist Party. In *Marx & Engels Collected Works (MECW) Volume 6*, 477–519. London: Lawrence & Wishart.

Menger, Carl. 1871. *Principles of Economics*. Auburn, AL: Ludwig von Mises Institute.

Mies, Maria. 2014. *Patriarchy and Accumulation on a World Scale: Women in the International Division of Labour*. London: Zed Books.

Mill, James. 1824. *Elements of Political Economy*. London: Baldwin, Cradock, and Joy. Second edition.

Mill, John Stuart. 1859. *On Liberty*. Lanham, MD: Rowman & Littlefield.

Mill, John Stuart. 1848. *Principles of Political Economy and Chapters on Socialism*. Oxford: Oxford University Press.

Mill, John Stuart. 1844. *Essays on Some Unsettled Questions of Political Economy*. Marston Gate: Amazon.

Mosco, Vincent. 2009. *The Political Economy of Communication*. London: Sage. Second edition.

O'Connor, James. 1998. *Natural Causes. Essays in Ecological Marxism*. New York: Guilford Press.

Piketty, Thomas. 2020. *Capital and Ideology*. Cambridge, MA: Harvard University Press.

Ricardo, David. 1824. *On the Principles of Political Economy and Taxation*. London: John Murray. Third edition.

Robinson, Cedric J. 2000. *Black Marxism. The Making of the Black Radical Tradition*. Chapel Hill, NC: The University of North Carolina Press. New edition.

Rudel, Thomas K., J. Timmons Roberts, and JoAnn Carmin. 2011. Political Economy of the Environment. *Annual Review of Sociology* 37: 221–238.

Santos, Boaventura de Sousa. 2017. *Decolonising the University. The Challenge of Deep Cognitive Justice*. Newcastle upon Tyne: Cambridge Scholars.

Smith, Adam. 1776. *The Wealth of Nations*. Two volumes. Indianapolis, IN: Liberty Fund.

Smith, Adam. 1759. *The Theory of Moral Sentiments*. Indianapolis, IN: Liberty Fund.

Smith, Dorothy E. 1989. Feminist Reflections on Political Economy. *Studies in Political Economy* 30: 37–59.

Steuart, James. 1767. An *Inquiry into the Principles of Political Economy. Volume I*. London: Millar and Cadell.

Thomas, Alex M. 2021. *Macroeconomics. An Introduction*. Cambridge: Cambridge University Press.

Walby, Sylvia. 1990. *Theorizing Patriarchy*. Oxford: Basil Blackwell.

Walras, Léon. 1874. *Elements of Pure Economics*. Abingdon: Routledge.

Williamson, Stephen D. 2018. *Macroeconomics. Global edition*. Harlow: Pearson. Sixth edition.

Wolff, Richard D. and Stephen A. Resnick. 2012. *Contending Economic Theories. Neoclassical, Keynesian, and Marxian*. Cambridge, MA: MIT Press.

Recommended Readings and Exercises

Readings

The following texts are recommended as accompanying readings to this chapter.

Vincent Mosco. 2009. *The Political Economy of Communication*. London: Sage. Second edition.
Chapter 2: What is Political Economy? Definitions and Characteristics
Chapter 3: What is Political Economy? Schools of Thought

James A. Caporaso and David P. Levine. 1992. *Theories of Political Economy*. Cambridge: Cambridge University Press.
Chapter 1: Politics and Economics
Chapter 2: The Classical Approach
Chapter 3: Marxian Political Economy
Chapter 4: Neoclassical Political Economy
Chapter 5: Keynesian Political Economy

Dorothy E. Smith. 1989. Feminist Reflections on Political Economy. *Studies in Political Economy* 30: 37–59.

Exercise 2.3   Neoliberalism and Neoclassical Political Economy 1

Milton Friedman (1912–2006) was one of the leading Neoclassical Political Economists. His main book is called "Capitalism and Freedom". Watch the video of his talk "Is Capitalism Humane?"

Milton Friedman: Is Capitalism Humane?
Cornell University, 27 September 1977
https://www.youtube.com/watch?v=27Tf8RN3uiM
https://miltonfriedman.hoover.org/objects/57281/is-capitalism-humane

Discuss:

What are Milton Friedman's main arguments?
What is his answer to the question: Is capitalism humane?

What are important elements of the version of Political Economy that Milton Friedman advances? Discuss example arguments from his talk and the discussion. What kind of Political Economy does he advocate? How do you assess his opinions and his approach?

Milton Friedman says in his talk that everything should be a commodity, a good that is sold on markets for money. What are the consequences for society when everything is a commodity? What happens when health care, education, the news and the Internet take on the commodity form? What is the role of the commodity in these realms? Should commodities play a role in these realms or not? Why respectively why not?

Exercise 2.4   Neoliberalism and Neoclassical Political Economy 2

Naomi Klein is a Canadian writer and filmmaker. She is known for books such as "No Logo", "The Shock Doctrine: The Rise of Disaster Capitalism", "This Changes Everything: Capitalism VS. The Climate".
"The Shock Doctrine" is a 2009 movie about Klein's book *"The Shock Doctrine. The Rise of Disaster Capitalism"*. Watch the following movie:

Whitecross, Mat and Michael Winterbottom (directors). 2009. The Shock Doctrine. Renegade Pictures, Revolution Films, Channel 4. Movie information: https://www.imdb.com/title/tt1355640/

In addition, read the following chapter in Naomi Klein's book:
Naomi Klein. 2007. *The Shock Doctrine. The Rise of Disaster Capitalism*. New York: Metropolitan Books.
Chapter 2: The Other Doctor Shock: Milton Friedman and the Search for a Laissez-Faire Laboratory.

Discuss:

How does Naomi Klein assess neoliberalism?
How does Naomi Klein assess Milton Friedman's thought?
What do you think about Naomi Klein's criticism?
With whose view do you more agree, Naomi Klein or Milton Friedman? Why? Try to give arguments for your opinion.

3 What is Media Economics?

What You Will Learn in This Chapter

- You will learn about the foundations of Media Economics;
- You will look at different definitions of Media Economics;
- You will engage with a model of Media Economics that outlines the various dimensions of what it means to study the media economy.

3.1 Introduction

Many of us consume media content such as news, music, films, video streams each day. We do so by making use of tablets, phones, laptops, and other hardware that is equipped with software. Hardware, software, and content are media products created in the media economy. Media Economics is a field of study that analyses how the media economy looks like. In this section, we discuss the foundations of this field.

The goal of this chapter is to provide a basic introduction to Media Economics. First, it engages with definitions of Media Economics (Section 3.2). Second, the chapter outlines a model of Media Economics (Section 3.3). Third, conclusions are drawn (Section 3.4).

3.2 Definitions of Media Economics

3.2.1 Foundations of Media Economics: What Are Media?

Humans are social and societal beings. This means that they live in and through relationships and relations with other human beings. Not only human beings and society, but all of nature and the world are relational. In dialectical philosophy, this is expressed by saying that the world consists of dialectical relations between moments, each of which has its own existence and influences the other, which results in dynamism, production of the new and reproduction of the overall context in which these moments are situated. The dialectical philosopher Hegel says that Something has an unmediated existence of its own – "it is so, because it is" – and it is at the same time

DOI: 10.4324/9781003391203-4

"*mediated* by a circle of circumstances, – it is so, because the circumstances are so" (Hegel 1830/2010, §149).

Media are structures that enable and condition the relation between two dialectical moments so that the One is reflected into an Other and the Other is reflected into the One. Mediation is the process of this reflection and interaction. Thus, cells reproduce themselves mediated by organs and the organism. The reproduction of the body of a living being is mediated by the brain, the nervous system, and the blood system, which regulate the interaction of the organs.

In society, we are interested in how humans together organise their everyday life. They do this by producing and reproducing social and societal relations. Human existence is mediated; it is made possible and conditioned by structures. Every relationship between humans is mediated. Humans, social systems, techno-social systems (such as communication technologies), subsystems of society (such as the economy, the political system, and culture), and society as a whole are forms of sociality that are mediators of communication. This means that sociality is produced and reproduced on the basis of existing social and societal structures. Jean-Paul Sartre (1960/2004, 106) puts it this way, that in society there are relations "through the mediation of a third party".

In the communication process, at least two humans interact with each other, sharing parts of their information and knowledge about the world, so that a social relationship is produced or reproduced. Communication is a production process in which humans produce or reproduce sociality, social relations, social structures, social systems, social relations, and ultimately society (Fuchs 2020, chapters 4 and 6). There is a dialectic of production and communication. We produce communication and communicate productively. Communication is always mediated. Where there is communication, there are mediators (media) and vice versa. Therefore, a strict distinction between Media Studies and Communication Studies does not make sense. Marx (1857/1858, 523) already spoke of the importance of the means of communication in capitalism and society as part of the productive forces, thus illustrating the connection between communication and media. For Raymond Williams (1980/2005, 53–72), means of communication are means of production. With the help of means of communication, humans produce meanings, information, news, entertainment, culture, worldviews, ideology, etc. Means of communication are "the institutions and forms in which ideas, information, and attitudes" are produced, mediated, and interpreted (Williams 1976, 9).

If means of communication are always also means of production, it becomes clear that the media always have an economic dimension. They are means of work and means of communication. Media are used to organise communication in the economy. With media like the computer, knowledge workers produce content that satisfies the human need for information. In capitalism, such content stands in the context of specific commodity forms such as media content, advertising, and media technologies as commodities.

Media as means of communication are "machines of social networking" that operate with symbols, codes, and signs, require media technologies, have form and content, transcend space and time, and are ubiquitous, that is omnipresent, in humans' everyday lives and in society (Winkler 2008, 11). Media are also machines of sign production and structure generation (Winkler 2008, 313).

In production, distribution, and reception, media play different roles as intermediaries, resulting in different types of media (Fuchs 2020, chapter 6). One important characteristic of the networked computer is that it enables the production and consumption of information at the same time, whereby consumers of information become producers, so-called prosumers. The computer is therefore a means of communication, as well as a means of work. The networked computer supports the blurring and liquefaction of the boundaries between spheres and phenomena such as work and leisure, labour and play, production and consumption, the public and the private, etc.. It is, therefore, a convergence technology. In modern society, media organisations have emerged in which media technologies, media content, media as infrastructures of society, etc. are produced. Media organisations are organisations where humans produce information that is made publicly available to society so that members of society can make interpretations of these contents. Media organisations have specific structures of ownership and production (economy), decision-making and governance (politics), and understandings of the world (culture). A media system is the totality of media organisations within a certain societal setting that features a common context consisting of common media laws and media regulations, a common economic system, a common cultural context, common standards and experiences of media work, and common audiences relating to different media organisations. Due to the importance of media organisations and media systems, the media economy has emerged as a subsystem of the modern economy. The media economy is thus a sub-aspect of the economy and society, the analysis of which is an important task for Media and Communication Studies.

Marx (1857/1858, 523) argues that the means of communication need special analysis "since they make up a form of fixed capital which has its own laws of realization". In the capitalist economy, means of communication are just like other means of production fixed for a longer time in the production process, which is why Marx speaks of fixed capital. The media system produces information and its infrastructure. A media organisation, therefore, has characteristics that make it different from, for example, a bank, a sausage factory or an oil company. Media Economics, therefore, is not a part of Business Studies, but rather is a distinct subfield of Media and Communication Studies that analyses the distinct characteristics and contradictions of the media, information, and communication as economic and societal phenomena.

3.2.2 The Academic Field of Media and Communication Studies

Media Economics is a subfield of Media and Communication Studies. Media and Communication Studies is itself an inter- and transdisciplinary field: When we study the media and communication, we do so from particular angles, such as political communication, media psychology, media ethics and philosophy, that connect the study of the media to other fields of study.

The next table gives an overview of some of the subfields of Media and Communication Studies (see also Beck 2020, 175; Pfau 2008). Each subfield emerges from the overlap and interaction of Media and Communication Studies and another field. The only one that is originally at home in Media and Communication Studies itself is Journalism Studies. The table just contains examples. Neither does it claim to be complete nor are the labels used for the subfields the definitive ones or the only ones in use (see Table 3.1).

According to the understanding shown in the table, Media Economics as a sub-aspect of Media and Communication Studies is a combination of the analysis of the media with aspects of Economics.

If Media and Communication Studies were a true interdiscipline and transdiscipline, then many of its subfields would constantly interact and work together. The field could then be visualised as a blossoming flower where the leaves intersect. But often the subfields operate rather separately, which is why Rosengren (1993) argues that Media and Communication Studies is not a field, but something that consists of isolated frog ponds. He argues that there is a lack of coherence and unity. The situation certainly is not that drastic today. There are cross-cutting themes such as the Internet and digital media that are treated from a variety of perspectives. Certain approaches such as the Political Economy of Communication are combinations of a variety of other subfields such as Media Economics, Political Communication, Media Policy Studies, Media Sociology, Media Philosophy, Communication Theory, and Media and Communication Ethics. Silvio Waisbord (2019) speaks of Media and Communication Studies as a postdiscipline. He argues that the plurality and diversity of the field is also something positive, but nonetheless calls for overcoming fragmentation and more co-operation. "To continue to wait for communication to become a cohesive field of inquiry is like waiting for Godot" (Waisbord 2019, 74). Waisbord argues:

> Communication studies embodies post-disciplinarity. It has been historically less concerned with disciplinary boundaries than the traditional disciplines. [...] Communication has been a meeting point for various disciplinary approaches within specific lines of research [...] A proto post-discipline even in its salad days, communication has been too diverse to succumb to a single vision of science or discipline, in the United States, Europe or other regions of the world. [...] Research within self-contained, ever-shrinking areas of specialization discourages addressing big, cross-cutting questions.[...] I want to conclude by proposing two analytical paths to cultivate cross-pollination [...] One way to address this is to think about big ideas that cross several areas of specialization: from information uncertainty management to news framing, from factors driving information sharing to mediatization, from effective message design to suitable conditions for democratic deliberation. Find

Table 3.1 Media and Communication Studies and some of its subfields

Media and Communication Studies	
	Journalism Studies
Anthropology	Media Anthropology
Arts	Film and Screen Studies, Media Arts, Media Aesthetics
Critical Race Theory, Racism Studies	Ethnicity and Race in Communication
Cultural Studies	Media and Popular Culture
Economics	Media Economics, Political Economy of Communication and the Media, Organisational Communication, Public Relations, Media Industry Studies, Media Management, Media Business Studies
Environmental Studies	Environmental Communication
Feminism, Gender Studies	Feminist Media and Communication Studies, Media and Gender
Geography	Geography of Media and Communication
Global and Area Studies	International and Global Media and Communication Studies
Health Science	Health Communication
History	Media History
Informatics	Digital Media Studies, Internet Research, Data Studies
Legal Studies	Media Policy Studies, Communication Law and Policy
Linguistics	Media Linguistics
Musicology	Popular Music Studies
Pedagogy	Media Education, Media Pedagogy
Philosophy	Media Philosophy, Media and Communication Ethics, Communication Theory, Digital Media Ethics
Political Science	Political Communication
Psychology	Media Psychology
Religious Studies	Media and Religion
Sociology	Media Sociology
Sport Studies	Media and Sports, Game Studies
...	...

what different slices of scholarship have in common and develop and refine cross-cutting arguments. [...] A second path to building bridges is to foreground communication problems of relevance across research clusters. [...] communication studies actually comprises several lines of research focused on many public problems, such as intolerance, lack of social empathy, misinformation, social exclusion, public health inequalities, institutional racism, sexism, and climate change.

(Waisbord 2019, 130, 131, 139, 140, 141)

A discipline is a distinct field of analysis that focuses on a certain aspect of the world, has its own theories, methods, publications such as journals and handbooks, academic conferences, study programmes. Media and Communication Studies has always had loose boundaries with connections to many other fields. At the same time, it has also become very specialised. Silvio Waisbord stresses that the field should more focus on the big global challenges of contemporary societies, which would help to overcome the fragmentation of Media and Communication Studies' into independent subfields.

Fuchs and Qiu (2018) argue that current important developments in Media and Communication Studies include the analysis of global media and communication, the importance of digital media and communication, a new critical and materialist turn, and praxis communication that analyses and challenges communication/media/digital injustices. "In our view, it is important for the field of communication studies to envision its future as being theoretically innovative and politically engaged, holistic instead of fragmented, truly global and interdisciplinary, reflexive and praxis-oriented" (Fuchs and Qiu 2018, 231).

Media Economics connects the field of Media and Communication Studies to the academic field of Economics. There are different ways of how this is done, which has resulted in different approaches to Media Economics.

3.2.3 Approaches to Media Economics

The economy has different dimensions. If we imagine that we look at the economy with a microscope, then we can zoom in and out of the economic system. This idea of zooming into and out of the economy allows us to distinguish different levels: the micro-economy, the meso-economy, and the macro-economy. The words "micro", "meso" and "macro" come from the Greek terms *mikrós, mésos* and *makrós*, respectively. *mikrós* means "small", *mésos* means "middle", and *makrós* means "large". We can distinguish between the study of the (media) economy at the micro-level, the meso-level, and the macro-level. Macroeconomics looks at the big picture of the economy. Microeconomics is focused on individual and organisational aspects of the economy. Mesoeconomics is a mid-range level of the economy that analyses economic institutions. Here is an overview of the three dimensions of Media Economics:

- **Microeconomic analysis of the media:**
  the analysis of individual and organisational aspects of the media economy, namely media organisations, and the individual and group behaviour of media workers/producers, media managers, media owners, media investors, media marketers, media advertisers, and media consumers;
- **Mesoeconomic analysis of the media:**
  the analysis of media institutions such as the media, cultural, digital and creative industries, media markets, the banking and monetary system, intellectual property rights, international trade agreements and organisations;
- **Macroeconomic analysis of the media (also called Political Economy of Communication and the Media):**
  the analysis of the big picture of the media economy, the analysis of the media economy in the context of society as a whole, and the analysis of media and communication in the context of capitalist society, the economy as a whole, the state, culture, and ideology.

There are different definitions of what the field of Media Economics is about. There are understandings and definitions that more focus on the microeconomic, the mesoeconomic or the macroeconomic dimensions. Here are some examples.

3.2.4 Microeconomic Definitions of Media Economics

- "Media economics provides a means to understand the activities and functions of media companies as economic institutions" (Albarran 2004, 303);
- "Media economics [...] (develops an) understanding of the way in which media businesses operate and are managed" (Doyle 2002, 2);
- "Media economics examines how the goods of information, entertainment and the dissemination of advertising messages are produced, distributed and consumed in mass media focused on current reporting"[1] (Heinrich 2001, 20);
- "Media economics is a term employed to refer to the business operations and financial activities of firms producing and selling output into the various media industries" (Owen, Carveth and Alison 1998, 5);
- "Media economics is concerned with how media operators meet the informational and entertainment wants and needs of audiences, advertisers and society with available resources. It deals with the factors influencing production of media goods and services and the allocation of those products for consumption" (Picard 1989, 7).

These definitions have in common that they focus on defining Media Economics as analysis of the operations of media companies and their products.

3.2.5 Mesoeconomic Definitions of Media Economics

- "Media economics is the study of how media industries use scarce resources to produce content [...] to satisfy various wants and needs" (Albarran 1996, 5);

- "The media economy is the study of how media firms and industries function across different levels of activity in tandem with other forces through the use of theories, concepts, and principles drawn from macroeconomic and microeconomic perspectives" (Albarran 2010, 17);
- "The object of knowledge of media economics are the economic relationships on media markets and in media companies"[2] (Beyer and Carl 2012, 9);
- Media Industry Studies is the "critical analysis of *how individuals, institutions, and industries produce and circulate cultural forms in historically and geographically contextualized ways*" (Herbert, Lotz and Punathambekar 2020, 7);
- "In our view, media economics primarily examines the institutional and organisational conditions of the production and distribution of news/reports, entertainment and advertising. Media economics is the stakeholder-theoretical analysis of the media. It sheds light on the economic conditions of journalistic professional action and analyses the possibilities and limits of the (economic, ethical, democratic, pedagogical, etc.) performance of the media"[3] (Karmasin 1998, 55);
- "Media economics is a specific application of economic laws and theories to media industries and firms, showing how economic, regulatory, and financial pressures direct and constrain activities and their influences on the dynamics of media markets" (Picard 2006, 23).

These understandings of Media Economics have in common that they focus on the analysis of media companies in the context of institutions such as media markets, legal frameworks, and the state.

3.2.6 Macroeconomic Definitions of Media Economics

The macroeconomic understanding of Media Economics is also often called Political Economy of Communication and the Media. Let us have a look at some definitions:

- Media Economics is "a sub-discipline of Journalism and Communication Studies that examines economic and journalistic phenomena of the media system in capitalist market economies with the help of economic theories. In describing the task, a distinction must again be made between a positive and a normative version of media economics. Positive media economics analyses and explains the economic and journalistic phenomena of the media system, normative media economics develops options for shaping society with a view to societal consensus on the goals of the media system"[4] (Kiefer 2001, 41; Kiefer and Steininger 2014, 51). Political Economy of Communication and the Media "attempts to explain overall interrelationships of political, sociological and economic factors (of the media). And it includes value judgements in its analysis"[5] (Kiefer 2001, 53). It asks "which steering and regulation mechanisms actually determine the media offer in our society and whether these mechanisms and the institutional arrangements on which they are based, make it at all likely that these, albeit vaguely defined, societal goals will be achieved"[6] (Kiefer 2001, 61). "Media Economics of the kind conceptualised here examines media systems in capitalist market economies"[7] (Kiefer 2001, 69).

These definitions have in common that they understand Media Economics as the analysis of the media in the context of society and societal contexts such as capitalist society.

A substantial number of macroeconomic approaches stress that it is not enough to analyse the micro- and meso-economic levels of the media and that the analysis of the media in the context of its broader societal context is important and should guide any analysis of the media and communication. For example, Manfred Knoche and Werner A. Meier stress this aspect:

- "Media economics should not be reduced to economics of the media (microlevel), but should be developed above all as a political economy of the mass media (partial-analysis and macrolevels)" (Knoche 1999, 86). "One of the basic questions of Media Economics in communication studies as a Critique of the Political Economy of the Media is the analysis of the relationship between the media industry and capitalist society, i.e. the role of the media for the entire material, economic, social, political and cultural human life. The central objects of investigation are thus, on the one hand, the specific developments of media production, distribution and consumption, and on the other hand, their functioning for the development of the entire capitalist economic and social system"[8] (Knoche 2002, 105);
- "The Political Economy of the Media has the task of analysing public communication processes as specifically societal. It has to work out in what way capitalist/market relations of production influence the societal communication carried out via mass media. [...] In contrast to traditional Media Economics, which provides a microanalysis of 'purely' economic processes in companies and on markets, the Political Economy of Public Communication captures the economic and political structural features of media and their relationships to each other from a macro perspective"[9] (Meier 2003, 229, 233).

In a nutshell, we can say that Media Economics as Political Economy of the Media and Communication analyses the relationship of media, economy, and society.

3.3 A Model of Media Economics

Altmeppen and Karmasin give a general definition of Media Economics:

Media Economics is a teaching and research programme that focuses on the foundations, forms and consequences of public communication with regard to its economic constitution. Media Economics focuses on the interplay between economic and journalistic factors. The economic

structures, services and functions of communication and its development are analysed with regard to their influence on the constitution of
the public sphere (private and institutional communication, individual
and mass communication).[10]

(Altmeppen and Karmasin 2003, 44; see also Altmeppen 2013, 218)

This definition is a bit too general. It does not identify different levels of
analysis and therefore does not make clear that there are different forms of
Media Economics that focus on different levels of analysis.

While macroeconomic and mesoeconomic analyses of the media often exclude a focus on society as a whole (Political Economy) and therefore operate
in a rather reductive manner, Political Economy approaches need to take into
account economic institutions, organisations, groups, and individuals in their
analyses. The upper level of analysis of the media encompasses, encapsulates
and envelops the lower levels, whereas lower-level analysis does not automatically include upper levels.

Based on the example definitions given above, we can now provide a syn-
thesis definition of Media Economics:

*Media Economics analyses communication processes and the production,
distribution and consumption of information and the media with respect to
media actors such as workers/producers, owners, managers, advertisers, marketing and public relations departments, consumers) and media organisations
(Media Microeconomics); media-economic institutions such as the media, cultural, digital and creative industries, media markets, the banking and monetary*

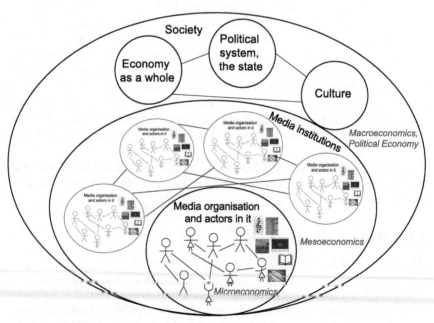

Figure 3.1 A model of Media Economics.

system, intellectual property rights, and international trade agreements and institutions (Media Mesoeconomics); and society as a whole including capitalist society, the economy as a whole, the state, culture and ideology (Media Macroeconomics, Political Economy of Communication and the Media).

Figure 3.1 provides a model of the three encapsulated levels of the media economy and its analysis. Media Macroeconomics, Media Mesoeconomics and Media Microeconomics are nested within each other.

3.4 Conclusion

This chapter presented foundations of Media Economics. We can summarise the main findings.

Finding 1: Media Economics

Media Economics analyses communication processes and the production, distribution and consumption of information and the media with respect to media actors such as workers/producers, owners, managers, advertisers, marketing and public relations departments, consumers and media organisations (Media Microeconomics); media-economic institutions such as the media, cultural, digital and creative industries, media markets, the banking and monetary system, intellectual property rights, and international trade agreements and institutions (Media Mesoeconomics); and society as a whole including capitalist society, the economy as a whole, the state, culture and ideology (Media Macroeconomics, Political Economy of Communication and the Media).

Finding 2: Media Economics Levels

There are different forms and analysis levels of Media Economics. Media Microeconomics and Media Mesoeconomics often do not take (capitalist) society as a whole into account in the context of the media and communication.

Notes

1 Translated from German: „Medienökonomie untersucht, wie die Güter Information, Unterhaltung und Verbreitung von Werbebotschaften in aktuell berichtenden Massenmedien produziert, verteilt und konsumiert werden".
2 Translated from German: „Das Erkenntnisobjekt der Medienökonomie sind die wirtschaftlichen Zusammenhänge auf Medienmärkten und in Medienunternehmen".
3 Translated from German:

> Medienökonomie untersucht in unserer Auffassung vor allem die institutionellen und organisatorischen Bedingungen der Produktion und der Verbreitung von Nachrichten/Berichten, Unterhaltung und Werbung. Medienökonomie ist die stakeholdertheoretische Analyse der Medien. Sie erhellt die ökonomischen Bedingtheiten journalistischen Berufshandelns und analysiert Möglichkeiten und Grenzen der (ökonomischen, ethischen, demokratischen, pädagogischen etc.) Leistungsfähigkeit von Medien.

4 Translated from German: Die Medienökonomik ist

> eine Teildisziplin der PKW [Publikzistik- und Kommunikationswissenschaft],
> die wirtschaftliche und publizistische Phänomene des Mediensystems kapi-
> talistischer Marktwirtschaften mit Hilfe ökonomischer Theorien untersucht.
> Bei der Aufgabenbeschreibung ist wieder zwischen einer positiven und einer
> normativen Version von Medienökonomie zu unterscheiden. Positive Medi-
> enökonomie analysiert und erklärt die wirtschaftlichen und publizistischen
> Phänomene des Mediensystems, normative Medienökonomie entwickelt
> Gestaltungsoptionen mit Blick auf gesellschaftlich konsentierte Ziele des
> Mediensystems.

5 Translated from German: Politische Ökonomie der Kommunikation und der
   Medien „versucht Gesamtzusammenhänge von politischen, soziologischen und
   ökonomischen Faktoren (der Medien) zu erklären. Und sie bezieht Werturteile in
   ihre Analyse ein“.

6 Translated from German: Es wird gefragt, „welche Steuerungsmechanismen das
   Medienangebot in unserer Gesellschaft eigentlich bestimmen und ob diese Steuerungsmechanismen und die ihnen zugrunde liegenden institutionellen Arrangements, eine Erreichung dieser, wenn auch nur vage definierten, gesellschaftlichen
   Ziele überhaupt wahrscheinlich machen“.

7 Translated from German: „Medienökonomie der hier konzeptualisierten Art untersucht Mediensysteme in kapitalistischen Marktwirtschaften“.

8 Translated from German:

> Zu den Grundfragen einer kommunikationswissenschaftlichen Medienökono-
> mie als Kritik der Politischen Ökonomie der Medien gehört die Analyse des
> Verhältnisses von Medienindustrie und kapitalistischer Gesellschaft, also der
> Rolle der Medien für das gesamte materielle, wirtschaftliche, gesellschaftli-
> che, soziale, politische und kulturelle menschliche Leben. Zentrale Untersu-
> chungsgegenstände sind also einerseits die spezifischen Entwicklungen der
> Medienproduktion, -distribution und -konsumtion, andererseits deren Funk-
> tionsweise für die Entwicklung des gesamten kapitalistischen Wirtschafts- und
> Gesellschaftssystems.

9 Translated from German:

> Der Politischen Ökonomie der Medien kommt die Aufgabe zu, öffentliche
> Kommunikationsprozesse als spezifisch gesellschaftlich zu analysieren. Sie
> hat herauszuarbeiten, auf welche Weise kapitalistische/marktwirtschaftliche
> Produktionsverhältnisse die über Massenmedien vollzogene gesellschaftliche
> Kommunikation beeinflussen. [...] Im Unterschied zur traditionellen Me-
> dienökonomie, die eine Mikroanalyse ‚rein‘ wirtschaftlicher Vorgänge bei
> Unternehmen und auf Märkten liefert, erfasst die Politische Ökonomie der
> öffentlichen Kommunikation die wirtschaftlichen und politischen Struk-
> turmerkmale von Medien und deren Beziehungen untereinander aus einer
> Makroperspektive.

10 Translated from German:

> Medienökonomie ist ein Lehr- und Forschungsprogramm, das die Grundlagen,
> Formen und Folgen der öffentlichen Kommunikation im Hinblick auf deren
> ökonomische Verfasstheit zum Inhalt hat. Im Zentrum der Medienökonomie
> steht das Zusammen- und Wechselspiel ökonomischer und publizistischer Fak-
> toren. Die ökonomischen Strukturen, Leistungen und Funktionen der Kommu-
> nikation und ihrer Entwicklung werden im Hinblick auf ihren Einfluss auf die
> Herstellung von Öffentlichkeit (private und institutionelle Kommunikation,
> Individual- und Massenkommunikation) erforscht.

References

Albarran, Alan B., ed. 2019. *A Research Agenda for Media Economics*. Cheltenham: Edward Elgar.

Albarran, Alan B. 2017. *The Media Economy*. New York: Routledge. Second edition.

Albarran, Alan B. 2010. *The Media Economy*. New York: Routledge. First edition.

Albarran, Alan B. 2004. Media Economics. In *The SAGE Handbook of Media Studies*, edited by John Downing, Denis McQuail, Philip Schlesinger, and Ellen Wartella, 291–307. London: Sage.

Albarran, Alan B. 1996. *Media Economics: Understanding Markets, Industries and Concepts*. Ames: Iowa State University Press.

Alexander, Alison et al., eds. 2004. *Media Economics. Theory and Practice*. Mahwah, NJ: Lawrence Erlbaum Associates. Third edition.

Altmeppen, Klaus-Dieter. 2013. Medienökonomie. In *Lexikon Kommunikations- und Medienwissenschaft*, edited by Günter Bentele, Hans-Bernd Brosius, and Otfried Jarren, 217–218. Second edition.

Altmeppen, Klaus-Dieter and Matthias Karmasin. 2003. Medienökonomie als transdisziplinäres Lehr- und Forschungsprogramm. In *Medien und Ökonomie. Band 1/1: Grundlagen der Medienökonomie: Kommunikations- und Medienwissenschaft, Wirtschaftswissenschaft*, edited by Klaus-Dieter Altmeppen and Matthias Karmasin, 19–51. Opladen: Westdeutscher Verlag.

Anderson, Simon P., Joel Waldfogel, and David Strömberg, eds. 2016. *Handbook of Media Economics*. Amsterdam: Elsevier.

Beck, Klaus. 2020. *Kommunikationswissenschaft*. Stuttgart: UTB. Sixth edition.

Beyer, Andrea and Petra Carl. 2012. *Einführung in die Medienökonomie*. München: UVK. Third edition.

Doyle, Gillian. 2013. *Understanding Media Economics*. Los Angeles: Sage. Second edition.

Doyle, Gillian. 2002. *Understanding Media Economics*. London: Sage. First edition.

Fuchs, Christian. 2020. *Communication and Capitalism: A Critical Theory*. London: University of Westminster Press. DOI: https://doi.org/10.16997/book45

Fuchs, Christian and Jack L. Qiu. 2018. Ferments in the Field: Introductory Reflections on the Past, Present and Future of Communication Studies. *Journal of Communication* 68 (2): 219–232.

Hegel, Georg Wilhelm Friedrich. 1830/2010. *Encyclopedia of the Philosophical Sciences in Basic Outline. Part I: Science of Logic*. Cambridge: Cambridge University Press.

Heinrich, Jürgen. 2001. *Medienökonomie. Band 1: Mediensystem, Zeitung, Zeitschrift, Anzeigenblatt*. Opladen: Westdeutscher Verlag.

Herbert, Daniel, Amanda D. Lotz, and Aswin Punathambekar. 2020. *Media Industry Studies*. Cambridge: Polity.

Hoskins, Colin, Stuart McFadyen, and Adam Finn. 2004. *Media Economics: Applying Economics to New and Traditional Media*. Thousand Oaks, CA: Sage.

Karmasin, Matthias. 1998. *Medienökonomie als Theorie (massen-)medialer Kommunikation*. Graz: Nausner & Nausner.

Kiefer, Marie Luise. 2001. *Medienökonomik*. München: Oldenbourg.

Kiefer, Marie Luise and Christian Steininger. 2014. *Medienökonomik*. München: Oldenbourg. Third edition.

Knoche, Manfred. 2002. Kommunikationswissenschaftliche Medienökonomie als Kritik der Politischen Ökonomie der Medien. In *Medienökonomie in der Kommunikationswissenschaft*, edited by Gabriele Siegert, 101–109. Münster: Lit.

Knoche, Manfred. 1999. Media Economics as a Subdiscipline of Communication Sciences. In *The German Communication Yearbook*, edited by Hans-Bernd Brosius and Christina Holtz-Bacha, 69–99. Cresskill, NJ: Hampton Press.

Marx, Karl. 1857/1858. *Grundrisse*. London: Penguin.

Meier, Werner A. 2003. Politische Ökonomie. In *Medien und Ökonomie. Band 1/1: Grundlagen der Medienökonomie: Kommunikations- und Medienwissenschaft, Wirtschaftswissenschaft*, edited by Klaus-Dieter Altmeppen and Matthias Karmasin, 215–243. Opladen: Westdeutscher Verlag.

Owen, James, Rod Carveth, and Alison Alexander. 1998. An Introduction to Media Economics Theory and Practice. In *Media Economics. Theory and Practice*, edited by Alison Alexander and Rod Varveth, 3–48. Mahwah: Lawrence Erlbaum.

Pfau, Michael. 2008. Epistemological and Disciplinary Intersections. *Journal of Communication* 58 (4): 597–602.

Picard, Robert. 2006. Historical Trends and Patterns in Media Economics. *In Handbook of Media Management and Economics*, edited by Alan B. Albarran, Sylvia M. Chan-Olmsted, and Michael O. Wirth, 23–36. Mahwah, NJ: Lawrence Erlbaum.

Picard, Robert G. 2001. *The Economics and Financing of Media Companies*. New York: Fordham University Press. Second edition.

Picard, Robert G. 1989. *Media Economics: Concepts and Issues*. London: Sage.

Rosengren, Karl Erik. 1993. From Field to Frog Ponds. *Journal of Communication* 43 (3): 6–17.

Sartre, Jean-Paul. 1960/2004. *Critique of Dialectical Reason. Volume 1: Theory of Practical Ensembles*. London: Verso.

Waisbord, Silvio. 2019. *Communication. A Post-Discipline*. Cambridge: Polity.

Williams, Raymond. 1980/2005. *Culture and Materialism*. London: Verso Books. S. 53–72.

Williams, Raymond. 1976. *Communications*. Harmondsworth: Penguin.

Winkler, Hartmut. 2008. *Basiswissen Medien*. Frankfurt am Main: Fischer.

Recommended Readings and Exercises

Exercise 3.1   Levels of Media Economics

Work in groups. Select a media phenomenon that your group is particularly interested in and that has recently been much discussed in public.

Create a list of Media Economics research questions that studies of this media phenomenon could focus on.

Order the research questions by the three levels of Media Economics (Media Macroeconomics/Political Economy of Communication and the Media, Media Mesoeconomics and Media Microeconomics).

Take care that you formulate at least five research questions at each of the three levels of analysis.

4 The Political Economy
of Communication and the Media

What You Will Learn in This Chapter

- You will read about what the Political Economy of Communication and the Media is all about;
- You will engage with principles of the Political Economy of Communication and the Media;
- You will learn how to apply principles of Political Economy to specific cases and examples.

4.1 Introduction

The analysis of the media and the media economy in the context of society has the advantage that it does not analyse the media in an isolated and uncritical manner that just describes what they are doing but takes large problems of society as the starting point for the analysis of the media and society. In this chapter, we introduce an approach to the analysis of the relationships between the media, the economy, and society – the Political Economy of Communication and the Media.

The goal of this chapter is to provide a basic introduction to the approach of the Political Economy of Communication. First, it engages with definitions of the Political Economy of Communication (Section 4.2). Second, it discusses principles and dimensions of the Political Economy of Communication (Section 4.3). Third, it presents an example of how to conduct a Political Economy of Communication analysis, namely the Political Economy of Facebook (Section 4.4). Fourth, conclusions are drawn (Section 4.5).

4.2 What is the Political Economy of Communication and the Media?

4.2.1 Definitions of the Political Economy of Communication and the Media

We will start with several classical definitions of the Political Economy of Communication. Later in this chapter, I will provide my own definition.

DOI: 10.4324/9781003391203-5

In the essay *On the Political Economy of Communications*, Dallas W. Smythe (1960, 564) gave an early definition of this very approach:

> The central purpose of the study of the political economy of communications is to evaluate the effects of communication agencies in terms of the policies by which they are organized and operated. Our concern will therefore be with the structure and policies of these communication agencies in their social settings.

Smythe points out that the Political Economy approach is interested in how media organisations operate in the broader context of society, focusing on how they operate in this setting and what role the state and policies play.

Vincent Mosco gives the following definition of the Political Economy of Communication:

> Political Economy of Communication *"is the study of the social relations, particularly the power relations, that mutually constitute the production, distribution, and consumption of resources, including communication resources"*.
>
> (Mosco 2009, 2)

This definition stresses that the approach's focus is on (a) the analysis of power relations in the context of media and communication (media power, communication power) and (b) that such power has an economic dimension as it has to do with the production, distribution, and consumption of information. What needs to be stressed is that in a Political Economy study, among the power relations studied, socio-economic relations, especially class relations, are considered to play a special role. It is assumed that in class societies, all power relations interact with and are influenced and constrained by class relations.

Robert W. McChesney's understanding of the Political Economy of Communication emphasises the analysis of class relations:

> The scholarly study of the political economy of communication entails two main dimensions. First, it addresses the nature of the relationship between media and communication systems on the one hand and the broader social structure of society. In other words, it examines how media and communication systems and content reinforce, challenge or influence existing class and social relations. It does this with a particular interest in how economic factors influence politics and social relations. Second, the political economy of communication looks specifically at how ownership, support mechanisms (e.g. advertising) and government policies influence media behavior and content. This line of inquiry emphasizes structural factors and the labor process in the production, distribution and consumption of communication. [...] Although the

political economy of communication can be applied to the study of precapitalist and postcapitalist societies and communication systems, it is primarily concerned with capitalist societies and commercial media systems, as these models dominate across the world.

(McChesney 2000, 110)

McChesney stresses that the Political Economy of Communication studies communication(s) in the context of society with a particular focus on class relations and the economy. What should be added to his understanding is that the analysis of class relations not just consists of the analysis of communication in the context of labour's position in the relations of production, that is the exploitation of labour and the production of surplus value, but also consists of the analysis of the actual and potential resistance of workers, that is class struggle.

Armand Mattelart and Seth Siegelaub stress the importance of class analysis in the Political Economy of Communication. They argue for a class analysis of communication (Mattelart 1979; Siegelaub 1979). Such an analysis includes for Mattelart (a) the analysis of the interaction of communication and the "basic economic, social, ideological and cultural forces", (b) the roles of communication practice and communication theory in the capitalist mode of production, and (c) the interaction of communication and "the struggle against exploitation and oppression" (Siegelaub 1979, 19).

Graham Murdock and Peter Golding provide the following understanding of the approach of the Political Economy of Communication:

The obvious starting point for a political economy of mass communications is the recognition that the mass media are first and foremost industrial and commercial organizations which produce and distribute commodities. [...] In addition to producing and distributing commodities, however, the mass media also disseminate ideas about economic and political structures. It is this second and ideological dimension of mass media production which gives it its importance and centrality and which requires an approach in terms of not only economics but also politics.

(Murdock and Golding 1973, 205–207)

Murdock and Golding stress that the Political Economy of Communication analyses the economic character of communication systems, which in capitalism means their role in the production, distribution, and consumption of commodities. They discuss phenomena whose analysis is important in this respect, including media concentration, crisis and media consolidation, horizontal and vertical integration, diversification, internationalisation, constricted choice as an implication of commercial media organisation, the control of information, or attempts to cement consensus in capitalism via the media. In addition, Murdock and Golding stress that media in capitalism have a double role in fostering (a) commodification and (b) ideologies.

Communication and communication systems (media) are peculiar goods in that they organise the production, distribution, and organisation of ideas. This means that organised as commodities, communication and communication systems are cultural commodities. Culture is the system and dimension of society where meanings are produced and circulated in society. While every commodity has a cultural dimension in that there are meanings associated with commodities that are created by mechanisms such as branding and advertising, communication and communication systems organise the production, distribution and consumption of ideas and content. A news programme is different from a pint of beer in that the first is a production, presentation, storage, and transmission of current information about society, whereas the beer does not contain information. Media and communication represent ideas and knowledge, which is why they play a particular role in the political constitution of society, the public sphere, and the question of whether or not and in what respects a society is democratic.

Manfred Knoche (2002, 103) stresses that the Critique of the Political Economy of the Media and Communication with the help of social theory and empirical social research analyses how "media production and consumption, over and above other commodity production, also fulfils elementary, indispensable macroeconomic and macro-societal political-ideological functions for securing the rule and safeguarding the capitalist economic and societal system as a whole".[1] Like Murdock and Golding, Knoche stresses that the Critique of Political Economy analyses the commodity character and the ideological character of communication(s) in capitalism.

In another essay, Murdock and Golding further specify the focus of analysis of the Critical Political Economy of Communication. It analyses

> the wider structures that envelop and shape everyday action, looking at how the economic organisation of media industries impinges on the production and circulation of meaning and the ways in which people's opinions for consumption and use are structured by their position within the general economic formation. [...] [It] starts with sets of social relations and the play of power. It is interested in seeing how the making and taking of meaning is shaped at every level by the structured asymmetries in social relations. [...] What marks critical political economy out as distinctive is that it always goes beyond situated action to show how particular micro contexts are shaped by general economic dynamics and the wider formations they sustain.
>
> (Murdock and Golding 2005, 61–62)

Murdock and Golding argue that Critical Political Economy analyses how inequality and power asymmetries play a role in the interaction of capitalism and communication. They point towards the circumstance that Critical Political Economy is not just a critical social theory and critical empirical social research but also a critical moral philosophy of communication.

4.2.2 A Definition of the Political Economy of Communication and Media

Based on such definitions, I want to give my own definition of the approach of the Political Economy of Communication and the Media:

Political Economy of Communication and the Media is an approach that uses social theory, empirical social research, and moral philosophy for analysing the roles of communication and communication systems (media, communications) in society, especially the interaction of politics and economy in the context of the media and communication. It studies how the interaction of communication, politics, and economy works and this interaction's roles in society. It sees the dialectical relationship between the economy and politics as the most important factor shaping communication and society. An important focus is the analysis of the production, distribution, and consumption of information in the context of society. Political Economy of Communication and the Media is often a critical analysis of how communication and communication systems work and are organised in capitalist society and how they impact on and interact with society and the lives of humans in society. *This critical analysis is also termed Critique of the Political Economy of Communication and the Media.* It gives particular attention to the analysis of the capitalist mode of producing information; communication labour; the production, distribution, and consumption of information and communication(s) as commodities; the space and time of communication; the interaction of politics and the media economy; ideology critique; communication in the context of class and social struggles; and alternatives to capitalist communication(s), non-capitalist communication(s). Figure 4.1 visualises the approach of the Political Economy of Communication and the Media.

The Political Economy of Communication and the Media differs from Media Business and Management Studies and Media/Creative/Cultural Industry Studies. Media Business and Management Studies have a focus on the analysis of media organisations. Media Industry Studies deals with the analysis of media industries. The Political Economy of Communication and the Media is also but not only an analysis of media organisations and media industries. It analyses media and communication – including media organisations, media industries, communication processes, media and communication systems, and communication technologies – in the context of the broader picture of society. It, therefore, takes into account the societal contexts of communication(s) such as capitalist society, class structures, the public sphere, the state, policies, globalisation, structures of inequality, ideology, domination.

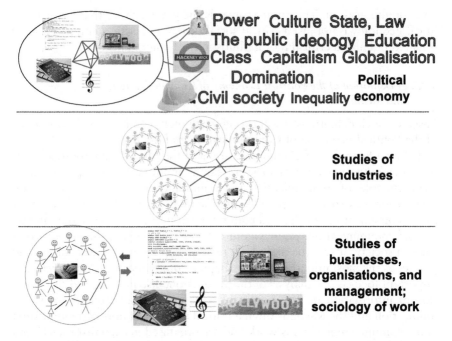

Power Culture State, Law
The public Ideology Education
Class Capitalism Globalisation
Domination   Political
Civil society Inequality economy

Studies of
industries

Studies of
businesses,
organisations, and
management;
sociology of work

Figure 4.1 Visualisation of the approach of the Political Economy of Communication
and the Media.

There have been several further definitions of the Political Economy of
Communication. Some of them shall be briefly mentioned. They do not add
anything new to what has already been said, but should also be mentioned.

Jonathan Hardy stresses that the approach of Critical Political Economy
analyses with a problem-oriented approach the interaction of the political
and the economic dimension of the media in the context of power:

> The political economy of communications describes all forms of en-
> quiry into the political and economic dimensions of communication.
> [...] I take the critical political economy approach to encompass studies
> that consider political and economic aspects of communications and
> which are critical in regard to their concerns with the manner in which
> power relations are sustained and challenged. [...] Critical political eco-
> nomic of communications is a critical realist approach that investigates
> problems connected with the political and economic organization of
> communication resources.
>
> (Hardy 2014, 3, 4, 14)

In the preface to Hardy's (2014) book, James Curran praises Hardy's introductory book to the Political Economy of Communication as being much
superior to the one by Vincent Mosco (2009). Hardy's own definition is not

different from Mosco's but a feasible reproduction of Mosco's understanding in other words.

Nicholas Garnham (1979, 127) writes that

> the purpose of a political economy of culture is to elucidate what Marx and Engels meant in the German Ideology by 'control of the means of mental production' [...] Further the political economy of mass-media is the analysis of a specific historical phase of this general development linked to historically distinct modalities of cultural production and eproduction.

Garnham focuses on the notion of control and the dynamic and historical character of Political Economy. There are economic forms of control of the media (such as control through ownership), political forms of control (such as state censorship, surveillance, and violence), and ideological forms of control. Garnham points out aspects of the Political Economy of Communication but does not provide a clear and distinct definition.

Having introduced some basic definitions of the Political Economy of Communication, we will next engage with classifications of its various approaches.

4.2.3 *Political Economy of Communication Approaches*

Dwayne Winseck (2011) distinguishes four approaches in the Political Economy of Communication and the Media:

1 Neoclassical Political Economy of the Media (based on Neoclassical and Neoliberal Economics);
2 Radical/Critical Political Economy of the Media (based on Marx and Marxian approaches);
3 Institutional Political Economy of the Media (focused on institutions such as the creative industries, the commons, networks, and markets);
4 The Cultural Industries School (focused on the unique characteristics of media and culture, e.g. the works of Miège 1979, 1987, 2011).

Winseck argues that Political Economy of Communication and the Media is not "a single field", which is why he uses the plural form "Political Economies". There are certainly different approaches within the field of Media Economics, basically the ones that Winseck lists, but not all of them characterise themselves as Political Economy. For example, various approaches that focus on "microeconomic issues" and "how media industries and companies can succeed, prosper, or move forward" (Wasko, Murdock and Sousa 2011) speak of themselves as "Media Economics" (e.g. Albarran 2017, 2019; Anderson, Waldfogel and Strömberg 2016; Doyle 2013; Hoskins, McFadyen and Finn 2004; Picard 1989, 2001), not as Political Economy. Robert Picard

(1989, 7) defines Media Economics as the analysis of "how media operators meet the informational and entertainment wants and needs of audiences, advertisers and society with available resources". Gillian Doyle outlines a predominantly microeconomic approach to Media Economics (Doyle 2013, 3). There is little point in characterising such approaches as Political Economy, as Winseck does, when they do not claim that label for themselves and do not give an important focus to moral philosophy.

> While competition may be assessed, little emphasis is placed on questions of ownership or the implications of concentrated ownership and control. These approaches avoid the kind of moral grounding adopted by political economists, as most studies emphasize description rather than critique.
>
> (Wasko, Murdock and Sousa 2011, 3)

Neoclassical approaches' understanding of Media Economics is too narrow, often ignoring the existence of the Political Economy of Communication. Political Economy of Communication certainly is a specific approach to Media Economics.

The approach of the Political Economy of Communication has been strongly influenced by Marx and Marxian thinking. Murdock and Golding (2005, 61) argue that the approach of the Political Economy of Communication has been "broadly marxisant". Reviewing the development of the approach of the Political Economy of Communication, Janet Wasko (2014, 260) argues that "often, those working within a political economic approach in media and communication studies have adopted a Marxist/neo-Marxist theoretical framework and thus a critical perspective". Political Economy of Communication is certainly not exclusively informed by the Critique of the Political Economy that Marx grounded and that has ever since been developed, but this critical approach is the dominant version of the Political Economy of Communication, which is why the terms Political Economy of Communication, Critique of the Political Economy of Communication and Critical Political Economy of Communication are often used synonymously.

> Meanwhile, institutional political economy represents an approach that focuses on technological and institutional factors that influence markets. While some work in communication studies draws on institutional analysis, a radical, critical or Marxian political economy is likely to be the tradition that is represented when one refers to 'the political economy of communication'.
>
> (Wasko 2005, 26)

There has been a variety of classifications of Media Economics approaches. We will now have a look at some of them.

Albarran (2010, 21) and Picard (2006, 28) distinguish between three theory traditions in Media Economics: Theoretical Media Economics, which is influenced by Neoclassical Economics; Applied Media Economics, which is industry-based and influenced by the Neoclassical approach; and Critical Approaches such as Marxism, British Cultural Studies and Political Economy.

Kiefer and Steininger (2014, 47) identify the following four approaches in Media Economics: Media Business Studies, Neoclassical and Neoliberal Media Economics, New Institutional Economics and New Political Economy of the Media, and Critical and Marxist Political Economy of the Media.

Meier (2003, 221) draws a distinction between Radical Political Economy and New Political Economy for characterising approaches to the Political Economy of Communication. According to Meier, New Political Economy has been influenced by Neoclassical Economics, Liberal Political Economy, and Institutional Political Economy and Radical Political Economy by Marxist Political Economy and Institutional Political Economy. Just and Latzer (2010, 73–76) identify the following approaches: Classical Political Economy, Neoclassical Political Economy, Critical and (Neo-)Marxist Political Economy, Institutional Political Economy, and New Political Economy.

In one way or another, all these classifications argue that one strand of Media Economics is Heterodox Media Economics (also called Radical Political Economy, Critical Political Economy, critical approach, etc.). In contrast, Manfred Knoche (1999) draws a fourfold distinction of approaches to Media Economics: Neoclassicism/Neoliberalism, New Institutional Economy/New Political Economy/Systems Theory, Critical Political Economy of the Media, and Marxist Political Economy of the Media/Critique of the Political Economy of the Media. In Knoche's classification, Critical Political Economy in contrast to the Critique of the Political Economy does not take Karl Marx's works as a starting point but tends to ignore or downplay their importance.

Other than Knoche, Sevignani (2016, 2022) does not distinguish between Critique of the Political Economy of the Media and Critical Political Economy of the Media. He tends to use the second term for a variety of approaches, to conflate the first term with the second, or to not use the first term at all. He thereby opens up the possibility for a pluralist, all-integrative, postmodern approach to Media Economics that can easily forget the importance of Marx and the tradition of analysis that has been based on Marx.

One important issue is the question of how to conduct a Political Economy analysis of a particular communication phenomenon that utilises social theory, empirical social research, and moral philosophy. For doing so, we require principles and dimensions of the Political Economy of Communication. We will in the next section discuss such principles and dimensions.

4.3 Principles and Dimensions of the Political Economy of Communication

4.3.1 *Principles of the Political Economy of Communication*

There are not just definitions of and a variety of approaches to the Political Economy of Communication. In addition, there are also principles that one uses in a Political Economy analysis of communication phenomena. We will first have a look at the principles and dimensions of analysis that the German Political Economist of the Media Horst Holzer introduced.

Horst Holzer (2017, 715–716) argues that the Critique of the Political Economy of the Media and Communication analyses five aspects of the media in capitalism:

1. *The capital-economic function*: Production and sale of media products (press products, broadcasting programmes, advertisements, advertising times, etc.);

2. *The function of commodity circulation*: The creation of a climate fostering consumption and the advertisement of specific products and services;

3. *The function of domination*: Legitimation and propagation of society's organisational principle, on which not just the media, but society as a totality is based;

4. *The function of regeneration and reproduction of labour-power*: Satisfaction of the audience's needs for information and entertainment that are oriented on the other functions;

5. *The media sales and media market function*: The media are markets for other media companies. We can call this aspect the media's sales and market function that has two manifestations: First, media organisations are buyers of relevant appliances, means of production and services (e.g. from the construction industry, the electrical industry, the chemical industry, the appliance industry, companies that produce films, television series and sound recordings). Second, especially broadcast organisations animate their audiences to act as buyers of receiving equipment.

Holzer argues that a Political Economy study of communication focuses on aspects of capital, commodities, ideology; advertising, marketing and sales; and consumer culture during leisure time. His five "functions" of communication in capitalism are not clearly delineated, so are overlapping. Furthermore, labour, class relations, and class struggles are not considered as analytical aspects. This means that Holzer advances a structuralist understanding of the Political Economy of Communication.

In the British and North American approaches to the Political Economy of Communication, there has also been an introduction of principles for the analysis of communication phenomena.

Mosco (2009, 2–4, 26–36) and Murdock and Golding (2005) define a total of seven principles of the Political Economy of Communication (PEC):

1 The commodity and commodification;
2 Space (local, regional, national, international, global);
3 Structuration (class, gender, racism);
4 History;
5 Social totality;
6 Moral philosophy;
7 Praxis.

4.3.2 Principle 1: The Commodity and Commodification

A commodity is a good or service that is exchanged on a market. The commodity is exchanged for a sum of money. A certain amount of a commodity is thereby put into an exchange relation with money: x commodity A = y money (x amount of the commodity A is exchanged for y monetary units of a certain currency). Commodification "is the process of transforming things valued for their use into marketable produces that are valued for what they can bring in exchange" (Mosco 2009, 2). In commodification, something is transformed into the commodity form x commodity A = y money. Commodification means that something that is not a commodity is turned into a commodity. The good thereby not just has a use-value whereby it satisfies human needs, but also has an exchange-value whereby it helps advance sales interests and capital accumulation interests.

Mosco argues that in the world of the media, we find three typical forms of the commodity: the commodification of content, the commodification of audiences, and the commodification of labour. Media companies sell various commodities, including media content, to make money. Advertising-funded media do often not primarily sell content, but provide free access to content to attract audience members. They sell access to a suited audience to advertisers, which is what Dallas W. Smythe (1977) terms the audience commodity. The commodification of labour means that in capitalism, humans are structurally forced by the labour market to sell their labour-power to survive. They become wage workers. There are workers in the communication industries. PEC studies their working conditions.

Here are three examples of how commodification works in the media industry: Software licences are mechanisms used by corporations such as Microsoft to commodify content, namely software such as Microsoft Office. Google is one of the world's largest advertising agencies. It sells access to its users as a commodity. Examples of communication workers who sell their labour-power as a commodity are journalists, software engineers, and PR workers.

4.3.3 *Principle 2: Spatialisation, Space (Local, Regional, National, International, Global)*

Spatialisation "is the process of overcoming the constraints of geographical space with, among other things, mass media and communication technologies" (Mosco 2009, 2). Space is the next-to-one-another organisation of matter. Production is organised in space-time. Local, national, regional, international, and global spaces matter in the analysis of communication. Globalisation is the process of stretching human practices over spatial distances. Communication technologies help communication to overcome distances. They are, among other things, technologies of globalisation. We have experienced the globalisation of the media (global media). Communication technologies are medium and outcome of globalisation.

4.3.4 *Principle 3: Structuration*

A structure is a relatively constant relationship between humans that exists over a longer period of time, in which there are certain roles, routinised (i.e. constantly repeated) actions, and certain outcomes. Structuration "is the process of creating social relations, mainly those organized around social class, gender, and race" (Mosco 2009, 2). Structuration has to do with power structures. Power is, generally speaking, the capacity of humans to influence changes in society. In asymmetric power structures, certain groups or individuals have the capacity to strongly influence what is happening in society or parts of it and to take advantage of this capacity at the expense of others.

PEC gives particular attention to the analysis of class structures, that is the relationship between private owners of means of production who have the power to force workers to produce surplus value and goods that are not the property of the producers but of the owners of the means of production. PEC sees class relations as the fundamental feature of class societies and communication in class societies. Class relations interact with other power structures, including gender relations and racism. PEC is therefore also interested in the analysis of communication in the context of the interaction of class and other forms of domination. Domination means that certain groups or individuals have coercive means at their disposal that allow them to derive advantages at the expense of others. Exploitation, patriarchal rule, sexism as well as racism are some of the important forms of domination.

4.3.5 *Principle 4: History*

PEC also analyses communication in the context of the historical development of the economy and society. It examines the dynamics and changes of capitalism brought about by crises and class struggles. It also wants to understand the role of revolutions in societal change (e.g. the French Revolution). It situates the analysis of communication in the analysis of the history of the media, capitalism, civil society, commodification, the state, ideology, technologies, etc. (Murdock and Golding 2005, 64).

4.3.6 Principle 5: Social Totality

PEC analyses communication in the context of the totality of society.

> Political economy has always believed that there is a big picture of so-
> ciety. [...] The political economist asks: How are power and wealth
> related and how are these in turn connected to cultural and social life?
> The political economist of communication wants to know how all of
> these influence and are influenced by our systems of mass media, infor-
> mation, and entertainment.
>
> (Mosco 2009, 4)

PEC is about how the big picture of society, the big issues, changes and developments in society shape the media landscape and communication and the
media and communication economy. Political Economy (of Communication)
is therefore also the analysis of society.

To study communication in the context of social totality means that PEC
analyses communication's role in society as a whole. PEC sees contemporary
societies as capitalist societies and argues that there is a capitalist world system. Also, the global dimension of society is a form of totality that forms a
context of communication that PEC analyses.

Capitalism is a type of society – a formation of society – where the mass of
humans is alienated from the conditions of economic, political and cultural
production, which means that they do not control the conditions that shape
their lives, which enables privileged groups' accumulation of capital in the
economy, decision-power in politics, and reputation, attention and respect in
culture (Fuchs 2022, chapter 1).

4.3.7 Principle 6: Moral Philosophy

Moral philosophy asks what a good society looks like and what a bad society
is and how the latter can be avoided. PEC is interested in moral philosophy
to discuss what good communication systems in a good society are and how
we can attain such forms of communication. PEC tends to value "extending
democracy to all aspects of social life" (Mosco 2009, 4), including politics,
economy, workplace culture, and everyday life. This form of democracy is
termed participatory democracy.

Mainstream Economics today rather ignores moral philosophy. Today's

> leading mainstream economists are less averse to using moral language
> in their economic discourse. [...] it is chiefly the heterodox schools of
> thought, rooted in political economy, that take up the moral concern.
> [...] The Marxian and institutional traditions are steeped in debates
> over the place of moral philosophy.
>
> (Mosco 2009, 34)

4.3.8 *Principle 7: Social Praxis*

Praxis means human and political activities and politics that change the world and make it a better place where all humans benefit and lead a good life. Praxis includes political reforms, policymaking, as well as class struggles and social movements' social struggles for a better society. PEC is interested in the analysis of the role of communication in struggles and the analysis of struggles for democratic communication(s) in a good society. It is interested in how humans (want to) change society, communicate transformations of society, and transform communication(s) and society. PEC is in this respect inspired by Karl Marx, who says in the eleventh Thesis on Feuerbach: "The philosophers have only *interpreted* the world, in various ways; the point is to *change* it" (Marx 1845, 5). This thesis means in the context of PEC that it conducts critical analyses of communication and society to inform the creation of a good society and democratic communication(s).

The seven principles discussed above are certainly important aspects of conducting a Political Economy analysis of communication phenomena. The focus on totality and history is an onto-epistemological feature of PEC. Ontology studies how the world looks like. Epistemology studies how humans create knowledge about the world. Onto-epistemology deals with how the world – in the case of the social sciences that is the social world of society – looks like and how humans create knowledge about the world. PEC is interested in the big picture of the world. It uses theory and empirical research for studying communication in society. And it asks normative, ethical, and moral questions about communication and society. This means that it combines theory, empirical research, and ethics/moral philosophy. The level of ethics/moral philosophy is sometimes also called axiology or praxeology. Axiology stems from the Greek word "axios", which means being worthy of and so points towards ethics, morality, norms, and moral values. Praxeology points towards the Greek word "praxis", which means that ethics is not just ideas but also action that puts ideas into reality.

Dialectics is an important feature of PEC's onto-epistemology. Dialectics is a form of analysis that analyses reality as contradictory, which means that it analyses how phenomena are constituted through their relations and how these relations look like, bringing about changes at different scales and the emergence of new moments and totalities. This means it studies history, crises, and transformations as dialectics of past/present and continuity/discontinuity. Furthermore, dialectics analyses dialectical relationships such as the ones between practices/structures, subjects/objects, productive forces/relations of production, good/evil (ethics, moral philosophy), production/consumption, working class/capitalist class, non-owners/owners, the poor/the rich, misery/wealth, use-value/exchange-value, concrete work/abstract labour, the simple form of value/the relative and expanded form of value, social relations of humans/relations of things, the fetish of commodities and money/fetishistic thinking, the circulation of commodities/the circulation of money, commodities/money, labour-power/wages, labour process/valorisation process, subject of labour (labour-power, worker)/the object of labour (the means of production), variable capital/constant capital, surplus labour/surplus product, necessary labour time/surplus labour time, the single worker/co-operation, single company/industry sector, single capital/competing capitals, etc.

4.3.9 Dimensions of the Political Economy of Communication

Based on using a dialectical onto-epistemology and moral philosophy, PEC studies the roles of media and communication in society and does so by giving particular attention to several aspects of analysis that are shown in Figure 4.2.

Figure 4.2 presents a model of the Political Economy of Communication. It shows what dimensions (D) PEC focuses on in its studies:

- D1: PEC analyses the *production of information*, the mode of the production of information (see also D6-D12);
- D2: PEC analyses the *circulation of information*: PEC analyses include media markets, advertising and branding, commodity sales, media concentration, the globalisation of markets and these processes' implications for society;
- D3: PEC analyses the *consumption of information*: PEC analyses consumer culture, which is about the consumption of commodities and non-commodified activities in everyday life, leisure time and leisure activities, and the reproduction of labour-power;
- D1-D3 together constitute the inner dynamics of the media and communication economy.
- D4: PEC analyses *the interactions between the media and communication economy and the political system*. PEC, therefore, analyses state politics and civil society politics in the context of media and communication, which includes the analysis of laws and policies that regulate the media and communication system and its economy, lobbying processes by which political and other actors want to influence the media, the ways of how political information makes it or does not make it into the media, social movements' relations to the media, social movements' communication forms, social movements' struggles for media reforms, and changes of the media and the public sphere;
- D5: PEC analyses *the interactions between the media and communication economy and the cultural system*. PEC, therefore, analyses how ideas, worldviews, ideologies, knowledge, meanings, and morality play a role in the media and communication economy, how media communicate ideas and ideologies, how users and audience members interpret Political Economy and how Political Economy, including capitalism, is represented in culture. This dimension includes ideology critique.

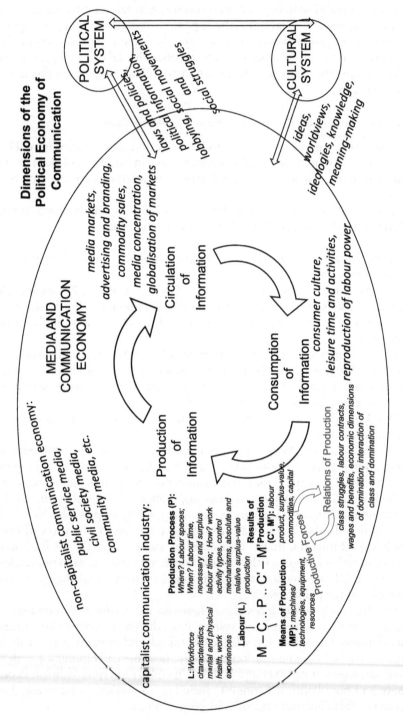

Figure 4.2 The Political Economy of Communication's dimensions of analysis.

- The analysis of production in the media and communication economy has several dimensions. In capitalist society, there are capitalist as well as non-capitalist media and communication organisations. PEC analyses both capitalist and non-capitalist media and communication organisations. Capitalist media organisations produce communication commodities for accumulating capital. Non-capitalist media organisations have a not-for-profit imperative. Their focus is on the media's use-value instead of their exchange-value and the profit imperative. PEC also analyses the media's productive forces and their relations of production. The productive forces consist of workers who utilise means of production for creating new goods and services, in the case of the media economy, these are informational goods and services. The relations of production are the social relations between groups and social practices in which humans organise the economy.

- D6: PEC analyses the *non-capitalist media and communication economy*. It studies how not-for-profit media organisations such as Public Service Media, civil society media, community media, media co-operatives, platform co-operatives, Public Service Internet platforms are organised and what roles they play in society and capitalism.

- D7: PEC analyses *the media and communication aspects of the (class and power) relations of production*. This includes the analysis of media and communication in the context of class struggles, labour contracts, wages and benefits, the economic dimensions of domination and the interaction of class and domination (including gender relations, racism, xenophobia, nationalism, patriarchy, sexism);

- D8: PEC analyses *the capitalist productive forces in the media and communication economy*. This means that it analyses how the capital accumulation process $M - C.. P.. C' - M'$ works in the context of the production of information, media, and communication as commodities driven by the profit interest and the logic of capital accumulation. The analysis of the capitalist media's productive forces includes several subdomains summarised in D9-D12;

- D9: PEC analyses the role of *the means of production in the media and communication economy* (objects utilised in the production process, constant capital such as machines/technologies, equipment, and resources).

- D10: PEC analyses features of *the workforce in the media and communication economy* (workforce characteristics, workers' mental and physical health, subjectivities and experiences).

- D11: PEC analyses *the production and labour process in the media and communication economy*, the where, when and how of production: labour spaces (the workplace, the spatial organisation of work, including the geographical division of labour, urban/rural aspects, local, regional, national, international, transnational and global aspects), labour time (types of work and surplus value production, typical working hours and overtime) as well as forms of labour control (types of management, surveillance, absolute and relative surplus value production, etc.).

• D12: PEC analyses the *products the labour process creates in the media and communication economy* (use-values, commodities, capital, profits, different types of information commodities, different types of capital operating in the media and communication economy, etc.).

Table 4.1 gives an overview of typical questions that PEC asks concerning its various dimensions of analysis.

Table 4.1 Types of research questions that the Political Economy of Communication approach asks

Dimension	Aspect	Question(s)
D2	The circulation of information: media markets	How do media markets look like and develop? How concentrated are they? What is the role of space and globalisation in media markets?
D2	The circulation of information: advertising, branding, commodity sales	How does capital try to increase commodity sales? How does it use media and communication in this context? How do advertising and branding operate? What is the role of advertising and branding in the media? What are the impacts of advertising and branding on society?
D3	The consumption of information	How does consumer culture work and advance commodity consumption? What are the roles of commodities, the mediation of commodities, commodity culture, and non-commodified culture in everyday life? How do the media and communication contribute to leisure time and the reproduction of labour-power?
D4	Interactions between the media and communication economy and the political system: the state, legislation, and policies	What laws and policies regulate the media and communication economy? What do they look like? What are the actors, processes, contents, and impacts of communication policies?
D4	Interactions between the media and communication economy and the political system: lobbying and political information	How do actors via lobbying and other mechanisms try to influence the news and media content? What political information is present or not present in the media? Why? How do the media report on politics?

(Continued)

Table 4.1 (Continued)

Dimension	Aspect	Question(s)
D4	Interactions between the media and communication economy and the political system: social movements and the media	How do social movements struggle for reforms and changes of the media and the public sphere? What is the relationship between social movement struggles and the media? What actors, processes, and social struggles are there in the transformation of the media and the public sphere? What aspects of praxis are there in the context of the analysed communication phenomenon?
D5	Interactions between the media and communication economy and the cultural system: ideology critique	Ideology critique: What are the roles of ideologies in capitalist society? How are such ideologies produced, and communicated? How do citizens interpret and react to ideologies?
D5	Interactions between the media and communication economy and the cultural system: ideas, worldviews, knowledge, meanings, and morality in and of Political Economy	How are ideas, worldviews, knowledge and meanings about Political Economy and capitalism produced, circulated, and interpreted? How are Political Economy and capitalism represented in culture? What are the roles of ideas, worldviews, knowledge and meanings in Political Economy and capitalism and the media economy? What aspect does moral philosophy play in understanding moral aspects of the studied communication phenomenon?
D6, D1	The non-capitalist communication economy	How do not-for-profit media organisations work? How do they differ from capitalist media organisations? What are their realities, opportunities, and challenges? What actors, processes, contents, and impacts on society do we find in non-capitalist media organisations? What roles do non-capitalist media organisations play in society? What roles do non-capitalist media organisations play in capitalism?
D7, D1	Relations of production: class struggles	What kind of class struggles are there in the analysed organisations and systems? What interests, strategies, practices, and class positions do the involved actors have? How do workers organise and engage in relations with capital? What is the role of worker protests, unions, and strikes? Is there a possibility that media workers form associations (freedom of association)? If so, do labour associations and trade unions exist and what do they do?

(*Continued*)

Table 4.1 (Continued)

Dimension	Aspect	Question(s)
		How does capital organise, enforce, and present its interests? Are there bargaining mechanisms between capital and labour? If so, how do they work and what are their impacts?
D7, D1	Relations of production: labour contracts, wages, and benefits	What kind of contracts do workers receive? What are the conditions defined in these contracts and what are their consequences? How high or low are the wage levels? What material, social or other benefits do workers lack or have?
D7, D1	Relations of production: the economic dimensions of domination and the interaction of class and domination	What is the role of structures of domination (including racism, nationalism, patriarchy, sexism, gender relations) in the context of the media? How do structures of domination shape labour processes, working conditions, and class relations? How do class and domination interact in the context of the media and communication in society?
D9, D1, D8	Means of production: machines and equipment	Which technologies are used in the production process with what goals and interests? What technologies or combinations thereof are being used during the agricultural, industrial and informational production processes that create media and content?
D9, D1, D8	Means of production: resources	What resources are used in the production process? What resources or combinations thereof are used during the agricultural, industrial and informational production processes of media and content?
D10, D1, D8	Labour: workforce characteristics	What are important characteristics of the workforce for example in terms of age, gender, ethnic background, education, class?
D10, D1, D8	Labour: mental and physical health	How do the employed means of production and the labour process impact the mental and physical health of workers?
D10, D1, D8	Labour: workers' subjectivity and experiences	How do workers experience and assess their working conditions?

(Continued)

Table 4.1 (Continued)

Dimension	Aspect	Question(s)
D11, D1, D8	Production process: workspaces	Where does the production process take place? How is the workplace organised? What spatial aspects of labour in the media and communication economy are there (local, regional, national, international, global, urban/rural differences, geographical division of labour)? Is there a spatial division of labour? If yes, what does it look like?
D11, D1, D8	Production process: labour time	How many working hours are common within a certain sector? How are working hours enforced? What is the relationship between work and free time? What is the relationship between necessary labour time (paid) and surplus labour time (unpaid)?
D11, D1, D8	Production process: work activity	What types of mental and/or physical activities are workers performing?
D11, D1, D8	Production process: control mechanisms, types of management, surveillance, absolute and relative surplus value production, etc.	What kind of control mechanisms of labour is there? What kind of management strategies and practices is there? Are there forms of economic surveillance? If yes, how do they work? Are methods of absolute surplus value production utilised? If yes, how do they work? Are methods of relative surplus value production utilised? If yes, how do they work? Are there forms of extending the working day (absolute surplus value production) and how do they work? Are there forms of technology use aimed at increasing the productivity of work? Are there forms of automation and how do they work? What are the impacts of control mechanisms on the workforce and society?
D12, D1, D8	Products of labour	Which kinds of media products or services do the relevant workers produce? Who are the owners of the produced commodities and capital (ownership structures)? How have the relevant profits and profit rates developed? What are the causes and sources of the crisis of the analysed capital?

4.3.10 *Some Explanatory Notes on the Dimensions of the Political Economy of Communication*

Some explanatory notes are needed on the foundational aspects of the PEC. Production, circulation, and consumption/interpretation of information are the three basic dimensions of the media and communication economy. They stand in dialectical relationships. This means that they require each other, and have identical and different aspects. In the "Introduction to the Critique of Political Economy", Karl Marx (1857) outlines the dialectics of production, circulation, and consumption: Production is the consumption of the means of production, circulation is the production of access to produced goods, and consumption is the production of satisfaction of needs, of additional need for production, and of the reproduction of labour-power.

> in production the members of society appropriate (create, shape) the products of nature in accord with human needs; distribution determines the proportion in which the individual shares in the product; exchange delivers the particular products into which the individual desires to convert the portion which distribution has assigned to him; and finally, in consumption, the products become objects of gratification, of individual appropriation. Production creates the objects which correspond to the given needs; distribution divides them up according to social laws; exchange further parcels out the already divided shares in accord with individual needs; and finally, in consumption, the product steps outside this social movement and becomes a direct object and servant of individual need, and satisfies it in being consumed. Thus production appears as the point of departure, consumption as the conclusion, distribution and exchange as the middle, which is however itself twofold, since distribution is determined by society and exchange by individuals.
>
> (Marx 1857, 89)

The Cultural Studies scholar Stuart Hall (1973/2003) interpreted Marx's "Introduction to the Critique of Political Economy". He stresses that the "Introduction" shows how Marx develops his dialectical method. Hall does not situate the dialectic of production, circulation, and consumption in the context of the media. Later, Cultural Studies works have done so by pointing out a dialectic of the production, circulation, and consumption of information in a model they term the circuit of culture (see du Gay, Hall, Janes, Mackay and Negus 1997, 3; Johnson 1986/1987). They do, however, not see the special role of production in society. Many Cultural Studies works have a privileged focus on information consumption and do not so much focus on the labour relations of media production. In contrast, Marx makes clear that production is the general dimension of the economy and society: "production, distribution, exchange, and consumption form a regular syllogism; production is the generality, distribution and exchange the particularity, and consumption the singularity in which the whole is joined together" (Marx 1857, 89). Political Economy of Communication is not a purely production- and labour-focused analysis. Rather, it also analyses the circulation and consumption of goods and commodities and sets these analyses into relation with class society and the relations of production.

The capitalist mode of production is focused on the accumulation of capital. Capital is money that capitalists try to increase by exploiting workers

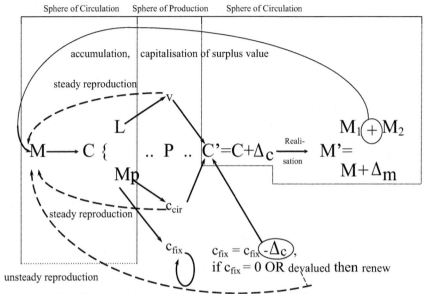

Figure 4.3 The process of the accumulation of capital.

who produce commodities that are sold for making a profit. Marx provides the formula M – C.. P.. C' – M' for analysing the capital accumulation process. PEC analyses the capital accumulation cycles of the media and communication economy and the relationship of the media and communication economy in the capital accumulation of other sectors of the economy. Let us have a look at the capital accumulation cycle (see Figure 4.3).

4.4.11 The Cycle of Capital Accumulation[2]

An explanation of the symbols in Figure 4.3:

M ... money
C ... commodities
L ... labour-power
Mp ... means of production
P ... production
C' ... a new commodity
M' ... more money
c_{cir} ... circulating constant capital
c_{fix} ... fixed constant capital
v ... variable capital

In *Capital Volume 2*'s chapter 1 "The Circuit of Money Capital", Marx (1885, 109) introduces the formula of capital accumulation: $M - C \, (Mp, L) .. P .. C' - M'$. Figure 4.3 visualises the capital accumulation process. Capitalists invest money capital M (that they often obtain from banks, to which they pay interest for loans) for buying labour-power L and means of production Mp. The monetary value of labour-power is called variable capital, and the monetary value of the means of production, constant capital. Marx distinguishes between two forms of constant capital: circulating constant capital and fixed constant capital. Circulating constant capital is resources that lose their value through full productive consumption in the production process. It includes raw and auxiliary materials, operating supply items, and semi-finished products. Fixed constant capital in contrast stays in the production process for a longer time and only gradually loses and transfers value to the commodity. One can count machines, buildings, and equipment to this form of capital.

In the production process P, workers conduct labour to transfer the value of parts of the means of production to a new commodity, and create the value of their labour-power, as well as new surplus value. The new commodity's value C' is $c + v + s$; it is larger than the value of the initial commodities. The commodity value has been increased by a surplus value (measured in hours of labour) and surplus product Δc. The new commodity C' is sold at a price M' that is larger than the initial capital M so that a monetary profit p emerges and $M' = M + p = M + \Delta m$. Part of the profit is reinvested for expanding economic operations; other parts are used for other purposes such as paying interest to banks and dividends to shareholders. The main goal and purpose of capitalism is that capital increases, that is capital is accumulated. Profit is generated by exploiting human labour.

Marx argues in *Capital Volume 3* that the general definition of the capitalist economy, that is its basic quality, is the combination of generalised commodity production and the exploitation of surplus value–generating labour so that capital is accumulated (Marx 1894, 1019–1021). For Marx, the capitalist economy is the system of expanded capital reproduction in the form $M - C .. P .. C' - M'$, in which capitalists buy with money M the commodities C (labour-power, means of production) so that labour creates in the production process a new commodity C' that contains a surplus value that upon sale on the market realises a profit p that increases the invested capital M by a surplus and allows capital to be accumulated and new investments to be made. For Marx, capitalism turns labour-power and means of production into instruments for the production of the end of accumulating capital, that is "money breeding money, value breeding value" (Marx 1885, 160).

The capitalist economy is a form of generalised commodity production: The commodity is the main form of the organisation of property. Labour is compelled to produce commodities that are sold so that capitalists can accumulate ever more capital, that is money that is intended to increase itself. The capitalist economy is a unity of many elements – money, the commodity, the exploitation of labour-power, the means of production, commodity production and capital. This functional unity has emergent qualities so that the sum of these elements is more than any of the elements. Capital accumulation is enabled by all of these elements, but is itself a new quality of capitalist society in comparison to other economic formations. Commodities are one of the cells of capitalism. The accumulation of capital is the whole body. Capital is a body that tries to increase its size by letting labour produce commodities that are sold on markets so that capital grows.

There is a difference between the capitalist economy and the capitalist society. Capitalism can signify a mode of the organisation of both the economy and society. One can argue that the capitalist mode of economic production shapes modern society at large: Modern society is a form of society dominated by the accumulation of money capital in the economy, power in politics, and reputation/ distinction in culture. These forms of accumulation are all interlinked. The economy shapes modern society and its subsystems in the form of the logic of accumulation that takes on specific forms with relative autonomy in each of these subsystems that mutually shape each other. Society's subsystems are therefore identical and different at the same time.

Marx argues that the working day consists of that part of the day during which the worker produces "the value of his labour-power" that is expressed and paid for by the wage. He calls this part of the day necessary labour time. The rest of the time is surplus labour time during which the worker "creates surplus value" that is in monetary terms present as profit (Marx 1867, 324–325). Surplus value is the value of the commodity that goes beyond necessary labour time.

Marx (1867, parts 3, 4, 5) distinguishes two forms of surplus value production: absolute and relative surplus value production. In absolute surplus value production, capital prolongs the working day without wage increases so that the workers produce absolutely more commodities and profits. In relative surplus value production, capital makes use of technologies to increase productivity so that labour produces during the same period as before relatively more commodities and profit.

In the next section, we will have a look at an example analysis of the Political Economy of Communication.

4.4 An Example Analysis: The Political Economy of Facebook

Here are some examples of typical political-economic questions for researching Facebook. To answer them, one needs a combination of social theory, empirical social research, and moral philosophy/ethics:

- What role do Facebook and the model of digital targeted advertising play in digital capitalism?
- What do users think of Facebook's economic model and its impacts on democracy and society?
- What is the role of surveillance in "surveillance capitalism" in general and specifically concerning Facebook's capital accumulation model?

- What alternatives to Facebook and the capitalist Internet can users imagine? What alternatives do they (not) want? How do users assess potential alternatives?

We want to point out what a Political Economy analysis of Facebook means along the following dimensions: D2, circulation; D3, consumption; D4, politics; D5, ideology; D6, non-capitalist; D7, relations of production; and D8, capital accumulation cycle.

Concerning circulation (*D2: circulation*), Political Economy research can focus on how Facebook's targeted advertising works and what its implications are for society. This requires a theoretical and practical understanding of digital advertising and its implications for society. Facebook is (after Google) the world's second-largest advertising agency. It sells targeted ads as a commodity. In 2023, Facebook according to estimates controlled 25.2% of the world's digital ad revenues.[3] Together, Facebook, and Google control more than half of this revenue[4] and therefore form a digital ad duopoly. Facebook's profit interests have threatened democracy. Facebook's focus on encouraging ever more data flows on its platforms to make profits has supported the spread of fake news, as in the case of the Cambridge Analytica scandal where right-wing demagogues collected massive amounts of personal Facebook data to target fake news to users in the context of the 2016 Trump campaign in the US presidential election and other elections.

Studies of Facebook use can conduct interviews, focus groups, etc. with users to learn more about how they assess the platform and how it practises digital capitalism (*D3: consumption*). Empirical studies have shown that Facebook users like Facebook's possibility to stay in touch with contacts and make new connections, the social use-value of Facebook. At the same time, they have strong concerns about Facebook's commodification of data, its digital surveillance, and privacy violations (see Allmer, Fuchs, Kreilinger and Sevignani 2014; Fuchs 2010a, 2010b).

Concerning Facebook in the context of politics (*D4: interaction of economy and politics),* PEC can conduct policy analyses of how state politics regulates or not regulates Facebook and similar digital giants. Topics discussed in the public include tax avoidance, the lax data protection and privacy regulation of Facebook, the lack of regulation of targeted advertising that has encouraged digital surveillance and threats to democracy as in the case of the Cambridge Analytica scandal. Concrete research can conduct news analysis of such aspects of Facebook and political regulation, interviews and focus groups with Facebook users on how they assess the regulation of Facebook, an analysis of the political messages transported by Mark Zuckerberg in the parliamentary hearings where he was interviewed, how Facebook makes use of lobbyists for trying to influence politics, etc. D4 also has to do with the relationship between social movements and Political Economy. There have been many public debates on Facebook's privacy violations. PEC researchers can, for example, study these debates.

An *ideology critique (D5)* of Facebook studies the way Facebook itself spreads ideology and how ideology is spread on Facebook. These are two aspects of ideology critique. Concerning the first aspect, one can use Critical Discourse Analysis as a method for analysing how Facebook and its managers such as Mark Zuckerberg present themselves to the public and the news. For example, Facebook advertises itself as a platform that "helps you connect and share with the people in your life".[5] Facebook presents itself as creating a better world where humans connect, share, and create. This is an ideology because such presentations try to distract attention from Facebook's negative side that involves mass surveillance of users as capital accumulation model, privacy violations, the spread of fake news on the platform, etc. (see Fuchs 2021, chapter 6).

There are non-capitalist alternatives to the digital giants. One task of PEC is to study alternatives (*D6: non-capitalist media and communication*). One alternative is platform co-operatives, which are self-managed Internet platforms where workers and users together own and govern the platform (see Fuchs 2021, sections 12.3 and 15.2; Sandoval 2020; Scholz and Schneider 2016). Such alternative projects within capitalism often lack the resources needed for surviving and competing with the capitalist incumbents that dominate the market, which often results in precarious, self-exploitative labour. PEC can study how platform co-operates work, their challenges and opportunities for society, and what users think about it by utilising interviews, focus groups, etc. Another alternative is Public Service Internet platforms. Public Service Internet platforms are digital platforms that are operated by Public Service Media organisations such as BBC and ARD on a not-for-profit basis and take the public service remit to foster high-quality news, entertainment, culture, educational content, citizenship, and democratic communication in the digital age by utilising digital platforms' affordances such as prosumption (productive consumption in the form of, e.g., user-generated content), participation, and convergence (see Fuchs 2021, section 15.3; Fuchs and Unterberger 2021).

PEC can study the challenges, realities, and opportunities of Public Service Media in digital capitalism, envision Public Service Internet platforms, conduct research that accompanies the development and introduction of such platforms, etc. The basic task of the PEC study of alternatives to Facebook is to learn from experiments to establish alternatives (such as Diaspora* or Mastodon) and how the logic of money and capital shapes the development of such projects.

An important aspect of a PEC study is the analysis of the *capital accumulation cycle (D1, D8)*. In the context of Facebook, such a study asks: How does Facebook accumulate capital? In 2022, Facebook was the world's 34th largest transnational corporation.[6] In the preceding year, it made profits of US$ 39.4 billion.[7] 2022 was a year where many countries faced economic difficulties having to do with factors such as heavy inflation, the war in Ukraine, global supply chain problems as a result of the COVID-19 pandemic. In 2022, real GDP growth was 1.8% in North America, 1.9% in Europe, and 3.2% in China, while in 2021, it was 5.5% in North America,

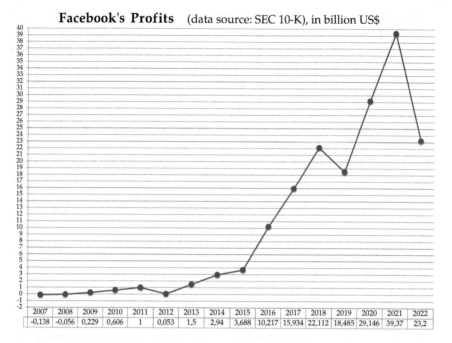

Facebook's Profits   (data source: SEC 10-K), in billion US$

2007	2008	2009	2010	2011	2012	2013	2014	2015	2016	2017	2018	2019	2020	2021	2022
-0,138	-0,056	0,229	0,606	1	0,053	1,5	2,94	3,688	10,217	15,934	22,112	18,485	29,146	39,37	23,2

Figure 4.4 The development of Facebook's profits.

5.4% in Europe, and 8.1% in China.[8] As a consequence, companies invested less money into advertising, which caused a decline of the profits of companies such as Facebook in 2022. In November 2022, Facebook laid off 11,000 employees, which was more than 10% of its staff.

Figure 4.4 shows the development of Facebook's profits. The key aspect of its capital accumulation model is that it does not sell access to the platform as a commodity, but commodifies user data that are obtained by user surveillance so that targeted ads can be personalised and targeted. Facebook's capital accumulation model is based on the sale of targeted ads and the valorisation of users' online activities (digital labour) (see Fuchs 2021, chapters 5 and 7). PEC research can study how user-workers assess and experience digital labour and Facebook's practices.

The *spatial organisation of labour* is another aspect of the capital accumulation cycle. Facebook users are digital workers. They are active globally in almost all countries except single ones such as China. In 2021, the largest share of Facebook users was 340 million in India, followed by 200 million in the USA, 140 million in Indonesia, 130 million in Brazil, and 98 million in Mexico.[9] PEC research could, for example, conduct comparative international research that studies how Facebook users assess their digital labour and Facebook in several selected countries.

Labour time is another important aspect of a PEC analysis. Such an analysis can, for example, analyse the working hours of Facebook's paid employees in the form of semi-structured interviews. Facebook accumulates capital by selling targeted advertisements. It has an interest in users spending ever more time on the platform and creating ever more content. Former Facebook employee Frances Haugen (2021) said in a testimony in US Congress that Facebook designs its algorithms in such a way that it attempts to make users spend more time on the platform by leading them towards sensationalist content. Haugen (2021) said Facebook uses "dangerous algorithms that [...] are picking up the extreme sentiments" and "pick out the content" that is most suited to make users "spend more time on their platform" so that "they make more money". "Soft interventions are about making slightly different choices to make the platform less viral, less twitchy. Mark [Zuckerberg] was presented with these options and chose to not remove" the current way algorithms work (Haugen 2021).

Haugen documented in her testimony that Facebook uses algorithms as a technology of absolute surplus value production that tries to make users spend more time on the platform, create more content and data, engage more with content, and potentially click on more ads whereby Facebook makes profits. "There is a pattern of behavior that I saw at Facebook of Facebook choosing to prioritize its profits over people" (Haugen 2021). PEC research can, for example, use semi-structured interviews, focus groups or surveys to analyse how users assess Facebook's ways of making profit and making its users create surplus value.

Concerning the *relations of production (D7)*, PEC asks what the class relations of Facebook look like. Facebook was founded by its now-CEO Mark Zuckerberg, who in 2021 owned 81.7% of Facebook's class B shares and controlled 52.9% of the total voting power.[10] In 2022, Zuckerberg controlled 84.7% of class B shares and 54.4% of the total voting power.[11] Facebook has become such a profitable company by its class character, namely by exploiting the digital labour of its billions of users and its more than 70,000 paid workers (as of 2022[12]). Given Facebook's value is largely created by unpaid workers who are not remunerated, it can achieve high profits and a high-profit rate. In 2020, Facebook's profit rate was 51%.[13] The profit rate is the mathematical relation of profit to investment costs (means of production and labour costs). The higher the profit rate, the more profit a company makes concerning its investment costs. A profit rate of 51% is extremely high.

Facebook's class structures interact with gender discrimination and racism. In 2021, while 65.4% of Facebook managers were white, only 3.1% of the managers and 1.5% of the employed technicians were black. In 2021, according to estimations, 77% of the technical Facebook personnel were male, and only 23% were female. 57.2% of the Facebook sales personnel were male, and 42.8% were female.[14] The highest paid Facebook jobs (managers, programmers) are controlled by white men (management), whereas women and black people are dominant in low-skill administrative jobs. PEC should analyse the relation of class and domination in the context of communication systems such as Facebook.

The analysis of class relations also includes aspects of *class struggles*. PEC scholars can analyse how Facebook has waged a class struggle against users as workers and how users have responded. A typical method is to interview users, campaigners, privacy activists, digital labour unionists, Facebook employees, policymakers, etc. The art project Wages for Facebook reformulated the feminist Wages Against Housework Manifesto written by Sylvia Federici (1975) by replacing "housework" and similar terms with "Facebook" use. The result shows and reminds us in an artistic activist manner that Facebook exploits its users. In 2019, Wikipedia co-founder Larry Sanger called for a #SocialMediaStrike, arguing for the demand for a decentralised social media system and protesting against Facebook's surveillance of users (Sanger 2019).

Protests against surveillance are informed by practical moral philosophy, which relates to the *interaction of culture and political economy (D5)*. Moral philosophy needs to ask about Facebook whether it alienates and expropriates users or advances public communication and social contacts. Facebook's public image has suffered, which has to do with critical news reports. One can empirically study such news reports.

Frances Haugen is a former Facebook product manager who worked in Facebook's civil integrity team. She went public to criticise Facebook's profit logic. Such testimonies are excellent sources for empirical data analysis. In a testimony in the US Senate, she said that Facebook's algorithms are programmed to lead users, including kids, to sensationalist content whereby Facebook is "buying its profits with our safety" (Milmo and Paul 2021). "We have a few choice documents that contain notes from briefings with Mark Zuckerberg where he chose metrics defined by Facebook like 'meaningful social interactions' over changes that would have significantly decreased misinformation, hate speech and other inciting content" (Milmo and Paul 2021). Arguing from the perspective of social totality, Zuboff (2019, 94) argues that Facebook and Google are key players in "a surveillance-based economic order" that she terms surveillance capitalism.

Public statements, interviews, etc. about Facebook that are focused on controversies are excellent starting points for moral philosophy. The basic moral question underpinning Facebook's organisational model is whether (a) Facebook is a great company that enters a fair deal with its users who exchange free access to being monitored, or (b) Facebook exploits users and endangers democracy.

4.5 Conclusion

This chapter presented foundations, definitions, principles, and dimensions of the approach of the Political Economy of Communication. We can summarise the main findings.

Finding 1: The Political Economy of Communication

Political Economy of Communication is an approach that uses social theory, empirical social research, and moral philosophy for analysing the roles of communication and communication systems (media, communications) in society, especially the interaction of politics and economy in the context of media and communication. It studies how the interaction of communication, politics, and economy works and this interaction's roles in society. It sees the dialectical relationship between the economy and politics as the most important factor shaping communication and society. An important focus is on the analysis of the production, distribution, and consumption of information in the context of society. Political Economy of Communication often is a critical analysis of how communication and communication systems work and are organised in capitalist society and how they impact on and interact with society and the lives of humans in society. *This critical analysis is also termed Critique of the Political Economy of Communication and the Media.* It gives particular attention to the analysis of the capitalist mode of producing information; communication labour; the production, distribution, and consumption of information and communication(s) as commodities; the space and time of communication; the interaction of politics and the media economy; ideology critique; communication in the context of class and social struggles; and alternatives to capitalist communication(s), non-capitalist communication(s).

Finding 2: Principles of the Political Economy of Communication

Principles of the approach of the Political Economy of Communication, as identified by Vincent Mosco (2009) and Graham Murdock and Peter Golding (2005), include the following:

P1: the commodity and commodification;
P2: space (local, regional, national, global);
P3: structuration (class, gender, racism);
P4: history;
P5: social totality;
P6: moral philosophy;
P7: praxis.

Finding 3: The Political Economy of Communication's Methodology

The approach of the Political Economy of Communication uses social theory, empirical research methods and moral philosophy to study the interaction of politics and the economy in the context of the media and communication. It is guided by dialectical thinking as a methodological approach that supports the production of insights about how the Political Economy of Communication works.

Finding 4: Dimensions of Political Economy of Communication

There are several dimensions of a Political Economy of Communication analysis:

D1: the production of information;
D2: the circulation of information;
D3: the consumption of information;
D4: the interactions between the media and communication economy and the political system;
D5: the interactions between the media and communication economy and the cultural system, which includes ideology critique;
D6: the non-capitalist media and communication economy;
D7: the media and communication aspects of the (class and power) relations of production;
D8: the capitalist productive forces in the media and communication economy;
D9: the means of production in the media and communication economy;
D10: the workforce in the media and communication economy;
D11: the production and labour process in the media and communication economy, the where, when, and how of production;
D12: the products the labour process creates in the media and communication economy (use-values, commodities, capital, profits).

In this chapter, we introduced the approach of the Political Economy of Communication. It is one of the approaches to Media Economics and an influential approach within the field of Media and Communication Studies. In the next chapter, we will situate this approach in the context of the critical tradition of analysing the media, communication, and society.

Notes

1 Translated from German: „Medienproduktion und -konsumtion über die übrige Warenproduktion hinausgehend auch elementare unverzichtbare gesamtökonomische und gesamtgesellschaftliche politisch-ideologische Funktionen für die Herrschaftssicherung und Absicherung des kapitalistischen Wirtschafts- und Gesellschaftssystems insgesamt erfüllt" (Knoche 2002, 103).
2 This section was first published in Fuchs (2020, 62–64). Reproduced based on the author agreement.
3 Data source: https://www.emarketer.com/content/duopoly-still-rules-global-digital-ad-market-alibaba-amazon-on-prowl, accessed on 22 October 2021.
4 Ibid.
5 Data source: https://www.facebook.com/, accessed on 21 October 2021.
6 https://www.forbes.com/lists/global2000, accessed on 3 December 2022.
7 Ibid.
8 Data source: IMF World Economic Outlook October 2022, https://www.imf.org/external/datamapper/, accessed on 13 February 2023.
9 Data source: https://www.statista.com/statistics/268136/top-15-countries-based-on-number-of-facebook-users/, accessed on 22 October 2021.
10 Facebook Proxy Statement 2021, https://www.sec.gov/Archives/edgar/data/1326801/000132680121000022/facebook2021definitiveprox.htm, accessed on 22 October 2021.
11 Meta Inc. Proxy Statement 2022, https://www.sec.gov/Archives/edgar/data/1326801/000132680122000043/meta2022definitiveproxysta.htm, accessed on 3 December 2022.

12 Data source: Meta Inc. SEC-Filings Form 10-K for financial year 2021.
13 Data source (Facebook profits and revenues): https://www.forbes.com/lists/global2000, accessed on 22 October 2021.
14 Data source: https://diversity.fb.com/read-report/, accessed on 22 October 2021.

References

Adorno, Theodor W. 1973/2004. *Negative Dialectics*. London: Routledge.
Albarran, Alan B., ed. 2019. *A Research Agenda for Media Economics*. Cheltenham: Edward Elgar.
Albarran, Alan B. 2017. *The Media Economy*. New York: Routledge. Second edition.
Albarran, Alan B. 2010. *The Media Economy*. New York: Routledge.
Allmer, Thomas, Christian Fuchs, Verena Kreilinger, and Sebastian Sevignani. 2014. Social Networking Sites in the Surveillance Society: Critical Perspectives and Empirical Findings. In *Media, Surveillance and Identity. Social Perspectives*, edited by André Jansson and Miyase Christensen, 49–70. New York: Peter Lang.
Anderson, Simon P., Joel Waldfogel, and David Strömberg, eds. 2016. *Handbook of Media Economics*. Amsterdam: Elsevier.
Black, Edwin. 2001. *IBM and the Holocaust: The Strategic Alliance between Nazi Germany and America's Most Powerful Corporation*. New York: Crown.
Doyle, Gillian. 2013. *Understanding Media Economics*. Los Angeles, CA: Sage. Second edition.
Du Gay, Paul, Stuart Hall, Linda Janes, Hugh Mackay, and Keith Negus. 1997. *Doing Cultural Studies: The Story of the Sony Walkman*. London: Sage.
Federici, Sylvia. 1975. *Wages against Housework*. Bristol: Falling Wall Press.
Fuchs, Christian. 2022. Introduction: What Is Digital Capitalism? In *Digital Capitalism*, Chapter 1, 3–37. London: Routledge.
Fuchs, Christian. 2021. *Social Media: A Critical Introduction*. London: Sage. Third edition.
Fuchs, Christian. 2020. *Marxism: Karl Marx's Fifteen Key Concepts for Cultural and Communication Studies*. New York: Routledge. Chapter 4: Commodities, Capital, Capitalism.
Fuchs, Christian. 2010a. Social Networking Sites and Complex Technology Assessment. *International Journal of E-Politics* 1 (3): 19–38.
Fuchs, Christian. 2010b. studiVZ: Social Networking Sites in the Surveillance Society. *Ethics and Information Technology* 12 (2): 171–185.
Fuchs, Christian and Klaus Unterberger, eds. 2021. *The Public Service Media and Public Service Internet Manifesto*. London: University of Westminster Press. Book version of http://bit.ly/psmmanifesto with accompanying chapters. DOI: https://doi.org/10.16997/book60
Garnham, Nicholas. 1979. Contribution to a Political Economy of Mass-Communication. *Media, Culture and Society* 1 (2): 123–146.
Hall, Stuart. 1973/2003. Marx's Notes on Method: A "Reading" of the "1857 Introduction". *Cultural Studies* 17 (2): 113–149.
Hardy, Jonathan. 2014. *Critical Political Economy of the Media: An Introduction*. Abingdon: Routledge.
Haugen, Frances. 2021. Frances Haugen's Testimony in the US Senate: Full Transcript. 5 October 2021. https://www.rev.com/blog/transcripts/facebook-whistleblower-frances-haugen-testifies-on-children-social-media-use-full-senate-hearing-transcript, accessed on 22 October 2021.

Herbert, Daniel, Amanda D. Lotz, and Aswin Punathambekar. 2020. *Media Industry Studies*. Cambridge: Polity.

Holzer, Horst. 2017. The Forgotten Marxist Theory of Communication. *tripleC: Communication, Capitalism & Critique* 15 (2): 686–725. DOI: https://doi.org/10.31269/triplec.v15i2.908

Hoskins, Colin, Stuart McFadyen, and Adam Finn. 2004. *Media Economics: Applying Economics to New and Traditional Media*. Thousand Oaks, CA: Sage.

Johnson, Richard. 1986/1987. What Is Cultural Studies Anyway? *Social Text* 16: 38–80.

Just, Natascha and Michael Latzer. 2010. Ökonomische Theorien der Medien. In *Theorien der Medien*, edited by Stefan Weber, 72–101. Konstanz: UVK. Second edition.

Kiefer, Marie Luise and Christian Steininger. 2014. *Medienökonomik*. München: Oldenbourg. Third edition.

Knoche, Manfred. 2002. Kommunikationswissenschaftliche Medienökonomie als Kritik der Politischen Ökonomie der Medien. In *Medienökonomie in der Kommunikationswissenschaft*, edited by Gabriele Siegert, 101–109. Münster: Lit.

Knoche, Manfred. 1999. Media Economics as a Subdiscipline of Communication Science. In *The German Communication Yearbook*, edited by Hans-Bernd Brosius and Christina Holtz-Bacha, 69–100. Cresskill, NJ: Hampton Press.

Marx, Karl. 1894. *Capital Volume Two*. London: Penguin.

Marx, Karl. 1885. *Capital Volume Two*. London: Penguin.

Marx, Karl. 1867. *Capital Volume One*. London: Penguin.

Marx, Karl. 1857. Introduction. In *Grundrisse*, 81–111. London: Penguin.

Marx, Karl. 1845. Theses on Feuerbach. In *Marx & Engels Collected Works (MECW) Volume 5*, 3–5. London: Lawrence & Wishart.

Mattelart, Armand. 1979. Introduction: For a Class Analysis of Communication. In *Communication and Class Struggle. Volume I: Capitalism, Imperialism*, edited by Armand Mattelart and Seth Siegelaub, 23–70. New York: International General.

McChesney, Robert W. 2000. The Political Economy of Communication and the Future of the Field. *Media, Culture & Society* 22 (1): 109–116.

Meier, Werner A. 2003. Politische Ökonomie. In *Medien und Ökonomie. Band 1/1: Grundlagen der Medienökonomie: Kommunikations- und Medienwissenschaft, Wirtschaftswissenschaft*, edited by Klaus-Dieter Altmeppen and Matthias Karmasin, 215–243. Opladen: Westdeutscher Verlag.

Miège, Bernard. 2011. Theorizing the Cultural Industries. Persistent Specificities and Reconsiderations. In *The Handbook of Political Economy of* Communications, edited by Janet Wasko, Graham Murdock, and Helena Sousa, 83–108. Chichester: Wiley.

Miège, Bernard. 1987. The Logics at Work in the New Cultural Industries. *Media, Culture and Society* 9 (3): 273–289.

Miège, Bernard. 1979. The Cultural Commodity. *Media, Culture and Society* 1 (3): 297–311.

Milmo, Dan and Kari Paul. 2021. Facebook Harms Children and Is Damaging Democracy, Claims Whistleblower. *The Guardian*, October 6, 2021.

Mosco, Vincent. 2009. *The Political Economy of Communication*. London: Sage. Second edition.

Murdock, Graham and Peter Golding. 2005. Culture, Communications and Political Economy. In *Mass Media and Society*, edited by James Curran and Michael Gurevitch, 60–83. London: Hodder Arnold.

Murdock, Graham and Peter Golding. 1973. For a Political Economy of Mass Communications. *Socialist Register* 10 (1973): 205–234. DOI: http://socialistregister.com/index.php/srv/article/view/5355#.Ud_T3lMWGP9

Neumann, Franz L. 1936. *European Trade Unionism and Politics*. New York: League for Industrial Democracy.

Picard, Robert G. 2006. Historical Trends and Patterns in Media Economics. In *Handbook of Media Management and Economics*, edited by Alban B. Albarran, Sylvia M. Chan-Olmsted, and Michael O. Wirth, 23–36. Mahwah, NJ: Lawrence Erlbaum Associates.

Picard, Robert G. 2001. *The Economics and Financing of Media Companies*. New York: Fordham University Press. Second edition.

Picard, Robert G. 1989. *Media Economics: Concepts and Issues*. London: Sage.

Sandoval, Marisol. 2020. Entrepreneurial Activism? Platform Co-Operativism between Subversion and Co-optation. *Critical Sociology* 46 (6): 801–817. DOI: https://doi.org/10.1177/0896920519870577

Sanger, Larry. 2019. Social Media Strike! https://larrysanger.org/2019/06/social-media-strike/

Scholz, Trebor and Nathan Schneider, eds. 2016. *Ours to Hack and to Own: The Rise of Platform Cooperativism, a New Vision for the Future of Work and a Fairer Internet*. New York: OR Books.

Sevignani, Sebastian. 2022. Critical Political Economy. In *Handbook of Media and Communication Economics*, edited by Jan Krone and Tassilo Pellegrini. Wiesbaden: Springer. DOI: https://doi.org/10.1007/978-3-658-34048-3_3-2

Sevignani, Sebastian. 2016. Kritische Politische Ökonomie. In *Handbuch Medienökonomie*, edited by Jan Krone and Tassilo Pellegrini. Wiesbaden: Springer. DOI: http://doi.org/10.1007/978-3-658-09632-8_3-1

Siegelaub, Seth. 1979. Preface: A Communication on Communication. In *Communication and Class Struggle. Volume I: Capitalism, Imperialism*, edited by Armand Mattelart and Seth Siegelaub, 11–21. New York: International General.

Smythe, Dallas W. 1977. Communications: Blindspot of Western Marxism. *Canadian Journal of Political and Social Theory* 1 (3): 1–27. https://journals.uvic.ca/index.php/ctheory/article/view/13715

Smythe, Dallas W. 1960. On the Political Economy of Communications. *Journalism & Mass Communication Quarterly* 37 (4): 563–572.

Wasko, Janet. 2014. The Study of the Political Economy of the Media in the Twenty-First Century. *International Journal of Media & Cultural Politics* 10 (3): 259–271.

Wasko, Janet. 2005. Studying the Political Economy of Media and Information. *Communicação e Sociedada* 7: 25–48.

Wasko, Janet, Graham Murdock, and Helena Sousa. 2011. Introduction: The Political Economy of Communications. Core Concerns and Issues. In *The Handbook of Political Economy of* Communications, edited by Janet Wasko, Graham Murdock, and Helena Sousa, 1–10. Chichester: Wiley.

Winseck, Dwayne. 2011. The Political Economies of Media and the Transformation of the Global Media Industries. In *The Political Economies of Media. The Transformation of the Global Media Industries*, edited by Dwayne Winseck and Dal Yong Jin, 3–48. London: Bloomsbury Academic.

Zuboff, Shoshana. 2019. *The Age of Surveillance Capitalism*. New York: PublicAffairs.

Recommended Readings and Exercises

Readings

The following texts are recommended as accompanying readings to this chapter:

Vincent Mosco. 2009. *The Political Economy of Communication*. London: Sage. Second edition.
Chapter 1: Overview of the Political Economy of Communication (pp. 1–20).

Graham Murdock and Peter Golding. 2005 (or previous editions: 1991, 1996, 2000). Culture, Communications and Political Economy. In *Mass Media and Society*, edited by James Curran and Michael Gurevitch, 60–83. London: Hodder Arnold.

Christian Fuchs. 2020. *Marxism: Karl Marx's Fifteen Key Concepts for Cultural and Communication Studies*. New York: Routledge.
Chapter 4: Commodities, Capital, Capitalism (pp. 38–76).

Graham Murdock and Peter Golding. 1973. For a Political Economy of Mass Communications. *Socialist Register* 10 (1973): 205–234. DOI: http://socialistregister.com/index.php/srv/article/view/5355#.Ud_T3lMWGP9

Exercise 4.1   Political Economy of Communication and Media Industry Studies

There have been debates about how to best study the media economy. The following readings engage with two of these debates that are focused on the difference between Media Industry Studies (operating primarily at the mesoeconomic level) and the Political Economy of Communication (that is stressing the interaction of levels and the importance of society as totality and the macroeconomy). Read the following texts and discuss them.

Read the following three texts:
David Hesmondhalgh. 2010. Media Industry Studies, Media Production Studies. In *Media and Society*, edited by James Curran, 145–163. London: Bloomsbury.
Timothy Havens, Amanda D. Lotz, and Serra Tinic. 2009. Critical Media Industry Studies: A Research Approach. *Communication, Culture & Critique* 2 (2): 234–253. DOI: https://doi.org/10.1111/j.1753-9137.2009.01037.x
Eileen R. Meehan and Janet Wasko. 2013. In Defence of a Political Economy of the Media. *Javnost – The Public* 20 (1): 39–53. DOI: https://doi.org/10.1080/13183222.2013.11009107

Discuss:
What are the main features of the approaches advocated by David Hes-
mondhalgh and Havens/Lotz/Tinic?
What are the main features of the approach advocated by Meehan and
Wasko?
What are the differences between these approaches? Where and why do
they disagree?
What is your assessment of this controversy? What is your own position?

Read the following texts:
Paul Dwyer. 2015. Theorizing Media Production: The Poverty of Po-
    litical Economy. *Media, Culture & Society* 37 (7): 988–1004. DOI:
    https://doi.org/10.1177%2F0163443715591667
Graham Murdock and Peter Golding. 2016. Political Economy and Me-
    dia Production: A Reply to Dwyer. *Media, Culture & Society* 38 (5):
    763–769. DOI: https://doi.org/10.1177%2F0163443716655094
Paul Dwyer. 2016. Understanding Media Production: A Rejoinder to
    Murdock and Golding. *Media, Culture & Society* 38 (8): 1272–
    1275. DOI: https://doi.org/10.1177%2F0163443716671495
Discuss:
What are the main features of the approach advocated by Dwyer?
What are the main features of the approach advocated by Murdock/
Golding?
What are the differences between these approaches? Where and why do
they disagree?
What is your assessment of this controversy? What is your own position?

**Exercise 4.2   The Political Economy of the World's Largest
Media and Digital Corporations**

Work in groups or individually.
Apply and discuss the seven principles (finding 1) and dimensions (finding 4) of the Political Economy of Communication to some of the world's
largest media and digital corporations. Make a list of questions that the
Political Economy of Communication asks concerning the studied phenomenon. Formulate at least one question for each of the seven PEC principles and each of the PEC dimensions. If you are in class or a study group,
I recommend that you form groups of 2–4 individuals, that each group
focuses on one company and that you present the results to each other.

Apple
Amazon

BBC
Samsung Electronics
Alphabet/Google
Microsoft
Verizon Communications
Alibaba Group
Comcast
SoftBank Group
Tencent Holdings
China Mobile
Facebook
Sony
Intel
Deutsche Telekom
IBM
Taiwan Semiconductor
Oracle
Cisco Systems
Charter Communications
Dell Technologies
Hon Hai Precision (Foxconn)

If you work in a larger class or a study group, you can form groups and each group can focus on one example. Compare the results.

Exercise 4.3   IBM and the Nazis

Work in groups or individually.
Apply and discuss the seven principles (finding 1) and dimensions (finding 4) of Political Economy of Communication to the example of IBM and the Nazis. Watch the suggested video as input for analysis and discussion.

Edwin Black is a journalist who wrote the book *IBM and the Holocaust*. He shows that the Nazi regime in Germany rented calculating machines from the IBM headquarters in New York for organising the transportation and annihilation of millions of Jews and other groups it saw as enemies. Black (2001, 9) says that there was a "conscious involvement – directly and through its subsidiaries –" of IBM "in the Holocaust, as well as […] in the Nazi war machine that murdered millions of others throughout Europe".

The Corporation is a 2003 documentary film directed by Mark Achbar and Jennifer Abbott.
Mark Achbar and Jennifer Abbott (directors). 2003. *The Corporation*. Big Picture Media Corporation. Movie information https://www.imdb.com/title/tt0379225/, https://thecorporation.com/film/about-film
Watch scene 19 "Taking the Right Side", which focuses on IBM and the Shoah/Holocaust. The movie is available on the site Cinema Politica https://vimeo.com/ondemand/thecorporationcp) and on DVD. There is also a book by Edwin Black on this topic that can be used as supplementary material:
Edwin Black. 2001. *IBM and the Holocaust: The Strategic Alliance between Nazi Germany and America's Most Powerful Corporation*. New York: Crown.

Discuss how the principles and dimensions of the Political Economy of Communication matter in the context of the example of IBM and the Nazis.
After individual work respectively group work, compare your results. Discuss aspects of morality and capitalism in the context of this example, specifically the question:Does IBM have a responsibility for the killing of Jews in the Nazis' gas chambers because it sold calculating machines helping to organise the Holocaust to the Nazis or not? Why respectively why not? Is IBM only selling machines and not responsible for their use? Or does it have to take care and look into the applications of these machines, especially in the context of war and totalitarian regimes? What is the connection between capitalism and fascism?

One discussion of PEC principles in the context of IBM and the Holocaust is provided in the appendix of this chapter. Conduct the exercise first yourself and read this appendix afterwards.

Appendix 4.1   IBM and the Holocaust

This appendix discusses a way of applying seven principles of Political Economy for the analysis of the example of IBM and the Holocaust (Exercise 4.2):

P1: the commodity and commodification;
P2: space (local, regional, national, international, global);
P3: structuration (class, gender, racism);
P4: history;
P5: social totality;
P6: moral philosophy;
P7: praxis.

P1: The Commodity and Commodification

Edwin Black's (2001) book *IBM and the Holocaust* and the scene from The Corporation show that IBM sold calculating machines to the Nazis who used them for organising the Shoah/Holocaust. IBM profited financially from the Holocaust. Its computers as a commodity had deadly implications for the Nazis' identified enemies because they were used as tools for the organisation of a mass-industrial annihilation project. The example shows the interaction of the economy and politics. IBM as an economic corporation traded with a fascist political system, namely Hitler's Nazi Germany.

P2: Space (Local, Regional, National, International, Global)

There is a national and an international/global dimension: IBM is a global corporation that engaged in international trade with Nazi Germany. Hitler's Nazi state started the Second World War. It was motivated by nationalism, racism and imperialism.

P3: Structuration (Class, Gender, Racism)

The example shows that Nazi fascism is an exterminatory, racist, anti-Semitic project and what role capitalist interests can play in totalitarian systems.

P4: History

The example shows that the history of computing stands in the context of genocide and war. It is a historical example that stands in the context of the history of the Second World War and the history of fascism and genocide.

P5: Social Totality

The example shows that there is a connection between computing and fascism, namely IBM's business and Nazi fascism as the social totality of Germany in the years from 1933 until 1945. The critical political theorist Franz L. Neumann saw fascism as a societal system, a social totality. He gave the following definition:

Fascism is "the dictatorship of the Fascist [...] party, the bureaucracy, the army, and big business, the dictatorship over the whole of the people, for complete organization of the nation for imperialist war" (Neumann 1936, 35).

Franz L. Neumann 1936. *European Trade Unionism and Politics*. New York: League for Industrial Democracy.

P6: Moral Philosophy

The movie "The Corporation" argues that the communications corporation IBM acted immorally because it made profits from the Nazis' killing of 6 million Jews by selling calculating machines to them that helped organise the Holocaust.

There are two basic moral positions:

1 IBM put its profit interests before human interests and therefore acted immorally. It played a role in the killing of Jews;
2 A corporation cannot be blamed for how its customers use its products. IBM is not to blame for how the Nazis used its computing machines.

In the movie excerpt, the then IBM Vice-President for Technology and Strategy Irving Wladawsky-Berger takes the first moral position:

> Generally, you sell computers and they are used in a variety of ways, and you always hope they are used in the more positive ways possible. If you ever found out they're used in ways that are not positive, then you would hope that you stop supporting that. But, do you always know? Can you always tell? Can you always find out?

Edwin Black in the movie and his book takes the second position:

> IBM would of course say that it had no control over its German subsidiary but here in October 9th of 1941 a letter is being written directly to Thomas J. Watson with all sorts of detail about the activities of the German subsidiary. None of these machines were sold, they were all leased by IBM. And they had to be serviced on site once a month. Even if that was at a concentration camp such as Dachau Buchenwald. This is a typical contract with IBM and the Third Reich, which was instituted in 1942. It's not with the Dutch subsidiary. It's not with the German subsidiary. It is with the IBM corporation in New York.

P7: Praxis

The example shows that fascism is a crime against humanity and that those wanting to defend humanity and democracy against fascism should engage in anti-fascist praxis. According to the critical theorist Theodor W. Adorno, anti-fascism means to create a society in which fascism and Auschwitz are no longer possible:

"A new categorical imperative has been imposed by Hitler upon unfree mankind: to arrange their thoughts and actions so that Auschwitz will not repeat itself, so that nothing similar will happen" (Adorno 1973/2004, 365).

Theodor W. Adorno. 1973/2004. *Negative Dialectics*. London: Routledge.

5   The Critical Tradition in the Analysis of Media, Communication, Economy, and Society

What You Will Learn in This Chapter

- You will learn more about the critical tradition in the study of media, communication, the economy, and society;
- You will learn about the relationship between class, capitalism, racism, and patriarchy in the context of the interaction of media, communication, economy, and society.

5.1 Introduction

Media are part of society. Society is a large interconnection of social relations between humans. Where many humans come together, there are questions of power about how decisions important to society should be made and who controls what and how much resources. Media as means of information and communication play an important role in society. Therefore, there are questions about how the media should be organised, who should decide about these organisations, how communicative resources should be distributed, etc. Critical media analysis deals with the analysis of media, communication, power, and society. The critical tradition in the analysis of media, communication, economy, and society emphasises economic aspects in the context of power, media, and communication in society.

This chapter discusses the critical tradition of research on media, economy, and society. It introduces the tradition of the Political Economy of Communication and the Media (Section 5.2), discusses the relationship of capitalism, patriarchy, and racism in the context of the Political Economy of Communication and the Media (Section 5.3), and draws conclusions (Section 5.4).

5.2 The Political Economy of Communication and the Media

The book at hand outlines an approach to the study of the Political Economy of Communication and the Media. It does not claim to be the ultimate or only feasible introduction. It is not so much interested in telling the history of the field of Political Economy of Communication and the Media and is more focused on the analysis of particular themes from a Political Economy

DOI: 10.4324/9781003391203-6

perspective that has been influenced by the works of Karl Marx and authors building on Marx. This approach is often also termed the Critique of the Political Economy of Communication and the Media.

5.2.1 The Approach's Name

The approach presented in this book has been named in various ways, including Political Economy of Communication (Garnham 1979, Garnham and Fuchs 2014; Mosco 2009), Critical Political Economy of the Media (Hardy 2014), Critique of the Political Economy of the Media (Knoche 2002), Political Economy of Communications (Gandy 1992; Murdock and Golding 1973; Smythe 1960; Wasko, Murdock and Sousa 2011), Political Economy of the Media (Fuchs and Mosco 2015a; Golding and Murdock 1997; McChesney 2008), Political Economy of Information (Mosco and Wasko 1988), Political Economies of the Media (Winseck and Jin 2011), Political Economy of Culture (Calabrese and Sparks 2004) or Cultural Political Economy (Sayer 2001; Sum and Jessop 2013).

Political Economy of Communication and the Media (PECM) encompasses a range of approaches that have in common the focus on the analysis of the interaction of the political and economic aspects of the media and communication. Communication is the process of symbolic human interaction where humans produce information about the world, create social relations by sharing information with each other, and make meaning of the world, society and each other. A medium is a structure that enables and constrains behaviour. Wherever there is communication in society, there is also a medium of communication. Media and information do not exclusively exist in the human realm. For example, the DNA of living beings stores genetic information, and the blood system is a medium through which a living system's organs interact. Speaking of the Political Economy of Communication and the Media makes evident that we are analysing processes in society. Wherever there is communication in society, there are also media of communication and vice versa, as well as information.

The term "communications" stands for communication systems and communication technologies. It is often used synonymously with the term of the media. Culture is often seen as a notion that is broader than the media, encompassing also live performances of music, theatre, poetry, etc. But face-to-face entertainment and communication are not unmediated, but rather make use of the media of the body, air, sound, and light. Speaking of media and communication always includes the meaning-making processes of culture and information that is stored, processed, encoded, and decoded.

There are certainly different approaches within the field of PECM, but pluralising the name as "Political Economies" (as suggested by Winseck and Jin 2011) is in my view a mistake as the plural a) distracts attention from the fact that there are not a vast variety of approaches in the field of PECM; b) disregards that PECM is primarily a critical approach so that critique is a relatively constant and universal feature in it; and c) does not acknowledge that the critical approach to Political Economy (Critique of the Political Economy) is the dominant strand of PECM.

In this book, I do not focus on telling the institutional story and history of Political Economy of Communication. I am not so much interested in presenting who is and was teaching and conducting research where about what, who held or was denied what positions, or what controversies there have been (Political Economy of Communication VS. Cultural Studies, Marxist Political Economy VS. Non-Marxist Political Economy, Political Economy of Communication VS. Media Production Studies, etc.). I find it more fruitful to engage with particular media-related issues that affect the lives of humans in society and how they can be analysed using a PECM framework.

5.2.2 The Approach's History

Mosco (2009, chapters 5 and 6) provides an overview of the institutional history of PECM. He distinguishes between a North American and a British tradition in PECM. Dallas W. Smythe and Herbert Schiller were the founding figures of PECM in North America, a tradition to which scholars such as Lee Artz, Benjamin Birkinbine, Enda Brophy, Andrew Calabrese, Paula Chakravartty, Noam Chomsky, Nicole Cohen, Greig de Peuter, Nick Dyer-Witheford, Oscar Gandy, Edward Herman, Sut Jhally, Dal Yong Jin, Micky Lee, Richard Maxwell, Robert McChesney, Catherine McKercher, Eileen Meehan, Vincent Mosco, Manjunath Pendakur, Victor Pickard, Dan Schiller, Gerald Sussman, Janet Wasko, Dwayne Winseck, Yuezhi Zhao, and many others have contributed in the USA and Canada. In the British tradition, there is on the one hand the Political Economy work and tradition created by Graham Murdock and Peter Golding, who worked at the University of Leicester and Loughborough University. On the other hand, there have been scholars practising PECM at the University of Westminster since the 1970s. They have included, among others, Miriyam Aouragh, Steven Barnett, Dimitris Boucas, Charles Brown, James Curran (who after a period at Westminster was involved in founding the Media, Communications and Cultural Studies Department at Goldsmiths where he has worked together with Natalie Fenton, Des Freedman, Gholam Khiabany, and others), Alessandro D'Arma, Christian Fuchs, Nicholas Garnham, Peter Goodwin, Jill Hills, Maria Michalis, Naomi Sakr, Jean Seaton, Jeanette Steemers, Colin Sparks, Pieter Verdegem, Xin Xin.

In the German-speaking world, Thomas Allmer, Jörg Becker, Franz Dröge, Christian Fuchs, Andrea Grisold, Horst Holzer, Wulf D. Hund, Bärbel Kirchhoff-Hund, Manfred Knoche, Christine Leidinger, Werner A. Meier, Sabine Pfeiffer, Dieter Prokop, Rudi Schmiede, Marisol Sandoval, Sebastian Sevignani, and Josef Trappel, among others, have contributed to the tradition of the Political Economy of Communication and the Media. Based on Marx's works, especially Holzer, Knoche, and Fuchs have grounded and developed the approach of the Critique of the Political Economy of Communication and the Media.

A good source of information for those interested in the development of the Political Economy of Communication and Media approach are the interviews conducted and published by John Lent and Michelle Amazeen in the two books *A Different Road Taken: Profiles in Critical Communication* (Lent 1995) and *Key Thinkers in Critical Communication Scholarship. From the Pioneers to the Next Generation* (Lent and Amazeen 2015). The first volume presents interviews with Dallas W. Smythe, George Gerbner, Herbert Schiller, James D. Halloran, and Kaarle Nordenstrengt; the second volume presents interviews with Noam Chomsky, Christian Fuchs, Edward S. Herman, John A. Lent, Robert W. McChesney, Eileen R. Meehan, Vincent Mosco, Graham Murdock, Manjunath Pendakur, Gerald Sussman, Janet Wasko, and Yuezhi Zhao.

5.2.3 The IAMCR's Political Economy Section

PECM is not limited to the UK and North America, but can be found in many countries today. The international character of PECM is evidenced by the history of the Political Economy Section of the International Association for Media and Communication Research (IAMCR, https://iamcr.org/s-wg/section/poe). Janet Wasko (2013) tells the institutional history of this Section, which was created in 1978.

In 2021, the IAMCR had 15 sections and 17 working groups. Out of these 32 units, the Political Economy Section was with 206 members the sixth largest one (see Table 5.1). This shows that Political Economy is a major field within the IAMCR and an important subfield of Media and Communication Studies. The IAMCR has traditionally attracted a large share of scholars who belong to the critical communication tradition. It has therefore been a fruitful ground for the development of a section focused on PECM. The International Communication Association (ICA) is in terms of its membership significantly larger than the IAMCR and much more US-focused. No group devoted to Political Economy developed in the ICA. Table 5.2 shows the number of members of the IAMCR Political Economy Section from specific countries in 2021.

The data shows that the two largest membership groups in terms of residence are the USA and the UK. Given that scholars in universities in poorer countries often do not have the resources required to attend conferences and pay membership fees, this is no surprise. The IAMCR is affected by structures of global inequality just like any other academic organisation. There is, however, a significant number of members from non-Western countries, including China, India, Argentina, Indonesia, Uruguay, Brazil, which reflects the IAMCR's efforts to organise its annual conferences also in non-Western countries and to make significant membership discounts for scholars from poor countries. In 2021, the regular annual membership fee for scholars

Table 5.1 The number of members of the IAMCR's units (sections and working groups)

IAMCR Section/Working Group Name	Number of Members (2021)
Audience Section	202
Communication Policy and Technology Section	198
Community Communication and Alternative Media Section	205
Emerging Scholars Network Section	166
Gender and Communication Section	271
History Section	115
International Communication Section	271
Journalism Research and Education Section	311
Law Section	50
Media, Communication and Sport Section	54
Media Education Research Section	135
Mediated Communication, Public Opinion and Society Section	207
Participatory Communication Research Section	229
Political Communication Research Section	236
Political Economy Section	212
Comic Art Working Group	30
Communication in Post- and Neo-Authoritarian Societies Working Group	61
Crisis, Security and Conflict Communication Working Group	91
Diaspora and Media Working Group	82
Digital Divide Working Group	147
Environment, Science and Risk Communication Working Group	128
Ethics of Society and Ethics of Communication Working Group	104
Global Media Policy Working Group	89
Health Communication Working Group	136
Islam and Media Working Group	48
Media Production Analysis Working Group	113
Media Sector Development Working Group	43
Music, Audio, Radio and Sound Working Group	35
Popular Culture Working Group	204
Public Service Media Policies Working Group	67
Religion and Communication Working Group	62
Rural Communication Working Group	61

Data source: https://iamcr.org/, accessed on 4 November 2021.

Table 5.2 The number of members from specific countries of the
IAMCR's Political Economy Section

Country	Members
USA	45
UK	21
China	13
Canada	12
Australia	10
Belgium	9
India	8
Spain	8
Argentina	5
Indonesia	5
Uruguay	5
Brazil	4
Germany	4
Ireland	4
South Africa	4
Austria	3
Denmark	3
Philippines	3
Portugal	3
Bangladesh	2
Colombia	2
Croatia	2
Czech Republic	2
France	2
Greece	2
Kenya	2
Mexico	2
New Zealand	2
Pakistan	2
Sweden	2
Taiwan	2
Turkey	2
Chile	1
Estonia	1

(*Continued*)

Table 5.2 (Continued)

Country	Members
Finland	1
Ghana	1
Israel	1
Italy	1
Jamaica	1
Korea	1
Malaysia	1
Martinique	1
Netherlands	1
Norway	1
Singapore	1
Switzerland	1
Taiwan	1
Thailand	1
Trinidad and Tobago	1
UAE	1
Total:	212

Data source: https://iamcr.org/, accessed on 4 November 2021.

from high-income economies was US$ 180; for scholars from middle-income economies, US$ 80; and for those from low-income economies, US$ 30.[1] From 2000 until 2022, the IAMCR conference took place 22 times, including in Singapore, Brazil, Taiwan, Egypt, Mexico, Turkey, South Africa, India, Colombia, Kenya, and China. In the same time period, the ICA conference took place nine times in the USA and almost always in Western countries.[2] This means that the IAMCR has taken active steps to reach out to scholars in poorer and non-Western countries.

5.2.4 Publications

A field of study also has publications that represent knowledge produced in it. There are collected volumes, textbooks, monographs, and journals that stand in the tradition of the Political Economy of Communication and the Media. We already mentioned the textbooks by Mosco (2009) and Hardy (2014). Collected volumes include *Communication and Class Struggle* (Mattelart and Siegelaub 1979, 1983), *Labor, the Working Class and the Media* (Mosco and Wasko 1983), *The Political Economy of Information* (Mosco and Wasko 1988), *Illuminating the Blindspots: Essays Honoring Dallas W. Smythe* (Wasko, Mosco and Pendakur 1993), *The Political Economy of the*

Media (Golding and Murdock 1997), *Culture Works: The Political Economy of Culture* (Maxwell 2001), *Sex & Money: Feminism and Political Economy in the Media* (Meehan and Riordan 2002), *Media in the Age of Marketization* (Murdock and Wasko 2007), *Global Communications: Toward a Transcultural Political Economy* (Chakravartty and Zhao 2008), *The Handbook of Political Economy of* Communications (Wasko, Murdock and Sousa 2011), *The Political Economies of Media* (Winseck and Jin 2011), *Marx and the Political Economy of the Media* (Fuchs and Mosco 2015a), *Marx in the Age of Digital Capitalism* (Fuchs and Mosco 2015b), *Global Media Giants* (Birkinbine, Gómez and Wasko 2017), *Political Economy of Media Industries: Global Transformations and Challenges* (Nichols and Martinez 2019), *Communicative Socialism/Digital Socialism* (Fuchs 2020b), *Engels@200: Friedrich Engels in the Age of Digital Capitalism* (Fuchs 2021b).

Media, Culture & Society is an academic journal published since 1979 that has in its history featured many articles that are based on the Political Economy of Communication and the Media (PECM) approach. It was never purely committed to PECM. In *Media, Culture & Society's* first issue, James Curran described the journal's focus as a "forum for research and discussion about the mass media (primarily, but by no means exclusively, the press and broadcasting) within their larger social, political, economic and cultural contexts" (Curran 1979, 1), the publication of articles that recognise "those wider contexts within which the media operate" (1). The journal said it wanted to encourage "research and debate within and between" (2) empirical inquiry and Marxist theory.

In a 1986 reader presenting selected essays from the journal, the editors said that an important feature of articles in *Media, Culture & Society* is that they situate the media in the context of "a range of institutional means by which, in any society, symbolic forms, and the meanings they create and carry, are produced, distributed and consumed" (Collins, Curran, Garnham, Scannell, Schlesinger and Sparks 1986, 1), which is one kind of definition of the Political Economy of the Media. The editors also say that the journal is "heavily influenced by an explicitly 'Marxist' tradition" (Collins, Curran, Garnham, Scannell, Schlesinger and Sparks 1986, 3) and is at the same time critical of Althusserianism and postmodernism. In another selection of essays from *Media, Culture & Society* published in 1992, the editors list "the political economy of the media" (Scannell, Schlesinger and Sparks 1992, 5) as an important concern of the journal and write that the journal is committed to an Enlightenment "critique of the present in the name of a better tomorrow".

The Political Economy of Communication and the Media and especially its versions inspired by Marx and Marxian theory are today not a dominant or specially featured approach in *Media, Culture & Society*. They are just one of many perspectives that appears in the journal. *Media, Culture & Society* of course has never been exclusively dedicated to PECM, but it will be hard to deny that today PECM plays a much less important role than in it than in the journal's early years.

In the meantime, two other journals that stand in the PECM tradition have emerged: *tripleC: Communication, Capitalism & Critique* and *The Political Economy of Communication*. *tripleC: Communication, Capitalism & Critique* (http://www.triple-c.at) is a journal founded in 2003 that is co-edited by the present author together with Marisol Sandoval and Thomas Allmer. It is a not-for-profit open access journal dedicated to the publication of critical analyses of communication in capitalism, which means that it is based on critical versions of PECM. The journal defines itself as "a forum to discuss the challenges humanity is facing in the capitalist information society today. *tripleC* is an open access journal focused on the critical study of capitalism and communication".[3]

The Political Economy of Communication (https://www.polecom.org/) is an open access journal associated with the IAMCR's (International Association for Media and Communication Research) Political Economy Section. It was founded in 2013 and describes its aims in the following manner: The journal "showcases original research from established and emerging scholars and commentaries on contemporary media-related issues. The journal especially invites contributions which reflect upon the political economy of communication as an evolving field of intellectual inquiry".[4]

Two other journals that have given significant space to PECM perspectives are *Democratic Communiqué* (https://journals.flvc.org/demcom/about), which is the journal of the North American–based Union for Democratic Communications, and the *Global Media Journal* (https://www.globalmediajournal.com/).

5.2.5 De-Westernisation and Decolonialisation

In 2000, James Curran and Myung-Jin Park (2000) called for de-Westernising Media Studies:

> This book is part of a growing reaction against the self-absorption and parochialism of much Western media theory. It has become routine for universalistic observations about the media to be advanced in English language books on the basis of evidence derived from a tiny handful of countries. Whether it be middle range generalization about, for example, the influence of news sources on reporting, or grand theory about the media's relationship to postmodernity, the same few countries keep recurring as if they are a stand-in for the rest of the world. These are nearly always rich Western societies, and the occasional honorary 'Western' country like Australia.
>
> (Curran and Park 2000, 2)

Curran and Park thus emphasise that many analyses of the media only include Western states. They say that it is time to analyse non-Western media systems as well. Similar calls have ever since been made under the slogans of "internationalizing Media Studies" (Thussu 2009), "de-Westernising communication research" (Wang 2011), and "decolonizing Media and Communication Studies" (Chakravartty, Kuo, Grubbs and McIlwain 2018; Chasi and Rodny-Gumede 2018; Chiumbu and Radebe 2020; Dutta 2020; Mano and milton 2021b; Mohammed 2021; Ngwenya 2022; Willems and Mano 2016).

Certain advances have been made in the development of what Paula Chakravartty and Yuezhi Zhao (2008) term a transcultural Political Economy of Communication and the Media that studies media and communication in the context of global capitalism, features scholars from poorer countries, and includes the media in poor countries as a focus of analysis. For example, there are monographs on and analyses of the Political Economy of the Media in Africa (Chuma 2019; Moyo and Chuma 2010; Salawu 2021; Teer-Tomaselli 2018), the Arab world (Della Ratta 2018; Della Ratta, Sakr and Skovgaard-Petersen 2015; Sakr 2007), Asia (George 2008), China (Hong 2011, 2017; Qiu 2009, 2017; Zhao 1998, 2008), India (Banaji 2017; Sulehria 2018; Thomas 2010), Indonesia (Masduki 2021; Tapsell 2017), Iran (Khiabany 2010; Sreberny-Mohammadi and Mohammadi 1994), Latin America (Artz 2017; Bolaño, Mastrini and Sierra, 2012; Martens, Vivares and McChesney 2014), Pakistan (Ashraf 2021; Sulehria 2018), Palestine (Aouragh 2012), Singapore (George 2012), South Africa (Ngwenya 2021; Olurunnisola and Tomaselli 2011; Radebe 2020), South Korea (Jin 2011), Turkey (Karlidag and Bulut 2020; Yesil 2016), Zambia (Hamusokwe 2018).[5]

Assessing 20 years of attempts to de-Westernise media and communication studies, Colin Sparks draws a pessimistic conclusion and stresses that de-Westernisation is not simply a moral issue of willingness but a question of Political Economy:

> the best-funded research universities remain in the Global North; the most important publishers are all headquartered there; the most-cited journals are all edited there; many of the most prestigious conferences take place there; the most ambitious of the new generation of scholars seek to study, to publish, and often to work, there. Even those few universities outside of that privileged environment which enjoy the funding and the freedom to pursue independent research agendas tend to be dominated by faculty educated in, and to recruit graduates from, the 'best' universities in the developed world. Certainly in China, and probably elsewhere, Presidents and Deans are fixated on university rankings and Social Science Citation Index impact factors.
>
> (Sparks 2018, 391)

Sparks is therefore critical of the project to de-Westernise media and communication studies. The project has largely failed so far and follows a neoliberal logic that is all about rankings, tuition fees, and citations.

Most international, non-Western and decolonised studies of media and communication, including studies of the Political Economy of Media and

Communication, are single-country studies. Methodological nationalism is the consequence of the nationalist organisation of research funding. Comparative international research on the Political Economy of the Media and Communication that is based on transnational and transdisciplinary methodologies and theories developed co-operatively by teams of international researchers based on dialectics of the universal and the particular is much needed. But conducting such research is time- and resource-intensive as scholars need to have the time, space, and resources needed for working together. Research funding is primarily based on the goals of national and regional governments to outcompete other nations and regions in the economy and along with it academia, science, and technology. Research funding agendas are largely driven by capitalist imperatives. As a consequence, there is little focus on funding truly transnational and transdisciplinary research.

Certainly, "a new kind of thinking is required which values ideas and perspectives emanating from non-metropolitan hubs of global knowledge centres" (Thussu 2009, 25), but developing such a framework, such projects, methodologies, theories, and studies is first and foremost not a moral issue or a "moral imperative" (Thussu 2009, 27) but a question of Political Economy. The primary problem is not disinterest, ignorance or a lack of willingness but rather a science and technology policy agenda that is driven by competition, neoliberalism, and instrumental reason instead of co-operation, solidarity, and critical reason. Thussu (2009, 27) gives a hint at what Political Economy changes are needed when writing that an "antidote is urgently needed to an unsustainable commercial model of media – a global public media benefiting from a global 'creative commons', where free access to knowledge is guaranteed". At the same time, we must also see that established scholars continue to edit journals published by commercial, for-profit publishing houses whose content is not made available for free and from which private owners benefit monetarily and undermine public interest and public access.

Neocolonialism has brought about what Boaventura de Sousa Santos (2018, 356) terms "university capitalism", the university as a "capitalist enterprise" and an organisation operating "according to criteria proper to capitalism". As a consequence, transnational, transdisciplinary, critical and convivial research and learning lack material preconditions, namely proper funding, infrastructures, and resources. A Media and Communication Studies that is critical, transdisciplinary, transnational, and convivial (see Mano and milton 2021a) requires abolishing the corporate university throughout the world and replacing it with the public interest, commons-oriented university (Fuchs 2022b, chapter 5).

To decolonise academia, we need to go from university capitalism towards the public interest and commons oriented university. This means a new policy agenda of commonification (the transformation of something into a common good), democratisation, and self-management as decolonisation of the academic field. Such a changed framework would enable and require decommodifying the academic publishing world so that academic knowledge is available globally to everyone as creative commons provided by publicly funded not-for-profit academic publishers and journals; the abolishment of academic rankings, metrics, and reputational hierarchies; the establishment of new transparent, inclusive, open and democratic forms of doing academia; publicly funded universities that throughout the world realise the human right to education, which includes the right of everyone to afford attending university and equitable access to higher education and requires proper taxation of capital and wealth to support the funding of higher education throughout the world; overcoming the gaps in wealth, reputation, influence, and resources between rich and poor universities; the proper global taxation of capital to fund public services, including public research and public higher education; the transformation of the neoliberal university into self-managed universities that are democratically managed by academic workers and students and that have no CEOs and executive boards; the creation of a classless higher education, research and academic system where class status does not determine the chances of humans to enter and succeed in respectively to be excluded from and fail in academia; more financial support for young people from poor and working-class families to attend university; and public funding not for projects that are public-private partnerships but for international research co-operations that take a critical approach for studying the world's pressing problems.

5.3 Capitalism, Patriarchy, Racism, and the Political Economy of Communication and the Media

5.3.1 Capitalism, Patriarchy, Racism

For anyone studying Political Economy, the question arises of how class and capitalism are related to gender and racism. In critical theories of society, there are different ways of how the relationship between class and markers of identity is theorised. One approach is outlined by the philosophers Michael Hardt and Antonio Negri (2018). They argue that racism and patriarchy are an inherent part of capitalism. They say that "racial and capitalist hierarchies are relatively autonomous, neither subordinate to or derivative of the other, and, on the other hand, the two have become intimately intertwined in contemporary society" (Hardt and Negri 2018, 443); "gender like race, although thoroughly interwoven with capitalist hierarchies, retains a relative autonomy" (443). Racism, patriarchy and capitalism have "equal weight and relative independence" (443–444) and are at the same time "mutually constitutive" (444). The implication is that capitalism is inherently patriarchal and racist, which is why Hardt and Negri speak of racial capitalism and patriarchal capitalism, whereby they want to express that racism and patriarchy are necessary constituents of capitalism. For Hardt and Negri, capitalism on the one hand and racism and patriarchy on the other hand form a multiplicity of contradictions that have relative autonomy.

The Political Economist and economic geographer David Harvey takes a different approach. Harvey (2014, 8) argues that the contradictions of capital form the "economic engine of capitalism".

> Contemporary capitalism plainly feeds of gender discriminations and violence as well as upon the frequent dehumanisation of people of colour. The intersections and interactions between racialisation and capital accumulation are both highly visible and powerfully present. But an examination of these tells me nothing particular about how the economic engine of capital works, even as it identifies one source from where it plainly draws its energy. [...] wars, nationalism, geopolitical struggles, disasters of various kinds all enter into the dynamics of capitalism, along with heavy doses of racism and gender, sexual, religious and ethnic hatreds and discriminations.
>
> (Harvey 2014, 8)

Harvey thus argues that there is an economic core to capitalism that interacts with different forms of domination such as patriarchy, violence, racism, war, nationalism. Racism and gender "are not specific to the form of circulation and accumulation that constitutes the economic engine of capitalism" (7–8). Whereas for Hardt and Negri, patriarchy and racism have become subsumed under capitalism and form integral parts of it, for Harvey, there is a dialectic of capitalism on the one side and racism and patriarchy on the other side, which means he situates racialisation and gender outside of capitalism. Harvey sees class and exploitation of labour as the primary aspects of capitalism. He does not reduce racism and patriarchy to the economy, but rather says that they are dialectically articulated with capital.

The term capitalist patriarchy emphasises "the mutually reinforcing dialectical relationship between capitalist class structure and hierarchical sexual structuring" (Eisenstein 1979, 5).

Nancy Fraser argues that class, racism, gender, and sexuality are independent but related; they "intersect":

> gender, 'race', sexuality, and class are not neatly cordoned off from one another. Rather, all these axes of subordination intersect one another in ways that affect everyone's interests and identities. No one is a member of only one such collectivity. And individuals who are subordinated along one axis of social division may well be dominant along another.
>
> (Fraser and Honneth 2003, 26)

Fraser advocates "a 'both/and' approach — both class *and* status, redistribution *and* recognition" (Fraser and Jaeggi 2018, 7). In her approach, class, racism, and gender are relatively independent and external to each other and are all equally important. In contrast to Harvey, she does not see class relations as primary, but postulates a multifactorial analysis of power where all factors are equally important. Sylvia Walby takes an approach comparable to the one by Fraser. In her theory, "gender shapes class as much as class shapes gender" (Walby 1997, 12) and "gender and class are mutually causative" (Walby 1997, 14). "Gender relations impact on the economy as a whole, and thus on class structure" (Walby 1997, 13).

In class societies, classes are the relations of production where workers produce surplus that is appropriated and owned by the dominant class. Relations of production are the economic dimensions of society. Social production is the fundamental feature of society (Fuchs 2020a). Class relations are economic relations of production. Racism and patriarchy are on the one hand part of the economy in the racist and patriarchal forms of exploitation. On the other hand, they are also relations of production that take place in the political and the cultural systems. This means that racism and patriarchy have an economic aspect that is immanent in the capitalist economy and they have an economic dimension of production that operates outside the economy as the production of gendered and racist political power, sexist ideology and racist ideology. In capitalism, racist labour relations are often forms of extreme exploitation and housework as the "sphere of reproduction" is "a source of value-creation and exploitation" (Federici 2004, 7). At the same time, there are political and ideological dimensions of racism and patriarchy that are related to the capitalist economy as the latter requires the regulation, justification and mystification of "the contradictions built into its social relations" (Federici 2004, 17).

5.3.2 Political Economy of Communication and the Media & Cultural Studies

The question of how class, racism, and gender are related has also played an important role in the controversy between PECM and Cultural Studies in the 1990s. Cultural Studies is another approach within Media and Communication Studies. It originated at the Centre for Contemporary Cultural Studies at the University of Birmingham in the 1960s. Stuart Hall (1932–2014), who led the Centre from 1969 until 1979, is the most influential Cultural Studies scholar. Cultural Studies originated in the UK and has diffused into many parts of the world. Well-known Cultural Studies scholars include, besides Hall, Paul Du Gay, John Fiske, Paul Gilroy, Lawrence Grossberg, John Hartley, Dick Hebdige, Henry Jenkins, Richard Johnson, David Morley, Angela McRobbie, and Paul Willis.

In the 1990s, there were controversies and debates between Political Economy and Cultural Studies. Basically, it was a conflict about the hegemony in Critical Media and Communication Studies. A core question was how we should think about the relationship between the economy and culture, as well as class politics and identity politics. One such controversy took place between Nicholas Garnham and Lawrence Grossberg in the journal *Critical*

Studies in Mass Communication (Garnham 1995a, 1995b; Grossberg 1995). Garnham argued:

> Political economy sees "class – namely, the structure of access to the means of production and the structure of the distribution of the economic surplus – as the key to the structure of domination, while cultural studies sees gender and race, along with other potential markers of difference, as alternative structures of domination in no way determined by class. [...] How is it possible to study multi-culturalism or diasporic culture without studying the flows of labor migration and their determinants that have largely created these cultures? [...] How is it possible to study advertising or shopping, let alone celebrate their liberating potential, without studying processes of manufacturing, retailing and marketing that make those cultural practices possible".
>
> (Garnham 1995a, 70, 71)

For Garnham, class issues are thus the main questions of contemporary society that critical media and communication studies must address. He does not reject dealing with racism and patriarchy in the context of the media, but stresses that such analyses must be integrated with class analyses. Grossberg has a different view and answered in the following way:

> For Garnham, apparently, capital determines in a mechanical way from start to finish. [...] [His] version of political economy is too reductionist and reflectionist for cultural studies. [...] [For] political economy, in every instance, in every context, somehow, almost magically, the economic appears to be the bottom line, the final and real solution to the problem, the thing that holds everything together and makes everything what it is. That is why, I believe, Hall argues that such reductionism and reflectionism are intrinsic to Marxism (and by extension, to political economy). Everything seems to be locked into place, guaranteed by economic relations. Garnham's own vocabulary betrays this.
>
> (Grossberg 1995, 76, 78, 79)

Grossberg accuses Garnham of reducing society and the media to economics. For Garnham, racism and gender relations are necessarily related to class, whereas for Grossberg, the economy operates relatively autonomously from other parts of society and class is relatively autonomous from gender and racism.

Douglas Kellner suggested a multiperspectival approach that includes both Political Economy and Cultural Studies, a "multicultural perspective of gender, race, and class" (Kellner 1997, 110). There is no denying that all three categories are important in many analyses, but a multiperspectival approach has the problem that it is a multifactor analysis that simply adds up factors without seeing relations of dominance between these factors. Political Economy in contrast argues that class is "the axial principle" of capitalism and "the locus of primary social difference" (Ferguson and Golding 1997, xxv). This does not mean that class relations are determining gender relations and racism, but that in capitalism, gender and racism necessarily stand in a relation to class and do not exist independently from capital and labour. The economy – and in capitalism that means class – determines, as Stuart Hall (1996, 44) says, society "in the first instance". Stuart Hall leaves open what this exactly means. I tend to understand this formulation as meaning, as Raymond Williams says, that the economy in society in general and class in class societies and capitalism in their relation to the non-economic, should be thought of as "the setting of limits and the exertion of pressure" (Williams 2005, 34). In addition, the economy operates outside of the economic system in the form of production processes inside other systems, which means that in class societies, class relations set limits, exert pressure and reach from the economy into other systems where they interact with other social relations.

Shortly before his death, Stuart Hall said that contemporary Cultural Studies often does not expand "a Marxist tradition of critical thinking – [...] and that is a real weakness" (Jhally 2016, 338) and "in its attempt to move away from economic reductionism, it forgot that there was an economy at all" (337). He called for a "return to what cultural studies should have been about and was during the early stages" (338).

Today, on the one hand, Cultural Studies tends to more focus on media consumption, audiences, reception, popular culture, fandom, youth culture, subcultures, racism and sexism in the media and culture, representation of identities in the media, and cultural struggles of interpretation than Political Economy. And Political Economy tends to more focus on media production, cultural labour, media corporations, class and the media, ideology critique, Public Service Media, and working-class struggles in the context of the media than Cultural Studies.

On the other hand, the boundaries between these two traditions have become more elastic and blurred and their objects of study have partly moved closer together. One important development in both Political Economy (e.g. Dyer-Witheford 2015; Fuchs 2014; Huws 2003; Mosco and McKercher 2008) and Critical Cultural Studies (e.g. Gill 2002, 2011; McRobbie 2016; Miller, Govil, Mcmurria, Maxwell and Wang 2004; Ross 2009) is the analysis of media, cultural and digital labour and the global division of labour in the context of neoliberalism and capitalism, which means that class is being taken seriously in both traditions. Vincent Mosco observes in this context that "a genuine labour standpoint has begun to emerge" in Media and Communication Studies (Mosco 2015, 45). We can add that both Political Economy and Cultural Studies scholars have made important contributions to this development (see also the contributions in *The Routledge Companion to Labor and Media*, Maxwell 2016).

5.3.3 The Political Economy of Communication and the Media & Feminism

The analysis of gender and racism in the context of the media is not external to but an aspect of the Political Economy of Communication and the Media. This becomes evident, for example, in Eileen R. Meehan and Ellen Riordan's collected volume *Sex & Money. Feminism and Political Economy in the Media* (Meehan and Riordan 2002). The editors describe the task of a Feminist Political Economy of the Media as follows:

> sex plus money equals power. Addressing this equation in media studies requires the integration of feminism and political economy. This integrative approach is not simply a matter of adding one to the other. Rather, we argue that all media structures, agents, processes, and expressions find their raison d'être in relationships shaped by sex and money.
>
> (Riordan and Meehan 2002, x)

Ellen Riordan (2002) argues that a Feminist Political Economy of the Media must analyse how media commodity production and consumption shapes women's lives. Micky Lee stresses the importance of applying Feminist Political Economy to the analysis of digital technologies and the information society: "women should be situated and understood in the context of unequal global wealth distribution, where they serve as resources in the production, distribution, and consumption process of the information society" (Lee 2006, 191).

Marx (1857) understood the method of Political Economy as the analysis of the dialectics of production, circulation and consumption. In communicative capitalism and contemporary digital capitalism, audiences of advertising-funded media and users of advertising-based Internet platforms are unpaid audience and digital workers. Feminist Political Economy has realised Riordan's (2002) methodological guideline that Feminist Political Economy of the Media should focus on both production and consumption of the media, which includes their dialectics as in the form of media prosumption. Feminist Political Economists have, for example, analysed the gendered commodity audience (Meehan 2002), digital labour as digital housework (Jarrett 2016), and the labour of social media producers such as influencers and bloggers who act in an environment of promotional culture and constant advertising (Duffy 2015, 2017).

5.3.4 The Political Economy of Communication and the Media & the Analysis of Racism

PECM has also analysed the relationship between capitalism, communication, and racism. Oscar H. Gandy (2007, 110) calls for "a political economy of communication that is sensitive to the role that identity plays in both production and consumption" and can thereby "further our understanding of the ways in which corporate control of media and other cultural institutions

[...] helps to reproduce inequality through the formation of an isolated racial class". Gandy's (1998) book *Communication and Race* is an outstanding example that sets out a theoretical and methodological framework as well as a research agenda. He interprets existing research results in the light of this framework. Gandy shows how racism shapes the production, distribution, and consumption of information in capitalism.

Gandy has analysed how surveillance, audience, consumer, and user measurement algorithms operate in capitalism and discriminate often along racialised lines. He has shown that social sorting is panoptic, capitalist, and racist and that these aspects intersect. Panoptic sorting is a surveillance system of surveillance power and disciplinary surveillance that identifies humans, classifies them, and assesses them (Gandy 2021, chapter 2).

> Identification focuses on the data processing and data storage of "persons with histories, records, and resources when those persons or agents of those persons present a card, form, signature, claim, or response, or when they present themselves at a particular place or time. [...] Classification involves the assignment of individuals to conceptual groups on the basis of identifying information. [...] Assessment represents a particular form of comparative classification. Individuals are compared with others. [...] Once classification has occurred, assessment frequently involves the examination of probabilities – that is, the likelihood that a person will act, react, or interact in a particular way to a situation or circumstance".
>
> (Gandy 2021, 29–30, 32)

So Gandy argues that panoptic sorting is discriminatory and therefore prone to racism. There are two main forms of panoptic sorting, "government information gathering" (Gandy 2021, 73) and "the corporate data machine" (78). Bias is built into many algorithms and systems that sort and monitor: "The panoptic sort institutionalizes bias because the blind spots in its visual field are compensated for by a common tendency to fill in the missing with the familiar or with that which is expected" (Gandy 2021, 31).

Gandy (2009) argues there is a connection between panoptic sorting and cumulative disadvantages: "Cumulative disadvantage refers to the ways in which historical disadvantages cumulate over time, and across categories of experience" (Gandy 2009, 12). Thus, membership in a targeted group and disadvantages in panoptic sorting can easily have negative effects. "People who have bad luck in one area, are likely to suffer from bad luck in other areas as well" (Gandy 2009, 116). If you are a person of colour, poor, unemployed, ill or a member of the working class living in a deprived area, the likelihood increases that a panoptic sorting system such as data mining discriminates against you. Predictive algorithms and sorting mechanisms based on certain characteristics and behaviours calculate that an individual is part of a risk group, which can easily result in discrimination such as the denial of certain services, offer of lower quality services at a higher price (e.g. a mortgage, a loan, a car) or the false classification of individuals as criminals. "Once they have been identified as criminals, or even as potential criminals, poor people, and black people, in particular, are systematically barred from the opportunities they might otherwise use to improve their status in life" (Gandy 2009, 141).

The analysis of the Political Economy of Racism and the Media has been further developed and advanced by works such as Safiya Noble's (2018) *Algorithms of Oppression*. She analyses the Political Economy of search engines, especially Google's algorithms, and shows how the interaction of digital capitalism, racism, and sexism has created what she terms "algorithms of oppression". She shows how Google's algorithm produces racist, sexist and other forms of discriminatory results. Google claims that its algorithms are neutral. Noble says in this context:

> As a result of the lack of African Americans and people with deeper knowledge of sordid history of racism and sexism working in Silicon Valley, products are designed with a lack of careful analysis about their potential impact on a diverse array of people. If Google software engineers are not responsible for the design of their algorithms, then who is?
>
> (66)

An algorithm is an expression of oppression if it "biases information – toward largely stereotypic and decontextualized results, at least when it comes to certain groups of people" (56). Such biases are often "buttressed by advertising profits" (116). Noble writes that "public search alternatives" (86) owned by the public and operated by public service organisations are part of ways to overcome algorithms of oppression. Comparable to Noble's approach but set in a different context, Meehan shows how advertising is often biased and discriminates "against anyone outside the commodity audience of white, 18 to 34-year-old, heterosexual, English-speaking, upscale men" (Meehan 2002, 220).

For Political Economy, the media are not just economic organisations, but at the same time also cultural and political organisations that as such interact with their economic character. This means that the profit orientation of capitalist media can have implications for what content is produced and not-produced and how it is produced. The critique of ideology is therefore an important aspect of the Political Economy of Communication and the Media. Representatives of the approach of Critical Discourse Analysis (CDA) such as Norman Fairclough and Ruth Wodak have analysed how ideology works and what roles it serves in society. CDA is in itself a tradition of research closely associated with linguistics (see, e.g., Fairclough 2015, as well as Wodak and Meyer 2001, for an overview). It is, however, a transdisciplinary approach, which is why Fairclough (2013, 484) argues that

> we need political economic analysis, and for discourse analysis to contribute to social research it needs to be embedded within transdisciplinary

frameworks which theorise and develop methodologies for analysing what I see as *dialectical* relations between discourse and other elements. Cultural political economy is just one such framework.

CDA has shown how racism, xenophobia, anti-Semitism, nationalism, neoliberalism, etc. work as ideologies. CDA has not emerged and developed from within but outside of the Political Economy of Communication and the Media (PECM), so it is not part of the latter tradition. We can, however, say that CDA is an important approach and method that should also be used and applied in studies dedicated to PECM (see, e.g., Fuchs 2018a, 2018b, 2020d, 2021a, 2022a). PECM is just like CDA a transdisciplinary approach that engages with a variety of critical approaches and traditions.

The discussion shows that the Political Economy of Communication and the Media has, among other research, advanced analyses of patriarchy and racism in the context of the media and capitalism. It neither ignores these important topics of analysis nor does it reduce them to class and the economy. It maintains that in capitalist society, gender relations and racism are always related to class, labour, and capital.

5.4 Conclusion

Finding 1: Political Economy of Communication and the Media

Political Economy of Communication and the Media (PECM) is a tradition situated within Media and Communication Studies. PECM exists in and is practised in many parts of the world today. It is institutionalised in the form of the International Association for Media and Communication Research's Political Economy Section (https://iamcr.org/s-wg/section/poe), modules taught in university courses, textbooks, monographs, collected volumes, and journals such as *tripleC: Communication, Capitalism & Critique* (http://www.triple-c.at) and *The Political Economy of Communication* (https://www.polecom.org/).

Finding 2: Class, Patriarchy and Racism in the Context of the Media

The Political Economy of Communication and the Media has, among other research, advanced analyses of patriarchy and racism in the context of the media and capitalism. It neither ignores these important topics of analysis nor does it reduce them to class and the economy. It maintains that in capitalist society, gender relations and racism are always related to class, labour and capital.

Notes

1 https://iamcr.org/membership-fees, accessed on 5 November 2021.
2 https://www.icahdq.org/page/PastFuture, accessed on 5 November 2021.
3 https://www.triple-c.at/index.php/tripleC/about/editorialPolicies#focusAndScope, accessed on 6 November 2021.

4 https://www.polecom.org/index.php/polecom/index, accessed on 6 November 2021.
5 This list is exemplary, so claims in no way to be complete. There are also multiple works in languages other than English. Ideally, works would be published in both national languages and English because national languages are spoken in daily life and it is a simple fact, for the better or the worse, that English is the academic lingua franca. The political economy of academia in capitalism results in an unequal distribution of resources, which is why multilanguage editions of academic works are the exception from the rule.

References

Aouragh, Miriyam. 2012. *Palestine Online: Transnationalism, the Internet and the Construction of Identity*. New York: I.B. Tauris.

Artz, Lee, ed. 2017. *The Pink Tide: Media Access and Political Power in Latin America*. Lanham, MD: Rowman & Littlefield.

Ashraf, Syed Irfan. 2021. *The Dark Side of News Fixing: The Culture and Political Economy of Global Media in Pakistan*. London: Anthem Press.

Banaji, Shakuntala. 2017. *Children and Media in India. Narratives of Class, Agency and Social Change*. New York: Routledge.

Birkinbine, Benjamin, Rodrigo Gómez, and Janet Wasko, eds. 2017. *Global Media Giants*. New York: Routledge.

Bolaño, César, Guillermo Mastrini, and Francisco Sierra, eds. 2012. *Political Economy, Communication and Knowledge: A Latin American Perspective*. Cresskill, NJ: Hampton Press.

Calabrese, Andrew and Colin Sparks, eds. 2004. *Toward a Political Economy of Culture. Capitalism and Communication in the Twenty-First Century*. Lanham, MD: Rowman & Littlefield.

Chakravartty, Paula, Rachel Kuo, Victoria Grubbs, and Charlton McIlwain. 2018. #CommunicationSoWhite. *Journal of Communication* 68 (2): 254–266.

Chakravartty, Paula and Yuezhi Zhao, eds. 2008. *Global Communications: Toward a Transcultural Political Economy*. Lanham, MD: Rowman & Littlefield.

Chasi, Colin and Ylva Rodny-Gumede. 2018. Decolonising Communication Studies: Advancing the Discipline through Fermenting Participation Studies. In *The Palgrave Handbook of Media and Communication Research in Africa*, edited by Bruce Mutsvairo, 55–71. Cham: Palgrave Macmillan.

Chiumbu, Sarah H. and Mandla Radebe. 2020. Towards a Decolonial Critical Political Economy of the Media: Some Initial Thoughts. *Communicatio* 46 (1): 1–20.

Chuma, Wallace. 2019. Political Economy of the Media in Africa. In *Media Studies: Critical African and Decolonial Approaches*, edited by Sarah Chiumbu and Mehita Iqani, 114–131. Cape Town: Oxford University Press Southern Africa.

Collins, Richard, James Curran, Nicholas Garnham, Paddy Scannell, Philip Schlesinger, and Colin Sparks, eds. 1986. *Media, Culture & Society. A Critical Reader*. London: SAGE.

Conor, Bridget, Rosalind Gill, and Stephanie Taylor. 2015. Gender and Creative Labour. *The Sociological Review* 63 (S1): 1–22.

Curran, James. 2014. Foreword. In *Critical Political Economy of the Media. An Introduction*, edited by Jonathan Hardy, x-xx. London: Routledge.

Curran, James. 1979. The Media and Politics. *Media, Culture & Society* 1 (1): 1–3.

Curran, James and Myung-Jin Park, eds. 2000. *De-Westernizing Media Studies*. London: Routledge.

Della Ratta, Donatella. 2018. *Shooting a Revolution: Visual Media and Warfare in Syria*. London: Pluto Press.

Della Ratta, Donatella, Naomi Sakr, and Jakob Skovgaard-Petersen, eds. 2015. *Arab Media Moguls*. London: I.B. Tauris.

Duffy, Brooke Erin. 2017. *(Not) Getting Paid to Do You Love: Gender, Social Media, and Aspirational Work*. New Haven, CT: Yale University Press.

Duffy, Brooke Erin. 2015. Gendering the Labor of Social Media Production. *Feminist Media Studies* 15 (4): 710–714.

Dutta, Mohan J. 2020. Whiteness, Internationalization, and Erasure: Decolonizing Futures from the Global South. *Communication and Critical/Cultural Studies* 17 (2): 228–235.

Dyer-Witheford, Nick. 2015. *Cyber-Proletariat: Digital Labour in the Global Vortex*. London: Pluto Press.

Eisenstein, Zillah. 1979. Capitalist Patriarchy and Socialist Feminism. In *Capitalist Patriarchy and the Case for Socialist Feminism*, edited by Zillah R. Eisenstein, 5–40. New York: Monthly Review Press.

Fairclough, Norman. 2015. *Language and Power*. London: Routledge. Third edition.

Fairclough, Norman. 2013. *Critical Discourse Analysis. The Critical Study of Language*. London: Routledge. Second edition.

Federici, Silvia. 2004. *Caliban and the Witch. Women, the Body and Primitive Accumulation*. Brooklyn, NY: Autonomedia.

Ferguson, Marjorie and Peter Golding. 1997. Cultural Studies and Changing Times: An Introduction. In *Cultural Studies in Question*, edited by Marjorie Ferguson and Peter Golding, xiii-xxvii. London: SAGE.

Fraser, Nancy and Axel Honneth. 2003. *Redistribution or Recognition? A Political-Philosophical Exchange*. London: Verso.

Fraser, Nancy and Rachel Jaeggi. 2018. *Capitalism*. Cambridge: Polity.

Fuchs, Christian. 2022a. *Digital Fascism. Media, Communication and Society Volume Four*. New York: Routledge.

Fuchs, Christian. 2022b. *Digital Humanism. A Philosophy for 21st Century Digital Society*. SocietyNow Series. Bingley: Emerald.

Fuchs, Christian. 2021a. *Communicating COVID-19. Everyday Life, Digital Capitalism, and Conspiracy Theories in Pandemic Times*. SocietyNow Series. Bingley: Emerald.

Fuchs, Christian, ed. 2021b. Engels@200: Friedrich Engels in the Age of Digital Capitalism. *tripleC: Communication, Capitalism & Critique* 19 (1): 1–194.

Fuchs, Christian. 2020a. *Communication and Capitalism. A Critical Theory*. London: University of Westminster Press. DOI: https://doi.org/10.16997/book45

Fuchs, Christian, ed. 2020b. Communicative Socialism/Digital Socialism. *tripleC: Communication, Capitalism & Critique* 18 (1): 1–285.

Fuchs, Christian. 2020c. *Marxism: Karl Marx's Fifteen Key Concepts for Cultural and Communication Studies*. New York: Routledge.

Fuchs, Christian. 2020d. *Nationalism on the Internet: Critical Theory and Ideology in the Age of Social Media and Fake News*. New York: Routledge.

Fuchs, Christian. 2018a. *Digital Demagogue: Authoritarian Capitalism in the Age of Trump and Twitter*. London: Pluto.

Fuchs, Christian. 2018b. *Nationalism 2.0. The Making of Brexit on Social Media*. London: Pluto.

124   *The Critical Tradition*

Fuchs, Christian. 2014. *Digital Labour and Karl Marx*. New York: Routledge.
Fuchs, Christian and Vincent Mosco, eds. 2015a. *Marx and the Political Economy of the Media*. Leiden: Brill.
Fuchs, Christian and Vincent Mosco, eds. 2015b. *Marx in the Age of Digital Capitalism*. Leiden: Brill.
Gandy, Oscar H. 2021. *The Panoptic Sort. A Political Economy of Personal Information*. Oxford: Oxford University Press. Second edition.
Gandy, Oscar H. 2009. *Coming to Terms with Chance. Engaging Rational Discrimination and Cumulative Disadvantage*. Farnham: Ashgate.
Gandy, Oscar H. 2007. Privatization and Identity: The Formation of a Racial Class. In *Media in the Age of Marketization*, edited by Graham Murdock and Janet Wasko, 109–130. Cresskill, NJ: Hampton.
Gandy, Oscar H. 1998. *Communication and Race. A Structural Perspective*. London: Arnold.
Gandy, Oscar H. Jr. 1992. The Political Economy Approach: A Critical Challenge. *Journal of Media Economics* 5 (2): 23–42.
Garnham, Nicholas. 1995a. Political Economy and Cultural Studies: Reconciliation or Divorce? *Critical Studies in Mass Communication* 12 (1): 62–71.
Garnham, Nicholas. 1995b. Reply to Grossberg and Carey. *Critical Studies in Mass Communication* 12 (1): 95–100.
Garnham, Nicholas. 1979. Contribution to a Political Economy of Mass-Communication. *Media, Culture and Society* 1 (2): 123–146.
Garnham, Nicholas and Christian Fuchs. 2014. Revisiting the Political Economy of Communication. *tripleC: Communication, Capitalism & Critique* 12 (1): 102–141. DOI: https://doi.org/10.31269/triplec.v12i1.553
George, Cherian. 2012. *Freedom from the Press. Journalism and State Power in Singapore*. Singapore: NUS Press.
George, Cherian, ed. 2008. *Free Press. Free Markets? Reflections on the Political Economy of the Press in Asia*. Singapore: Asian Media Information and Communication Centre.
Gill, Rosalind. 2011. "Life is a Pitch": Managing the Self in New Media Work. In *Managing Media Work*, edited by Mark Deuze, 249–262. London: SAGE.
Gill, Rosalind. 2002. Cool, Creative and Egalitarian? Exploring Gender in Project-Based New Media Work in Europe. *Information, Communication & Society* 5 (1): 70–89.
Golding, Peter and Graham Murdock, eds. 1997. *The Political Economy of the Media. Two volumes*. Cheltenham: Edward Elgar.
Grossberg, Lawrence. 1995. Cultural Studies vs. Political Economy: Is Anybody Else Bored with This Debate? *Critical Studies in Mass Communication* 12 (1): 72–81.
Hall, Stuart. 1996. The Problem of Ideology: Marxism without Guarantees. In *Stuart Hall: Critical Dialogues in Cultural Studies*, edited by David Morley and Kuan-Hsing Chen, 24–45. London: Routledge.
Hamusokwe, Basil N. 2018. Theoretical Perspectives: Towards a Zambian Political Economy of Communication. *Communicatio* 44 (2): 1–19. DOI: https://doi.org/10.1080/02500167.2018.1493522
Hardt, Michael and Toni Negri. 2018. The Multiplicities within Capitalist Rule and the Articulation of Struggles. *tripleC: Communication, Capitalism & Critique* 16 (2): 440–448. DOI: https://doi.org/10.31269/triplec.v16i2.1025
Hardy, Jonathan. 2014. *Critical Political Economy of the Media: An Introduction*. Abingdon: Routledge.

Harvey, David. 2014. *Seventeen Contradictions and the End of Capitalism.* London: Profile.

Hong, Yu. 2017. *Networking China: The Digital Transformation of the Chinese Economy.* Urbana: University of Illinois Press.

Hong, Yu. 2011. *Labor, Class Formation, and China's Informationized Policy of Economic Development.* Lanham, MD: Lexington Books.

Huws, Ursula. 2003. *The Making of a Cybertariat. Virtual Work in a Real World.* New York: Monthly Review Press.

Jarrett, Kylie. 2016. *Feminism, Labour and Digital Media. The Digital Housewife.* New York: Routledge.

Jhally, Sut. 2016. Stuart Hall: The Last Interview. *Cultural Studies* 30 (2): 332–345. DOI: https://doi.org/10.1080/09502386.2015.1089918

Jin, Dal Yong. 2011. *Hands On/Hands Off. The Korean State and the Market Liberalization of the Communication Industry.* Cresskill, NJ: Hampton Press.

Karlidag, Serpil and Selda Bulut, eds. 2020. *Handbook of Research on the Political Economy of Communications and Media.* Hershey, PA: IGI Global.

Kellner, Douglas. 1997. Overcoming the Divide: Cultural Studies and Political Economy. In *Cultural Studies in Question*, edited by Marjorie Ferguson and Peter Golding, 102–120. London: SAGE.

Khiabany, Gholam. 2010. *Iranian Media: The Paradox of Modernity.* New York: Routledge.

Knoche, Manfred. 2002. Kommunikationswissenschaftliche Medienökonomie als Kritik der Politischen Ökonomie der Medien. In *Medienökonomie in der Kommunikationswissenschaft. Bedeutung, Grundfragen und Entwicklungsperspektiven. Manfred Knoche zum 60. Geburtstag*, edited by Gabriele Siegert, 101–109. Münster: Lit.

Lee, Micky. 2006. What's Missing in Feminist Research in New Information and Communication Technologies? *Feminist Media Studies* 6 (2): 191–210.

Lent, John A., ed. 1995. *A Different Road Taken: Profiles in Critical Communication.* Boulder, CO: Westview Press.

Lent, John A. and Michelle A. Amazeen, eds. 2015. *Key Thinkers in Critical Communication Scholarship. From the Pioneers to the Next Generation.* Basingstoke: Palgrave Macmillan.

Mano, Winston and viola c. milton. 2021a. Afrokology of Media and Communication Studies. Theorising from the Margins. In *Routledge Handbook of African Media and Communication Studies*, edited by Winston Mano and viola c. milton, 19–42. London: Routledge.

Mano, Winston and viola c. milton. 2021b. Decoloniality and the Push for African Media and Communication Studies: An Introduction. In *Routledge Handbook of African Media and Communication Studies*, edited by Winston Mano and viola c. milton, 1–18. London: Routledge.

Martens, Cheryl, Ernesto Vivares, and Robert W. McChesney, eds. 2014. *The International Political Economy of Communication. Media and Power in South America.* Basingstoke: Palgrave Macmillan.

Marx, Karl. 1857. Introduction. In *Grundrisse*, 81–111. London: Penguin.

Masduki. 2021. *Public Service Broadcasting and Post-Authoritarian Indonesia.* Singapore: Palgrave Macmillan.

Mattelart, Armand and Seth Siegelaub, eds. 1983. *Communication and Class Struggle. Volume 2: Liberation, Socialism.* New York: International General.

Mattelart, Armand and Seth Siegelaub, eds. 1979. *Communication and Class Struggle. Volume 1: Capitalism, Imperialism*. New York: International General.

Maxwell, Richard, ed. 2016. *The Routledge Companion to Labor and Media*. New York: Routledge.

Maxwell, Richard, ed. 2001. *Culture Works: The Political Economy of Culture*. Minneapolis: University of Minnesota Press.

McChesney, Robert W. 2008. *The Political Economy of Media. Enduring Issues, Emerging Dilemmas*. New York: Monthly Review Press.

McRobbie, Angela. 2016. *Be Creative. Making a Living in the New Culture Industries*. Cambridge: Polity.

Meehan, Eileen R. 2002. Gendering the Commodity Audience. In *Sex & Money. Feminism and Political Economy in the Media*, edited by Eileen R. Meehan and Ellen Riordan, 209–222. Minneapolis: University of Minnesota Press.

Meehan, Eileen R. and Ellen Riordan, eds. 2002. *Sex & Money. Feminism and Political Economy in the Media*. Minneapolis: University of Minnesota Press.

Miller, Toby, Nitin Govil, John Mcmurria, Richard Maxwell, and Ting Wang. 2004. *Global Hollywood 2*. London: British Film Institute.

Mohammed, Wunpini Fatimata. 2021. Decolonizing African Media Studies. *Howard Journal of Communications* 32 (2): 123–138.

Mosco, Vincent. 2015. The Political Economy of Communication: A Living Tradition. In *Power, Media, Culture. A Critical View from the Political Economy of Communication*, edited by Luis A. Albornoz, 35–57. Basingstoke: Palgrave Macmillan.

Mosco, Vincent. 2009. *The Political Economy of Communication*. London: SAGE. Second edition.

Mosco, Vincent and Catherine McKercher. 2008. *The Labouring of Communication. Will Knowledge Workers of the World Unite?* Lanham, MD: Lexington Books.

Mosco, Vincent and Janet Wasko, eds. 1988. *The Political Economy of Information*. Madison: The University of Wisconsin Press.

Mosco, Vincent and Janet Wasko, eds. 1983. *Labor, the Working Class and the Media*, Norwood, NJ: Ablex.

Moyo, Dumisani and Wallace Chuma, eds. 2010. *Media Policy in a Changing Southern Africa. Critical Reflections on Media Reforms in the Global Age*. Pretoria: University of South Africa Press.

Murdock, Graham and Peter Golding. 1973. For a Political Economy of Mass Communications. *Socialist Register* 10 (1973): 205–234. DOI: http://socialistregister.com/index.php/srv/article/view/5355

Murdock, Graham and Janet Wasko, eds. 2007. *Media in the Age of Marketization*. Cresskill, NJ: Hampton.

Ngwenya, Blessed. 2022. Is Marxism Clad in Eurocentric Garb? A Decolonial Political Economy of the Media. In *Marxism and Decolonization in the 21st Century: Living Theories and True Ideas*, edited by Sabelo J. Ndlovu-Gatsheni and Morgan Ndlovu, 248–263. London: Routledge.

Ngwenya, Blessed. 2021. *Media Power and Hegemony in South Africa: The Myth of Independence*. London: Routledge.

Nichols, Randy and Gabriela Martinez, eds. 2019. *Political Economy of Media Industries: Global Transformations and Challenges*. London: Routledge.

Noble, Safiya Umoja. 2018. *Algorithms of Oppression: How Search Engines Reinforce Racism*. New York: New York University Press.

Olurunnisola, Anthony and Keyan G. Tomaselli, eds. 2011. *Political Economy of Media Transformation in South Africa*. Cresskill, NJ: Hampton Press.

Qiu, Jack L. 2017. *Goodbye iSlave: A Manifesto for Digital Abolition*. Urbana: University of Illinois Press.

Qiu, Jack L. 2009. *Working-Class Network Society. Communication Technology and the Information Have-Less in Urban China*. Cambridge, MA: The MIT Press.

Radebe, Mandla J. 2020. *Constructing Hegemony: The South African Commercial Media and the (Mis)Representation of Nationalisation*. Pietermaritzburg: University of KwaZulu-Natal Press.

Riordan, Ellen. 2002. Intersection and New Directions: On Feminism and Political Economy. In *Sex & Money. Feminism and Political Economy in the Media*, edited by Eileen R. Meehan and Ellen Riordan, 3–15. Minneapolis: University of Minnesota Press.

Riordan, Ellen and Eileen R. Meehan. 2002. Introduction. In *Sex & Money. Feminism and Political Economy in the Media*, edited by Eileen R. Meehan and Ellen Riordan, ix-xiii. Minneapolis: University of Minnesota Press.

Ross, Andrew. 2009. *Nice Work If You Can Get It. Life and Labour in Precarious Times*. New York: New York University Press.

Sakr, Naomi. 2007. *Arab Television Today*. London: I.B. Tauris.

Salawu, Abiodun, ed. 2021. *African Language Media: Development, Economics and Management*. Abingdon: Routledge.

Santos, Boaventura de Sousa. 2018. *The End of the Cognitive Empire. The Coming of Age of Epistemologies of the South*. Durham, NC: Duke University Press.

Sayer, Andrew. 2001. For a Critical Cultural Political Economy. *Antipode* 33 (4): 687–708.

Scannell, Paddy, Philip Schlesinger, and Colin Sparks, eds. 1992. *Culture and Power. A Media, Culture & Society Reader*. London: SAGE.

Smythe, Dallas W. 1960. On the Political Economy of Communications. *Journalism & Mass Communication Quarterly* 37 (4): 563–572.

Smythe, Dallas W. and Tran Van Dinh. 1983. On Critical and Administrative Research: A New Critical Analysis. *Journal of Communication* 33 (3): 117–127.

Sparks, Colin. 2018. Changing Concepts for a Changing World. *Journal of Communication* 68 (2): 390–398.

Sreberny-Mohammadi, Annabelle and Ali Mohammadi. 1994. *Small Media, Big Revolution. Communication, Culture, and the Iranian Revolution*. Minneapolis: University of Minnesota Press.

Sulehria, Farooq. 2018. *Media Imperialism in India and Pakistan*. New York: Routledge.

Sum, Ngai-Ling and Bob Jessop. 2013. *Towards a Cultural Political Economy. Putting Culture in Its Place in Political Economy*. Cheltenham: Edward Elgar.

Tapsell, Ross. 2017. *Media Power in Indonesia. Oligarchs, Citizens and the Digital Revolution*. London: Rowman & Littlefield International.

Teer-Tomaselli, Ruth. 2018. The Four-Leafed Clover: Political Economy as a Method of Analysis. In *The Palgrave Handbook of Media and Communication Research in Africa*, edited by Bruce Mutsvairo, 131–152. London: Palgrave Macmillan.

Thomas, Pradip Ninan. 2010. *Political Economy of Communications in India. The Good, the Bad and the Ugly*. New Delhi: SAGE.

Thussu, Daya, ed. 2009. *Internationalizing Media Studies*. London: Routledge.

Walby, Sylvia. 1997. *Gender Transformations*. London: Routledge.

Wang, Georgette, ed. 2011. *De-Westernising Communication Research: Altering Questions and Changing Frameworks*. London: Routledge.

Wasko, Janet. 2013. The IAMCR Political Economy Section: A Retrospective. *The Political Economy of Communication* 1 (1): 4–8.

Wasko, Janet, Vincent Mosco, and Majunath Pendakur, eds. 1993. *Illuminating the Blindspots: Essays Honoring Dallas W. Smythe*. Norwood, NJ: Ablex, 1993.

Wasko, Janet, Graham Murdock, and Helena Sousa, eds. 2011. *The Handbook of Political Economy of* Communications. Chichester: Wiley.

Willems, Wendy and Winston Mano. 2016. Decolonizing and Provincializing Audience and Internet Studies: Contextual Approaches from African Vantage Points. In *Everyday Media Culture in Africa: Audiences and Users*, edited by Wendy Willems and Winston Mano, 1–26. London: Routledge.

Williams, Raymond. 2005. *Culture and Materialism. Selected Essays*. London: Verso.

Winseck, Dwayne and Dal Yong Jin, eds. 2011. *The Political Economies of Media. The Transformation of the Global Media Industries*. London: Bloomsbury Academic.

Wodak, Ruth and Michael Meyer, eds. 2001. *Methods of Critical Discourse Analysis*. London: SAGE.

Yesil, Bilge. 2016. *Media in New Turkey. The Origins of an Authoritarian Neoliberal State*. Urbana: University of Illinois Press.

Zhao, Yuezhi. 2008. *Communication in China: Political Economy, Power, and Conflict*. Lanham, MD: Rowman & Littlefield.

Zhao, Yuezhi. 1998. *Media, Market, and Democracy in China. Between the Party Line and the Bottom Line*. Urbana: University of Illinois Press.

Recommended Readings and Exercises

Readings

The following texts are recommended as accompanying readings to this chapter.

Vincent Mosco. 2009. *The Political Economy of Communication*. London: SAGE. Second edition.
Chapter 4: The Development of a Political Economy of Communication (pp. 65–81).
Chapter 5: The Political Economy of Communication: Building a Foundation (pp. 82–103).
Chapter 6: The Political Economy of Communication Today (pp. 104–126).

Janet Wasko. 2013. The IAMCR Political Economy Section: A Retrospective. *The Political Economy of Communication* 1 (1): 4–8.

John A. Lent. 1995. *A Different Road Taken: Profiles in Critical Communication*. Boulder, CO: Westview Press.

John A. Lent and Michelle A. Amazeen, eds. 2015. *Key Thinkers in Critical Communication Scholarship. From the Pioneers to the Next Generation*. Basingstoke: Palgrave Macmillan.

Oscar H. Gandy. 2007. Privatization and Identity: The Formation of a Racial Class. In *Media in the Age of Marketization*, edited by Graham Murdock and Janet Wasko, 109–130. Cresskill, NJ: Hampton.

Janet Wasko. 2014. The Study of the Political Economy of the Media in the Twenty-First Century. *International Journal of Media & Cultural Politics* 10 (3): 259–271.

Vincent Mosco. 2015. The Political Economy of Communication: A Living Tradition. In *Power, Media, Culture. A Critical View from the Political Economy of Communication*, edited by Luis A. Albornoz, 35–57. Basingstoke: Palgrave Macmillan.

Exercise 5.1 Studying The Political Economy of Communication And The Media

Work in groups or individually.

Search for all articles, books and chapters from the Political Economy of Communication and the Media tradition that were published during a recent calendar year. Use databases such as Google Scholar, Web of Science, Scopus, University book search engines, WorldCat.org.

Use keyword combinations such as "Political Economy" AND (communication OR media OR culture OR communications* OR digital OR Internet).

Read the articles you found.

Discuss:

What topics did representatives of the approach of Political Economy of Communication and the Media (PECM) analyse during the time period you focus on? What were the main research topics?
What are the characteristics of studies that use PECM?
What research questions are asked in the analysed works?
What methodological and theoretical approaches have been used?
How does PECM differ from other approaches?
Have a look at one particular article you found that uses PECM. Ask yourself: What kind of research questions would someone ask about the same topic using the Lasswell Formula? What is the difference between traditional Media and Communication Research that uses the Lasswell Formula and research that uses PECM?

Part II
Applications

6 The Political Economy of Media Concentration

What You Will Learn in This Chapter

- You will learn about capital strategies of media concentration;
- You will learn about the causes and consequences of media concentration;
- You will learn how to use the C4 Ratio and the Herfindahl-Hirschman Index for measuring media concentration.

6.1 Introduction

Markets are dynamic economic systems where commodities are traded. Their development is unpredictable. In the capitalist economy, there is a tendency that monopolies emerge. One also speaks of the tendency of economic concentration. Given the special nature of media organisations as producing and publishing information, a capitalist or authoritarian media monopoly where one economically, politically or ideologically controlled media organisation dominates, impedes negatively on and destroys democracy. There is an inherent connection of questions of media concentration and democracy. Media concentration is, therefore, an important topic for the Political Economy of Communication.

This chapter asks: How does the political economy of media concentration work? What are the causes, impacts, and problems of media concentration?

Section 6.2 discusses strategies of media concentration; Section 6.3, causes and impacts of media concentration; and Section 6.4, how to define and measure media concentration. Section 6.5 draws conclusions.

6.2 Strategies of Media Concentration

Economic concentration means that there are only a small number of companies that dominate specific markets, own the majority of property and capital operating in these markets, and control the majority of labour-power and sales made in that market. Media concentration is economic concentration taking place in the media industry.

DOI: 10.4324/9781003391203-8

6.2.1 An Example: Internet Search

Let us have a look at an example. Table 6.1 shows the global share of Internet searches conducted using specific search engines.

Google holds a monopoly in the world of online search. There are few other players, and they only control very small shares of global online searches. Google was established in 1998. Its search technology was superior to other algorithms used at this time, which brought the company advantages in the market. It branded itself as the world's key search engine, which helped expand its market share. In addition, Google attracted users by developing ever more free-to-use services such as Gmail (webmail, launched in 2004), Google Maps (navigation, launched in 2005), Google Docs (word processing, launched in 2006), Google Sheets (spreadsheets, launched in 2006), Google Forms (online surveys, launched in 2008), Google Drive (cloud storage, launched in 2012),. Free services attract users to Google's core search service. In 2015, the company renamed itself from Google Inc. to Alphabet Inc. Google/Alphabet also owns YouTube, the world's dominant user-generated video-sharing platform. YouTube was launched in 2005.

By providing freely accessible services combined with the capital accumulation model of targeted online advertising, where lots of data is collected about users' online behaviour and ads are presented to them that reflect their interests, Google's capital was rapidly growing. According to the Forbes 2000 List of the World's Biggest Public Companies, Google/Alphabet was in 2021 the world's thirteenth largest corporation and in 2022 the eleventh largest.[1] A good way of finding out more about the financial operations of transnational corporations is to read their annual financial reports. Companies listed on a stock market, such as Google, normally provide such reports with financial data. In the case of companies trading shares in the USA, the

Table 6.1 Share of searches conducted on desktop and laptop computers, tablets, and mobile phones from 4/2022 until 3/2023

Rank	Search Engine	Share of Global Searches (%)	Company	Country
1	Google	71.61	Google/Alphabet	USA
2	Bing	21.11	Microsoft	USA
3	Yahoo!	2.53	Verizon	USA
4	Yandex	2.27	Yandex	Russia
5	Baidu	1.56	Baidu	China
6	DuckDuckGo	0.59	DuckDuckGo	USA
7	Ecosia	0.10	Ecosia GmbH	Germany
8	Naver	0.09	Naver Corp	South Korea
9	Other	0.14		

Data source: http://www.netmarketshare.com.

respective form is called the SEC 10-K form. SEC is the Securities and Exchange Commission and regulates the USA's financial economy. Often, the financial reports of companies can be found on their websites in a section called "Investor Relations".

According to Google's 2020 annual financial report, it in 2020 made revenues of US$ 182.5 billion and profits (also called "net income") of US$ 40.2 billion.[2] Google makes the vast majority of its revenues from digital ads. In 2020, global ad sales amounted to US$ 665.9 billion and global digital ad sales to US$ 391.7 billion.[3] This means that digital advertising amounted to 58.8% of worldwide ad sales. Google accounted for 27.4% of the world's ad revenues and 46.6% of the global digital ad revenues. Facebook is after Google the world's second-largest advertising agency. In 2020, its revenues were US$ 86.0 billion and its profits were US$ 29.1 billion.[4] In 2020, Google and Facebook with combined ad sales of US$ 268.5 billion accounted for 40.3% of the world's ad sales and 68.5% of the global digital ad sales. The two companies are not primarily tech companies, but the world's largest advertising agencies. They form a digital advertising duopoly, which means that Google and Facebook together control the majority of capital and sales in the digital ad industry.

In 2021, global ad revenues amounted to US$ 772.41 billion and global digital ad revenues were US$ 521.02 billion.[5] In 2021, Alphabet's profits were US$ 76.0 billion and its revenues were US$ 257.6 billion.[6] Facebook renamed itself to Meta Platforms in 2021. That same year, its revenues were US$ 117.9 billion and its profits were US$ 39.4 billion.[7] According to this data, Alphabet and Meta in 2021 together controlled 38.5% of the world's ad revenues and 57.0% of the global digital ad revenues. In comparison to 2020, these shares had increased. Alphabet and Meta are digital advertising giants and the world's largest advertising companies.

In 2017, the EU fined Google 2.4 billion Euro for the abuse of monopoly power. It said that Google manipulated the search results for shopping so that its own shopping platform Google Shopping was privileged. In 2018, the EU fined Google 4.34 billion Euro because according to the EU, Google required phone and tablet manufacturers who wanted to run Google's Android operating system to also pre-install Google's web browser Chrome and its search app. In 2019, the EU fined Google 1.5 billion Euro. It argued that Google used exclusivity clauses in contracts with companies participating in Google's AdSense programme. These contracts prohibited these Google partners to use other online ad services.

The three examples show that monopoly capital has immense power to control customers' and users' behaviour in order to try to expand its own corporate power.

6.2.2 Concentration Strategies

There are four strategies of concentration that companies use for trying to increase their control of economic power:

- Horizontal integration;
- Vertical integration;
- Conglomeration;
- Strategic alliances.

Horizontal integration means that one company acquires companies in the same economic sector (Doyle 2013, 36–37; Hesmondhalgh 2013, 30; McChesney 2004, 177). **Vertical integration means** that one company buys companies in neighbouring economic sectors (Doyle 2013, 37–38; Hesmondhalgh 2013, 30, 200–204; McChesney 2004, 180; Turow 2010, 198). In the media sector, an example is the integration of media content companies and media technology companies, that is media production and distribution. **Conglomeration** means that one company operates in very different business areas and expands into these or further ones (Doyle 2013, 37; Hesmondhalgh 2013, 195–200; McChesney 2004, 183–185; Turow 2010, 207–209). **In strategic alliances,** companies co-operate in order to save money, avoid competition, share risks or compete against another player (Hesmondhalgh 2013, 212–215).

6.2.3 *The Example of Rupert Murdoch*

Let us have a look at examples of these media concentration strategies. News Corporation is the communication empire owned by media mogul Rupert Murdoch. The Murdoch family owns newspapers such as *The Sun* and *The Times* in the UK, and *The Wall Street Journal* and the *New York Post* in the USA; TV stations such as Fox and Fox News; and the book publisher HarperCollins. Many of Murdoch's media are notorious for their partiality, tabloid style, sensationalism, and the propagation of right-wing ideology. Murdoch's empire dominates the UK press. A survey about the press conducted in seven European countries (Britain, Denmark, Finland, France, Germany, Norway, and Sweden) found that "Britain's media is viewed as having a right-wing bias" concerning reporting on the topics of crime, Economics, health, housing, and immigration and that the British press is the most right wing in Europe (Dahlgreen 2016).

In 2020, before his Twitter profile was deleted, Donald Trump had more than 85 million followers. He followed 50 other users. Among them were many Fox News hosts and anchors such as @SeanHannity, @TuckerCarlson, @JudgeJeanine, @MariaBartiromo, @JesseBWatters, @DiamondandSilk and the Fox News shows @FoxandFriends. All of these are loyal Trump followers who delivered pro-Trump propaganda day by day. When in March 2020, protests and riots broke out in the light of the police killing of George Floyd in Minneapolis, Trump tweeted:

> ...These THUGS are dishonoring the memory of George Floyd, and
> I won't let that happen. Just spoke to Governor Tim Walz and told

him that the Military is with him all the way. Any difficulty and we will assume control but, when the looting starts, the shooting starts. Thank you!

Trump was widely criticised for threatening to use the military against US citizens. One of those who supported Trump was Fox News talk show host Sean Hannity, who tweeted on 29 May 2020: "MINNEAPOLIS UPDATE: President Trump Says Military Available to Stop Looting, Restore Peace". The example shows how aligned many of those working for FOX News are with far-right ideology and how they make use of television news and talk shows for advancing right-wing propaganda. The phrase "when the looting starts, the shooting starts" has a racist background. In 1967, Miami Police Chief Walter Headley used it in the light of the unrest in black neighbourhoods (Rosenwald 2020).

News Corporation has its origins in the Australian company News Limited, which was founded in 1923. News Limited became News Corporation in 1979. News Corp expanded its economic and cultural power through strategies of media concentration. On the one hand, it acquired newspapers, the core business in which it already operated in Australia. On the other hand, among these acquisitions were *News of the World* (1969), *New York Post* (1976), *The Times* (1981), and Dow Jones & Company Inc. (2007), which operates the *Wall Street Journal*.

An example of vertical integration is Murdoch's expansion into the film production industry. 20th Century Fox was created as a merger of 20th Century Studios and Fox, on the one hand, a film production studio, and on the other hand TV channels that distribute programmes. Before the creation of 20th Century Fox, Murdoch was only active in the print industry and focused on newspapers.

In 1985, Murdoch acquired the film studio 20th Century Fox for a total of US$ 575 million. In 1985, News Corp bought Metromedia's TV stations for US$ 3.5 billion. In 1986, Murdoch launched Fox Television Stations. The basic idea was that vertical integration allows to increase profits by making money from both film production and television channels, the commodification of content and content distribution. Murdoch's empire produced popular content such as Star Wars, Ice Age, Planet of the Apes, The Simpsons, American Idol, X-Files, Family Guy and made profits not only from movie screenings but also from ads run on TV stations while such content was broadcast.

Murdoch's media empire developed from a single-medium corporation focused on the press into a conglomerate. Murdoch used conglomeration for expanding into different economic sectors in order to increase his profits.

News Corp first focused on print, but increasingly became active in broadcasting and the Internet. In 1985, the purchase of Metromedia TV stations enabled the creation of the Fox Broadcasting Company. Murdoch continued the expansion into broadcasting by, for example, acquiring Star TV in Hong

Kong. The Murdoch empire since the Millennium expanded into the Internet economy by acquiring the entertainment website International Gaming Network in 2005, the social networking site MySpace in 2005, the social media news agency and content aggregator Storyful in 2013, and the real estate company Move Inc. in 2014 that operates real estate platforms such as realtor.com.

Hulu.com is an example of a strategic alliance. It is a video platform that tries to compete with Google's YouTube. Hulu was formed in 2007 as a strategic alliance of NBCUniversal (now owned by Comcast), News Corporation, and Walt Disney formed Hulu.com. In 2016, Time Warner bought parts of Hulu. In 2018, Time Warner was acquired by AT&T in 2018. In 2019, Disney acquired AT&T's share and the one of 21st Century Fox. In 2021, Disney owned 67% of Hulu, and Comcast owned 33%. Hulu was never able to compete with YouTube. The latter has for a long time been among the three most accessed web platforms. In 2021, YouTube was the second most accessed web platform[8] and Hulu the 205th most accessed one.[9]

6.2.4 *The Walt Disney Corporation*

Disney's acquisition of 20th Century Fox in 2019 is also an example of horizontal integration. Disney operates in the film and television business and acquired film studios and film rights held by 20th Century Fox by taking over the latter.

20th Century Fox was the Murdoch company's film production and television subdivision. It consisted of television stations (Fox, Fox News, National Geographic TV channels, etc.), movie production and distribution, and cable network programming. In 2019, the Walt Disney Company acquired parts of 20th Century Fox for US$ 71 billion, including the Hulu stake, cable and satellite TV stations, and the 20th Century film studios. Murdoch held on to parts of the TV business and formed the Fox Corporation, which owns the Fox TV channels. Disney in 2019 launched its video streaming platform Disney+. It wants to compete with Netflix and Amazon Prime. For doing so, the acquisition of 20th Century Fox was a strategic move as it gives Disney access to popular content such as the X-Men film series, Avatar, Star Wars.

> The acquisition of Fox was especially significant in expanding Disney's direct-to-consumer offerings, not only with the addition of 21st Century Fox's entertainment content, but a controlling interest in Hulu. Disney's own streaming services include ESPN+ (started in 2018) and Disney+ (launched in 2019), which has become the streaming site for new releases from companies in the Disney Multiverse.
>
> (Waoko 2020, 15)

Table 6.2 shows the world's best-selling movies. Disney is the key player, but 20th Century Fox plays also a very important role with movies such as

Table 6.2 The best-selling movies of all time.

Rank	Movie Title	Year	Lifetime Gross Sales	Distributor
1	Avatar	2009	$2,922,917,914	20th Century Fox
2	Avengers: Endgame	2019	$2,797,501,328	Disney
3	Titanic	1997	$2,201,647,264	Paramount Pictures, 20th Century Fox
4	Star Wars VII – The Force Awakens	2015	$2,069,521,700	Disney
5	Avengers: Infinity War	2018	$2,048,359,754	Disney
6	Spider-Man: No Way Home	2021	$1,916,306,995	Sony Pictures Entertainment
7	Jurassic World	2015	$1,671,537,444	Universal Pictures
8	The Lion King	2019	$1,663,250,487	Disney
9	The Avengers	2012	$1,518,815,515	Disney
10	Furious 7	2015	$1,515,341,399	Universal Pictures
11	Top Gun: Maverick	2022	$1,488,576,503	Paramount Pictures
12	Frozen II	2019	$1,450,026,933	Disney
13	Avengers: Age of Ultron	2015	$1,402,809,540	Disney
14	Black Panther	2018	$1,382,248,826	Disney
15	Harry Potter and the Deathly Hallows: Part 2	2011	$1,342,359,942	Warner Bros.
46	Star Wars Episode I	1999	$1,027,082,707	20th Century Fox
67	Bohemian Rhapsody	2018	$910,809,311	20th Century Fox
73	Ice Age: Dawn of the Dinosaurs	2009	$886,686,817	20th Century Fox
76	Ice Age: Continental Drift	2012	$877,244,782	20th Century Fox
79	Star Wars Episode III	2005	$868,390,560	20th Century Fox
91	Independence Day	1996	$817,400,891	20th Century Fox

Data source: https://www.boxofficemojo.com/chart/top_lifetime_gross/?area=XWW, accessed on 14 December 2021.

Avatar, Titanic, Star Wars or Ice Age. By acquiring 20th Century Fox, Disney controls a vast archive of movies that it uses for advancing its capital accumulation strategies and interests.

In 2018, 20th Century Fox controlled 9.1% of the global movie box office sales,[10] and Disney, 26.2%. In 2019, the year of Disney's acquisition of 20th Century Fox, Disney's share increased to 33.2%.[11]

Table 6.3 Companies dominating the global movie box office sales, 1995–2022.

Rank	Distributor	Movies	Total Box Office	Tickets	Sales Share (%)
1	Walt Disney	598	$41,951,258,961	5,912,438,870	17.06
2	Warner Bros.	838	$37,263,551,533	5,309,160,933	15.16
3	Sony Pictures	770	$30,686,033,541	4,465,171,923	12.48
4	Universal	557	$29,633,843,336	4,174,115,294	12.05
5	20th Century Fox	526	$25,882,657,988	3,795,188,109	10.53
6	Paramount Pictures	509	$25,684,175,588	3,791,238,296	10.45
7	Lionsgate	432	$9,724,601,619	1,231,397,462	3.96
8	New Line	208	$6,195,248,024	1,116,404,118	2.52
9	DreamWorks SKG	77	$4,278,649,271	760,431,349	1.74
10	Miramax	385	$3,836,019,208	714,108,890	1.56
11	MGM	242	$3,709,722,832	664,477,969	1.51
12	Fox Searchlight	227	$2,608,358,365	364,761,933	1.06
13	Focus Features	219	$2,506,967,392	324,009,468	1.02
14	Weinstein Co.	173	$2,207,186,458	279,587,721	0.90
15	Summit Entertainment	40	$1,667,022,795	217,204,346	0.68

Data source: https://www.the-numbers.com/current/market/distributors, accessed on 14 December 2022.

Table 6.3 shows the world's dominant companies in movie box office sales in the years from 1995 until 2021. Disney is the dominant corporation in movie ticket sales. By acquiring 20th Century Fox, it got access to the movie catalogue of the fifth and twelfth best-selling movie distributors (20th Century Fox, Fox Searchlight).

Political economist of communication Janet Wasko has conducted Political Economy studies of Disney and Hollywood (Wasko 2003, 2020). She points out that Disney is a megacorporation that dominates the entertainment sector:

> The Disney company, however, represents one of the best examples of the synergy that takes place through the cross-ownership of media and entertainment outlets and the recycling of products across these businesses. [...] What exists now is a mega corporation that dominates much of the entertainment industry.
>
> (Wasko 2020, 262, 264)

Disney has been criticised as ideological content that advances unrealistic pictures of reality and consumerism. Ariel Dorfman and Armand Mattelart argue:

> all the relationships in the Disney world are compulsively consumerist; commodities in the marketplace of objects and ideas. [...] The Disney industrial empire itself arose to service a society demanding entertainment; it is part of an entertainment network whose business it is to feed leisure with more leisure disguised as fantasy. The cultural industry is the sole remaining machine which has purged its contents of society's industrial conflicts, and therefore is the only means of escape into a future which otherwise is implacably blocked by reality. It is a playground to which all children (and adults) can come, and which very few can leave.
>
> (Dorfman and Mattelart 1991, 96)

Alan Bryman characterises the globalisation of consumer culture, branding, merchandising, control and surveillance of the workforce, and emotional, precarious labour as the Disneyisation of society. Disneyisation is "the process by which *the principles* of the Disney theme parks are coming to dominate more and more sectors of American society as well as the rest of the world" (Bryman 2004, 1).

Following the discussion of media concentration strategies, we will next ask: What are the causes of media concentration? What impacts does media concentration have on society?

6.3 Causes and Impacts of Media Concentration

6.3.1 Causes of Media Concentration

Critical Political Economy argues that capital concentration is an inherent feature and outcome of capital accumulation. Competition has monopolistic tendencies, the very logic of competitive markets and exchange drives corporations to search for strategies that allow them to reduce investment costs, and increase productivity so that they can produce cheaper than competitors, which in the long run results in bankruptcy of the less productive corporations and a tendency for capital concentration.

Marx argues that technologically induced productivity increases, the credit system and financialisation are factors advancing the centralisation of capital:

> The battle of competition is fought by the cheapening of commodities. The cheapness of commodities depends, all other circumstances remaining the same, on the productivity of labour, and this depends in turn on the scale of production. Therefore the larger capitals beat the smaller. It will further be remembered that, with the development of the capitalist mode of production, there is an increase in the minimum amount

of individual capital necessary to carry on a business under its normal conditions. The smaller capitals, therefore, crowd into spheres of production which large-scale industry has taken control of only sporadically or incompletely. Here competition rages in direct proportion to the number, and in inverse proportion to the magnitude, of the rival capitals. It always ends in the ruin of many small capitalists, whose capitals partly pass into the hands of their conquerors, and partly vanish completely. Apart from this, an altogether new force comes into existence with the development of capitalist production: the credit system. In its first stages, this system furtively creeps in as the humble assistant of accumulation, drawing into the hands of individual or associated capitalists by invisible threads the money resources, which lie scattered in larger or smaller amounts over the surface of society; but it soon becomes a new and terrible weapon in the battle of competition and is finally transformed into an enormous social mechanism for the centralization of capitals.

(Marx 1867, 777–778)

Marx (1894) writes that credit and financialisation give "rise to monopoly in certain spheres and hence provokes state intervention", which "reproduces a new financial aristocracy" and creates "an entire system of swindling and cheating with respect to the promotion of companies, issue of shares and share dealings". Monopoly is "the abolition of the capitalist mode of production within the capitalist mode of production" (569). Capitalism's monopoly tendency "accelerates the violent outbreaks of this contradiction, crises" (572).

The media/information/communication economy involves on the one hand the peculiarity that content is produced. On the other hand, this sector also produces hardware (information and communication technologies) and communication services. There are five features of the information sector that favour capital concentration in the media/information/communication economy (see also Micklethwait 1989):

1 The Sunk Cost Rule:

The creation of information and knowledge as a commodity has high initial development and investment costs. These initial costs are sunk in the product and need to be recovered by sufficient sales. Think for example of a movie. According to data, the average cost of producing a major movie was US$ 65 million in 2020 (Mueller 2020). Few corporations can obtain the large amount of capital needed for such production, which assists that only a few companies are active and competitive in the information economy.

2 The Nobody Knows Anything Rule:

The entertainment, cultural, and media industry is a highly unpredictable industry. It is also highly uncertain and unknown in advance if audiences and users will have an interest in a specific book, film, record, software, television series, advertisement, mobile phone, etc. because human tastes and cultural preferences are complex and cannot be calculated. Producing a cultural/information/entertainment/media commodity is therefore not just expensive, but also high risk. Not many companies are willing to take such big risks, which is a factor that favours capital concentration.

3 The Hit Rule:

In the entertainment and popular culture sector, not every produced good has high sales. Single "hits" create a large share of the sales and profits, whereas other products make a loss or only result in modest profits. The Hit Rule is another aspect of uncertainty that makes it a high risk to be active in the media industry and favours capital concentration.

4 The "Piracy" Rule:

Information is a good that is intangible and is therefore not used up physically in consumption. The Theory of Public Goods says that such goods are non-rivalrous in consumption. It also uses the term subtractability and says that public goods have low subtractability, which means that multiple use does not subtract from the good's usability. It can still be used after multiple uses and can even be used in parallel by different individuals. If you eat an apple, then your friend cannot eat the same apple. But both of you can at the same time listen to the same piece of music. It is also difficult to exclude others from the access to information because it can easily be copied and distributed. The Theory of Public Goods says that such goods involve the non-exclusion of others from consumption. As a consequence of these peculiar features of information, the history of the information economy is also a history of users copying and sharing information ("pirating") and the industry trying to circumvent such sharing by intellectual property laws, criminalisation, surveillance, and security technologies. As a consequence, selling information as a commodity involves the risk of an income loss because of "pirating". This is another high risk of selling information as a commodity that can reduce the number of companies active in the market willing to take such risks, which in turn favours capital concentration. Trying to circumvent "piracy" is expensive as it requires personnel, time and financial resources. Only large companies can make such investments.

5 The Advertising-Circulation-Spiral:

Advertising is an important feature of the capitalist media industry. There are on the one hand media corporations that almost fully rely on advertising as a capital accumulation model. Examples are corporations such as

Facebook and Google that use targeted online advertising, free newspapers, or freely accessible commercial television and radio stations. Advertising is a political-economic mechanism that tends to advance media concentration. On the other hand, in Media Economics literature, one in this context speaks of the advertising-circulation-spiral (see Furhoff 1973): Advertisers are interested to buy ads from media that reach large audiences. They will therefore tend to go for the big commercial media that offer access to such audiences. Those media that have large circulation reach have larger audiences than their competitors. There is a tendency that larger audiences mean more advertising clients and the sale of more ads than competitors, which translates into more ad-related profits. More profits allow more effective and efficient capital reinvestment into strategies for increasing audience shares. If these strategies work, then the audience share increases, which attracts further advertising clients. Large audiences and advertising then reinforce each other in a spiral with positive feedback. The advertising-circulation-spiral advances the concentration of capital in the media industry.

Figure 6.1 shows the basic model advanced by the Theory of Public Goods.

In the Theory of Public Goods, there are four types of goods that are shown in Figure 6.1:

- Public goods are those that have low subtractability and where exclusion is difficult;
- Common goods are those that have high subtractability and where exclusion is difficult;

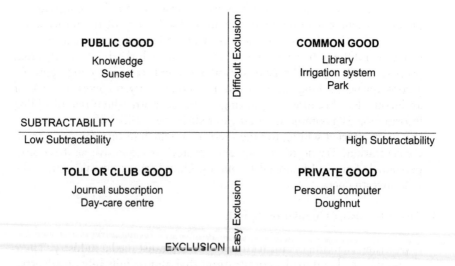

Figure 6.1 The Theory of Public Goods.

Source: Based on Hess and Ostrom (2003, 9).

- Toll or club goods are those that have low subtractability and where exclusion is easy;
- Private goods are those that have high subtractability and where exclusion is easy.

Figure 6.1 shows examples. Concerning the information and media economy, the Theory of Public Good says that information is a public good; a library, a common good; a subscription-based journal or newspaper, a toll club accessible only to a club of users; and a personal computer, a private good. Gillian Doyle (2013, 12–13) outlines why media content is in her view a public good:

> If one person watches a television broadcast, it doesn't diminish someone else's opportunity of viewing it. Because it is not used up as it is consumed, the same content can be supplied over and over again to additional consumers. So television and radio broadcasts exhibit one of the key features of being a 'public good'. Other cultural goods such as works of art also qualify as public goods because the act of consumption by one individual does not reduce their supply to others. Public goods contrast with normal or private goods in that private goods (such as a loaf of bread, jar of honey or pint of Guinness) *will* get used up as they are consumed. As soon as one person consumes a loaf of bread it is no longer available to anyone else. A loaf of bread can only be sold once. But when an idea or a story is sold, the seller still possesses it and can sell it over and over again.

The Institutional Political Economists Marie Luise Kiefer and Christian Steininger (2014, 136) point out that television

> can be both: terrestrially broadcast a pure public good, organised as pay-TV a club good. [...] A film broadcast on terrestrial television is a pure public good for all broadcast subscribers in the distribution area of the broadcaster, the same film broadcast in the cinema or on pay-TV is a club good for the respective paying audience. [...] According to the definitions of the Theory of Public Goods, only broadcasting that is distributed wirelessly and without distortion is a pure public good. Non-excludability (at economically reasonable cost) and non-rivalry in consumption are fully given for media content and carriers. However, the carrier has the characteristics of a public good only in the audience market, not in the market for frequencies and orbital positions, where the definition and enforcement of property rights is in principle possible. [...] Cable television and cable radio as well as all forms of pay-TV or pay-radio are club or toll goods, i.e. public goods in the narrower sense.[12]
>
> (Kiefer and Steininger 2014, 136, 156, 157)

The Theory of Public Goods is widely accepted in contemporary Microeconomics and is part of what is taught in Microeconomics. For example, Hal R. Varian, who in 2002 became Google's Chief Economist and is a representative of Neoclassical Economics, in his introductory textbook *Microeconomic Analysis* distinguishes between private goods "whose consumption only affects a single economic agent" such as bread; and goods "that are not excludable and are nonrival" and are called "public goods; other examples are police and fire protection, highways, national defense, lighthouses, television and radio broadcasts, clean air, and so on" (Varian 1992, 414).

The basic issue with the Theory of Public Goods is that it naturalises the notions of "public" and "private" based on immanent characteristics of goods. A different approach is that class relations that determine ownership are seen as determining factors of what is a public or a private good. The Theory of Public Goods is a consumption-oriented theory, whereas Critical Political Economy is a production-oriented. A good is private if the means of production and capital used for its production are privately owned. And it is a public good if the means of production are publicly owned by public service organisations and the good is provided to all members of the public.

Terrestrial television that is freely accessible to everyone is not always a public good. It is a public good if operated by a Public Service Media organisation. It is, however, a private good if operated by a privately owned for-profit company that makes content available as a "free lunch" (Smythe 1977, 5) and sells ads in order to make a profit.

6.3.2 Impacts of Media Concentration on Society

Critics of media concentration argue that media power should be limited by, for example, measures such as unbundling, asset stripping, public services, and government aid for small suppliers (Kleinsteuber 2004; Kleinsteuber and Thomaß 2004, 144) and/or that the principles of competition and profit have to be overcome (Knoche 2004, 2005, 2013, 2021). Robert McChesney (2004, 175) writes in this context that the "problem with market regulation is not merely a matter of economic concentration – even competitive markets are problematic. Perhaps we should not even expect the market to be the appropriate regulator for the media system" (McChesney 2004, 175).

Manfred Knoche distinguishes between an apologetic-normative theory of competition and a critical-empirical theory of concentration. The first argues that competition is a normative goal and that concentration is an exception from the competitive rule that can be avoided, whereas the second sees "the actual economic *rivalry* of individual capital owners associated with *profit maximisation*" as "a systematic, regular cause of concentration processes that have negative consequences for the freedom of information, the freedom of opinion and the diversity of the media" (Knoche 2021, 384). Capital concentration and market concentration, Knoche argues, are the rule of capitalism, not an exception from the rule.

Figure 6.2 visualises the two theories of media concentration that Knoche distinguishes.

Apologetic-normative theories assume that private media corporations' profit interests result in economic competition and competitive markets.

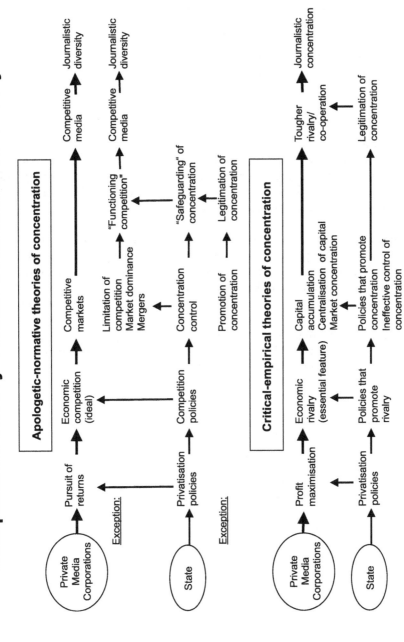

Figure 6.2 Two theories of media concentration.

Source: Knoche 2021, reprinted with permission by the journal tripleC.

Market dysfunctionalities would be irregularities that could be resolved by the state in the form of competition policies that make competition function again. The market would safeguard the diversity of the media and its content. In contrast, critical-empirical theories of concentration argue that the centralisation of capital and market concentration are immanent in media corporations' profit imperative and that economic rivalry has an inherent monopoly tendency that results in the concentration of the media.

There are several effects of corporate media monopolies and media concentration processes on society.

- Ideological power:

  Corporations that produce or organise content have the power to define what people can consider as correct and valuable views of reality and as truth. Corporate monopolies hence have an ideological function; they can potentially lead to the simplification of complex realities. This ideological power stems from the fact that the media

  connect a productive system rooted in private ownership to a political system that presupposes a citizenry whose full social participation depends in part on access to the maximum possible range of information and analysis and to open debate on contentious issues.

  (Murdock 1990, 311)

  Media owners can ideologically influence media output, and conglomerate owners can use their media for their marketing initiatives and influencing the public (Murdock 1990, 314–315).

- Political power:

  In capitalism, money is entangled with political power; hence, monopolies enable the political influence of small groups of people.

- Threats to democracy and the public sphere:

  Media monopolies have ideological and political power. They control who and what is visible and gains attention in the public sphere. They, therefore, centralise not just capital but also visibility and attention in the public sphere. As a consequence, media monopolies limit the freedom of speech, the freedom of opinion, and the freedom of the media and the press.

- Labour standards:

  Monopoly corporations can set low labour standards (especially concerning wages) in their industry sector.

- Control of prices:

  Monopolies have the economic power to control the prices of goods and services.

- Control of technological standards:

  Monopolies have the power to define and control technological standards. For example, Lawrence Lessig (2002) argues that monopolies like the one held by Microsoft in the areas of operating systems, intellectual property rights on technology and software patents destroy the original idea of the Internet that is based on an existing common architecture – code, that is protocols and software that makes protocols run – everyone can create applications and content. Monopolists like Microsoft or AOL would aim at monopolising technological systems and limiting the potential diversity of code, content and applications. Monopolisation would threaten the existence of free software code and free content.

- Customers' dependency:

  Monopoly control of the power to define technological standards also means that the need of customers to buy ever more media technologies to remain up to date can be generated. Hence, a potential result is an increasing dependency of users and consumers on commodities produced by one corporation and increasing monopoly profits.

- Economic centralisation:

  Monopolies derive others of economic opportunities.

- Lack of quality:

  A monopolist might care less about quality because there are no alternatives to choose from for consumers.

- Consumer surveillance and censorship:

  If content and applications are monopolised, that is most users have to rely on certain products of single companies, operations of surveillance (i.e. monitoring, statistically evaluating, and recording of audience and user behaviour, which content they create, consume, and how and what they communicate) and censorship can be carried out easily and more completely than in the case of several competing companies. This concerns especially communication technologies, such as phones and the Internet.

6.3.3 *The Structural Transformation of the Public Sphere: Rich Capitalist Media, Poor Democracy*

In his book *The Structural Transformation of the Public Sphere*, Jürgen Habermas (1991) shows that with the rise of advertising-funding of the press, there was a shift of the media to being "primarily a business" (184). There was a transition from the politically and ideologically motivated press to the commercially motivated press. The

> newspaper, as it developed into a capitalist undertaking, became en-meshed in a web of interests extraneous to business that sought to exer-cise influence upon it. The history of the big daily papers in the second half of the nineteenth century proves that the press itself became ma-nipulable to the extent that it became commercialized.
>
> (185)

The press "became the gate through which privileged private interests in-vaded the public sphere" (185). These developments came along with the rise of monopoly capital. In

> the measure that the public sphere became a field for business advertis-ing, private people as owners of private property had a direct effect on private people as the public. In this process, to be sure, the transforma-tion of the public sphere into a medium of advertising was met halfway by the commercialization of the press. Conversely. however, the latter was also propelled by the needs of business advertising that indepen-dently emerged out of economic configurations.
>
> (189)

James Curran summarises Habermas's insights into how capitalism structur-ally transformed the public sphere in the following way:

> Modern media fell under the sway of public relations, advertising and big business. Whereas the early press had facilitated participation in reasoned public debate, the new mass media encouraged consumer apa-thy, presented politics as a spectacle and provided pre-packaged, con-venience thought. The media, in short, managed the public rather than expressed the public will.
>
> (Curran 2002, 34)

Robert McChesney summarises the negative impact of capitalist media monopolies on the public sphere in the formula "rich media, poor democracy":

> the media have become a significant *anti-democratic* force in the United States and, to varying degrees, worldwide. The wealthier and more powerful the corporate media giants have become, the poorer

the prospects for participatory democracy. I am not arguing that *all* media are getting wealthier, of course. Some media firms and sectors are faltering and will falter during this turbulent era. But, on balance, the dominant media firms are larger and more influential than ever before, and the media *writ large* are more important in our social life than ever before. Nor do I believe the media are the sole or primary cause of the decline of democracy, but they are a part of the problem and closely linked to many of the other factors. Behind the lustrous glow of new technologies and electronic jargon, the media system has become increasingly concentrated and conglomerated into a relative handful of corporate hands. This concentration accentuates the core tendencies of a profit-driven, advertising-supported media system: hypercommercialism and denigration of journalism and public service. It is a poison pill for democracy.

(McChesney 2015, 2)

Having discussed the causes and impacts of media concentration, we will in the next section ask: What is media concentration and how should we define it? How can we measure media concentration?

6.4 Defining and Measuring Media Concentration

Media concentration means "an increase in the presence of one or a handful of media companies in any market as a result of various possible processes: acquisitions, mergers, deals with other companies, or even the disappearance of competitors" (Sánchez-Tabernero 1993, 7; see also Kiefer and Steininger 2014, 109–114; Meier and Trappel 1998, 41).

Picard (1988) lists the following indicators for measuring media concentration:

the number of outlets owned by the largest chain; the total circulation controlled by the largest chain; the ratio of the total sales or assets of the single top or top four or top eight firms to all firms (concentration ratio); the Herfindahl Index (that takes into account the total number of firms in the market and the amount of the industry accounted for by each firm).

Sánchez-Tabernero (1993, 7–8) mentions measuring turnover, profits, the number of employees, the number of titles/providers in a market, and market shares as indicators for media concentration.

Josifides (1997) discusses the following methods of measuring media concentration: political and cultural influence, the number of licences controlled by a single operator, the number of media outlets under a single controller, total revenues (advertising revenues, consumer expenditures on the media), the total expenditures on creating programmes or publishing, influence based on cross-subsidisation (the ability to finance losses by with revenues from other controlled businesses from other sectors), audience share/circulation share/listenership share/daily average contacts (online).

Manfred Knoche (2021) distinguishes between the measurement of capital and market concentration on the one hand and journalistic concentration on the other hand. And each has an absolute and a relative dimension that can be measured. "*Concentration in the media sector includes economic concentration, which appears as market concentration and as capital concentration, as well as journalistic concentration, which refers to the concentration of editorial units as well as to the homogenisation of content*" (Knoche 2021, 377).

Capital concentration can absolutely be measured as the number of corporations in the market and their profits, revenues, capital assets, and financial market values. The measurement of relative capital concentration assesses specific companies' share of total turnover, profits, etc. in the specific industry they are part of. The absolute measurement of journalistic concentration determines the absolute number of journalistic units. The relative measurement of journalistic concentration is focused on circulation rates and audience rates. "The main advantages of applying a revenue-based measure are first that it is a long established and tested method for measuring market concentration, and second that it provides a common currency of measurement across media" (Josifides 1997, 660). In practical terms, how media concentration is measured is often dependent on what data is available.

Next, I will introduce two measures of media concentration, the C4 Ratio and the Herfindahl-Hirschman Index. Both measures can be applied to financial data and audience data, depending on what data is available.

6.4.1 The C4 Ratio

The C4 Ratio is calculated in the following manner (Noam 2009, 47).
C4 Ratio:

$$C4_j = \sum_{i=1}^{4} S_{ij}$$

S_{ij} = firm i's market share of a given industry j.

The C4 Ratio is the sum of the market shares of the four largest ownership groups. The higher the C4 Ratio, the more concentrated the market. It is important methodologically in this context that one looks at who the owners of specific media are and organises the data according to ownership groups. In the UK press landscape, Rupert Murdoch's News UK owns both the country's biggest tabloid *The Sun* and the broadsheet *The Times*. In Germany, Axel Springer SE owns both the country's biggest newspaper, the tabloid *Bild-Zeitung*, and the broadsheet *Die Welt*. It is a mistake to consider market shares of such units separately. The data needs to be organised based on companies. For each company in the market, one determines the total market share, then organises the data from the highest to the lowest share, and sums up the market shares of the four largest companies.

6.4.2 The Herfindahl-Hirschman Index

The Herfindahl-Hirschman Index is calculated in the following way (see Noam 2009, 47).

Herfindahl-Hirschman Index (HHI)

$$HHI_j = \sum_{i=1}^{f} S_{ij}^2$$

f = number of firms participating in the analysed industry,
S_{ij} = the firm i's market share in the analysed industry j.
Interpretation of HHI:
low level of concentration: HHI < 1,000;
medium level of concentration: 1,000 < HHI < 1,800;
high level of concentration: HHI > 1,800.

For calculating the HHI, one first organises the data based on companies. This means that data of companies owning multiple media operating in the analysed market is summed up. Once one has the market data organised by companies, one calculates the relative market share of each company in percentage. The sum of all market shares should add up to 100%. The HHI can only be calculated with data for an entire market. One squares the market share of each company and sums up these squared values. The resulting number is the HHI. Depending on how large the HHI is, the market is considered as having a low, medium or high degree of concentration.

6.4.3 Calculating Media Concentration: The British Press Market

Let us now conduct an example calculation that shows how to calculate the C4 Ratio and the HHI. The data in Table 6.4 show the daily reach of UK newspapers.

We first have to organise the data based on corporations so that the market shares for those companies that own multiple newspapers are summed up. The reorganised data are shown in Table 6.5.

The C4 Ratio is the sum of the market share of the four largest companies:

C4 Ratio = 28.6% + 28.5% + 22.9% + 12.8% = 92.8%

We can conclude that the British press market is highly concentrated.

The C4 Ratio had the disadvantage that it does not include in its calculation all market players' economic power. In our example, data for the Telegraph Media Group must be left out. The HHI has the advantage that it

Table 6.4 Daily reach of national UK newspapers

Newspaper	Owner	Type	Average Daily Reach (1000s)	Share (%)
The Sun	News UK	Tabloid	9,440	22.5
Daily Mail	Daily Mail and General Trust	Tabloid	8,503	20.3
Daily Mirror	Reach plc	Tabloid	6,641	15.8
Daily Telegraph	Telegraph Media Group	Quality	3,020	7.2
The Times	News UK	Quality	2,580	6.1
The Guardian	Guardian Media Group	Quality	5,360	12.8
Daily Express	Reach plc	Tabloid	3,739	8.9
Daily Star	Reach plc	Tabloid	1,564	3.7
I	Daily Mail and General Trust	Quality	1,123	2.7
			Total: 41,970	100

Data source: PAMCO 1/2021, April 2019-March 2020, news reach includes access to news in print, on desktop computers and via phones and tablets.

Included are all newspapers that are published nationwide in print and online (excluding free commuter papers that are funded by advertising-only, which is a different business model than the combination of ads and sales).

Table 6.5 Reorganised data of British national newspapers' daily reach

Company	Daily Audience Reach	Market Share (%)	s^2
News UK	12,020	28.6	817.96
Reach plc	11,944	28.5	812.25
Daily Mail and General Trust	9,626	22.9	524.41
Guardian Media Group	5,360	12.8	163.84
Telegraph Media Group	3,020	7.2	51.84
Total:	13,350	100.0	

is calculated based on the market shares of all companies competing in the market. Let us now calculate the HHI for the British press market. Table 6.5 shows the squared values of all market shares. To calculate the HHI, we have to sum up these squared values:

$$HHI = 28.6^2 + 28.5^2 + 22.9^2 + 12.8^2 + 7.2^2 = 817.96 + 812.25 + 524.41 + 163.84 + 51.84 = 2370.3$$

HHI values above 1,800 mean high concentration. With an HHI of 2370.3, the British national newspaper market is highly concentrated.

6.4.4 Calculating Media Concentration: The German Press Market

Let us have a look at a second example: the German market of national newspapers. Table 6.6 displays relevant data.

We again have to reorganise the data based on the company's total market shares. It becomes evident that Axel Springer SE dominates the German national newspaper market. The reorganised data is shown in Table 6.7.

The C4 Ratio of the German newspaper industry is

C4 Ratio = 71.3% + 11.6% + 8.2% + 4.6% = 95.7%

Such a high C4 Ratio shows that this industry is highly concentrated.

Table 6.6 The reach of German national newspapers

Newspaper	Reach (in million)	Owner	Market Share (%)
Bild	7.35	Axel Springer SE	63.9
Süddeutsche Zeitung	1.33	Süddeutsche Zeitung GmbH	11.6
Frankfurter Allgemeine Zeitung (FAZ)	0.94	Frankfurter Allgemeine Zeitung GmbH	8.2
Die Welt	0.85	Axel Springer SE	7.4
Handelsblatt	0.53	Handelsblatt Media Group (DvH Medien, Verlagsgruppe Holtzbrinck GmbH)	4.6
TAZ	0.3	taz Verlags- und Vertriebs GmbH	2.6
Neues Deutschland	0.197	Neues Deutschland Druckerei und Verlags GmbH	1.7
Total:	11.497		100.0

Data source: *ma Presse 2022/II,* https://www.ma-reichweiten.de/reach, *data for Neues Deutschland:* https://www.nd-aktuell.de/kontakt/9, accessed on 10 April 2023.

Table 6.7 Reorganised data of German national newspapers' daily reach

Company	Market Share (%)	s^2
Axel Springer SE	71.3	5087.0
Süddeutsche Zeitung GmbH	11.6	133.8
Frankfurter Allgemeine Zeitung GmbH	8.2	66.8
Handelsblatt Media Group (DvH Medien, Verlagsgruppe Holtzbrinck GmbH)	4.6	21.3
taz Verlags- und Vertriebs GmbH	2.6	6.8
Neues Deutschland Druckerei und Verlags GmbH	1.7	2.9

The HHI is: HHI = $71.3^2 + 11.6^2 + 8.2^2 + 4.6^2 + 2.6^2 + 1.7^2 = 5318.6$

An HHI of around 5,400 is an indication of a very highly concentrated industry. The Springer corporation dominates the German newspaper market. Its tabloid *Bild-Zeitung* is by far the most widely read newspaper in Germany. It is notorious for its sensationalism (see https://bildblog.de/) and comparable in terms of reporting, worldview, and dominance to Murdoch's *Sun* in the UK.

6.4.5 Calculating Media Concentration: Search Engines

Table 6.8 shows data on the global use of search engines.

Google dominates the world of online search. It accounts for the vast majority of searches conducted on desktop and laptop computers, tablets, and mobile phones. The C4 Ratio of the search engine industry is

C4 Ratio = 71.61 + 21.11 + 2.53 + 2.27 = 97.52%

And the HHI is

HHI > $71.61^2 + 21.11^2 + 2.53^2 + 2.27^2 + 1.56^2 + 0.59^2 + 0.10^2 + 0.09^2 + 0.14^2 = 5127.9921 + 445.6321 + 6.4009 + 5.1529 + 2.4336 + 0.3481 + 0.01 + 0.0081 + 0.0196 > 5587$

Both the C4 Ratio and the HHI show that online search is a highly concentrated industry.

Table 6.8 Share of searches conducted on desktop and laptop computers, tablets, and mobile phones from April 2022 until March 2023

#	Company	Search Engine	Country	Search Share (%)	s^2
1	Google/Alphabet	Google	USA	71.61	5127.9921
2	Microsoft	Bing	China	21.11	445.6321
3	Verizon	Yahoo!	USA	2.53	6.4009
4	Yandex	Yandex	USA	2.27	5.1529
5	Baidu	Baidu	Russia	1.56	2.4336
6	DuckDuckGo	DuckDuckGo	South Korea	0.59	0.3481
7	Ecosia GmbH	Ecosia	USA	0.10	0.01
8	Naver Corp	Naver		0.09	0.0081
9		Other		0.14	0.0196
					HHI > 5587

Data source: http://www.netmarketshare.com.

6.5 Conclusion

This chapter introduced the Political Economy of media concentration. Let us now summarise the main findings.

Finding 1: Four Concentration Strategies

There are four strategies of concentration that companies use for trying to increase their control of economic power: horizontal integration, vertical integration, conglomeration, and strategic alliances.

Finding 2: Five Features of the Information Sector That Favour Capital Concentration

There are five features of the information sector that favour capital concentration in the media/information/communication economy:

The Sunk Cost Rule;
The Nobody Knows Anything Rule;
The Hit Rule;
The "Piracy" Rule;
The advertising-circulation-spiral.

Finding 3: Media Concentration's Negative Impacts on Society

Media concentration has multiple negative impacts on society. Above all, it is a threat to democracy and the public sphere. Media monopolies have ideological and political power. They control who and what is visible and gains attention in the public sphere. They, therefore, centralise not just capital but also visibility and attention in the public sphere. As a consequence, media monopolies limit the freedom of speech, the freedom of opinion, and the freedom of the media and the press. Rich, profitable, monopolistic media are a threat to democracy.

Finding 4: The Measurement of Media Concentration

Media concentration can be measured absolutely and relatively, as well as based on financial data (revenues, profits) and consumer-focused data (audience/user numbers and shares, circulation rates and shares, reach).

Finding 5: Two Methods of Measuring Media Concentration

The C4 Ratio and the Herfindahl-Hirschman Index are two important methods for measuring media concentration.

Notes

1 Data source: https://www.forbes.com/lists/global2000/, accessed on 31 October 2021 and on 14 December 2022.
2 Data source: Alphabet SEC-Filings 10-K for financial year 2020, accessed via https://www.sec.gov/ on 31 October 2021.
3 Data source: World Advertising Research Center, https://www.warc.com/data/adspend, data accessed on 31 October 2021.
4 Data source: Facebook SEC-Filings 10-K for financial year 2020, accessed via https://www.sec.gov/ on 1 November 2021.
5 Data sources: https://www.statista.com/statistics/236943/global-advertising-spending/, https://www.statista.com/statistics/237974/online-advertising-spending-worldwide/, accessed on 14 December 2022.
6 Data source: Alphabet SEC-Filings 10-K for financial year 2021, accessed via https://www.sec.gov/ on 14 December 2022.
7 Data source: Facebook SEC-Filings 10-K for financial year 2021, accessed via https://www.sec.gov/ on 14 December 2022.
8 Data source: https://www.alexa.com/topsites, accessed on 25 October 2021.
9 Data source: https://www.alexa.com/, accessed on 25 October 2021.
10 https://www.the-numbers.com/market/distributor/20th-Century-Fox, accessed on 1 November 2021.
11 Ibid.
12 Translation from German:

beides sein kann: terrestrisch verbreitet ein reines öffentliches Gut, als Pay-TV organisiert ein Clubgut. [...] Ein Film, ausgestrahlt im terrestrischen Fernsehen, ist ein reines öffentliches Gut für alle Rundfunkteilnehmer im Verbreitungsgebiet des Senders, derselbe Film, ausgestrahlt im Kino oder im Pay-TV, ist ein Club-gut für das jeweilige zahlende Publikum. [...] Ein reines öffentliches Gut ist nach den Definitionen der ökonomischen Güterlehre nur der drahtlos und unverzerrt verbreitete Rundfunk. Nichtausschließbarkeit (zu ökonomisch vernünftigen Kosten) und Nichtrivalität im Konsum sind in vollem Umfang für Medieninhalte und Träger gegeben. Der Träger hat die Eigenschaften eines öffentlichen Gutes allerdings nur auf dem Publikumsmarkt, nicht auf dem Markt der Frequenzen und Orbitalpositionen, wo die De- finition und Durchsetzung von Eigentumsrechten im Prinzip möglich ist. [...] Kabelfernsehen und Kabelhörfunk sowie alle Formen von Pay-TV oder Pay-Radio sind Club- oder Mautgüter, also öffentliche Güter im engeren Sinn.

References

Bryman, Alan. 2004. *The Disneyization of Society*. London: SAGE.
Curran, James. 2002. *Media and Power*. London: Routledge.
Dahlgreen, Will. 2016. British Press "Most Right-Wing" in Europe. *YouGov*, 7 February 2016. https://yougov.co.uk/topics/politics/articles-reports/2016/02/07/british-press-most-right-wing-europe
Dorfman, Ariel and Armand Mattelart. 1991. *How to Read Donald Duck. Imperialist Ideology in the Disney Comic*. New York: International General.
Doyle, Gillian. 2013. *Understanding Media Economics*. London: SAGE. Second edition.
Furhoff, Lars. 1973. Some Reflections on Newspaper Concentration. *Scandinavian Economic History Review* 21 (1): 1–27.
Habermas, Jürgen. 1991. *The Structural Transformation of the Public Sphere. An Inquiry into a Category of Bourgeois Society*. Cambridge, MA: The MIT Press.

Hesmondhalgh, David. 2013. *The Cultural Industries.* London: SAGE. Third edition.

Hess, Charlotte and Elinor Ostrom. 2003. Ideas, Artefacts, and Facilities: Information as a Common-Pool Resource. *Law and Contemporary Problems* 66 (1/2): 111–145.

Josifides, Petros. 1997. Methods of Measuring Media Concentration. *Media, Culture & Society* 19 (4): 643–663.

Kiefer, Marie Luise and Christian Steininger. 2014. *Medienökonomik.* Munich: Oldenbourg Verlag. Third edition.

Kleinsteuber, Hans J. 2004. Konzentrationsprozesse im Mediensektor. *spw – Zeitschrift für sozialistische Politik und Wirtschaft* 138: 22–24.

Kleinsteuber, Hans J. and Barbara Thomaß. 2004. Medienökonomie, Medienkonzerne und Konzentrationskontrolle. In *Medien und Ökonomie. Band 2: Problemfelder der Medienökonomie*, edited by Klaus-Dieter Altmeppen and Matthias Karmasin, 123–158. Wiesbaden: VS Verlag für Sozialwissenschaften.

Knoche, Manfred. 2021. Media Concentration. A Critical Political Economy Perspective. *tripleC: Communication, Capitalism & Critique* 19 (2): 371–391. DOI: https://doi.org/10.31269/triplec.v19i2.1298

Knoche, Manfred. 2013. Medienkonzentration. In *Mediensysteme im internationalen Vergleich*, edited by Barbara Thomaß, 135–160. Konstanz: UVK. Second edition.

Knoche, Manfred. 2005. Medienkonzentration als Macht- und Legitimationsproblem für Politik und Wissenschaft. Kritisch-empirische Konzentrationstheorie versus apologetisch-normative Wettbewerbstheorie. In *Internationale partizipatorische Kommunikationspolitik*, edited by Petra Ahrweiler and Barbara Thomaß, 117–140. Münster: LIT.

Knoche, Manfred. 2004. Konkurrenz, Konzentration und Regulierung in der Medienindustrie. In *Effiziente Medienregulierung. Marktdefizite oder Regulierungsdefizite?* edited by Mike Friedrichsen and Wolfgang Seufert, 157–171. Baden-Baden: Nomos.

Lessig, Lawrence. 2002. *The Future of Ideas.* New York: Vintage Books.

Marx, Karl. 1894. *Capital. Volume 3.* London: Penguin.

Marx, Karl. 1867. *Capital. Volume 1.* London: Penguin.

McChesney, Robert. 2015. *Rich Media, Poor Democracy. Communication Politics in Dubious Times.* New York: The New Press. New edition.

McChesney, Robert W. 2004. *The Problem of the Media.* New York: Monthly Review Press.

Meier, Werner A. and Josef Trappel. 1998. Media Concentration and the Public Interest. In *Media Policy: Convergence, Concentration & Commerce*, edited by Denis McQuail and Karen Siune, 38–59. London: SAGE.

Micklethwait, John. 1989. The Entertainment Industry. *The Economist*, 23 December 1989 (Supplement): 3–4.

Mueller, Annie. 2020. Why Movies Cost So Much to Make. *Investopedia*, 28 April 2020. https://www.investopedia.com/financial-edge/0611/why-movies-cost-so-much-to-make.aspx

Murdock, Graham. 1990. Redrawing the Map of the Communications Industries. Concentration and Ownership in the Era of Privatization. In *The Political Economy of the Media. Volume I*, edited by Peter Golding and Graham Murdock, 308–323. Cheltenham: Edward Elgar.

Noam, Eli. 2009. *Media Ownership and Concentration in America*. Oxford: Oxford University Press.

Picard, Robert. 1988. Measures of Concentration in the Daily Newspaper Industry. *Journal of Media Economics* 1 (1): 59–71.

Rosenwald, Michael S. 2020. "When the Looting Starts, the Shooting Starts": Trump Quotes Miami Police Chief's Notorious 1967 Warning. *The Washington Post*, 29 May 2020. https://www.washingtonpost.com/history/2020/05/29/when-the-looting-starts-the-shooting-starts-trump-walter-headley/

Sánchez-Tabernero, Alfonso. 1993. *Media Concentration in Europe*. London: John Libbey.

Smythe, Dallas W. 1977. Communications: Blindspot of Western Marxism. *Canadian Journal of Political and Social Theory* 1 (3): 1–27.

Turow, Joseph. 2010. *Media Today*. New York: Routledge.

Varian, Hal R. 1992. *Macroeconomic Analysis*. New York: W. W. Norton & Company. Third edition.

Wasko, Janet. 2020. *Understanding Disney. The Manufacture of Fantasy*. Cambridge: Polity. Second edition.

Wasko, Janet. 2003. *How Hollywood Works*. London: SAGE.

Recommended Readings and Exercises

Readings

The following texts are recommended as accompanying readings to this chapter:

John D. H. Downing. 2011. Media Ownership, Concentration, and Control. The Evolution of Debate. In *The Handbook of the Political Economy of Communications*, edited by Janet Wasko, Graham Murdock, and Helena Sousa, 140–168. Chichester: Wiley-Blackwell.

Manfred Knoche. 2021. Media Concentration. A Critical Political Economy Perspective. *tripleC: Communication, Capitalism & Critique* 19 (2): 371–391. DOI: https://doi.org/10.31269/triplec.v19i2.1298

Eli Noam. 2009. *Media Ownership and Concentration in America*. Oxford: Oxford University Press.
Chapter 3: Seeking the Answers.

Jonathan Hardy. 2014. *Critical Political Economy of the Media. An Introduction*. Abingdon: Routledge.
Chapter 4: Concentration, Conglomeration, Commercialisation

Exercise 6.1   Rich Media, Poor Democracy

First, read the following chapter in Robert McChesney's book "Rich Media, Poor Democracy":

Robert McChesney. 2015. *Rich Media, Poor Democracy. Communication Politics in Dubious Times*. New York: The New Press. New edition. Introduction: The Media/Democracy Paradox (pp. 1–11)

Second, watch the following documentary about McChesney's book:

Sut Jhally (producer). 2003. Rich Media, Poor Democracy. Media Education Foundation. Movie information: https://shop.mediaed.org/rich-media-poor-democracy-p118.aspx
Transcript: https://www.mediaed.org/transcripts/Rich-Media-Poor-Democracy-Transcript.pdf

Third, discuss in groups the following questions respectively think about them individually:

What problems does a highly concentrated media system cause?
How could alternatives to a highly concentrated media system look like? How can they be achieved?
What suggestions for alternatives do media reform movements make (see, e.g., http://www.mediareform.org.uk/wp-content/uploads/2012/09/time-for-media-reform.pdf, https://www.freepress.net/)? How do you assess these suggestions?

Exercise 6.2   Media Concentration Measurement in the Internet Industry

Work with the following data for the Internet platform industry. Calculate the C4 Ratio and the Herfindahl-Hirschman Index (HHI). As indicator use the revenue data. These are the total sales per year measured in US$.

Consider the data provided in the table as one market of Internet services provided by large transnational corporations, which means that the total revenues of this market are the sum of the single-company revenues provided in the list.

Table. The world's largest transnational Internet companies

Rank	Company Name	Country	Employees	Previous Rank	Revenues (US$ million)	Profits (US$ million)	Assets (US$ million)
9	Amazon.com	USA	1,298,000	6	386,064	21,331	321,195
21	Alphabet/Google	USA	135,301	8	182,527	40,269	319,616
59	JD.com	China	314,906	43	108,087	7,160.2	64,718.4
63	Alibaba Group Holding	China	251,462	69	105,865.7	22,224	257,977.7
86	Facebook/Meta Platforms	USA	58,604	58	85,965	29,146	159,316
132	Tencent Holdings	China	85,858	65	69,864.2	23,166.2	204,356.3
484	Netflix	USA	9,400	-	24,996.0	2,761.0	39,280.0

Data source: Fortune Global 500 List for the year 2021, https://fortune.com/global500/search/, accessed on 3 November 2021.

Another calculation example is shown below, namely the transnational Internet companies listed in the Fortune Global 500 List for the year 2022.

Table: The world's largest transnational Internet companies

Rank	Company Name	Country	Employees	Previous Rank	Revenues (US$ million)	Profits (US$ million)	Assets (US$ million)
2	Amazon.com	USA	1,608,000	9	469,822	33,364	420,549
17	Alphabet/Google	USA	156,500	21	257,637	76,033	359,268
46	JD.com	China	385,357	59	147,526	-552	78,164
55	Alibaba Group Holding	China	254,941	63	132,936	9,701	267,467
71	Facebook/Meta Platforms	USA	71,970	86	117,929	39,370	165,987
121	Tencent Holdings	China	112,771	132	86,836	34,854	253,832
481	Netflix	USA	11,300	484	29,698	5,116	44,585

Data source: Fortune Global 500 List for the year 2022, https://fortune.com/global500/search/, accessed on 13 February 2023.

The calculation results are shown in Appendix 1 of this chapter. Conduct your own calculations (without reading the appendix). Once you have arrived at the results, compare them to the data in Appendix 1.

Exercise 6.3   Media Concentration Measurement in the Music Industry

Work with the following data for the global music industry. The data shows a ranking of the world's most sold music albums and indicates each album's certified sales. The ranking includes all albums with a total certified sales number larger than 10 million units.

Calculate the C4 Ratio and the Herfindahl-Hirschman Index (HHI). As indicator use the number of sold albums. There are some albums where more than one company acted as releasing label. In such cases, use as sales share for each involved music company the number of sold copies divided by the number of involved record companies. For example, if an album sold 18 million copies and three different music companies are involved in the release, then each music company's share is 18 million / 3 = 6 million units.

Table: The world's most sold music albums with sales of more than 10 million

Rank	Artist	Album	Released	Genre	Label	Certified Sales (in million)
1	Michael Jackson	Thriller	1982	Pop, post-disco, funk, rock	Sony Music Entertainment	51.2
2	Eagles	Their Greatest Hits (1971–1975)	1976	Country rock, soft rock, folk rock	Warner Music Group	41.2
3	Eagles	Hotel California	1976	Soft rock	Warner Music Group	31.8
4	Shania Twain	Come On Over	1997	Country, pop	Universal Music Group	30.4
5	Led Zeppelin	Led Zeppelin IV	1971	Hard rock, heavy metal, folk rock	Warner Music Group	30.4

(Continued)

Table: (Continued)

Rank	Artist	Album	Released	Genre	Label	Certified Sales (in million)
6	AC/DC	Back in Black	1980	Hard rock	Warner Music Group, BMG (Bertelsmann Group)	30.1
7	Fleetwood Mac	Rumours	1977	Soft rock	Warner Music Group	29.3
8	Whitney Houston / Various Artists	The Bodyguard	1992	R&B, soul, pop, soundtrack	Sony Music Entertainment	28.7
9	Adele	21	2011	Pop, soul	Sony Music Entertainment, XL Recordings	27.1
10	Alanis Morissette	Jagged Little Pill	1995	Alternative rock	Warner Music Group	25.4
11	Pink Floyd	The Dark Side of the Moon	1973	Progressive rock	Universal Music Group	24.8
12	Various Artists	Dirty Dancing	1987	Pop, rock, R&B	Sony Music Entertainment	24.1
13	The Beatles	1	2000	Rock	Apple Corps, Warner Music Group, Universal Music Group	23.2
14	Bob Marley & The Wailers	Legend: The Best of Bob Marley & The Wailers	1984	Reggae	Universal Music Group	22.9

(Continued)

Table: (Continued)

Rank	Artist	Album	Released	Genre	Label	Certified Sales (in million)
15	Guns N' Roses	Appetite for Destruction	1987	Hard rock	Universal Music Group	22.8
16	Metallica	Metallica	1991	Heavy metal	Warner Music Group	22.7
17	Bee Gees / Various Artists	Saturday Night Fever	1977	Disco	Universal Music Group	22.1
18	Meat Loaf	Bat Out of Hell	1977	Hard rock, glam rock, progressive rock	Sony Music Entertainment	22.0
19	Bruce Springsteen	Born in the USA	1984	Heartland rock	Sony Music Entertainment	22.0
20	ABBA	Gold: Greatest Hits	1992	Pop, disco	Universal Music Group	21.6
21	Michael Jackson	Bad	1987	Pop, rhythm and blues, funk and rock	Sony Music Entertainment	21.2
22	Celine Dion	Falling into You	1996	Pop, soft rock	Sony Music Entertainment	21.1
23	Dire Straits	Brothers in Arms	1985	Roots rock, blues rock, soft rock	Universal Music Group	21.1
24	Santana	Supernatural	1999	Latin rock	Sony Music Entertainment	20.8
25	Elvis Presley	Elvis' Christmas Album	1957	Christmas, pop, gospel, rock and roll	Sony Music Entertainment	20.8
26	Queen	Greatest Hits	1981	Rock	Warner Music Group	20.6

(Continued)

Table: (Continued)

Rank	Artist	Album	Released	Genre	Label	Certified Sales (in million)
27	Celine Dion	Let's Talk About Love	1997	Pop, soft rock	Sony Music Entertainment	20.5
28	Norah Jones	Come Away with Me	2002	Jazz	Universal Music Group	19.9
29	Britney Spears	...Baby One More Time	1999	Pop	Sony Music Entertainment	19.9
30	Madonna	The Immaculate Collection	1990	Pop, dance	Warner Music Group	19.8
31	Eminem	The Eminem Show	2002	Hip hop	Universal Music Group	19.1
32	Elton John	Greatest Hits	1974	Pop	Universal Music Group	19.1
33	Adele	25	2015	Soul, pop, R&B	Sony Music Entertainment, XL Recordings	19.0
34	Pink Floyd	The Wall	1979	Progressive rock	Universal Music Group, Sony Music Entertainment	18.9
35	Backstreet Boys	Millennium	1999	Pop	Sony Music Entertainment	18.4
36	The Beatles	Sgt. Pepper's Lonely Hearts Club Band	1967	Rock	Warner Music Group, Universal Music Group	18.3

(Continued)

Table: (Continued)

Rank	Artist	Album	Released	Genre	Label	Certified Sales (in million)
37	James Horner	Titanic: Music from the Motion Picture	1997	Film score	Sony Music Entertainment	18.1
38	Boston	Boston	1976	Arena rock, hard rock	Sony Music Entertainment	18.1
39	Mariah Carey	Music Box	1993	Pop, R&B	Sony Music Entertainment	17.8
40	Nirvana	Nevermind	1991	Grunge, alternative rock	Universal Music Group	17.8
41	Phil Collins	No Jacket Required	1985	Pop rock	Warner Music Group	17.7
42	Whitney Houston	Whitney Houston	1985	Pop, R&B	Sony Music Entertainment	17.6
43	Eminem	The Marshall Mathers LP	2000	Hip hop	Universal Music Group	17.5
44	Linkin Park	Hybrid Theory	2000	Nu metal, rap metal, alternative metal	Warner Music Group	17.2
45	Michael Jackson	Dangerous	1991	New jack swing, R&B and pop	Sony Music Entertainment	17.0
46	Eric Clapton	Unplugged	1992	Acoustic rock, acoustic blues	Warner Music Group	17.0
47	The Beatles	Abbey Road	1969	Rock	Apple Corps	16.9

(Continued)

Table: (Continued)

Rank	Artist	Album	Released	Genre	Label	Certified Sales (in million)
48	U2	The Joshua Tree	1987	Rock	Universal Music Group	16.7
49	Spice Girls	Spice	1996	Pop	Universal Music Group	16.4
50	Madonna	Like a Virgin	1984	Pop, dance	Warner Music Group	16.2
51	Prince and The Revolution	Purple Rain	1984	Pop rock, new wave, R&B	Warner Music Group	15.7
52	Bon Jovi	Slippery When Wet	1986	Hard rock, glam metal	Universal Music Group	15.3
53	Michael Jackson	HIStory: Past, Present and Future, Book I	1995	R&B, pop and hip hop	Sony Music Entertainment	15.2
54	Mariah Carey	Daydream	1995	Pop, R&B	Sony Music Entertainment	15.2
55	Carole King	Tapestry	1971	Pop	Universal Music Group	15.1
56	Various Artists	Grease: The Original Soundtrack from the Motion Picture	1978	Rock and roll	Universal Music Group	15.0
57	Green Day	Dookie	1994	Pop punk, punk rock, alternative rock	Warner Music Group	14.6
58	Madonna	True Blue	1986	Pop, dance	Warner Music Group	14.5
59	Shania Twain	The Woman in Me	1995	Country, pop	Universal Music Group	14.5

(Continued)

Table: (Continued)

Rank	Artist	Album	Released	Genre	Label	Certified Sales (in million)
60	Ace of Base	*Happy Nation/ The Sign*	1993	Pop	Universal Music Group, Warner Music Group	14.4
61	Celine Dion	*All the Way… A Decade of Song*	1999	Pop	Sony Music Entertainment	14.4
62	Britney Spears	*Oops!… I Did It Again*	2000	Pop	Sony Music Entertainment	14.4
63	Whitney Houston	*Whitney*	1987	Pop, R&B	Sony Music Entertainment	14.4
64	George Michael	*Faith*	1987	Pop, R&B, funk, soul	Sony Music Entertainment	13.9
65	Def Leppard	*Hysteria*	1987	Hard rock, glam metal	Universal Music Group	13.9
66	Lauryn Hill	*The Miseducation of Lauryn Hill*	1998	Neo Soul, R&B and Hip Hop	Sony Music Entertainment	13.7
67	Tracy Chapman	*Tracy Chapman*	1988	Folk rock	Warner Music Group	13.3
68	Simon & Garfunkel	*Bridge over Troubled Water*	1970	Folk rock	Sony Music Entertainment	12.5
69	Lionel Richie	*Can't Slow Down*	1983	Pop, R&B, soul	Universal Music Group	12.3

(Continued)

Table: (Continued)

Rank	Artist	Album	Released	Genre	Label	Certified Sales (in million)
70	Michael Jackson	Off the Wall	1979	Disco, pop, funk and R&B	Sony Music Entertainment	11.7
71	Bon Jovi	Cross Road	1994	Hard rock, glam metal	Universal Music Group	11.6
72	Fugees	The Score	1996	Alternative hip hop	Sony Music Entertainment	11.6
73	Oasis	(What's the Story) Morning Glory?	1995	Britpop, rock	Sony Music Entertainment	11.6
74	Celine Dion	The Colour of My Love	1993	Pop	Sony Music Entertainment	11.1
					Total:	1444.20

Data source: https://en.wikipedia.org/wiki/List_of_best-selling_albums, accessed on 23 April 2023.

The calculation results are shown in Appendix 2 of this chapter. Conduct your own calculations (without reading the appendix). Once you have arrived at the results, compare them to the data in the appendix.

Appendix 1   Solution to Exercise 6.2

Example 1

Rank	Company Name	Country	Employees	Previous Rank	Revenues (US$ million)	Revenue Share (%)	s^2
9	Amazon.com	USA	1,298,000	6	386,064	40.07	1605.95
21	Alphabet/ Google	USA	135,301	8	182,527	18.95	358.98
59	JD.com	China	314,906	43	108,087	11.22	125.88
63	Alibaba Group Holding	China	251,462	69	105,865.7	10.99	120.76
86	Facebook	USA	58,604	58	85,965	8.92	79.63
132	Tencent Holdings	China	85,858	65	69,864.2	7.25	52.59
484	Netflix	USA	9,400	484	24,996.0	2.59	6.73
				Total:	963,368.9	100	2350.52

C4 Ratio = 40.07% + 18.95% + 11.22% + 10.99% = 81.23%

HHI = $40.07^2 + 18.95^2 + 11.22^2 + 10.99^2 + 8.92^2 + 7.25^2 + 2.59^2 = 2350.52$

Both the C4 Ratio and the HHI indicate that the Internet services industry is highly concentrated.

Example 2

C4 Ratio = 37.82% + 20.74% + 11.87% + 10.70% = 81.13%

HHI = $37.82^2 + 20.74^2 + 11.87^2 + 10.70^2 + 9.49^2 + 6.99^2 + 2.39^2 = 2260.26$

Both the C4 Ratio and the HHI indicate that the Internet services industry is highly concentrated.

Rank	Company Name	Country	Employees	Previous Rank	Revenues (US$ million)	Revenue Share (%)	s^2
2	Amazon.com	USA	1,608,000	9	469,822	37.82	1430.06
17	Alphabet	USA	156,500	21	257,637	20.74	430.04
46	JD.com	China	385,357	59	147,526	11.87	141.00
55	Alibaba Group Holding	China	254,941	63	132,936	10.70	114.49
71	Facebook/Meta Platforms	USA	71,970	86	117,929	9.49	90.10
121	Tencent Holdings	China	112,771	132	86,836	6.99	48.85
481	Netflix	USA	11,300	484	29,698	2.39	5.71
				Total:	1,242,384	100	2260.26

Appendix 2   Solution to Exercise 6.3

	Sales (in million)	Sales Share (%)	s^2
Sony Music Entertainment	571.50	39.57	1565.95
Universal Music Group	423.43	29.32	859.64
Warner Music Group	386.53	26.76	716.34
Apple Corps	24.63	1.71	2.91
XL Recordings	23.05	1.60	2.55
BMG	15.05	1.04	1.09
	1444.20	100.00	

C4 Ratio = 39.57 + 29.32 + 26.76 + 1.71 = 97.36%

HHI = 1565.95 + 859.64 + 716.34 + 2.91 + 2.55 + 1.09 = 3148.47

The results indicate that the music industry is very highly concentrated. It is dominated by the "big 3" corporations: Sony Music Entertainment, Universal Music Group and Warner Music Group.

7 The Political Economy of Advertising

What You Will Learn in This Chapter

- You will learn how to define, assess, and criticise advertising;
- You will learn about advertising's roles in capitalism;
- You will learn how to analyse the ideological aspects of advertising.

7.1 Introduction

Advertising is present in many spaces of private and public life in contemporary societies. There are online ads as well as ads on television, radio, in newspapers and magazine, in and before movies, and in public space. In contemporary societies, advertising has become an important industry. Advertisements are often displayed via media. They are therefore part of the media industry. They connect the media economy to other realms of society such as the economy, politics, and culture. Economic, political, and cultural organisations pay for advertisements in order to be able to reach a wide public with their messages. They want to sell commodities, shape public opinion, and present their worldviews and ideologies to the public via advertisements. The aim of advertising is always to get the audience to react in a certain way. For example, commercial advertising aims to get consumers to buy certain goods. And politically and culturally oriented advertisements aim to get people to share certain attitudes.

This chapter provides an introduction to the political economy of advertising. It deals with the following questions: What is the role of advertising in capitalism? What are the problems of advertising for society?

Section 7.2 discusses how we should define advertising. Section 7.3 analyses the development of advertising in capitalism. Section 7.4 discusses the political economy of advertising by introducing Dallas Smythe's concepts of the audience commodity and audience labour. Section 7.5 discusses positive and critical views of advertising. Section 7.6 is focused on advertising as ideology. Section 7.7 examines protest and resistance against advertising. Section 7.8 presents conclusions.

DOI: 10.4324/9781003391203-9

7.2 What Is Advertising?

Conduct the following exercise (Exercise 7.1).

Exercise 7.1   Consumer Goods

Have a look at the following lists of products:
https://us.pg.com/brands/
https://en.wikipedia.org/wiki/List_of_Procter_%26_Gamble_brands

Make an estimated guess: How many of these products have you bought during the past month?
If you are studying in a group, compare the results.

7.2.1 Procter & Gamble

The commodities you encountered in Exercise 7.1 have one thing in common: They are produced by the US consumer goods corporation Procter & Gamble (P&G). Many of the commodities that many shoppers in the world buy in supermarkets are from P&G. P&G is one of the world's largest advertisers (Doyle 2013, 149; Picard 2011, 42) and one of the largest producers of household products such as detergents, toilet paper, cosmetics, shampoos, coffee, snacks, sanitary towels, toothpaste, pet food, water filters, and medicine. With profits of US$ 13.8 billion and revenues of US$ 120.1 billion, P&G was in 2021 the world's 46th largest transnational corporation.[1] In 2022, P&G was the world's 63rd-largest company.[2] Table 7.1 gives an overview of some of P&G's financial data.

In the analysed years (Table 7.1), P&G on average spent 10.9% of its revenues on advertising. That P&G spends vast amounts of money on branding its products, and buying ads shows the importance of advertising in capitalism. Advertising is a mechanism that tries to spur the purchase and consumption of commodities and thereby the transformation of commodity capital into money capital and profits. Marx (1885) speaks of the sales process as the realisation process of surplus value. Advertising helps to turn commodities into money capital that contains profit.

7.2.2 Definitions of Advertising

Let us have a look at some definitions of advertisements and advertising:

- An advertisement is

    a kind of text – carried by electronic or print media – that attracts attention to, stimulates a desire for, and in some cases leads to the purchase of a product or service. The convention is that commercial

Table 7.1 Procter & Gamble financial data

Financial Year	Revenues (US$ billion)	Profits (US$ billion)	Ad Spending (US$ billion)	Share of Ad Spend in Revenues (%)
2022	80.2	14.8	7.9	9.9
2021	76.1	14.4	8.2	10.8
2020	70.9	13.1	7.3	10.3
2019	67.7	4.0	6.8	10.0
2018	65.1	15.4	7.1	11.0
2017	65.3	10.6	7.2	11.0
2016	76.3	7.1	8.3	10.9
2015	83.1	11.8	9.2	11.1
2014	82.6	11.4	9.6	11.6
2013	82.0	10.9	9.2	11.2
2012	79.4	11.9	9.2	11.6
2011	75.8	12.8	8.5	11.2
Average	75.4	11.5	8.2	10.9

Data source: P&G, SEC Filings, form 10-K, various years.

messages in print are called advertisements and those in electronic media are called commercials.

(Berger 2011, 197)

- "The term 'advertising' came to be defined as paid-for mass-media communication, rather than all promotional activity. It became a means to the marketing ends of managing and controlling the consumer markets at the least cost" (Brierley 1995, 2).
- Firms "spend money on advertising in the hope of persuading consumers to buy their products. The general aim behind advertising expenditure is to try to increase sales and to reinforce consumers' loyalty to particular brands" (Doyle 2013, 143–144).
- "Advertising is designed to spur consumption of specific goods and services. [...] When the amount of goods increased and differences between products appeared, advertising began being directed toward consumers to attract their attention and influence their choices" (Picard 2011, 139–140).
- Advertising is "[p]aid communication by companies and individuals designed to develop interest in, understanding of, purchases of, and uses of the goods and services they offer" (Picard 2011, 253).
- Advertising is "the activity of explicitly paying for media space or time in order to direct favorable attention to certain goods or services" (Turow 2010, 593).

- Advertising

  has a function, which is to sell things to us. But it has another function, which I believe in many ways replaces that traditionally fulfilled
  by art or religion. It creates structures of meaning. [...] Advertisements must take into account not only the inherent qualities and
  attributes of the products they are trying to sell, but also the way in
  which they can make those properties *mean something to us*.

  (Williamson 1979, 11–12)

In the most general sense, an advertisement is a paid-for message communicated to the public that aims at making certain information known to the
public or creating certain effects or changes. Advertising is the process of the
production and distribution of advertisements. Advertisements are promotion messages sold as commodities, which means that the advertiser pays an
advertising company for the publication of the advert. Adverts can promote
information of primarily economically, politically or culturally motivated individuals or organisations. For example, some ads promote the purchase of
certain commodities, ads that promote political parties and programmes, and
ads that promote certain ideas (such as the availability of scientific reports).
These dimensions can also be overlapping, for example when companies use
the promotion of lifestyles (cultural dimension) for at the same time promoting their commodities (economic dimension) and implicating that these commodities help consumers to better realise certain lifestyles. Both for-profit and
not-for-profit organisations can purchase and use ads, such as companies on
the one hand and governments, non-governmental organisations (NGOs),
and associations on the other hand. But in capitalist societies, the use of advertising for advancing capitalist purposes, namely the sale and the consumption of commodities, tends to be the primary role of advertising in society.

On the one hand, it is true, as Joseph Turow (2010) says that advertising
is as old as markets. In the Roman Empire, "criers were paid to scream out
messages about products for sale" (Turow 2010, 593). On the other hand,
when making such arguments as Turow does, there is also a danger that
one naturalises advertising as a necessary feature of all societies. Commodities, markets and commodity logic are not part of all social relations and
not features of all societies. Gifts, co-operation, and solidarity are alternatives to commodities, competition, and markets. Societies can exist without
commodities and competition, but they cannot exist without co-operation
and solidarity. This thought experiment shows that gifts, co-operation, and
solidarity are more substantial than commodities, competition, and markets.

7.2.3 *Marx on Advertising in Capitalism*

Marx describes the capital accumulation process as the process $M - C.. P.. C' - M'$: Capitalist companies invest money capital M for buying labour-power and
means of production as commodities C. In the production process P, workers

use the means of production for creating new commodities C'. The commodities C' are sold on the market. If the sale succeeds, then money capital M' is generated that is larger than the invested money M. M' contains a profit Δm. Parts of the profit are reinvested to accumulate more capital. Advertising plays a role in the process C' – M', the sales process of commodities. C' – M' is "the transformation of commodity capital into money capital" (Marx 1885, 189). Advertising operates as a mechanism that supports capital in transforming commodity capital into money capital. It is located in the process C' – M'.

One of the sources of the economic crisis of a company and the capitalist economy is the lack of commodity sales:

> If C'-M' comes to a halt in the case of one portion, for example, if the commodity is unsaleable, then the circuit of this part is interrupted and its replacement by its means of production is not accomplished; the successive parts that emerge from the production process as C' find their change of function barred by their predecessors. If this continues for some time, production is restricted and the whole process brought to a standstill.
>
> (Marx 1885, 183)

Advertising is a mechanism that capital uses sell commodities by ideologically promoting them to try to stabilise accumulation and circumvent economic crises at the level of individual companies, industries and the economy as a whole. Marx and Engels did not write much about advertising because it was only by the 20th century that advertising became such an important economic mechanism in the course of the rise of Fordist mass production and mass consumption. Engels characterised advertising as "importunate charlatanry" (Engels 1894, 109). In *Capital Volume III*, part 4 (chapters 16–20) is focused on commercial capital, capital that is active in the sale of commodities.

The main focus is on capital that sells commodities and the workers it employs. Examples are supermarkets and their employees. "Commercial capital [...]creates neither value nor surplus-value, at least not directly" (Marx 1894, 392). It contributes to "shortening the circulation time" (392), which means that commercial capital helps to speed up and organise the sales process of commodities. It "can indirectly help the industrial capitalist to increase the surplus-value he produces" (392) and is "enabling capital to operate on a bigger scale" (393). Marx argues that workers employed by commercial capital, such as salespersons in supermarkets, create commercial capital's "ability to appropriate surplus-value" from commodity producers (407). The "unpaid labour of the commercial employee" according to that approach creates "a share in that surplus-value [of industrial capital] for commercial capital" (407–408). One could now argue that advertising labour is comparable to commercial labour and is therefore according to Marx not value-generating, but value-transferring.

Advertising became ever more prevalent with the rise of consumer culture (Turow 2010, chapter 15), which resulted in the emergence of advertising agencies, brands, ad campaigns, direct marketing, audience and marketing research, and the ratings industry. WPP (USA), Omnicom (USA), Dentsu (Japan), Publicis (France), Interpublic (USA), Hakuhodo (Japan), Advantage Solutions (USA), and Clear Channel Communications (USA) are some of the world's largest advertising agencies that are ranked in lists of the world's largest transnational corporations such as Forbes 2000 and Fortune 500. In the 20th century, advertising developed into a relatively autonomous capitalist industry. Advertising as an industry developed as part of the establishment of Fordist capitalism in the 20th century. Fordism was based on the principle of mass consumption and mass production of commodities (see Jessop 1992). It is named after the US industrialist Henry Ford (1863–1947) who owned the Ford Motor Company and contributed to the production of the car as a mass commodity, that is a commodity that was purchased by a large share of the population. A key factor in this stage of the development of capitalism was the deliberate improvement of the material situation of the working class, including wage increases, so that it had better living conditions. This was on the one hand a result of the struggles of the working class for better wage conditions and on the other hand a deliberate concession by politicians influenced by Keynesianism and capitalists who saw mass consumption as a means of increasing profits. As a consequence, the working class could afford to buy more commodities, which increased demand and commodity production. Advertising developed into a separate specialised industry in Fordist capitalism that provided ideas and ideologies for the sale of mass-produced commodities.

Exercise 7.2   Advertising Agencies

Search for advertising agencies represented in lists of the world's largest corporations (such as Forbes 2000 and Fortune 500). Inform yourself about the financial data development of these corporations (revenues, profits, etc.) during the past years.

Have a look at what big ad campaigns these agencies conducted. For what companies did they work? What did these campaigns look like?

What kind of criticisms of ad agencies is there? Search for information in quality newspapers and magazines and online sources. Document the results.

Advertising has on the one hand become a separate industry that sells advertisements as commodities. Companies such as Procter & Gamble invest large amounts of money and shares of their sales and profits into creating illusionary commodity meanings and stories about their commodities that promise great lifestyle enhancement to consumers who buy and consume these commodities. Given that lots of labour goes into branding and advertising commodities, capitalists charge for that labour as part of the commodity prices. This means that advertising and branding labour is reflected in commodity prices.

In *Capital Volume II*, Marx analyses in part 1 the metamorphoses of capital, which includes the analysis of circulation time (chapter 5) and circulation costs (chapter 6). In chapter 6, there is a section about transport costs. Marx argues that transport labour changes the nature of the commodity and is of key importance in the sales process.

> The capitalist mode of production reduces the transport costs for the individual commodity by developing the means of transport and communication, as well as by concentrating transport – i.e. by increasing its scale. It increases the part of social labour, both living and objectified, that is spent on commodity transport, firstly by transforming the great majority of all products into commodities, and then by replacing local by distant markets. The 'circulating' of commodities, i.e. their actual course in space, can be resolved into the transport of commodities. The transport industry forms on the one hand an independent branch of production, and hence a particular sphere for the investment of productive capital. On the other hand it is distinguished by its appearance as the continuation of a production process *within* the circulation process and *for* the circulation process.
> (Marx 1885, 228–229)

Marx here stresses that the means of transport and communication play an important role in the transport and circulation of commodities. Advertising is a communication industry as it produces and communicates commodity ideology. It has become an important, relatively autonomous industry that is mediated by other realms of commodity and capital production. The capital accumulation process requires the transport of commodities from commodity producers to consumers. In the case of tangible products, transport requires the physical transport of goods. In the case of personal services, the producer and the consumer need to be in one joint space at the same time. In the case of knowledge products and services, ideas need to be transported from producers to consumers. In the 20th century, capitalism based on the mass production and mass consumption of commodities emerged. Later, mass-produced commodities became diversified so that commodities are produced that appeal to a vast amount of different tastes and that are partly personalised and manufactured according to individual ideas and tastes. In this consumer-oriented capitalism, ideas are produced and circulated for selling commodities. The sales process of a commodity is therefore not just the transport of the commodity itself from producer to consumer but also the transport of ideas, namely commodity ideologies that appeal to consumers' lifestyles. Advertisements transport commodity ideologies to consumers. The labour involved in advertising is the ideological transport labour of commodities that transports commodity ideology to consumers. Based on this approach, labour in advertising is value-generating labour. Marx's analysis of transport labour also applies to labour in advertising:

> The quantity of products is not increased by their transport. The change in their natural properties that may be effected by transport is also, certain exceptions apart, not an intended useful effect, but rather an unavoidable evil. But the use-value of things is realized only in their consumption, and their consumption may make a change of location necessary, and thus also the additional production process of the transport industry. The productive capital invested in this industry thus adds value to the products transported, partly through the value carried over from the means of transport, partly through the value added by the work of transport. This latter addition of value can be divided, as with all capitalist production, into replacement of wages and surplus-value.
>
> (Marx 1885, 226–227)

7.2.4 Advertising and Deception

One of Procter & Gamble's commodities is Prilosec, a heartburn relief. In advertisements, P&G argued that one pill relieves heartburn for a full day: "ONE PILL EACH MORNING. 24 HOURS. ZERO HEARTBURN".[3] A rival consortium of companies, namely Johnson & Johnson-Merck Pharmaceuticals, sued P&G with respect to this ad for false advertising.

In September 2003, the US District Court of New York argued that the claim of the ad that the one pill stops heartburn for 24 hours was false and deceptive and ruled that the ad, therefore, had to be stopped:

> The District Court found, with substantial support in the record, that a single pill of Prilosec OTC does not provide relief for a period of four to five hours after ingestion. Furthermore, the court rejected P&G's claim that once effective, a single pill provides a full 24 hours of relief.[4]

The injunction made use of § 43(a) of the Lanham Act that outlaws false advertising, namely the publishing of content in the form of "commercial advertising or promotion" that "misrepresents the nature, characteristics, qualities, or geographic origin of his or her or another person's goods, services, or commercial activities".[5]

The Prilosec example shows that commercial advertising is a form of economic positivism that only disseminates positive information about commodities and leaves out talking about problems associated with commodities. To advertise their goods, producers of ads try to create positive feelings and associations among consumers. This is why critics of advertising argue that advertising tries to manipulate, deceive and create false needs. For example, the philosopher Herbert Marcuse writes:

> We may distinguish both true and false needs. 'False' are those which are superimposed upon the individual by particular social interests in his repression: the needs which perpetuate toil, aggressiveness, misery, and injustice. Their satisfaction might be most gratifying to the individual, but this happiness is not a condition which has to be maintained and protected if it serves to arrest the development of the ability (his own and others) to recognize the disease of the whole and grasp the chances of curing the disease. The result then is euphoria in unhappiness. Most of the prevailing needs to relax, to have fun, to behave and consume in accordance with the advertisements, to love and hate what others love and hate, belong to this category of false needs.
>
> (Marcuse 1964, 7)

Conduct the following exercise.

Exercise 7.3   Deceptive Advertising

Have a look at the following two advertisements for Crest Pro Health, a mouthwash produced by Procter & Gamble:

http://www.ispot.tv/ad/7ZlZ/crest-pro-health-check-up
http://www.ispot.tv/ad/7ZCC/crest-pro-health-clinical-dentist-didnt-know-what-to-do

In case one or both of these adverts are no longer available, search on-line for alternative television ads for Crest Pro Health.

Also, have a look at the product page:

https://crest.com/en-us/oral-care-products/toothpaste/pro-health-clean-mint#:~:text=Crest%20Pro%2DHealth%20Toothpaste%20is%20the%20first%20and%20only%20toothpaste,found%20in%20other%20sensitivity%20toothpastes.

Ask yourself and discuss:

How does Procter & Gamble present its toothpaste in ads? What are the key features of the presentation?
What are the key messages?

What is not being said?
How realistic respectively deceptive is the content of the ads?

Concerning Crest Pro Health, there have been complaints by consumers and consumer protection organisations claiming that the product can result in stained teeth and a loss of the sense of taste:

http://www.youtube.com/watch?v=bWh8bfX3Ews

Others reported that it can cause long-term dependence and intensify the symptoms when you stop using the drug:

http://www.youtube.com/watch?v=a8xCV4_d1c8

Ask yourself and discuss:

How do you assess the story of Crest Pro Health having negative effects on the consumer, but conveying very positive images of itself in advertisements ("My dentist was so proud of my teeth today. I've been using Crest Pro Health for a few weeks. I feel brighter, fresher, cleaner"; "My mouth is so clean, my dentist almost didn't know what to do")?
Why is it that companies try to foreground the positive aspects of the commodities they sell and downplay, deny or exclude discussion of negative aspects?
Is deception and manipulation in advertisements the exception from the rule or part of advertising as such?
What can and should be done against deceptive advertisements?

Exercise 7.2 provides indications that commercial advertisements and capitalist companies present commodities only in a positive manner and leave out, deny or downplay negative impacts on society. In the example, being confronted with the fact that P&G's mouthwash resulted in brownly stained teeth of some customers, the P&G spokesperson says that the stain "in some people" can "also be a sign that the product is working" and that "99.99% of the people who have purchased this product have not reported this issue to us".

Critical analysts of advertising argue that such examples show that advertising is not mere product information that communicates what goods are available on the market to consumers. Kaptan in an introductory book to advertising provides such a definition: Advertising is "a channel of information from manufacturers to Consumers" that merely "tells where to find what you want" (Kaptan 2002, 28).

In her critical analysis of advertising *Decoding Advertisements: Ideology and Meaning in Advertising*, Judith Williamson provides a criticism of such definitions. She argues that they overlook the ideological character of advertising:

> What an advertisement 'says' is merely what it *claims* to say; it is part of the deceptive mythology of advertising to believe that an advertisement is simply a transparent vehicle for a 'message' behind it. Certainly, a large part of any advertisement *is* this 'message': we are told something about a product, and asked to buy it. The information that we are given is frequently untrue, and even when it is true, we are often being persuaded to buy products which are unnecessary; products manufactured at the cost of damaging the environment and sold to make a profit at the expense of the people who made them.
>
> (Williamson 1979, 17)

7.3 The Development of Advertising in Capitalism

Advertising expenditure as part of GDP reflects the development of the general economy and is higher in richer countries because they are heavier consumer societies (Doyle 2013, 150–154).

Figure 7.1 shows the development of the shares of specific types of advertising in global advertising revenues. The period is from 1980 until 2021. From 1980 until 2000, newspaper ads accounted for the largest share of global ad revenues. These types of ads developed from a share of 46.3% in 1980 to one of 4.4% in 2021, which is a drastic fall. Television advertising has maintained a constantly important role during the entire analysed period with a share between 24.4% at the lower end (the year 1980) and 41.3% at the upper end (the year 2010). The most dramatic change in the ad industry in the late 20th century and the 21st century has to do with digital capitalism. Since the late 1990s, the share of digital advertising in the global ad revenues started to rise, first at a modest pace, and since 2010 rapidly. The digital ad share increased from 0.1% in 1999 to 58.8% in 2021. Digital advertising became the dominant form of advertising. Given digital advertising is controlled by two companies – Google and Facebook – the advertising market has become more concentrated. At the same time, ad-financed newspapers have struggled to survive. Those who advertise seem to trust digital advertising as a medium that helps them sell more commodities than print advertising. Digital advertising is highly targeted to individual consumer preferences that are collected with the help of the big data-based surveillance of Internet users (Fuchs 2021).

Table 7.2 shows the distribution of global ad revenues by medium in the year 2024. The previous trends have continued. In 2024, Internet advertising accounted for almost two thirds of the global ad revenues and broadcast advertising (radio and television) for roughly a quarter. Other forms of advertising (print advertising, outdoor advertising, cinema advertising) only had small shares.

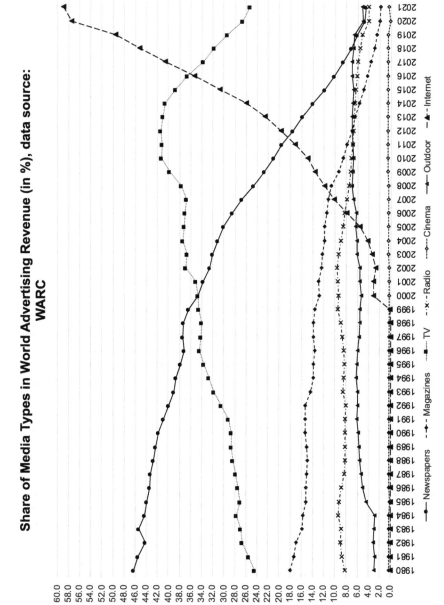

Figure 7.1 The development of the share of media-specific types of advertising in the global advertising revenues.

Table 7.2 Share of certain media in global advertising revenues in 2024

Medium	Share (%)
Internet	65.13
Television	20.80
Outdoor advertising	5.22
Radio	3.56
Newspapers	3.09
Magazines	1.75
Cinema	0.45
Reorganised data:	
Internet	65,13
Broadcasting (television, radio)	24,36
Outdoor advertising	5,22
Print	4,84
Cinema	0,45

Data source: Statista, https://www.statista.com/statistics/269333/distribution-of-global-advertising-expenditure/, accessed on 13 February 2023.

7.3.1 The Historical Development of Advertising in Capitalism

Graham Murdock (2013) provides a historical overview of the development of advertising in capitalism. Table 7.3 summarises the main results. We "can think of the production of commodity culture as a process in which developments in the organisation of retailing are accompanied by new media of popular communication and both are organised around a succession of common principles" (Murdock 2013, 131). I added to Murdock's typology phases of capitalist development that shaped the development of specific forms of communication technologies and advertising.

In the 19th century, advertising was dominated by the principle of utility. Advertising was based on basic information about the commodities' use-values in classified newspaper ads and local grocery stores' shop windows. The use-value of a commodity is its basic characteristics that enable the satisfaction of human needs. "Neither space paid much attention to visual display. Press advertisements relied wholly or mainly on printed text offering unvarnished descriptions" (Murdock 2013, 131).

In the late 19th century, department stores became very popular and displayed commodities that were for purchase. The cinema emerged as a new medium that besides movies started to also display advertising. According to Murdock, display became the central advertising principle. The first movies displayed in the UK were films by the Lumière brothers such as "Workers Leaving the Factory". The first such British screening of a Lumière took place on

Table 7.3 The development of advertising in capitalism

Medium	Retail Environment	Central Principle	Capitalism
Newspapers	Local shops, markets	Utility	Competitive capitalism (19th century)
Cinema	Department stores	Display	Imperialist capitalism (late 19th century until the end of the Second World War)
Commercial Network Television	Supermarkets	Flow	Fordist, Keynesian capitalism (after Second World War until the mid-1970s)
Multi-Channel Television	Malls	Immersion	Global, flexible, neoliberal, financial capitalism (the mid-1970s until 2000)
Web 2.0	Retail destinations	Integration	Digital capitalism (since 2000)

Source: Based on Murdock (2013, 130).

21 February 1896 at the Polytechnic in London's Regent Street, which is today the main building of the University of Westminster. On 28 December 1895, the Lumière Brothers made the world's first movie screening at the Grand Café in Paris. The Lumières sent their movies around the world, which, for example, on 11 August 1896 also resulted in the first movie screening in China. In Germany, the first movie was screened on 1 November 1895 at the Wintergarten in Berlin. It was a film by the brothers Max and Emil Skladanowsky. The 1890s marked the advent of the "age of advertising" (Staiger 1990, 4), which resulted first in the advertising of movies (including newspaper ads and national ad campaigns) and then also in the advertising of general commodities at the movies. One of the earliest forms of movie advertising was the slide ad, which means that non-moving advertising images "appeared between entertainment reels" (Segrave 2004, 3). In the USA, there are reports of such slide ads in movie theatres in the 1910s (Segrave 2004, 3–4). Longer moving advertisements were not used during the silent film area. "Reportedly Alka-Seltzer began using such ads around 1922, but it would be the late 1930s before the minute-ad would start to become more prevalent" (4). One of the first Hollywood product placements, namely for tires and gasoline, appears in the movie *The Garage* from 1920 (Maher 2016). Murdock (2013, 133) reports that there was already product placement for soap in an 1896 Lumière Brothers movie.

After the Second World War, the principle of flow started to dominate advertising and retail. Commercial television that broadcasts flows of regular content interspersed by advertisements became popular. In 1916, the Piggly Wiggly store in Memphis, Tennessee, was the world's first self-service supermarket (Murdock 2013, 134). Self-service supermarkets became ever more popular, which resulted in flows of customers purchasing commodities.

Television changed significantly during the 1980s. The VCR, as well as cable and satellite television, became very popular. The multichannel transition occurred.

> Beginning in the 1980s, the television industry experienced two decades of gradual change. New technologies, including the remote control, videocassette recorder, and analog cable systems, expanded viewers' choice and control; [...] nascent cable channels and new broadcast networks added to viewers' content choices and eroded the dominance of ABC, CBS, and NBC; subscription channels launched [...]; and methods for measuring audiences grew increasingly sophisticated with the deployment of Nielsen's People Meter.
>
> (Lotz 2014, 25)

In 1992, the first mega shopping mall opened in Bloomington, Minnesota (Murdock 2013, 135).

> Mega malls provided multiple entertainments as well as shopping opportunities. Cable television packages offered home shopping channels alongside film, sports, and entertainment services. Increasing reliance on corporate sponsorship and product placement expanded the paid-for opportunities to integrate commodities into programming.
>
> (Murdock 2013, 135–136)

Both in shopping malls and in their homes where they watched cable television, consumers became immersed in consumer culture and advertising as lifestyles.

Since around 2005, integration has become a major principle of advertising and retail. Social media and Internet platforms, as well as mobile apps, have become the most popular form of information and entertainment among young people. Many of them are based on targeted, personalised advertising. Advertising has thereby become a constant feature of online life and everyday life. In the world of retail, mega malls are often no longer limited to single buildings, but turn into streets, districts, and cities – what Murdock (2013, 140) characterises as retail destinations that integrate shopping and capitalist consumer cultures into urban life and urban space. In Bristol, Cabot Circus opened in 2008. It was conceived as a shopping part of the city. Outlet villages have emerged. In the Chinese city of Chengdu, the world's then-largest building, the New Century Global Center was opened in 2013. It contains a shopping mall so large that it is more of a shopping village. Such changes have been part of changes in urban life, which has also called forth protests against gentrification and the commodification of urban space. The opening of Cabot Circus in Bristol resulted in protests against gentrification that stressed the loss of green spaces, pubs, community meeting spaces, cycle paths, and public parks. A demonstration call read: "Please show your opposition to the destruction of our places, spaces and culture, before its [sic!] too late".[6]

7.3.2 Advertising and the Development of Capitalism

Murdock (2013) provides an excellent overview of the development of advertising and consumer culture. I want to add a dimension to that analysis, namely the interaction of advertising and retail with the development of capitalism (see Table 7.3, column 4).

19th-century capitalism was competitive, industrial capitalism. Advertising was in an early stage, which is reflected by its focus on utility. Capital was much less concentrated than it became in the early 20th century.

Imperialist capitalism was focused on the combination of finance capitalism (the merger of banking capital and industrial capital), transnational capital investments (capital export), capitalist monopolies, and the competition of nation-states for economic and political influence that resulted in the First World War. This stage of capitalism saw the rise of advertising campaigns and the constitution of advertising as a relatively autonomous industry. Monopoly corporations used advertising as a means for advancing the concentration of capital.

Ernest Mandel describes the competitive and imperialist stages of capitalism as follows:

> The "beginnings of the first two successive stages in the history of industrial capitalism – the stage of free competition and the stage of imperialism or classical monopoly capitalism [...] appear as two phases of accelerated accumulation. *The movement of capital exports unleashed by the quest for surplus-profits, and the cheapening of circulating constant capital, led to a temporary rise in the average rate of profit in the metropolitan countries, which in turn explains the colossal increase in the accumulation period 1893–1914*, after the long period of stagnation from 1873–93 which was dominated by the falling rate of profit".
> (Mandel 1975, 82–83)

New phases of capitalist development that are characterised by new models of capital accumulation, regulation, and ideology are often the result of major crises of capitalism. Such a crisis also took place in the world economy from 1929 until 1939. After the Second World War, a new stage of capitalist development emerged – Fordist, Keynesian capitalism. Its main feature was the combination of the Fordist principles of mass production and mass consumption of commodities with the establishment of Keynesian welfare states that improved the working class and general population's living conditions and thereby also stabilised capitalism. Commercial television and supermarkets organising flows of commodities, consumers, and advertisements were characteristic of this stage. Mass consumption required massive investments in advertising. Bob Jessop describes Fordist, Keynesian capitalism in the following manner:

> As an accumulation regime, i.e., a macroeconomic regime sustaining expanded reproduction, Fordism involves a virtuous circle of growth based on mass production and mass consumption. [...] the Fordist state is a Keynesian welfare state which has two key functions in promoting the virtuous circle of Fordism. It manages aggregate demand so that the relatively rigid, capital-intensive investments of Fordist firms are worked close to capacity and firms have enough confidence to undertake the extended and expensive R&D as well as the subsequent heavy capital investment involved in complex mass production; and it generalizes mass consumption norms so that most citizens can share in the prosperity generated by rising economies of scale. Where the latter function involves only limited state provision for collective consumption, the state must ensure adequate levels of demand through the transfer of incomes. More intense intervention is likely both as Fordism rises to dominance and during its declining years.
>
> (Jessop 1992, 43, 45)

In the mid-1970s, there was a major global crisis of capitalism that resulted in the emergence of global, flexible, neoliberal, financial capitalism. It was characterised by the massive increase in transnational capital, flexible modes of production, the global outsourcing of labour, the creation of precarious labour to increase profits, high-risk financial capital, privatisation, accumulation by dispossession, and the commodification of (almost) everything. Along with massive commodification and privatisation came the emergence of mega malls and omnipresent commercial media. More and more humans became constantly immersed in commodity culture. David Harvey characterises this stage of capitalism in the following manner.

> Flexible, global, neoliberal, financialised capitalism "is characterized by the emergence of entirely new sectors of production, new ways of providing financial services, new markets, and, above all, greatly intensified rates of commercial, technological, and organizational innovation. It has entrained rapid shifts in the patterning of uneven development, both between sectors and between geographical regions, giving rise, for example, to a vast surge in so-called 'service-sector' employment as well as to entirely new industrial ensembles in hitherto underdeveloped regions (such as the 'Third Italy', Flanders, the various silicon valleys and glens, to say nothing of the vast profusion of activities in newly industrializing countries). It has also entailed a new round of what I shall call 'time-space compression' [...]

in the capitalist world – the time horizons of both private and public decision-making have shrunk, while satellite communication and declining transport costs have made it increasingly possible to spread those decisions immediately over an ever wider and variegated space. These enhanced powers of flexibility and mobility have allowed employers to exert stronger pressures of labour control on a work force in any case weakened by two savage bouts of deflation, that saw unemployment rise to unprecedented postwar levels in advanced capitalist countries (save, perhaps, Japan). Organized labour was undercut by the reconstruction of foci of flexible accumulation in regions lacking previous industrial traditions, and by the importation back into the older centres of the regressive norms and practices established in these new areas".

(Harvey 1990, 147)

The main substantive achievement of neoliberalization, however, has been to redistribute, rather than to generate, wealth and income. I have elsewhere provided an account of the main mechanisms whereby this was achieved under the rubric of 'accumulation by dispossession'.

(Harvey 2005, 159)

Digital capitalism is not a stage following global capitalism. It has rather developed as a dimension of and in interaction with global capitalism since the 1970s and may very well postdate global capitalism. New digital technologies such as the personal computer, the World Wide Web, social media, the mobile phone, and cloud computing were the medium and outcome of the crisis and volatility of capitalism. New technologies were needed to organise the global organisation of capitalism, a new phase of automation, global finance capital, and mass surveillance. As part of the attempts to stabilise capitalism, new forms of advertising and retail, namely digital targeted advertising and retail destinations that integrated commodity culture as an almost constant real-time feature into everyday communication and everyday life, emerged. Harvey argues in this context:

Information technology is the privileged technology of neoliberalism. It is far more useful for speculative activity and for maximizing the number of short- term market contracts than for improving production. Interestingly, the main arenas of production that gained were the emergent cultural industries (films, videos, video games, music, advertising, art shows), which use IT as a basis for innovation and the marketing of new products.

(Harvey 2005, 159)

In 1993, *Forbes* magazine announced the coming "age of digital capitalism" (Lenzner and Heuslein 1993). In 1999, political economist Dan Schiller

(1999) published the book *Digital Capitalism. Networking the Global Market System*. What is digital capitalism?

> Digital capitalism has been a particular dimension of capitalist society in the 20th and 21st centuries. In the mid-1970s, capitalism experienced a profound multidimensional crisis that resulted in the rise of neoliberal capitalism, a new round of political-economic globalisation, and the advancement of new digital technologies as means of production and communication (Fuchs 2008). The rise of capitalism's digital technological paradigm was a response to the crisis of capitalist society.
>
> Digital capitalism is the dimension of capitalist society where processes of the accumulation of capital, decision-power and reputation are mediated by and organised with the help of digital technologies and where economic, political and cultural processes result in digital goods and digital structures. Digital labour, digital capital, political online communication, digital aspects of protests and social struggles, ideology online, and influencer-dominated digital culture are some of the features of digital capitalism. In digital capitalism, digital technologies mediate the accumulation of capital and power.
>
> One characteristic of networked computing is that it supports the transcendence of boundaries and helps to produce and reproduce relations. For example, the World Wide Web is a network of interlinked texts, sites, and platforms. At the level of social systems and society, digitalisation enables the production and reproduction of relations between objects and human subjects, between structures and human practices. Digital capitalism as a societal formation neither operates just as a practice nor just as a structure. Digital capitalism is not just a digital practice and not just a digital structure, it is the totality of the dialectics of digital practices and digital structures that take place in capitalist society. For example, Facebook's and Google's server farms are technological structures that store massive amounts of big personal data. Google and Facebook are only social and meaningful through the human practices of searching, clicking, liking, commenting, uploading, etc. These practices produce and reproduce data structures that condition – enable and constrain – further digital practices. Google's and Facebook's profits are based on the valorisation of this dialectic of digital structures and practices so that they exploit their users' digital labour [...]. Digitalisation affects both the productive forces and the relations of production and the dialectic of forces and relations.
>
> Digital capitalism has enabled and required new forms of marketing and advertising. Only a global information system such as the Internet enables the real time surveillance of vast shares of user behaviour that results in big data that is used for micro-targeted, individualised and personalised advertising.
>
> (Fuchs 2022, 28–29)

The financialisation of capitalism resulted in a major economic crisis in 2007 and 2008. The result was not a new stage of capitalist development, but an intensification of neoliberalism combined with the strengthening of authoritarian and fascist forces in many societies. The 2020/2021 COVID-19 crisis brought about forced lockdowns of societies and shutdowns of economies, which created crisis tendencies to which governments had to react with massive state expenditures. At the time of writing, it is not clear if this crisis will bring about a new phase of capitalist development such as a neo-Keynesian model of capitalism that is less global in character and more regulated.

7.3.3 Measuring Advertising

Political economists have since a long time conducted empirical analyses of advertising. In the 1950s, Dallas Smythe (1954) conducted content analyses of commercial TV programming in New York, Los Angeles, and New Haven. He wanted to find out how much advertising there is on commercial television. Programme time measurement was done with the help of stopwatches. There were no video recorders, digital storage technologies, etc. at that time, so research required teams that constantly watched television and conducted measurements.

The content analysis used the following categories: drama, variety, dance, music, personalities; quiz, stunts, and contests; fine arts, sports, news, weather, information, cooking; arts, crafts, and hobbies; shopping and merchandise, personal care, public issues, public events, public institutional, religion, personal relations, pre-school entertainment.

The main finding was that already in the early phase of television, there was lots of advertising on US television: Advertising "occupies about one of every five minutes of big city television program time and about of every four minutes of smaller-city program time" (Smythe 1954, 66). Entertainment "constitutes three out four minutes of total time. One might say that the chief element in television programs is the representation of reality as entertainment [...] Information-type programs amount to slightly less than one-fifth of total program time" (Smythe 1954, 66).

Raymond Williams (1921–1988) established a critical approach that he termed Cultural Materialism. It is often presented as a version of Cultural Studies but is in fact quite close to Political Economy (see Fuchs 2017). Williams (1974) wrote a classical book about television. In it, he among other things analysed the role of entertainment and advertising on British and US television. He conducted a content analysis of one week of programming (3–9 March 1973) on five television stations (Williams 1974, 40): BBC 1 and BBC 2 (Public Service Broadcasting) and ITV Anglia (commercial) in the UK; and KQED (Public Service Broadcaster) and Channel 7 (commercial) in San Francisco. Tables 7.4 and 7.5 show the results.

On the three public service stations, there was no advertising. On the two commercial channels, more than 10% of the programming time was filled by

Table 7.4 Raymond Williams' content analysis of television programming

3–9 March 1973	BBC 1 (%)	BBC 2 (%)	ITV Anglia (%)	KQED (%)	Channel 7 (%)
News and public affairs	24.5	12.0	13.0	22.5	14.0
Features and documentaries	6.5	20.0	6.3	6.0	0.5
Education	23.0	29.5	12.5	26.0	2.0
Arts and music	1.0	2.5	0	5.0	0
Children's programmes	11.5	6.5	8.0	27.0	4.0
Drama – plays	4.5	4.5	3.1	0	0
Drama – series and serials	7.0	4.0	16.6	5.0	17.0
Movies	6.5	11.0	12.0	5.5	18.0
General entertainment	7.5	7.5	9.5	0	24.5
Sport	6.0	1.5	6.2	2.0	4.5
Religion	1.0	0	0.6	0	0.5
Publicity	1.0	1.0	1.5	1.0	1.0
Commercials	0	0	10.7	0	14.0

Source: Based on Williams (1974, 83).

Table 7.5 Raymond Williams' content analysis of television programming recoded data

3–9 March 1973	BBC 1 (%)	BBC 2 (%)	ITV Anglia (%)	KQED (%)	Channel 7 (%)
Type A: public service content	71	75	42.9	86	20.5
Type B: commercial content	21	22.5	38.1	10.5	59.5

Source: Based on Williams (1974, 84).

advertisements. Williams recoded the data (see Table 7.5). He distinguished between two types of programmes:

- type A programming: public service content focused on education, learning, public and general interest (news and public affairs, features and documentaries, education, arts and music, children's programmes, plays);
- type B programming: commercial content focused on entertainment (drama series and serials, movies, general entertainment).

Williams's analysis shows that commercial television stations that use advertising tend to much more rely on entertainment than on public service content as it tends to be easier to sell ads with type B (entertainment) content. As a consequence, more commercial television stations tend to act more like tabloids where entertainment and sensationalism replace or reduce more serious and more engaging information.

7.4 Dallas Smythe: The Audience as Commodity

7.4.1 Advertising's Political Economy

Dallas Smythe (1977) wrote a classical article on the Political Economy of advertising where he introduces the notions of audience labour and the audience as a commodity (audience commodity). He argues that advertising-funded media do not sell content, but provide content for free to attract audiences that they sell as a commodity to advertisers. His starting point is that the analysis of labour in the context of advertising is a blindspot of critical analyses: "The mass media of communications and related institutions concerned with advertising, market research, public relations and product and package design represent a blindspot in Marxist theory in the European and Atlantic basin cultures" (Smythe 1977, 1). Smythe criticised that a lot of critical and administrative scholars analysed commercial media in terms of messages, information, images, meaning, entertainment, orientation, education, manipulation, and ideology. He then asks in his seminal article what the commodity is in advertising:

> I submit that the materialist answer to the question – What is the commodity form of mass-produced, advertiser-supported communications under monopoly capitalism? – is audiences and readerships (hereafter referred to for simplicity as audiences). The material reality under monopoly capitalism is that all non-sleeping time of most of the population is work time. This work time is devoted to the production of commodities-in-general (both where people get paid for their work and as members of audiences) and in the production and reproduction of labour power (the pay for which is subsumed in their income). Of the off-the-job work time, the largest single block is time of the audiences which is sold to advertisers.
>
> (Smythe 1977, 3)

What is the nature of the content of the mass media in economic terms under monopoly capitalism? The information, entertainment and 'educational' material transmitted to the audience is an inducement (gift, bribe or "free lunch") to recruit potential members of the audience and to maintain their loyal attention. The appropriateness of the analogy to the free lunch in the old-time saloon or cocktail bar is manifest: the free lunch consists of materials which whet the prospective audience members' appetites and thus (1) attract and keep them attending to the programme, newspaper or magazine, and (2) cultivate a mood conducive to favourable reaction to the explicit and implicit advertisers' messages.

(Smythe 1977, 5)

The work which audience members perform for the advertiser to whom they have been sold is to learn to buy particular 'brands' of consumer goods, and to spend their income accordingly. In short, they work to create the demand for advertised goods which is the purpose of the monopoly capitalist advertisers. While doing this, audience members are simultaneously reproducing their own labour power.

(Smythe 1977, 6)

Smythe argues that advertising-funded media sell access to audiences as a commodity to advertising clients. According to Marx, workers create the value of commodities. Smythe's logical conclusion is that audiences work for advertising-funded media, which is why he speaks of audiences conducting the audience labour of giving attention to and consuming commercial media. In the age of digital capitalism, where digital ads play an important role, Smythe's analysis remains highly topical for the analysis of the Political Economy of digital advertising (Fuchs 2012).

Karl Bücher, one of the founders of journalism studies in Germany, made an argument that is comparable to Smythe's approach:

By taking up advertising, the newspaper got into a peculiar hybrid position. It no longer merely publishes news and opinions for the subscription price, to which a general interest is attached, but it also serves private intercourse and private interests through advertisements of every kind, for which it is specially remunerated. It sells new news to its readers, and it sells its readership to every solvent private interest.[7]

(Bücher 1893/1917, 258)

Smythe identifies four purposes of the commercial, advertising-funded mass media:

1 Supply of consumers:
   "The prime purpose of the mass media complex is to produce people in audiences who work at learning the theory and practice of consumership for civilian goods and who support (with taxes and votes) the military demand management system";
2 The diffusion of the ideology of possessive individualism:
   "The second principal purpose is to produce audiences whose theory and practice confirms the ideology of monopoly capitalism (possessive individualism in an authoritarian political system)";

3 The creation of support for state politics:
   The third principal purpose is to produce public opinion supportive of the strategic and tactical policies of the state (e.g. presidential candidates, support of Indochinese military adventures, space race, détente with the Soviet Union, rapprochement with China and ethnic and youth dissent);
4 The maintenance of media as profitable enterprises:
   "Necessarily in the monopoly capitalist system, the fourth purpose of the mass media complex is to operate itself so profitably as to ensure unrivalled respect for its economic importance in the system" (Smythe 1977, 20).

7.4.2 *The Ratings Industry*

Selling the audience commodity requires determining its size. As a consequence, the ratings industry has emerged as part of the advertising industry:

> How are advertisers assured that they are getting what they pay for when they buy audiences? A sub-industry sector of the consciousness industry checks to determine. The socio-economic characteristics of the delivered audience/ readership and its size are the business of A.C. Nielsen and a host of competitors who specialize in rapid assessment of the delivered audience commodity. The behaviour of the members of the audience product under the impact of advertising and the 'editorial' content is the object of market research by a large number of independent market research agencies as well as by similar staffs located in advertising agencies, the advertising corporation and in media enterprises.
>
> (Smythe 1977, 4–5)

Eileen Meehan (2002) analyses gender aspects of the audience commodity. She speaks of the gendered commodity audience: Advertisers are primarily interested in bona fide consumers who have "the disposable income, access, and desire to loyally purchase brand names and to habitually make impulse purchases" (Meehan 2002, 213). "The larger the number of bona fide consumers viewing, the higher the price charged by networks" (Meehan 2002, 213).

> The overvaluing of a male audience reflects the sexism of patriarchy as surely as the overvaluing of an upscale audience reflects the classism of capitalism. [...] From this perspective, television is structured to discriminate against anyone outside the commodity audience of white, 18- to 34-year-old, heterosexual, English-speaking, upscale men. [...] television is an instrument of oppression.
>
> (Meehan 2002, 220–221)

The ratings industry consists of companies such as Nielsen, Comscore, Traffic Audit Bureau, Audit Bureau of Circulation, and Simmons/MRI. In Germany, Gesellschaft für Konsumforschung (GfK) is the dominant actor in measuring television audiences. Rating companies measure audience sizes and thereby try to influence the prices of audience commodities.

There is a relationship between advertising price and audience size: Picard (2009) conducted an analysis of the relationship between the circulation and advertising prices of a random sample of 160 daily newspapers. He found that the average advertising price increases with higher circulation.

7.4.3 Capital Accumulation in the Advertising Industry

Figure 7.2 shows the capital accumulation processes in the advertising industry.

The advertising industry consists of ad agencies that sell ad campaigns and branding as commodities, rating companies that sell audience ratings, and advertising companies that sell ads. These processes constitute three capital accumulation cycles that are interacting and are mediated with the capital accumulation of regular companies. At the bottom of Figure 7.2, we see the capital accumulation process of advertising-funded media. The workers in such companies produce a product P1 (content) that is not or is only partly

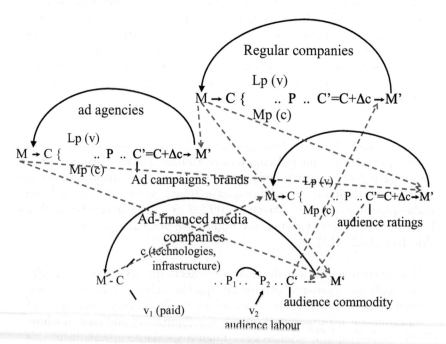

Figure 7.2 Capital accumulation in the advertising industry.

a commodity. Audiences (v2) act as workers who produce a commodity C', namely the audience commodity that is sold as a commodity. The capital accumulation cycle of ad-financed media is coupled to regular companies via the investments the latter make into the first by purchasing ads, as well as by the advertisements' influence on the sales process C' – M' of regular companies that try to sell commodities to consumers.

Regular companies either have their own PR and ad departments or often invest money into ad and branding campaigns where they make use of the services offered by ad agencies. Ad agencies sell advertising campaigns and brands as commodities. They receive money from regular companies, purchase audience ratings, and purchase ad spaces from ad-financed media. Rating companies such as Nielsen produce audience ratings. They sell such data to media, and others who have an interest in finding out how attractive or unattractive certain ads are for particular audiences.

Horkheimer and Adorno argue that advertising is an important aspect of capitalism: "Culture is a paradoxical commodity. It is so completely subject to the law of exchange that it is no longer exchanged [...] Advertising is its [the culture industry's] elixir of life" (Horkheimer and Adorno 2002, 131). Manfred Knoche (2005) argues there are three dimensions of advertising as capitalism's elixir of life:

1 Prevention:
   Advertising prevents overproduction, overaccumulation, and capital accumulation problems;
2 Advancement:
   Advertising advances market concentration, capital concentration, the gap between the rich and the poor and the gap between the powerful and the dependent. At the company level, companies use advertisements for trying to advance commodity sales, capital accumulation, and profitability;
3 Stabilisation:
   Advertising stabilises the capital-labour relation, the regime of accumulation, commercial media, and capitalism.

7.5 Assessing Advertising

Political Economy also has to do with moral philosophy. It wants to understand how advertising works in capitalism and also what negative impacts it can have on society. The book *Advertising and Society: An Introduction* (Pardun 2014) presents debates on the positive and negative impacts of advertising on society. In each book section, two people who hold opposing views discuss a certain aspect of advertising in society. Let us summarise some of the arguments made in favour and against advertising (see Doyle 2013, 146–147; Pardun 2014).

7.5.1 Legitimation

Legitimating positions on advertising typically argue the following:

- Advertising is essential information for customers to know which products are available;
- Advertising is a form of communication between companies and customers that makes the market system work and enables customers' choice and sovereignty;
- Without advertising, products and services would be more expensive and consumers would make less informed purchase choices;
- Advertising helps to make choices and to reduce complexity in a consumer society with high levels of offer and demand.

Advertising associations are associations of companies making money in the ad business. They lobby for more advertising, a positive view of advertising in society, and favourable treatment of advertisers by governments. The International Advertising Association was founded in 1938. It opposes proper regulation of advertising and therefore favours self-regulation, which means that advertising companies make their own rules of behaviour and commit to respecting them. The IAA defines one of its goals and values as "[a]dvocacy to protect and advance the freedom of commercial speech and consumer choice, while defending the responsible communications industry against unwarranted bans and restrictions".[8]

In Germany, the German Advertising Federation (Zentralverband der Deutschen Werbewirtschaft, ZDW) argues that advertising "is an integral part of the free market economy and an indispensable factor in a diverse and independent media landscape" and that it wants to defend and promote "the freedom of commercial advertising, and in particular disproportionate product-specific or media-specific prohibitions and restrictions on commercial communication".[9]

To speak of the "freedom of commercial speech" (IAA) or "freedom of commercial advertising" are polite formulations of the view that advertisers should be allowed to make whatever claims they want to make about their commodities, even if these are lies.

In the report *How Advertising Fuels the UK Economy*, the Advertising Association (AA) (Advertising Association 2013, 6) claims that advertising brings a lot of advantages:

> advertising drives price competition, advertising funds media and the creative industries, advertising promotes innovation and differentiation, advertising enables the digital economy, advertising encourages market growth, advertising's social contribution has an economic value, advertising spend supports a wide range of employment, advertising supports exports.

Such arguments are mainly of an economic nature. They are based on the neoliberal view that advertising is good as it has the potential to increase the GDP. But what is meant by such arguments is that advertising is a way to increase profits. There is no talk about the potential and actual negative impacts of advertising on society. The focus is purely on economic goals, and questions of social justice and democracy, as well as the negative effects of advertising on society, do not play a role in such propaganda for advertising.

There are also critics of advertising. Let us summarise some of their arguments.

7.5.2 *Critical Positions on Advertising*

- Advertising is product propaganda that conceals actual or possible negative features of products;
- Advertising only presents the products and ideologies of powerful companies and discriminates against competing products, views and less powerful actors, especially non-commercial and non-profit organisations;
- Advertising advances the concentration of the economy;
- Advertising advances media concentration via the advertising-circulation-spiral (see the discussion of this spiral in chapter 6, section 6.3);
- Advertisers try to manipulate humans' needs, desires, tastes, and purchasing and consumption decisions;
- Advertising is mainly aimed at wealthy consumers;
- Advertising structures the corporate media as a filter in such a way that criticisms of corporate behaviour are avoided in order not to face loss of advertising clients;
- Advertisers try to calculate and make purely mathematical assumptions about human behaviour and interests (e.g. a person lives in a certain area, has a specific skin colour and age => has low income, no loan should be offered). It statistically sorts consumers and users into groups and tends to discriminate especially the weak, people with low purchasing power, and people of colour who as a consequence have disadvantages in society;
- Advertisements frequently contain and tend to enforce stereotypes, prejudices, and biases. Examples are classist, racist, and patriarchal stereotypes;
- Advertisements present women frequently in a sexist way;
- Advertising tends to violate consumer privacy and to use sensitive personal data for commercial purposes;
- Advertising fosters mass consumption of mostly non-renewable resources that end up as waste in nature. Advertising aggravates the ecological crisis;
- Advertising fosters the programming of light entertainment and thereby advances the tabloidisation of the media, as well as the undermining of Public Service Media/content.
- Advertising can advance consumer debt, which was an important factor in economic crises such as the 2007/2008 world economic crisis.

7.6 Advertising as Ideology

7.6.1 *Diamonds Are Capitalism's Best Friend...*

De Beers is a Luxembourg-based producer and retailer of diamonds and diamond rings. It was founded in 1888 and is one of the world's largest and most profitable diamond producers. Conduct the following exercise. It is focused on one of De Beers' diamond advertisements.

Exercise 7.4   De Beer's Diamond Ring Advert

Have a look at the following advert by diamond trading company De Beers (in case one of the links no longer works, use another one, or alternatively conduct an image search online for: De Beers right-hand ring campaign 2003):

https://www.pinterest.com/pin/453808099921650217/
https://i1.wp.com/dataintherough.com/wp-content/uploads/2016/07/DeBeers-Right-Hand-Ring-Campaign.jpg?ssl=1
https://dataintherough.com/tag/de-beers/.

The image shows a businesswoman with a shiny diamond ring. The accompanying text reads:

YOUR LEFT HAND SAYS "WE". YOUR RIGHT HAND SAYS "ME". YOUR LEFT HAND LOVES CANDLELIGHT. YOUR RIGHT HAND LOVES THE SPOTLIGHT. YOUR LEFT HAND ROCKS THE CRADLE. YOUR RIGHT HAND RULES THE WORLD. WOMEN OF THE WORLD, RAISE YOUR RIGHT HAND.

Discuss:
What is the basic message of this advert?
What characteristics does De Beers imply its diamond rings have?
In what respects is this advert ideological?

7.6.2 *What Is Ideology?*

Terry Eagleton (1991) gives an introduction to the concept of ideology. He shows that there are general definitions that equate ideology with worldviews, as well as critical definitions of ideology that are focused on aspects of deception, manipulation, legitimation of class interests, distortion, and dissimulation (Eagleton 1991, 28–31). Marx stresses in this context that an ideology makes reality appear different than it really is. He writes that "in all ideology men and their relations appear upside-down as in a *camera obscura*" (Marx and Engels 1845/1846, 36). Ideology is "an *inverted consciousness of the world*" and functions as the "*opium* of the people" (Marx 1843, 250).

Ideology can in a critical approach be understood as thoughts, practices, ideas, words, concepts, phrases, sentences, texts, belief systems, meanings, representations, artefacts, institutions, systems or combinations thereof that represent and justify one group's or individual's domination and power by misrepresenting, one-dimensionally presenting or distorting reality in symbolic representations. "Ideology is a reified and mystified semiotic representation of the world" (Fuchs 2020a, 221).

The De Beer's advert presents the diamond ring it sells as the key to women's success in the business world and the world in general. It communicates that women should buy the company's diamond rings and that wearing these rings will make them self-confident and successful leaders and managers in the business world. The diamond ring, which is a thing, is presented as a magic item that has the power to positively transform the lives of the women of the world. In reality, we know that things such as rings do not bring about changes in society. The advert is an ideology that promises women's success through the purchase of luxury goods. The makers of the advert are interested in advancing the sale of diamond rings and increasing De Beer's profits. They do, however, not say so but present an imaginary, invented story about the diamond ring's supposed magic. Like religion, scammers or charlatans, advertising makes empty promises that are not in line with reality.

7.6.3 Commodity Fetishism

Marx stresses that ideologies are practices and modes of thought that make claims that do not accord to reality or present aspects of human existence that are historical and changeable as eternal and unchangeable. In *Capital Volume 1*, Marx (1867, chapter 1.4) devotes a section to *The Fetishism of the Commodity and its Secret*. He analyses commodity fetishism. Commodity fetishism is an aesthetic and ideological dimension of commodities that makes social relations appear as things or as relations between humans and things. In commodity-purchase, we are confronted by money and commodities (things) and do not see the workers who produced the commodities and their working conditions. The economy appears to us in the form of money and commodities. In the world of commodities, the "social relation between" humans takes on "the fantastic form of a relation between things" (Marx 1867, 165). The De Beers advert is an expression of the ideological dimension of commodity fetishism: It promises that a thing will bring about positive changes in women's lives that in reality can only be brought about by humans in social relations. The advert presents the thing (the ring) as a magic transformer and neglects social relations to try to make consumers buy diamond rings.

Sut Jhally (2006) argues that in capitalism, the division of labour makes people work only on one part of the product (see also Jhally 1987). There is a division between mental and physical labour. Commodities come to us through markets; we do not understand their origins. "The social relations of production embedded in goods are systematically hidden from our eyes. The real meaning of goods, in fact, is *emptied* out in capitalist production and consumption" (Jhally 2006, 88). "Production empties. Advertising fills" (Jhally 2006, 89). Advertising is so powerful because it tells stories and provides meanings about goods and the economy that are not presented in other forms. It uses various strategies for doing so, for example, the strategy of black magic: "persons undergo sudden physical transformations", "the commodity can be used to entrance and enrapture other people" (Jhally 2006, 91). "The real function of advertising is not to give people information but to make them feel good" (Jhally 2006, 92). Advertising is a secular form of religion and God. Advertising is a system of commodity fetishism: It promises satisfaction and happiness through the consumption of things (Jhally 2006, 102).

In a way comparable to Jhally, Raymond Williams (1980) argues that advertising is a magic system that promises that the purchase and consumption of commodities magically transform the lives of consumers.

> You do not only buy an object: you buy social respect, admiration, health, beauty, success, power to control your environment. The magic obscures the real sources of general satisfaction because their discovery would involve radical change in the whole common way of life.
>
> (Williams 1980, 189)

Advertising is propaganda that promotes the ideology of human happiness through the consumption of commodities.

De Beer's advert for diamond rings builds on the fact that humans do not know how these rings have been produced as commodity fetishism hides the relations of production. There are no automatic stories associated with De Beer's diamond rings. It uses this void to invent stories, namely the story that wearing its rings makes women successful business leaders. The company uses the advertising strategy of black magic. By buying a De Beer's ring, consumers do not simply buy a ring, but a brand that makes them feel good, important, beautiful, powerful, successful, admirable, etc. In reality, all of these features do not derive from things but from social relations. Advertising is commodity propaganda. It is an ideology that tells stories to try to advance the sale of commodities (see Sussman 2012, 475).

7.6.4 Herman and Chomsky: The Propaganda Model

In their book *Manufacturing Consent. The Political Economy of the Mass Media*, Edward Herman and Noam Chomsky (1994) outline how the Political Economy acts as a filter that creates a kind of economic censorship of the media. They identify five such filters that they together call the Propaganda Model:

(f1) Profit orientation;
(f2) Advertising;

(f3) Dominant information sources;
(f4) Flak;
(f5) Ideology.

The media's profit orientation can have negative effects on reporting (f1). For example, for-profit media might tend to report negatively about those who are critical of the profit principle. Media may rely on dominant information sources and leave out the voices of those who are not powerful (f3). "Flak" were aircraft defence cannons used by the Germans in the Second World War. Herman and Chomsky use the term for arguing that powerful organisations invest money into public relations and lobbying to work against their negative representation in the public sphere and the media (f4). Ideology can shape the mindset of editors and journalists and thereby result in a particular political direction of the medium (f5).

Advertising is one of the five Political Economy filters that Herman and Chomsky discuss (f2). They argue that there is a danger that advertising-funded media distort reality. They make three basic arguments in this context:

1 Advertising fosters concentration and disadvantages for ad-free media:

> With the growth of advertising, papers that attracted ads could afford a copy price well below production costs. This puts papers lacking in advertising at a serious disadvantage: their prices would tend to be higher [...] an advertising-based system will tend to drive out of existence or into marginality the media companies and types that depend of revenue from sales alone.
>
> (Herman and Chomsky 1994, 14)

2 The advertising-circulation-spiral:

> A market share and advertising edge on the part of one paper or television station will give it additional revenue to compete more effectively – promote more aggressively, buy more salable features and programs – and the disadvantaged rival must add expenses it cannot afford to try to stem the cumulative process of dwindling market (and revenue) share.
>
> (Herman and Chomsky 1994, 15)

More media concentration tends to be the consequence of the advertising-circulation-spiral;

3 Conservatism: Advertisers

> choose selectively among programs on the basis of their own principles. With rare exceptions these are culturally and politically conservative. Large corporate advertisers on television will rarely sponsor

programs that engage in serious criticisms of corporate activities, such as the problem of environmental degradation, the workings of the military-industrial complex, or corporate support of and benefits from Third World tyrannies.

(Herman and Chomsky 1994, 17)

The Propaganda Model certainly has limits. It, for example, does not provide a systematic model and does not take aspects of labour into account. Nonetheless, it remains an important mechanism for the analysis of economic censorship (see Fuchs 2018; Pedro-Carañana, Broudy and Klaehn 2018).

7.6.5 Branding

Advertising is always ideological. Branding is an extended type of advertising and therefore of ideology that tries to associate particular lifestyles with certain commodities. "A brand is a name and image associated with a particular production" or company (Turow 2010, 594).

The journalist Naomi Klein is one of the critics of branding. She argues:

The "role of branding has been changing, particularly in the past fifteen years: rather than serving as a guarantee of value on a product, the brand itself has increasingly become the product, a free-standing idea pasted on to innumerable surfaces. The actual product bearing the brand-name has become a medium, like radio or a billboard, to transmit the real message. The message is: It's Nike. It's Disney. It's Microsoft. It's Diesel. It's Caterpillar".

(Klein 2000b)

Savvy ad agencies began to think of themselves as brand factories, hammering out what is of true value: the idea, the lifestyle, the attitude. Out of this heady time, we learnt that Nike was about 'Sport', not shoes; Microsoft about 'Communications', not software; Starbucks about 'Community', not coffee; Virgin about a 'Fun-loving Attitude', not an airline, a record label, a cola, a bridal gown line, a train – or any of the other brand extensions the company has launched. My favourite is Diesel, whose chief executive says he has 'created a movement', not a line of clothes.

(Klein 2000b)

The formula for these brand-driven companies is pretty much the same: get rid of your unionised factories in the west and buy your products from Asian or Central American contractors and sub-contractors. Then, take the money you save and spend it on branding - on advertising, superstores, sponsorships.

(Klein 2000b)

There are several impacts of branding on society (Klein 2000a, 2000b):

1 Branding advances the privatisation of social and cultural infrastructure (e.g. in the form of schools sponsored by brands);
2 Branding restricts choice and advances the concentration of the economy;
3 Branding is expensive and therefore advances the race to save production costs. The consequences are outsourced labour in export-processing zones with low wages, long working hours, military management, toxic workplaces, hazardous work, and a lack of trade unions.

Jim McGuigan (2009) argues branding has been accompanied by the rise of "cool capitalism": Companies present themselves as selling brands that enable a cool lifestyle. Cool capitalism is an expression of:

• Post-Fordist, flexible capitalism (Harvey 1990):
    In contemporary capitalism, products are not mass-produced, but specialised, targeted, personalised, and individualised. This is also characterised by terms such as flexible specialisation and the flexible regime of accumulation;
• Neoliberalism (Harvey 2005):
    Neoliberalism is a form of politics that is based on the privatisation of public goods and services, the commodification of everything, and the individualisation of risk;
• The new spirit of capitalism (Boltanski and Chiapello 2005; see also Chapter 14 in this book):
    The values of 1968, such as anti-authoritarianism, rebellion, authenticity, creativity, freedom, and autonomy, have become part of marketing strategies.

7.7 Protest and Resistance Against Advertising, Branding, and Commodity Culture

There are several strategies that citizens have used for questioning and resisting advertising and consumer capitalism.

7.7.1 Consumer Movements

First, there are consumer movements. The basic idea of consumer protection is to create organisations that lobby for consumer laws that protect consumers from harm caused by corporations. For example, in Germany, there are organisations such as Stiftung Warentest, Verbraucherzentrale Bundesverband, Deutscher Konsumentenbund, Foodwatch or Deutsche Umwelthilfe. In the UK, there are consumer advocacy groups such as Citizen's Advice Bureau or Which? Consumers International is a world federation of consumer groups that has more than 200 member organisations in more than 100 countries. It describes itself as follows:

> We believe in a world where everyone has access to safe and sustainable products and services. [...] [We] empower and champion the rights of consumers everywhere. We are their voice in international policy-making forums and the global marketplace to ensure they are treated safely, fairly and honestly. We are resolutely independent, unconstrained by businesses or political parties.[10]

The United Nations Guidelines for Consumer Protection define 11 consumer rights:

> 1. Access by consumers to essential goods and services; 2. The protection of vulnerable and disadvantaged consumers; 3. The protection of consumers from hazards to their health and safety; 4. The promotion and protection of the economic interests of consumers; 5. Access by consumers to adequate information to enable them to make informed choices according to individual wishes and needs; 6. Consumer education, including education on the environmental, social and economic consequences of consumer choice; 7. Availability of effective consumer dispute resolution and redress; 8. Freedom to form consumer and other relevant groups or organizations and the opportunity of such organizations to present their views in decision-making processes affecting them; 9. The promotion of sustainable consumption patterns; 10. A level of protection for consumers using electronic commerce that is not less than that afforded in other forms of commerce; 11. The protection of consumer privacy and the global free flow of information.
>
> (UNCTAD 2016, 7–8)

7.7.2 Protest: The Example of Adbusters

Second, there are protest movements that among other things question corporations' use of branding and advertising. An example is the consumer advocacy group Adbusters (https://www.adbusters.org/) that edits the popular *Adbusters Magazine* and has engaged in a variety of campaigns and protest actions that question the power of corporations and advertising.

> Since 1989, our international collective of artists, designers, writers, musicians, poets, punks, philosophers and wild hearts has been smashing ads, fighting corruption and speaking truth to power. As a not-for-profit, we put every dollar we raise back into our magazine – and into funding activist campaigns. From Buy Nothing Day to Occupy Wall Street, we've been at the helm of some of our era's defining tone-shifting moments.[11]

The BlackSpot Collective is Adbuster's activist branch (see https://www.ad-busters.org/campaigns). Adbusters frequently produces and publishes spoof ads, which are parodies and fictional advertisements that use the aesthetics of real advertising and branding but are sharp commentaries on capitalism, advertising, and corporate power. Examples can be seen here: https://www.adbusters.org/spoof-ads. In 2011, Adbusters also initiated the Occupy Wall Street movement.

In September 2018, Adbusters organised #OccupySiliconValley, a one-day boycott of Facebook, Google, Apple, and Amazon. The call to action read as follows:

WE
SHUT DOWN
BIG TECH
FOR A
DAY

Big Tech competes for one thing: our attention. They exploit our basic human instincts in the pursuit of unprecedented financial and cultural control.
Facebook claims to connect us, but promotes individualism to its most divisive extreme.
Amazon endorses endless consumption, prodding people to milk mother earth for all she's worth.
Apple infiltrates every strata of our lives, with the HomePod to the Apple Watch, ensuring its role in everything we do.
Google outsources our desires, fears, and thoughts, narrowing the great mystery of life into a manipulating machine.
How do we take on the largest and most corrupt corporate Goliaths to ever exist?
IN 4 STEPS:

1 Google No Search Day
   The ONLY thing we search is: does google do evil?
   We force the megabot to do some soul-searching. [...]

2 Boycott Bezos
   We fill our Amazon shopping carts with giant orders, then abandon them before checkout.
   We flood their servers with imaginary orders never to be fulfilled. [...]

3 Fine Facebook
   We "Report a Problem" and attach an invoice detailing the personal cost of mental health and mutated memory, the hours of time wasted – billed to CEO Mark Zuckerberg.
   We demand payback for the billions of ad dollars Facebook has made from us over the years. [...]

4 Accessorise Apple Stores
   We go to Apple stores and cover their glossy windows with subver-
   sive stickers, slogans, and symbols.[12]

Given that audiences of ad-funded media are workers and users of ad-funded
Internet platforms are digital workers who create ad value, #OccupySilicon-
Valley was not just a consumer boycott, but a digital labour strike (see Fuchs
2020b, chapter 11).

7.7.3 Corporate Watchdogs

Third, there are critical journalists, media, and civil society organisations
that document what corporations do, and what crimes and injustices they
commit. Examples are corporate watchdog organisations such as Corporate Watch (https://corporatewatch.org) and CorpWatch (https://www.cor-
pwatch.org/).

Adbusters is an example of the second and third strategy of consumer
protection. Its spoof ads are an example of culture jamming. Culture jamming is "the practice of parodying advertisements and hijacking billboards
in order to drastically alter their messages" (Klein 2000a, 280). Culture jammers "introduce noise into the signal as it passes from transmitter to receiver,
encouraging idiosyncratic, unintended interpretations. Intruding on the in-
truders, they invest ads, newscasts, and other media artifacts with subver-
sive meanings; simultaneously, they decrypt them, rendering their seductions
impotent" (Dery 2010).

Besides Adbusters, Reverend Billy Talen and the Church of Stop Shopping,
and The Yes Men (https://en.wikipedia.org/wiki/The_Yes_Men) are examples of culture jammers. The Yes Men produced movies such as *The Yes Men*,
The Yes Men Fix the World, and *The Yes Men Are Revolting* where they
document their culture-jamming actions that are not just political statements
and actions but are at the same time funny and satirical.

7.7.4 Regulation

Fourth, there is the potential for governments to pass laws that realise strong
protections for consumers and workers (regulation). This requires, however,
governments that have a strong commitment to workers' rights and consumer rights and is therefore a question of political power in society.

7.7.5 Non-Commercial Alternatives to Advertising-Funded Media

Fifth, non-commercial not-for-profit alternatives to commercial media are
possible and needed. Examples are community media as well as Public Service
Media without advertising.

Public service media (PSM) can provide a countervailing force to advertiser influence not only by sustaining non-commercial media, but by shaping media cultures in ways that influence private media too, for instance through movements of professionals and values between sectors, and by influencing consumer expectations, cultural and policy environments.

(Hardy 2014, 154)

Sixth, there is the possibility that society and its citizens decide that society works better beyond the logic of commodity culture and that they decommodify life and society, which drives back advertising or makes it entirely unnecessary.

7.8 Conclusion

This chapter introduced the Political Economy of advertising. Let us now summarise the main findings.

Finding 1: Defining Advertisements

An advertisement is a paid-for message communicated to the public that aims at making certain information known to the public or creating certain effects or changes. Advertising is the process of the production and distribution of advertisements. Advertisements are promotion messages sold as commodities, which means that the advertiser pays an advertising company for the publication of the advert. In capitalist societies, the use of advertising for advancing capitalist purposes, namely the sale and consumption of commodities, tends to be the primary role of advertising in society.

Finding 2: Advertising and Capitalism

Advertising has developed together with capitalism. Crises of capitalism have often resulted in new phases of capitalist development and along with it in new principles of advertising and retail. Advertising aims at preventing crises, advancing profitability, and stabilising capitalism.

Finding 3: The Audience Commodity

Dallas Smythe (1977) argues in a classical Political Economy of Communication article that in advertising, the audience produces attention as a commodity to programmes and adverts. He says that audiences of ad-financed media are audience workers who produce an audience commodity that advertisers sell to their ad clients. The larger the audience of a medium and its attention, the more interesting it is for advertisers to buy ads that are presented to this audience.

Finding 4: Advertising as Ideology

Advertising is a form of economic positivism that companies use for propagating positive messages about their commodities. They want to make consumers feel good and promise that the purchase and consumption of the advertised commodities have positive impacts on the lifestyle of consumers. Commodity fetishism deprives commodities of meaning by hiding the social relations of the production of commodities. Adverts fill this void by inventing stories that promote commodity sales and consumption. Advertising is a secular form of religion and God. Advertising is a system of commodity fetishism: It promises satisfaction and happiness through the consumption of things.

Finding 5: Resistance Against Advertising, Branding and Commodity Culture

Protest strategies against advertising, branding, and commodity culture include consumer movements, protests, corporate watchdogs, the regulation of advertising, the strengthening of non-commercial not-for-profit alternatives such as Public Service Media and community media, and the decommodification of society.

Notes

1 Data source: Forbes 2000 List of the World's Biggest Public Companies, year 2021, https://www.forbes.com/lists/global2000/, accessed on 10 November 2021.
2 Data source: Forbes 2000 List of the World's Biggest Public Companies, year 2022, https://www.forbes.com/lists/global2000/, accessed on 15 December 2022.
3 https://www.ispot.tv/ad/nkq7/prilosec-otc-how-prilosec-otc-provides-24-hour-heartburn-protection-with-one-pill-a-day, https://m.media-amazon.com/images/I/81s-y37r95L._AC_SL1500_.jpg, accessed on 15 December 2022.
4 https://law.justia.com/cases/federal/district-courts/FSupp2/285/389/2577208/, accessed on 15 December 2022.
5 https://www.bitlaw.com/source/15usc/1125.html, accessed on 15 December 2022.
6 https://www.brh.org.uk/site/2008/04/stop-the-gentrification-of-central-bristol/, accessed on 15 December 2022.
7 Translated from German: „Durch die Aufnahme des Inseratenwesens geriet die Zeitung in eine eigentümliche Zwitterstellung. Sie bringt für den Abonnementpreis nicht mehr bloß Nachrichten und Ansichten zur Veröffentlichung, an die sich ein allgemeines Interesse knüpft, sondern sie dient auch dem Privatverkehr und dem Privatinteresse durch Anzeigen jeder Art, welche ihr speziell vergolten werden. Sie verkauft neue Nachrichten an ihre Leser, und sie verkauft ihren Leserkreis an jedes zahlungsfähige Privatinteresse".
8 https://www.iaaglobal.org/about/mission-and-values, accessed on 14 November 2021.
9 https://zaw.de/about-zaw/, accessed on 14 November 2021.
10 https://www.consumersinternational.org/who-we-are/, accessed on 15 December 2022.
11 https://www.adbusters.org/about-us, accessed on 14 November 2021.
12 https://www.adbusters.org/campaigns/occupy-silicon-valley, accessed on 14 November 2021.

References

Advertising Association. 2013. How Advertising Fuels the UK Economy. London: Advertising Association.

Berger, Arthur Asa. 2011. *Ads, Fads and Consumer Culture. Advertising's Impact on American Character and Society*. Lanham, MD: Rowman & Littlefield. Fourth edition.

Boltanski, Luc and Ève Chiapello. 2005. *The New Spirit of Capitalism*. London: Verso.

Brierley, Sean. 1995. *The Advertising Handbook*. London: Routledge.

Bücher, Karl. 1893/1917. *Die Entstehung der Volkswirtschaft: Vorträge und Aufsätze*. Tübingen: Verlag der H. Laupp'schen Buchhandlung. Zehnte Auflage.

Dery, Mark. 2010. Culture Jamming: Hacking, Slashing, and Sniping in the Empire of Signs. http://markdery.com/?page_id=154 (2010 version).

Doyle, Gillian. 2013. *Understanding Media Economics*. London: Sage. Second edition.

Eagleton, Terry. 1991. *Ideology: An Introduction*. London: Verso.

Engels, Friedrich. 1894. Preface. In Karl Marx: *Capital. Volume 3*, 91–111. London: Penguin.

Fuchs, Christian. 2022. *Digital Capitalism. Media, Communication and Society Volume Three*. London: Routledge.

Fuchs, Christian. 2021. *Social Media: A Critical Introduction*. London: Sage. Third edition.

Fuchs, Christian. 2020a. *Communication and Capitalism. A Critical Theory*. London: University of Westminster Press. DOI: https://doi.org/10.16997/book45

Fuchs, Christian. 2020b. *Marxism: Karl Marx's Fifteen Key Concepts for Cultural and Communication Studies*. New York: Routledge.

Fuchs, Christian. 2018. Propaganda 2.0: Herman and Chomsky's Propaganda Model in the Age of the Internet, Big Data and Social Media. In *The Propaganda Model Today: Filtering Perception and Awareness*, edited by Joan Pedro-Carañana, Daniel Broudy, and Jeffery Klaehn, 71–91. London: University of Westminster Press. DOI: https://doi.org/10.16997/book27.f

Fuchs, Christian. 2017. Raymond Williams' Communicative Materialism. *European Journal of Cultural Studies* 20 (6): 744–762. DOI: https://doi.org/10.1177%2F1367549417732998

Fuchs, Christian. 2012. Dallas Smythe Today – The Audience Commodity, the Digital Labour Debate, Marxist Political Economy and Critical Theory. Prolegomena to a Digital Labour Theory of Value. *tripleC: Communication, Capitalism & Critique* 10 (2): 692–740. DOI: https://doi.org/10.31269/triplec.v10i2.443

Fuchs, Christian. 2008. *Internet and Society. Social Theory in the Information Age*. New York: Routledge.

Hardy, Jonathan. 2014. *Critical Political Economy of the Media: An Introduction*. Abingdon: Routledge.

Harvey, David. 2005. *A Brief History of Neoliberalism*. Oxford: Oxford University Press.

Harvey, David. 1990. *The Condition of Postmodernity. An Enquiry into the Origins of Cultural Change*. Cambridge, MA: Blackwell.

Herman, Edward and Noam Chomsky. 1994. *Manufacturing Consent. The Political Economy of the Mass Media*. London: Vintage Books.

Horkheimer, Max and Theodor W. Adorno. 2002. *Dialectic of Enlightenment. Philosophical Fragments*. Standford, CA: Stanford University Press.

Jessop, Bob. 1992. Fordism and Post-Fordism. A Critical Reformulation. In *Pathways to Regionalism and Industrial Development*, edited by Allen J. Scott and Michael J. Storper, 43–65. London: Routledge.

Jhally, Sut. 2006. *The Spectacle of Accumulation. Essays in Culture, Media, & Politics*. New York: Peter Lang.

Jhally, Sut. 1987. *The Codes of Advertising*. New York: Routledge.

Kaptan, S.S. 2002. *Advertising: New Concepts*. New Delhi: Sarup & Sons.

Klein, Naomi. 2000a. *No Logo. No Space, No Choice, No Job*. London: Flamingo.

Klein, Naomi. 2000b. The Tyranny of Brands. *New Statesman*, 24 January 2000. https://www.afr.com/companies/media-and-marketing/the-tyranny-of-brands-20000211-jl9yw

Knoche, Manfred. 2005. Werbung – ein notwendiges „Lebenselixier" für den Kapitalismus: Zur Kritik der politischen Ökonomie der Werbung. In *Theorie und Praxis der Werbung in den Massenmedien*, edited by Wolfgang Seufert and Jörg Müller-Lietzkow, 239–255. Baden-Baden: Nomos.

Lenzner, Robert and William Heuslein. 1993. The Age of Digital Capitalism. *Forbes* 151 (7): 62–72.

Lotz, Amanda D. 2014. *The Television Will Be Revolutionized*. New York: New York University Press. Second edition.

Maher, Michael. 2016. The Evolution of Product Placement in Film. *Premiumbeat*, 25 March 2016, https://www.premiumbeat.com/blog/product-placement-in-films/

Mandel, Ernest. 1975. *Late Capitalism*. London: NLB.

Marcuse, Herbert. 1964. *One-Dimensional Man. Studies in the Ideology of Advanced Industrial Society*. London: Routledge.

Marx, Karl. 1894. *Capital. Volume 3*. London: Penguin.

Marx, Karl. 1885. *Capital. Volume 2*. London: Penguin.

Marx, Karl. 1867. *Capital. Volume 1*. London: Penguin.

Marx, Karl. 1843. Contribution to the Critique of Hegel's Philosophy of Law: Introduction. In *Marx & Engels Collected Works (MECW) Volume 3*, 19–539. London: Lawrence & Wishart.

Marx, Karl and Friedrich Engels. 1845/1846. The German Ideology. In *Marx & Engels Collected Works Volume 6*, 19–539. London: Lawrence & Wishart.

McGuigan, Jim. 2009. *Cool Capitalism*. London: Pluto.

Meehan, Eileen R. 2002. Gendering the Commodity Audience. In *Sex & Money. Feminism and Political Economy in the Media*, edited by Eileen R. Meehan and Ellen Riordan, 209–222. Minneapolis, MN: University of Minnesota Press.

Murdock, Graham. 2013. Producing Consumerism: Commodities, Ideologies, Practices. In *Critique, Social Media and the Information Society*, edited by Christian Fuchs and Marisol Sandoval, 125–143. New York: Routledge.

Pedro-Carañana, Joan, Daniel Broudy and Jeffery Klaehn. 2018. *The Propaganda Model Today*. London: University of Westminster Press. DOI: https://doi.org/10.16997/book27

Picard, Robert G. 2011. *The Economics and Financing of Media Companies*. New York: Fordham University Press. Second edition.

Picard, Robert G. 2009. A Note on the Relations between Circulation Size and Newspaper Advertising Rates. *Journal of Media Economics* 11 (2): 47–55.

Schiller, Dan. 1999. *Digital Capitalism. Networking the Global Market System.* Cambridge, MA: The MIT Press.

Segrave, Kerry. 2004. *Product Placement Hollywood Films. A History.* Jefferson, NC: McFarland & Company.

Smythe, Dallas W. 1977. Communications: Blindspot of Western Marxism. *Canadian Journal of Political and Social Theory* 1 (3): 1–27.

Smythe, Dallas W. 1954. Reality as Presented by Television. In *Counterclockwise. Perspectives on Communication,* 61–74. Boulder, CO: Westview Press.

Staiger, Janet. 1990. Announcing Wares, Winning Patrons, Voicing Ideals: Thinking about the History and Theory of Film Advertising. *Cinema Journal* 29 (3): 3–31.

Sussman, Gerald. 2012. Systemic Propaganda as Ideology and Productive Exchange. tripleC: *Communication, Capitalism & Critique* 10 (2): 474–487. DOI: https://doi.org/10.31269/triplec.v10i2.370

Turow, Joseph. 2010. *Media Today. An Introduction to Mass Communication.* New York: Routledge. Third edition.

UNCTAD (United Nations Conference on Trade and Development). 2016. *United Nations Guidelines for Consumer Protection.* New York: United Nations.

Williams, Raymond. 1980. Advertising: The Magic System. In *Culture and Materialism,* 170–194. London: Verso.

Williams, Raymond. 1974. *Television. Technology and Cultural Form.* Abingdon: Routledge.

Williamson, Judith. 1979. *Decoding Advertisements: Ideology and Meaning in Advertising.* London: Marion Boyars.

Recommended Readings and Exercises

Readings

The following texts are recommended as accompanying readings to this chapter:

Graham Murdock. 2013. Producing Consumerism: Commodities, Ideologies, Practices. In *Critique, Social Media and the Information Society*, edited by Christian Fuchs and Marisol Sandoval, 125–143. New York: Routledge. Chapter 7.

Dallas W. Smythe. 1977. Communications: Blindspot of Western Marxism. *Canadian Journal of Political and Social Theory* 1 (3): 1–27. Can be downloaded from: https://journals.uvic.ca/index.php/ctheory/article/view/13715

Christian Fuchs. 2020. *Marxism: Karl Marx's Fifteen Key Concepts for Cultural and Communication Studies.* New York: Routledge.
Chapter 9: Ideology (pp. 178–204).
Chapter 11: Class Struggles (pp. 247–279).

Sut Jhally. 1989. Advertising as Religion: The Dialectic of Technology and Magic. In *Cultural Politics in Contemporary America*, edited by Sut Jhally and Ian H. Angus, 217–229. London: Routledge.

Also in: Sut Jhally. 2006. *The Spectacle of Accumulation. Essays in Culture, Media, & Politics*. New York: Peter Lang. pp. 85–98.

Naomi Klein. 2000. *No Logo. No Space, No Choice, No Job*. London: Flamingo.
Chapter 12: Culture Jamming: Ads under Attack (pp. 279–310).

Eileen R. Meehan. 2002. Gendering the Commodity Audience. In *Sex & Money. Feminism and Political Economy in the Media*, edited by Eileen R. Meehan and Ellen Riordan, 209–222. Minneapolis, MN: University of Minnesota Press.
Also published in:
Eileen Meehan. 2006. Gendering the Commodity Audience. Critical Media Research, Feminism, and Political Economy. In *Media and Cultural Studies. KeyWorks*, edited by Meenakshi Gigi Durham and Douglas Kellner, 311–321. Malden, MA: Blackwell. Revised edition Chapter 19.

Jim McGuigan. 2009. *Cool Capitalism*. London: Pluto.
Chapter 3: Consumer Culture (pp. 83–128).

Jonathan Hardy. 2014. *Critical Political Economy of the Media: An Introduction*. Abingdon: Routledge.
Chapter 6: Marketing Communications and Media (pp. 135–156).

Exercise 7.5   Assessing Advertising's Roles in Society

Part 1

Think about the following question:
What arguments will a manager of an advertising agency or of a marketing/advertising department of a large company have if asked "Why do we need advertising? What are the advantages of advertising?"

Write down these arguments.

If you study in a group, then compare the arguments to each other.

Part 2

If you work alone:
Your task is to formulate an argument that a critic of advertising and marketing might make against the ad manager who makes the first argument in favour of advertising. Ask yourself: What dangers of

advertisements do critics of advertising see for society and the individual? Respond to the arguments in the first part by formulating a counter-argument that is critical of and opposed to advertising.

If you work in a group of students:
Each student comments on the argument made by another student (in the role of an advertising manager) in the first part. Your task is to formulate an argument that a critic of advertising and marketing might make against the ad manager who makes the first argument in favour of advertising.

Ask yourself: What dangers of advertisements do critics of advertising see for society and the individual? How do you assess those arguments that speak in favour of advertising and those that are critical of advertising?

If you need some help with this exercise, then you can search online for the pros and cons, advantages and challenges/risks of advertising. You should, however, formulate arguments in your own words. You can also have a look at the chapters in the following book:

Carol J. Pardun, ed. 2014. *Advertising and Society. An Introduction.* Malden, MA: Wiley Blackwell. Second edition.

Exercise 7.6   How Ideology Works in Advertisements

Ideology is about deception and the attempt to manipulate. An ideology tries to deceive humans so that they believe certain things that are not true. Advertising is an ideology that tries to make consumers believe that they need a certain commodity and that a commodity and the company producing it will improve the consumers' lives. In this exercise, you analyse how ideology works in an example advertisement you choose yourself.

Follow the steps of this exercise.

Step 1:
Choose one large transnational corporation. Choose one that uses lots of advertisements to market its commodities (e.g. in magazines, on

television, online ads, targeted digital ads, posters). It is best you first check if a company you are interested in has ads that are worth analysing. You can, for example, choose one of the world's 2,000 largest companies that are listed in the Forbes 2000 List or the Fortune Global 500 List:

https://fortune.com/global500/2019/search/
https://www.forbes.com/global2000/

The companies in these two lists are the world's biggest and most powerful global corporations. But you can also choose any other transnational corporation that uses lots of advertisements.

Step 2:
Search for an advertisement of this company that makes promises that are deceptive and that seem to be ideological. Document this advertisement: If it's an online ad, download it or make a screenshot. If it's a poster in a public space, take a picture of it with your mobile phone. If it's a video ad, download the video or take a screen recording of the video.

Step 3:
Analyse what ideologies are present in the ad and how ideology is communicated in it.
Use the Advertising Analysis Guide that you find in Annex 7.1 to this chapter. It documents how to analyse ideology in advertisements.
Also, remember the discussion of how ads work in Chapter 7.

Step 4:
Write around 200–800 words that analyse the selected ad and how ideology works in it.

Step 5:
Create a blog post that contains the following:

* a description of the selected company
* a description (and if it exists) a link to the analysed ad(s)
* your description and analysis of the ad (200–800 words)

Exercise 7.7   The Political Economy of Brands

Sut Jhally (director). 2003. *No Logo: Brands. Globalization. Resistance.*
Media Education Foundation.
Movie information:
https://www.imdb.com/title/tt0373193
https://shop.mediaed.org/no-logo-p115.aspx

Naomi Klein is a Canadian journalist, author, filmmaker and activist.
She became well-known after publishing the book *No Logo*, which
deals with the impacts of brands and advertising on society. The Media
Education Foundation produced a documentary about the book.

Watch the film *No Logo*. In addition, you can read some or all of the
chapters in the accompanying book:

Naomi Klein. 2000. *No Logo. No Space, No Choice, No Job.* London:
Flamingo.

Discuss the following questions in groups.

* Why do you think some consumers are so interested in buying brand-
  name commodities?

* Are there certain brands that you particularly like or are a fan of?
  Why?

* Are there certain brands you would never buy? If so, why?

* Try to give some examples of lifestyle branding. What are the effects
  of lifestyle branding on society? How do you assess lifestyle branding?

* Imagine a society without brands and advertising. How is this society
  different from contemporary societies?

Exercise 7.8   The Yes Men

The Yes Men are a group of culture jammers. Watch one of their movies.

Dan Ollman, Sarah Price, and Chris Smith (directors). 2005. *The Yes
Men.* Yes Men Films LLC. Movie information: https://www.imdb.com/
title/tt0379593/

Andy Bichlbaum, Mike Bonanno, and Kurt Engfehr (directors). 2009. *The Yes Men Fix the World*. ARTE, Article Z, Renegade Pictures Movie information: https://www.imdb.com/title/tt1352852/

Andy Bichlbaum, Mike Bonanno, and Laura Nix (directors). 2014. *The Yes Men Are Revolting*. Gebrüder Beetz Filmproduktion, Chili Film, Pieter Van Huystee Film and Television. Movie information: https://www.imdb.com/title/tt2531282

Select one movie scene that you found particularly interesting. Discuss:

What is culture jamming?
What are the particular features of the Yes Men's version of culture jamming?
How do you assess The Yes Men's movies and strategy?

Exercise 7.9   Create a Political Economy Meme

Work in groups or individually. Create a meme about a transnational media company. A meme is an "an image, a video, a piece of text, etc. that is passed very quickly from one internet user to another, often with slight changes that make it humorous" (Oxford English Dictionary: https://www.oxfordlearnersdictionaries.com/definition/english/meme, accessed on 15 December 2022)

Choose one transnational media corporation. Create a satirical meme about this company that criticises an aspect of this company.

Meme tools:
https://imgflip.com/memegenerator
http://www.makeameme.org/memegenerator
http://memebetter.com/generator

There can be more than one meme per company, so don't worry if there is already a meme about the company you are interested in, you can create another one. Try to spread your meme on the Internet and social media.

Annex 7.1   Advertising Analysis Guide: Ideology in Advertisements

Ask yourself:

* To **whom** does the ad appeal/speak? To whom does it **not** appeal to?

* **What** meanings does it communicate? What does it want the viewer to think and do?

* **How** does it communicate these meanings?

* **Which moral values** does it consciously or unconsciously address and appeal to? Which moral values does it **exclude**?

* What **false promises** does the advertisement make? How does it make such promises?

* Does the advertisement try to **deceive or manipulate** the audience? If so, how?

* Do **ideologies** such as consumerism/consumer culture, sexism, racism, nationalism play a role in the advertisement? If so, how is ideology represented?

You can also ask some of the following questions:

Which company owns the magazine you analyse? Which other media does it own? Who are the owners of the company? In which countries does the company operate? Is it a rather small or large company (employees, profits, etc.)?

Which media company runs the ad that you analyse? What kind of products does this company sell (make a list by looking at its website)? Is it only active in one industry or in multiple ones, in which one(s)? How large are the annual profits of the company and its advertising spending (see: company website, company annual report, SEC-filings form 10-K, forms 10-Q)?

Which group does the ad you analyse address? Which groups does it not address/exclude? What are the typical socio-demographic characteristics of the group that the ad appeals to (gender, class, income, age, education, jobs, location, place of living (home owner, etc.), origin/ethnicity, lifestyles, consumer behaviour, mobility, typical goods that this group possesses and is interested in, etc.)?

Which product or service is advertised? What is the role of this product or service in society?

What is the main message of the ad? Which visual and textual elements and strategies does it use for communicating this message? Does the ad use metaphors, symbols and hidden meanings that are represented in specific forms? If so, which ones? How are they expressed in visual and textual form?

Information: Typical elements in ads that have a specific meaning can include characteristics of the persons shown (hair colour, hairstyle, hair length, eye colour, facial expressions, body type, age, gender, race, body language, make-up, clothes, eyeglasses, earrings, body adornments), settings, social relationships shown or implied, power relationships between the persons or groups shown, spatiality, signs of education level, signs of occupations, shown objects, activities, background, lightning (sound, music), colours, typefaces, design, words used, questions asked, textual metaphors, associations, use of negations in texts, use of affirmations in texts, arguments, appeals, slogans, headlines, paradoxes, tone and style of the text, the way the reader/viewer is addressed, angle of photographs.

Make a list of five values that you consider important for life and society.

Are there any specific values expressed in the advertisement (e.g. individualism, individuality, sexual desire, jealousy, hard work, patriotism, nationalism, success, power, good taste)? How are these values expressed? Why are they expressed and what picture of society do they communicate? Compare the values in the ad to your values listed previously. Are there commonalities/differences? Are there any myths, biases, ideologies or stereotypes present in the ad? If so, which ones?

What image of society does the company express in this ad? How does it present society in the ad? Do you agree or disagree with this presentation of reality? Is it a realistic picture of society as it is or not? Are there important dimensions of society that are left out? If so, which ones?

Does the ad appeal to any specific conscious or subliminal human wishes, desires and fantasies? If so, how?

8   The Political Economy
of Global Media

What You Will Learn in This Chapter

- You will learn why capitalism is a global system;
- You will learn what global media corporations are all about;
- You will learn about how to think about global capitalism in the context of the media and culture.

8.1 Introduction

Think of a news organisation such as CNN. It has its headquarters in the USA but operates globally and tries to cover all parts of the world. Other global news organisations include Al Jazeera, BBC World Service, CGTN, Deutsche Welle, France 24, and Russia Today. With the globalisation of societies and the economy since the 1970s, also the world of the media has become more globalised. The media have for a long time had an international dimension, which has been intensified since the 1970s. The emergence of the Internet as global information and communication technology has played an important role in this context. This chapter is focused on the global and international dimension of the media.

This chapter asks: How does the political economy of global media look like?

Section 8.2 deals with the question: What is globalisation? Section 8.3 discusses global media. Section 8.4 is focused on cultural imperialism. Section 8.5 analyses China in the context of the world system and the media. Section 8.6 presents some conclusions.

8.2 What Is Globalisation?

Conduct Exercise 8.1.

DOI: 10.4324/9781003391203-10

Exercise 8.1   David Harvey: Crises of Capitalism

David Harvey is one of the most-cited social scientists and one of the
primary representatives of Critical/Marxist Political Economy. Watch
the RSA Animate video "Crises of Capitalism", an animation of parts
of a talk by David Harvey. RSA Animate is a project by the Royal
Society of Arts. "The RSA Animate series was conceived as an innovative, accessible and unique way of illustrating and sharing [...] world-
changing ideas" (http://www.thersa.org/events/rsaanimate, accessed on
21 November 2021).

RSA Animate: David Harvey: "Crises of Capitalism":
https://www.youtube.com/watch?v=qOP2V_np2c0

Discuss:

How does Harvey analyse the 2007/2008 crisis of capitalism?
What has been the role of globalisation and how does Harvey mention
it in the context of capitalism since the 1970s?
What is global capitalism?

Harvey (2010, 47) says that capital "cannot abide [...] limits" (Harvey
2010, 47).

> Capitalism has so far survived in the face of many predictions of its
> imminent demise. This record suggests that it has sufficient fluidity and
> flexibility to overcome all limits, though not, as the history of periodic
> crises also demonstrates, without violent corrections.
>
> (Harvey 2010, 46)

Harvey here reflects an insight by Marx: "Capital is the endless and limitless
drive to go beyond its limiting barrier" (Marx 1857/1858, 334).

8.2.1 Globalisation and Capital Accumulation

Figure 8.1 visualises the process of the accumulation of capital as Marx
(1867, 1885) analysed it.
   An explanation of the symbols in Figure 8.1:

M ... money
C ... commodities
L ... labour-power
Mp ... means of production

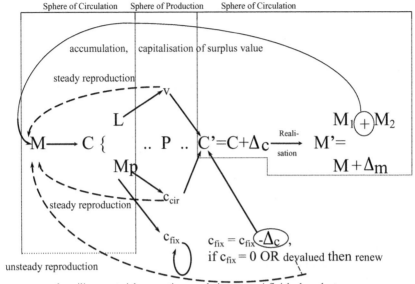

Sphere of Circulation   Sphere of Production   Sphere of Circulation

Figure 8.1 The accumulation of capital.

P ... production
C' ... a new commodity
M' ... more money
c_{cir} ... circulating constant capital
c_{fix} ... fixed constant capital
v ... variable capital

In capitalist production, capitalists invest money M for purchasing labour-power L (variable capital v) and means of production Mp (constant capital c). In the production process P, workers use the means of production for producing new commodities C' that are more than the initially purchased commodities. These commodities are offered on markets. If their sale succeeds, then a sum of money capital M' is generated that is larger than the invested capital M. A profit over the investment costs has been realised. Parts of the achieved capital and the profit are reinvested so that more commodities can be produced and offered for sale.

In the accumulation process M – C .. P .. C' – M', capital requires the following:

1 labour-power;
2 means of production (raw materials, technologies, infrastructure);
3 commodity markets;
4 capital, capital investment.

Marx describes capitalism's goal in the following manner:

> Accumulate, accumulate! That is Moses and the prophets! [...] Accumulation for the sake of accumulation, production for the sake of production: this was the formula in which classical economics expressed the historical mission of the bourgeoisie in the period of its domination.
>
> (Marx 1867, 742)

"Accumulation is the engine which powers growth under the capitalist mode of production. The capitalist system is therefore highly dynamic and inevitably expansionary" (Harvey 2001, 237).

Capital drives beyond national boundaries and organises itself on a transnational scale in order to find

1 cheap labour;
2 cheap means of production;
3 commodity markets; and
4 investment opportunities.

Competition drives capitalists to seek ever-cheaper spaces of production: "The coercive laws of competition push capitalists to relocate production to more advantageous sites" (Harvey 2006, 98). New transport and communication technologies are the medium and outcome of the globalisation of capitalism:

> The "revolution in the modes of production of industry and agriculture made necessary a revolution in the general conditions of the social process of production, i.e. in the means of communication and transport. [...] the means of communication and transport gradually adapted themselves to the mode of production of large-scale industry by means of a system of river steamers, railways, ocean steamers and telegraphs".
>
> (Marx 1867, 505–506)

It is no accident that the Internet became so important in a new phase of the globalisation of capitalism. The Internet is medium and outcome of the globalisation of capitalism since the 1970s. This phase of capitalist globalisation required appropriate means of communication and transport, which enforced the development and diffusion of the Internet. This means that the Internet was an outcome of the drive to globalise capitalism. At the same time, it is one of the means that was used for globalising capitalism.

The globalisation of production lengthens the turnover time of capital, the total time it takes to produce and sell commodities, because the commodities have to be transported from one place to another (Harvey 2001, 244). Therefore, capitalists try to develop technological innovations in transport and communications in order to speed up the production and distribution of commodities and the circulation of capital. "Economy of time, to this all economy ultimately reduces itself" (Marx 1857/1858, 173).

Marx analyses the connection between the globalisation of capitalism and the means of communication and transport in the following manner:

> The more production comes to rest on exchange value, hence on exchange, the more important do the physical conditions of exchange – the means of communication and transport – become for the costs of circulation. Capital by its nature drives beyond every spatial barrier. Thus the creation of the physical conditions of exchange – of the means of communication and transport – the annihilation of space by time – becomes an extraordinary necessity for it. Only in so far as the direct product can be realized in distant markets in mass quantities in proportion to reductions in the transport costs, and only in so far as at the same time the means of communication and transport themselves can yield spheres of realization for labour, driven by capital; only in so far as commercial traffic takes place in massive volume – in which more than necessary labour is replaced – only to that extent is the production of cheap means of communication and transport a condition for production based on capital, and promoted by it *for that reason*.
> (Marx 1857/58, 524–525)

Harvey (2000) argues that capitalism has been undergoing a new phase of globalisation that consists of four recent interconnected developments:

- financial deregulation;
- a new wave of technological innovation;
- the rise of the Internet;
- technological innovation has continuously cheapened transport and communications.

The globalisation of society and communication is not new. In 1866, the transatlantic cable enabled rapid communication across continents. Already in the late 19th and early 20th centuries, transnational communication organisations emerged such as the big news agencies Haves (France), Reuters (UK), and Wolff (Germany).

Vincent Mosco (2009, 170) gives an example that shows that modern technologies have enabled humans to cross spatial distances at an accelerating speed: The distance between London and Edinburgh is 530 kilometres. In 1658, the journey by stagecoach took 20,000 minutes, which is 333 hours 20 minutes or almost 2 weeks. In 1840, travel on the modernised stage took 2,500 minutes, which is 41 hours and 40 minutes. In 1850, travelling from London to Edinburgh by rail took 800 minutes, which is 13 hours and 20 minutes. In 1970, air travel from the one to the other city took 3 hours and 20 minutes. In 2013, the London-Edinburgh destination by plane took 1 hour and 20 minutes, and in 2021, 1 hour and 15 minutes.

8.2.2   *Capitalist Globalisation's Consequences*

The globalisation of capitalism has several consequences:

- The global outsourcing of labour and the creation of precarious jobs:

  Offshore production that began in the 1960s suddenly became much more general. [...] The geographical dispersal and fragmentation of production systems, divisions of labor, and specializations of tasks ensued, albeit often in the midst of an increasing centralization of corporate power through mergers, takeovers, or joint production agreements which transcended national boundaries. Corporations have more power to command space, making individual places much more vulnerable to their whims.

  (Harvey 2000, 63)

- Global migration;
- Hyper-urbanisation;
- Neoliberal competition states (Jessop 2002):

  "In its neo-liberal configuration, the state functions more clearly now as an 'executive committee of capitalist class interests' than at any other time in history" (Harvey 2006, 106);

- Global environmental and political problems and risks:

  Ulrich Beck argues that a world risk society (Beck 1999) has emerged. One should, however, add that there is a capitalist world risk society where the rich can avoid and manage many risks with their money, while the poor cannot escape risks. There are the globalised rich and the localised poor (Bauman 1998);

- The globalisation of culture:

  Cultural goods circulate globally, which means that there is also a globalisation of cultural practices. Benjamin Barber (2003) speaks in the context of a cultural antagonism between Jihad and McWorld. The globalisation of capitalist culture ("McDonaldisation", "CocaColonisation", "Disneyfication", "cultural imperialism") creates a global culture on the one hand and opposition to it on the other hand, such as in the form of religious fundamentalism and terrorism;

- Spatial agglomeration (Mosco 2009, 169–175):

> "The need to minimize circulation costs as well as turnover times pro-
> motes agglomeration of production within a few large urban centers
> which become, in effect, the workshops of capitalist production" (Har-
> vey 2001, 245). Geographical expansion goes hand in hand with geo-
> graphical concentration (Harvey 2001, 246).

The economic globalisation of capitalism has been accompanied by the
emergence of global cities that are agglomerations of capital, companies,
banks, infrastructure, corporate headquarters, service industries, international financial services, telecommunication facilities, etc. Both the rich and
the very poor can be found in these cities; the hierarchically segmented social
space is reflected in a segmented urban space where one can find protected
rich areas besides ghettos. "The more globally the economy becomes, the
higher the agglomeration of central functions in a relatively few sites, that is,
the global cities" (Sassen 1991, 5). Global cities "concentrate the infrastructure and the servicing that produce a capability for global control" (Sassen
1995, 63). Examples of global cities are New York, London, Tokyo, Paris,
Frankfurt, Zurich, Amsterdam, Los Angeles, Sydney, São Paulo, Mexico
City, and Hong Kong. "[S]patial agglomeration enforces new hierarchies
that concentrate wealth and power in some cities while others decline"
(Mosco 2009, 174).

Neoliberalism is an ideology and policy regime that sees private
ownership, the commodity form and commercialism as the best forms for
providing goods and services. It combines four processes: commercialisation, liberalisation, privatisation as well as the internationalisation of
capital.

Commercialisation means the introduction of for-profit logic and companies that sell commodities in order to achieve profit. Liberalisation refers to
the creation of markets where capitals compete against each other. Privatisation means that public services and nationalised industries are turned into
privately owned for-profit companies. The internationalisation of capitalism
is the creation of transnational corporations that invest, exploit labour, and
sell commodities at the international level.

8.2.3 The Commercialisation, Liberalisation and Globalisation of Telecommunications

Let us have a look at the example of telecommunications in the UK. British
Telecom (BT) was founded in 1846 as Electric Telegraph Company. It was
the world's first public service telegraph company. Public telecommunications companies have universal service obligations that ensure that basic
communications services are available to all citizens at an affordable price.

Such an obligation is more difficult to realise when for-profit logic is applied. In 1984, BT was privatised, and along with it, commercial logic was introduced. A market for telecommunications was introduced, which means that for-profit companies were allowed to compete for the sales of telecommunications connections as a commodity. This was the process of the *commercialisation* and *liberalisation* of telecommunications. It was enacted by the Telecommunications Act 1984. In the European Union, EU Directive 96/19/ EC *enforced the liberalisation of telecommunications markets in the EU member states.* The British telecommunications industry was the first nationalised industry that the Conservative Thatcher government *privatised.* In 1984, more than 50% of BT were sold as shares. In 1991, the British government sold half of its shares, reducing its stake to 21.8%. In 1993, the rest of the publicly owned shares were sold. The UK telecommunications market has also been *internationalised.* In 2021, the largest mobile operators were BT, O2 (global operator, owned by the Spanish telecommunications company Telefónica), Vodafone (global operator with headquarters in the UK), and Three (telecommunications company with headquarters in Hong Kong).

After the end of the Nazi regime in Germany and the Second World War, the new democratic German state created the Deutsche Bundespost (German Federal Post Office) in 1947. It also held a telecommunications monopoly with a universal service obligation. In 1989, the Post Reform Act I (Postreform I) split Deutsche Bundespost into three companies, one focused on the postal service, one on the post office bank, and one on telecommunications. In 1993, the *internationalisation* of German telecommunications started when Deutsche Telekom acquired parts of the Hungarian telecom company Matáv. Telekom thereby became an internationally operating company. In 1994, the Post Reform Act II (Postreform II) created Deutsche Telekom AG. In 1996, Deutsche Telekom made an initial public offering. It became a publicly traded company, which meant its *privatisation.* In 1996, the Post Reform Act III (Postreform III) *liberalised* the German telecommunications market. The German government thereby realised the European Union's Directive 96/19/EC that enforced *the liberalisation of telecommunications markets in its member states. The liberalisation also brought along the commercialisation of telecommunications so that for-profit oriented companies started to compete for customers to whom they sell access to communication networks as commodities. In 2021, the German state held 31.9% of Deutsche Telekom's shares and the largest private shareholder was the Japanese SoftBank Group,*[1] *which is another aspect of internationalisation. In 2021, the three largest mobile phone network providers were Deutsche Telekom, Vodafone (transnational telecommunications corporation with headquarters in the UK), and Telefónica Deutschland (subsidiary of the Spain-based international telecom corporation Telefónica).*[2]

8.3 Global Media

8.3.1 The Power of Transnational Corporations

The Forbes 2000 List is an annual list of the world's biggest public companies. In 2021, the total sales of these 2,000 companies were US$ 47.8 trillion; in 2020, US$ 39.8 trillion; and in 2019, US$ 42.3 trillion.[3] The world GDP was US$ 96.1 trillion in 2021, US$ 84.9 in 2020 and US$ 87.7 in 2019.[4] We can therefore calculate the share of the world's largest 2,000 corporations' revenues in world GDP:

2021: 49.7%;
2020: 46.9%;
2019: 48.3%.

Table 8.1 shows similar values for the years from 2007 until 2021.

The share of revenues of the world's largest 2,000 corporations in the global GDP has continuously been around 50%, which shows the power of transnational corporations.

Table 8.1 Share of the revenues of the world's largest 2,000 corporations in the global GDP

Year	Share (%)
2007	51.0
2008	50.0
2009	49.3
2010	48.6
2011	49.0
2012	50.9
2013	49.6
2014	48.9
2015	46.8
2016	46.2
2017	47.9
2018	47.6
2019	48.3
2020	46.9
2021	49.7

Data source: Forbes 2000, 2008–2021 (revenues), WDI (world GDP in current US$, accessed on 15 December 2022).

8.3.2 The Transnationality Index

The question arises how *global* large corporations, including media corporations, actually are. Some scholars have voiced doubts. Kai Hafez (2007, 159) argues: "Media capital's lack of global reach is [...] the key reason why the globalization of the media today is taking place to a far more modest degree and at a far slower pace than is generally assumed". Terry Flew (2007, 87) lists data on the foreign asset share, the Transnationality Index, and the foreign revenue share of Time Warner, Disney, News Corporation, and Viacom for the year 2005 in order to argue that "media corporations are less globalized than major corporations in other sectors", that globalisation of media and entertainment is moving slowly, and that News Corporation is the only truly global media company (Flew 2007, 87–88). Colin Sparks (2007, 172–174) analyses the foreign assets and sales of News Corporation, Viacom, and Time Warner (for 2002 respectively 2004) and argues that global media are "centred in a single 'home' country" (Sparks 2007, 174).

The Transnationality Index (TNI) is published in the World Investment Report. It is a composite index that is calculated for a company as the average of its foreign asset share, foreign revenue share, and foreign employee share. Table 8.2 displays the average TNI for the world's largest 100 transnational corporations (TNCs) and all the informational TNCs under these 100 TNCs. Table 8.3 shows how the average TNI of informational TNCs for the year 2020 has been calculated. For calculating these shares, I treated all companies (respectively information companies) as a totality (what Marx termed "collective capital"; Marx 1867, 344) so that the shares were calculated based on aggregated values.

Table 8.2 Average Transnationality Index of the world's largest TNCs and informational TNCs

	100 TNCs (%)	Informational TNCs
2001	55.7	60.2%, N = 26
2002	57.0	55.0%, N = 22
2003	55.8	55.3%, N = 21
2004	56.8	55.9%, N = 21
2005	59.9	59.5%, N = 20
2006	61.6	61.7%, N = 18
2011	54.4	58.6%, N = 22
2012	67.1	64.8%, N = 16
2020	60.5	52.8%, N = 21
2021	61.6	52.8%, N = 21

Data source: World Investment Report 2012, 2013, 2021 and 2022.

Table 8.3 TNI of informational TNCs

Ranking by TNI	Corporation	Home Economy	Industry	TNI (in %)
28	Deutsche Telekom AG	Germany	Telecommunications	76.8
11	Vodafone Group Plc	UK	Telecommunications	89.2
4	Hon Hai Precision Industries	Taiwan	Electronic components	97.5
77	Microsoft Corporation	USA	Computer and Data Processing	44.6
79	Huawei Investment & Holding Co., Ltd	China	Communications equipment	43.5
81	Apple Inc	USA	Computer Equipment	38.4
86	Alphabet Inc	USA	Computer and Data Processing	36.3
37	Telefonica SA	Spain	Telecommunications	74.5
62	Samsung Electronics Co., Ltd.	Korea, Republic of	Communications equipment	56.8
99	Tencent Holdings Limited	China	Computer and Data Processing	15.4
94	Amazon.com, Inc	USA	E-Commerce	24.7
88	Nippon Telegraph & Telephone Corporation	Japan	Telecommunications	34.1
31	SAP SE	Germany	Computer and Data Processing	76.2
74	Sony Group Corp	Japan	Consumer electronics	48.0
93	Comcast Corp	USA	Telecommunications	25.2
73	Orange SA	France	Telecommunications	48.2
78	IBM Corp	USA	Computer and Data Processing	43.9
66	Intel Corporation	USA	Electronic components	53.5
67	Oracle Corporation	USA	Computer and Data Processing	53.2
64	Legend Holdings Corporation	China	Computer and data processing	56.1
96	Comcast Corp	USA	Telecommunication	72.4
			Average:	52.8

Data source: World Investment Report 2022, N = 21.

The data shows that there is a bit of variation of the Transnationality Index over the years, but by and large, we can see that on average the majority of the assets, revenues, and employees are located outside of the country in which the company headquarters are located.

The data shows that the TNI of the largest information corporations has overall been quite close to the total average and that the information companies covered by the TNI are more global than local in their operations, which casts doubt on the assumption (made by Flew, Hafez, and others) that there are no global media corporations.

8.3.3 Global Media

Edward Herman and Robert McChesney (1997; see also McChesney 1999, 78–118) argue that global media advance corporate expansion by advertising and create an ideological environment for a global profit-driven social order. Neoliberalism and mergers and acquisitions would have resulted in a tiered global media system dominated by a small number of colossal, vertically integrated media conglomerates (measured by annual sales). The main feature of the global media system is for Herman and McChesney (1997, 152) the global implantation of a model of privately owned commercial media. Possible negative effects would be the global spread of consumption as lifestyle, the displacement of the public sphere with entertainment, the strengthening of conservative political forces, and the erosion of local cultures (Herman and McChesney 1997, 154–155). The "global media system is best perceived as one that best represents the needs of investors, advertisers, and the affluent consumers of the world" (McChesney 1999, 107). What is new is an "increasing TNC control over media distribution and content within nations. Prior to the 1980s and 1990s, national media systems were typified by nationally owned radio and television systems, as well as domestic newspaper industries" (McChesney 1999, 80).

Herman and McChesney (1997, 34–38) argue that a global corporate ideology has spread that consists of the following elements:

- The market is the best means for organising the economy;
- Government intervention and regulation should be minimised;
- Profit growth is the most important goal in society;
- Privatisation is desirable.

Tables 8.4 and 8.5 show an analysis of financial data of the world's largest 2,000 transnational corporations for the years 2013 and 2018. The company-level data has been reorganised and combined at the level of industries.

Transnational capitalism is dominated by finance capital, followed by information capital, energy capital, and mobility capital. Global capitalism is not only informational capitalism, but also finance capitalism, hyperindustrial capitalism, and mobility capitalism.

Table 8.4 Share of the five largest industries in the capital assets of the world's 2000 largest companies

Rank	Industry	Number of Companies	Share of Capital Assets (%)
1	Finance	496	73.9
2	Information	253	4.6
3	Oil and gas	139	4.1
4	Transport	153	3.2
5	Utilities	93	2.6

Data source: Forbes 2000 List of the World's Largest Public Companies, 2013 list.

Table 8.5 Share of specific industries in the profits, revenues and assets of the world's largest 2000 transnational corporations

Industry	No. of Companies	Share of Sales (%)	Share of Profits (%)	Share of Assets (%)
Conglomerates	36	2.0	1.1	0.9
Culture and Digital	260	14.6	17.7	5.1
Energy and Utilities	199	14.3	9.8	5.7
Fashion	26	1.0	0.9	0.0
FIRE (finance, insurance, and real estate)	634	22.5	33.7	74.8
Food	86	3.6	5.8	1.2
Manufacturing and Construction	352	15.2	13.1	5.4
Mobility and Transport	169	11.6	9.4	3.6
Pharmaceutical and Medical	105	7.2	4.9	1.9
Retail	86	6.9	2.5	0.9
Security	1	0.0	0.0	0.0
Various Services	46	1.1	1.1	0.4

Data source: Forbes 2000 List of the World's Largest Public Companies, year 2018.

Klaus Beck (2018, 361–366) identifies three levels of the globalisation and internationalisation of the media: the micro-level (audience), the meso-level (media companies and their services), the macro-level (media structures and media markets).

At the micro-level, media globalisation is about the consumption of media by the audience. The consumption of press, TV news, and radio is very local, regional and national, and film and music are much more international.

At the meso-level, media globalisation is about internationalisation through the export of media products, international licensing of media products, joint ventures, and foreign direct investment.

At the macro-level, we find, for example, the internationally oriented film and music markets and international capital investments in media companies.

8.3.4 Examples of Global Media

Bertelsmann is a global media company based in Gütersloh, Germany, with over 130,000 employees. There are eight divisions: Arvato (business services), Bertelsmann Education Group, Bertelsmann Investments, Bertelsmann Printing Group (printing industry), BMG (music), Gruner+Jahr (magazines and newspapers), Penguin Random House (250 publishers), and RTL Group (TV, radio, TV rights, Internet, content production).[5]

Penguin Random House is part of Bertelsmann and the largest book publishing group in the world (over 200 publishers). It operates globally. Its published authors include Jane Austen, George Orwell, and Aldous Huxley. BMG is a global music publisher and subsidiary of Bertelsmann. Musicians distributed include the Rolling Stones, David Bowie, Nena, and Iggy Pop.

Deutsche Telekom is active in more than fifty countries and has more than 200,000 employees.[6] Bertelsmann and Deutsche Telekom are examples of German companies that operate internationally.

8.3.5 The Development of the World Economy

Let us now have a look at how the world economy has developed.

Table 8.6 shows absolute data for global economic processes, namely the global GDP, the value of global exports and global capital investments. In 2020, the year the COVID-19 pandemic emerged, all three of these

Table 8.6 The world economy in the COVID-19 pandemic

in million US$	2018	2019	2020	2021
Global GDP	86,139,293 (86.1 trillion)	87,436,705 (87.4 trillion)	84,577,963 (84.6 trillion)	96,100,091 (96.1 trillion)
Global Exports (goods and services)	25,257,368	24,810,350	22,030,531	27,897,707
Global FDI Outward Flows	870,715	1,220,432	739,872	1,707,594

Data source: GDP: World Development Indicators, other: UNCTAD Stat, data for 2018–2020 accessed on 15 December 2021, data for 2021 accessed on 15 December 2022.

economic variables significantly declined, which is an indication of the global shrinking of the world economy during the pandemic. The social shutdown of societies was also an economic shutdown.

Figure 8.2 shows the development of the global capital investments since 1970. Capital export is in Macroeconomics also called foreign direct investments (FDI). There are outward and inward investments. Outward investments are those that go from one country into others. Inward investments are those that are made from other countries to one country. There are FDI stocks and flows. FDI stocks is the total capital invested abroad (e.g. in a certain country) that has been accumulated over the years. FDI flows is the newly invested and exported capital during one period of time such as one financial year.

Figure 8.2 shows that there has been a significant growth of global capital export in the period from the early 1970s until 2008, which indicates that capitalism became more global. Since the world economic crisis 2008 and the COVID-19 pandemic 2020, global capital exports have contracted somewhat, which shows a certain de-globalisation tendency of capitalism.

Figure 8.3 shows the development of the value of world exports in the global GDP. Export activities as share of the global GDP have significantly grown from the 1980s until the start of the world economic crisis 2008, which indicates a certain globalisation of world trade. Since the start of that crisis, there is a certain de-globalisation tendency of exports so that the level of global exports has relatively decreased.

Figure 8.4 shows how the share of developing and developed countries in FDI outward flows has developed. In the early 1970s, capital export was almost entirely dominated by developed countries. Since 2000, the share of developed countries has significantly decreased, which primarily has to do with China's role in capital export. China has become an important exporter

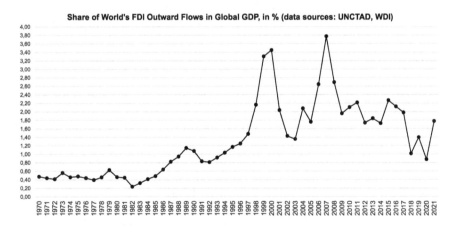

Share of World's FDI Outward Flows in Global GDP, in % (data sources: UNCTAD, WDI)

Figure 8.2 The development of the share of the world's foreign direct investment (FDI) outward flows in the global GDP, in % (data accessed on 15 December 2021, except for year 2021: accessed on 15 December 2022).

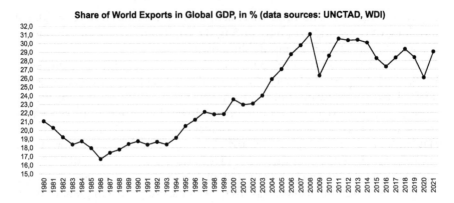

Figure 8.3 The development of the share of world exports in the global GDP (data accessed on 15 December 2021, except for year 2021: accessed on 15 December 2022).

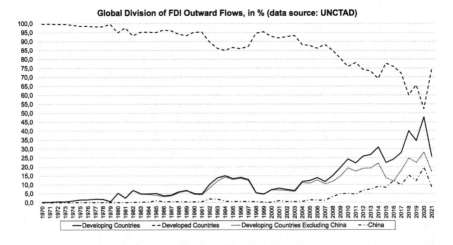

Figure 8.4 The development of the global division of FDI outward flows.

of capital. In 2021, in the light of the attempts to de-globalise the world economy in the context of COVID, the Ukraine war and China's economic crisis that had to do with its COVID lockdowns, China's share of global capital investments decreased significantly.

Table 8.7 shows the dominant countries in capital export stocks in various years. The data shows their share of the capital export stocks in the specific year. China has, since the early 1980s when its capital exports were negligent, become the third-largest exporter of capital in 2020. The USA has lost power in capital export but has remained the world's largest exporter of capital. The shares of the UK and Germany have also decreased in recent years, but both have remained important exporters of capital. The Netherlands' share has significantly increased after 2010.

Table 8.7 Countries with the largest shares of the world's FDI outward stocks, in %, listed are all countries that had a share of > 4% in one of the displayed years

	1980	2000	2010	2017	2020	2021
Brazil	6.9		0.7	0.7	0.7	0.7
Canada	4.2	6.0	4.8	4.7	5.0	5.4
Mainland China		0.4	1.6	5.5	6.0	6.2
China, Hong Kong	0.0	5.1	4.6	5.5	5.0	5.0
France	4.4	4.9	5.7	4.4	4.4	3.7
Germany	7.7	6.5	6.7	5.0	5.0	5.1
Japan	3.5	3.8	4.0	4.6	5.1	4.7
Netherlands	9.5	4.1	4.7	6.6	9.7	8.0
Switzerland, Liechtenstein		3.1	5.1	4.3	4.2	3.8
UK	14.4	12.7	8.3	5.7	5.2	5.2
USA	38.5	36.4	23.5	23.9	20.7	23.5

Data source: UNCTAD, accessed on 8 November 2021 (years 1980, 2000, 2010, 2017, 2020) and 16 December 2022 (year 2021).

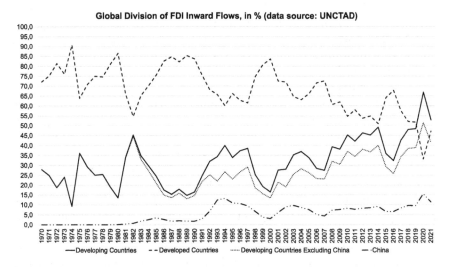

Figure 8.5 The development of the global division of foreign direct investment inward flows.

Figure 8.5 visualises the development of the global division of FDI inward flows since 1970. The development has been running in waves. Overall, the very large share of developing countries in the 1970s has significantly decreased, especially since around 2000. China as the location of capital exports has played a significant role in the increase of developing countries'

Table 8.8 Countries with the largest shares of the world's FDI inward stocks, in %, listed are all countries that had a share of > 4% in one of the displayed years

	1980	2000	2010	2017	2020	2021
Canada	7.7	4.4	4.9	2.8	2.7	3.6
Mainland China	0.2	2.6	2.9	4.5	4.6	4.5
China, Hong Kong	25.4	5.9	5.4	5.8	4.6	4.4
France	4.5	2.5	3.2	2.5	2.3	2.2
Germany	5.2	6.4	4.8	2.9	2.6	2.5
Ireland	5.1	1.7	1.4	3.2	3.3	3.0
Netherlands	3.5	3.3	3.0	4.6	7.0	5.7
Singapore	0.8	1.5	3.2	4.4	4.5	4.4
Switzerland, Liechtenstein		1.4	3.3	4.3	3.7	3.0
UK	9.0	6.0	5.4	5.7	5.3	5.8
USA	11.9	37.7	17.2	23.4	26.1	30.0

Data source: UNCTAD, accessed on 8 November 2021 (years 1980, 2000, 2010, 2017, 2020) and 16 December 2022 (year 2021).

FDI inward flows. In 2020 and 2021, the COVID pandemic resulted in fluctuations in developing and developed countries' shares in FDI inward flows.

Table 8.8 shows the countries with the largest shares of the world's foreign direct investment inward stocks. The USA has continuously been the world's country with the largest share of capital imports. China together with Hong Kong plays an important role. The Netherlands has significantly increased its share in the course of the COVID-19 pandemic. The shares of Germany, the UK, France, Ireland, and Canada have decreased since the 1980s, but all four countries remain important in capital import. Singapore has since the 1980s significantly increased its importance in capital import.

The world economy entered a major crisis in the middle of the 1970s. Capital export and the global outsourcing of labour were part of a new regime of capital accumulation that was the result of and response to this crisis. Neoliberal politics drove these developments. The goal was to cheapen labour and resources in order to maximise profits. Wage repression was an important means of increasing profit rates. The globalisation of capitalism was one of the consequences. The situation has somewhat changed since the 2008 world economic crisis that brought about certain de-globalisation tendencies of capitalism:

- In many countries, the 2008 world economic crisis resulted in austerity politics, the bail-outs of companies and banks and a kind of hyper-neoliberalism that increased inequalities and the power of capital over labour. But what followed were political crises. Extreme inequalities supported the intensification of nationalism and authoritarianism. The political legitimacy crises slowed down the globalisation of economies, and a de-globalisation tendency of capitalism emerged;

- It became more common to use tariffs in world trade;
- The success of right-wing demagogues such as Vladimir Putin (Russia), Donald Trump (USA), Recep Erdoğan (Turkey), Narendra Modi (India), and Viktor Orbán (Hungary) included nationalist ideology, including opposition to foreign capital accompanied by the glorification of national capital;
- The 2008 world economic crisis triggered a debt crisis in Southern European economies. Greece was especially hard hit. The European Union showed no solidarity with Greece and implemented austerity politics in Greece, which advanced the political legitimacy crisis of the EU;
- Britain's referendum on leaving the EU ("Brexit") was accompanied by anti-immigration rhetoric and the scapegoating of migrants as benefit scroungers, social parasites, etc. As a result of Brexit, the EU and the UK's markets became less focused on free trade. The UK strictly limited the freedom of movement of workers;
- The EU had no co-ordinated response to the 2015 refugee crisis, which advanced the rise of nationalism, closed borders, anti-refugee xenophobia, and the success of right-wing parties;
- The COVID-19 pandemic resulted in the lockdown of economies and societies throughout the world, which included limiting global trade and global investments. The lack of ventilators and protective gear in many countries put the global outsourcing of labour into question. In addition, nation-states had to invest large sums of money into supporting workers and national capital, which made state intervention in the economy more common. As a result of COVID-19, the development of a neo-Keynesian mode of regulation and more nationally and more strictly regulated oriented economies has become more likely;
- In 2022, Russia's invasion of Ukraine, its use of gas supply as a strategic political means and the increased political polarisation of the world showed that the globalisation of trade and investments had created economic dependencies on resources such as gas and other energy forms. Realising that such dependencies can in situations of war and global conflict be utilised as means of warfare further advanced de-globalisation processes.

8.4 Cultural and Media Imperialism

8.4.1 Cultural Imperialism and American Empire

Herbert Schiller's (1969/1992) book *Mass Communications and American Empire* played an important role in the establishment of the concept of cultural imperialism:

> A powerful communication system exists to secure" the identification of the "American presence" in the world "with freedom – freedom of trade, freedom of speech and freedom of enterprise.
>
> (Schiller 1969/1992, 47)

The United States communications complex [...] now directly impinges on peoples' lives everywhere.

(Schiller 1969/1992, 60–61)

The concept of cultural imperialism today best describes the sum of the processes by which a society is brought into the modern world system and how its dominating stratum is attracted, pressured, forced, and sometimes bribed into shaping social institutions to correspond to, or even promote, the values and structures of the dominating center of the system.

(Schiller 1975/1976, 9)

The rise of an American Empire would especially concern film and radio/TV programming: The "growing American influence in global communications" results "in the propagation and extension of the American business system and its values to all corners of the international community" (Schiller 1969/1992, 136). In the "emergent imperial society", messages "'made in America' radiate across the globe and serve as the ganglia of national power and expansionism" (Schiller 1969/1992, 191–192). Cultural imperialism has been characterised as the propagation of commercial culture and the American way of life.

Cultural imperialism is a more general term than media imperialism. It includes besides the media also sports, food, religion, clothing (Sparks 2007, 96). The context of the analysis of cultural imperialism as the US Empire included the Cold War between the USA and the Soviet Union, that there were nations outside of this conflict that the USA and Russia tried to pull over to their sides, as well as national liberation struggles in the Global South (Schiller 1969/1992, 1–2).

8.4.2 Criticisms of Cultural/Media Imperialism Theory

There have been several points of criticism of the concept of cultural imperialism (see Golding and Harris 1997; Sparks 2007):

- Theories of cultural imperialism show a lack of attention to counter-power. They underestimate resistance;
- Economic power is equated with culture;
- Passive audiences: Audiences are seen as passive, and no active interpretation capacities are part of the model;
- Cultural nationalism: National cultures in developing countries are seen as authentic or superior;
- Lack of contextualisation: Theories of cultural imperialism underestimate the emergence and diffusion of local and regional cultures, local and regional cultural industries, and hybrid forms of culture that foster diversity and variety;
- Global cultural products also originate in parts of the world other than the USA (Bollywood, Nollywood, Japanese video games, Brazilian and

Mexican telenovelas, news provided by Al-Jazeera, the BBC, CGTN, Russia Today, etc.);
- Cultural flows are quite global today so one cannot think of cultural imperialism as one state dominating the culture of another one.

8.4.3 Herbert Schiller: Transnational Cultural Domination

Herbert Schiller took such debates seriously and responded to them in his article "Not-Yet the Post-Imperialist Era" (Schiller 1991). He argues that there were important changes since he published the book on American Empire in 1969, including the breakdown of the Soviet system, the dependence of Third World countries on the world market and Western creditors and the emergence of transnational corporate cultural domination. He speaks of the "enormous growth of transnational corporate power in the last twenty years" (Schiller 1991, 252), which includes the globalisation of the capitalist model, profit making, capital accumulation, the privatisation (of communications and other services), inequalities, advertising, cultural sponsorship, public relations, and consumerism. Consequently, global media companies are hardly "distinguishable from the same services at the disposal of American-owned corporations" (Schiller 1991, 249). "What is emerging, therefore, is a world where alongside the American output of cultural products are the practically identical items marketed by competing national and transnational groups" (Schiller 1991, 254). For example, Brazilian soaps have the same purpose as US soaps – to sell products produced by "transnational corporations who advertise in Brazil as well as in the United States" (Schiller 1991, 255).

This means that Schiller reconceptualised cultural imperialism as the globalisation of capitalism and the application of the capitalist model to culture on the national, international, and global level.

8.4.4 Global Capitalism

Global capitalism means capitalist society and its logics of accumulation operating at the international, transnational or global level. Global capitalist society involves the transnational accumulation of money capital in the economy, the accumulation of political decision-power and influence at the international level in politics, and the accumulation of international reputation and respect in culture. Capitalist society globalises as one of the responses to economic, political, and cultural crises. The development of global capitalism is the attempt of a spatial fix to such crises.

Global capitalism is an international system of political-economic rivalries for the economic, political, and ideological control of territories where rival powers use violent and/or non-violent methods for trying to advance the accumulation and centralisation of the dominant class's economic power, as well as the accumulation and global centralisation of political and ideological power. The biggest danger of competing forces in global capitalism is that rivalry, nationalism and the friend/enemy-logic that are part of global capitalism intensify to such a level that a World War is the consequence.

Rosa Luxemburg argues that "severe competition" between capitalist countries can become very violent and ruthless (Luxemburg 1913/2003, 426). For Luxemburg, a world war is "the product of the imperialistic rivalries between the capitalist classes of the different countries for world hegemony and for the monopoly in […] exploitation and oppression" (Luxemburg 1970, 329). The situation of world politics in the 21st century is not completely dissimilar from the one before the First World War when Luxemburg (1913/2003) was writing her book *The Accumulation of Capital*. We again find competing and colliding forces in global capitalism that seem to be willing to not just compete economically but also use the means of military violence. The danger of a new world war and along with it the danger of the nuclear annihilation of humanity and life on Earth has increased in recent years.

The danger of the situation the world is in today, namely the danger of a new World War, arises from the global rivalry of dominant powers. Table 8.9 shows how powerful contemporary great powers are with respect to several variables.

Let us briefly discuss two examples of the aspects shown in the table above. The data presented in the tables below shows that Russia and the USA control the vast amount of the world's nuclear bombs. China has the world's largest army, which increases its military power (data source: https://www.statista.com/statistics/264443/the-worlds-largest-armies-based-on-active-force-level/#:~:text=In%202022%2C%20China%20had%20the,the%20top%20five%20largest%20armies, accessed on 30 January 2023). The USA is home to the largest number of top transnational corporations, followed by China and the EU. Russia has a relatively small number of such corporations (see Tables 8.10 and 8.11).

What makes the world situation so dangerous today is the collision of political-economic powers. Such a constellation has resulted in World Wars before with the difference that nuclear arsenals did not exist in the First World War and only started to emerge during the Second World War. A Third World War would be an absolute catastrophe that is likely to result

Table 8.9 The power of the contemporary world's competing political-economic forces

Country	Economic Power	Military Power	Cultural, Political and Ideological Influence
USA	High	High	High
China	High	Medium	Medium
European Union	Medium	Low	Medium
Russia	Low	High	Low

Table 8.10 The world's nuclear arsenal

Country	Nuclear Bombs
Russia	5,977
USA	5,428
China	350
France	290
UK	225
Pakistan	165
India	160
Israel	90
North Korea	20

Data source: https://www.sipri.org/yearbook/2022/10, accessed on 30 January 2023.

Table 8.11 Absolute share of the world's largest 100 corporations that are headquartered in selected regions and countries

Country	Top Transnational Corporations
USA	38
China	17
EU	14
Switzerland	6
Japan	5
UK	5
Russia	2

Data source: Forbes 2000 List for the year 2022.

in the end of humanity and the end of life on Earth. A global democratic, humanist, socialist system is a way of overcoming, containing and reducing this threat. "Only when we have the power in our hands will there be an end to wars and barracks"[7] (Luxemburg 1914, 847). In such a system, there is the maximisation of benefits for all, the largest-possible degree of co-operation, the minimisation of mutual harm, as well as peaceful co-existence where co-operation is not feasible for both sides.

8.4.5 Media and Global Capitalism

Fuchs (2010) argues that media and cultural imperialism should not only be understood as the spread of capitalism at the level of media and cultural content. Rather, global capitalism has a media and cultural dimension. It also is the dimension of imperialism that relates to the media and culture, which means that media, culture, and digital technologies play a role in the reorganisation and globalisation of capitalism. Global capitalism combines global capital export, the dominance of finance capital, monopoly capital and capital concentration, global geographical inequalities and global stratification, and political-economic conflicts over influence in the world, which includes warfare.

Fuchs stresses the following aspects of global capitalism that are related to media, culture, and the digital:

- Capital export:
  Finance, mining/quarrying/petroleum, trade, and information are the most important economic sectors of foreign direct investment. Finance is the dominant sector in both FDI and world trade;
- Finance capital:
  Financialisation, hyper-industrialisation by the continued relevance of fossil fuels and the car, and informatisation are three important economic trends of global capitalism. Financialisation is the dominant factor;
- Capital concentration:
  Information sectors such as publishing, telecommunications and the manufacturing of communication equipment are among the most concentrated economic sectors, although finance is the most concentrated sector;
- Global stratification:
  Transnational information corporations do not operate entirely globally. They are grounded in national economies, but a certain degree of their operations, assets, employees, sales, profits and affiliates are located beyond their home economies so that a national-transnational nexus is established. Transnationality is an emergent quality, a measure, degree and tendency. Transnational corporations have created global inequalities;
- Political-economic conflicts and wars:
  Media, computers and the Internet are arenas and mediators of global political and economic conflicts. Competing, escalating struggles of competing forces can result in wars for international and global hegemony, which means political, economic, and cultural dominance. Therefore, the media and computers also play a role in global capitalism in the form of the mediation of war and digital weapon systems (see Table 8.12).

The global film market is dominated by big media corporations: In 2009, News Corporation was involved in the distribution of five of the top 20 movies: Warner in four; Viacom, Sony and Disney in three each; and Comcast in two. In 18 out of 20 cases, the main distributor was a corporation that had its headquarters in the USA.

Tables 8.13 8.14, and –8.15 show data for the globally best-selling movies in 2019, 2020, and 2021.

Table 8.12 Globally best-selling movies in 2009

#	Film	Distribution Company	Headquarters of Main Company	Revenues
1	Avatar	20th Century Fox (News Corporation)	USA	$2,743,577,587
2	Harry Potter and the Half-Blood Prince	Warner Bros. (Time Warner)	USA	$933,959,197
3	Ice Age: Dawn of the Dinosaurs	20th Century Fox (News Corporation)	USA	$886,686,817
4	Transformers: Revenge of the Fallen	Paramount (Viacom)	USA	$836,303,693
5	2012	Columbia Pictures (Sony)	Japan	$769,679,473
6	Up	Walt Disney	USA	$735,099,082
7	The Twilight Saga: New Moon	Summit Entertainment (Lions Gate Entertainment)	USA	$709,827,462
8	Sherlock Holmes	Warner Bros. (Time Warner)	USA	$524,028,679
9	Angels & Demons	Columbia Pictures (Sony)	Japan	$485,930,816
10	The Hangover	Warner Bros. (Time Warner)	USA	$468,812,793
11	Alvin and the Chipmunks: The Squeakquel	20th Century Fox (News Corporation)	USA	$443,140,005
12	Night at the Museum: Battle of the Smithsonian	20th Century Fox (News Corporation)	USA	$413,106,170
13	Star Trek	Paramount Pictures (Viacom)	USA	$385,680,446
14	Monsters vs. Aliens	Paramount Pictures (Viacom)	USA	$381,509,870
15	X-Men Origins: Wolverine	20th Century Fox (News Corporation)	USA	$373,062,864
16	Terminator Salvation	Warner Bros (Time Warner) & Sony Pictures	USA, Japan	$371,353,001
17	Fast & Furious	Universal Pictures (Comcast)	USA	$360,364,265
18	Prince of Persia: The Sands of Time	Walt Disney	USA	$336,365,676
19	A Christmas Carol	Walt Disney	USA	$325,286,646
20	Inglourious Basterds	The Weinstein Company, Universal Pictures (Comcast)	USA	$321,455,689
				Total: $12.8 billion

Data source: https://www.boxofficemojo.com/year/world/2009/, accessed on 23 November 2021.

Table 8.13 Globally best-selling movies in 2019

Rank	Movie	Main Distributor	Headquarters of Distributor	Global Box Office 2020
1	Avengers: Endgame	Walt Disney	USA	$2,797,501,328
2	The Lion King	Walt Disney	USA	$1,656,943,394
3	Frozen II	Walt Disney	USA	$1,450,026,933
4	Spider-Man: Far from Home	Sony	Japan	$1,131,927,996
5	Captain Marvel	Walt Disney	USA	$1,128,274,794
6	Joker	Warner Bros (Warner Media, AT&T)	USA	$1,074,251,311
7	Star Wars: Episode IX - The Rise of Skywalker	Walt Disney	USA	$1,074,144,248
8	Toy Story 4	Walt Disney	USA	$1,073,394,593
9	Aladdin	Walt Disney	USA	$1,050,693,953
10	Jumanji: The Next Level	Sony	Japan	$800,059,707
11	Fast & Furious Presents: Hobbs & Shaw	Universal Pictures (Comcast)	USA	$759,056,935
12	Ne Zha	Beijing Enlight Pictures	China	$726,063,471
13	The Wandering Earth	China Film Group Corporation	China	$699,856,699
14	How to Train Your Dragon: The Hidden World	Universal Pictures (Comcast)	USA	$521,799,505
15	Maleficent: Mistress of Evil	Walt Disney	USA	$491,730,089
16	It Chapter Two	Warner Bros (Warner Media, AT&T)	USA	$473,093,228
17	My People, My Country	Huaxia Film Distribution	China	$450,064,993
18	Pokémon Detective Pikachu	Warner Bros (Warner Media, AT&T), Toho	USA, Japan	$433,005,346
19	The Secret Life of Pets 2	Universal Pictures (Comcast)	USA	$430,051,293
20	The Captain	Bona Film Group Limited	China	$417,282,021
				Total: $18.6 billion

Data source: https://www.boxofficemojo.com/year/world/2019/, accessed on 23 November 2021.

Table 8.14 Globally best-selling movies in 2020

Rank	Movie	Main Distributor	Headquarters of Distributor	Global Box Office
1	The Eight Hundred	Huayi Brothers, China Media Capital	China	$461,421,559
2	Demon Slayer: Mugen Train	Toho, Aniplex	Japan	$452,974,619
3	Bad Boys for Life	Sony Pictures Releasing (Sony Entertainment)	Japan	$426,505,244
4	My People, My Homeland	Huaxia Film Distribution	China	$422,390,820
5	Tenet	Warner Brothers (WarnerMedia, AT&T)	USA	$363,656,624
6	Sonic the Hedgehog	Paramount Pictures (ViacomCBS)	USA	$319,715,683
7	Dolittle	Universal Pictures (Comcast)	USA	$245,438,444
8	Legend of Deification	Beijing Enlight Pictures	China	$240,663,149
9	A Little Red Flower	HG Entertainment	UK	$216,000,000
10	The Croods: A New Age	Universal Pictures (Comcast)	USA	$215,905,815
11	Birds of Prey	Warner Brothers (WarnerMedia, AT&T)	USA	$201,858,461
12	Shock Wave 2	Universe Films Distribution	China (Hong Kong)	$198,921,659
13	Wonder Woman 1984	Warner Brothers (WarnerMedia, AT&T)	USA	$166,534,027
14	The Sacrifice	China Film Group Corporation	China	$161,047,608
15	The Invisible Man	Universal Pictures (Comcast)	USA	$143,151,000
16	Onward	Walt Disney Studios (Walt Disney Company)	USA	$141,940,042
17	Warm Hug	Shaw Organisation	Singapore	$129,240,236
18	Soul	Walt Disney Studios (Walt Disney Company)	USA	$120,957,731
19	The Call of the Wild	Walt Disney Studios (Walt Disney Company)	USA	$111,105,497
20	Caught in Time	Emperor Motion Pictures	China (Hong Kong)	$80,543,319
				Total: $4.8 billion

Data source: https://www.boxofficemojo.com/year/world/2020/, accessed on 23 November 2021.

Table 8.15 Globally best-selling movies in 2021

Rank	Movie	Main Distributor	Headquarters of Distributor	Global Box Office
1	Spider-Man: No Way Home	Sony Pictures Releasing (Sony Entertainment)	USA	US$1,538,282,364
2	The Battle at Lake Changjin	CMC Pictures	China	US$902,540,914
3	Hi, Mom	China Film Co.	China	US$822,009,764
4	No Time to Die	Universal Pictures (Comcast), United Artists (MGM)	USA	US$774,034,007
5	F9: The Fast Saga	Universal Pictures (Comcast)	USA	US$726,229,501
6	Detective Chinatown 3	Wanda Pictures	China	US$686,257,563
7	Venom: Let There Be Carnage	Sony	Japan	US$501,138,437
8	Godzilla vs. Kong	Warner Bros (WarnerMedia, AT&T), Toho	USA, Japan	US$467,863,133
9	Shang-Chi and the Legend of the Ten Rings	Walt Disney	USA	US$432,233,010
10	Eternals	Walt Disney	USA	US$401,836,070
11	Dune	Warner Bros (WarnerMedia, AT&T)	USA	US$397,024,576
12	Black Widow	Walt Disney	USA	US$379,631,351
13	Free Guy	20th Century Studios (Walt Disney)	USA	US$331,503,757
14	A Quiet Place Part II	Paramount Pictures (ViacomCBS)	USA	US$297,372,261
15	Cruella	Walt Disney	USA	US$233,274,812
16	My Country, My Parents	Huaxia Film Distribution	China	US$221,701,823
17	Jungle Cruise	Walt Disney	USA	US$220,889,446
18	Encanto	Walt Disney	USA	US$216,116,977
19	Raging Fire	Emperor Motion Pictures (Emperor Group)	China (Hong Kong)	US$205,838,889
20	The Conjuring: The Devil Made Me Do It	Warner Bros (WarnerMedia, AT&T)	USA	US$201,965,074
				Total: US$ 10.0 billion

Data source: https://www.boxofficemojo.com/year/world/2021/, accessed on 12 January 2022.

In 2019, the vast majority of the best-selling movies were distributed by transnational US corporations. Walt Disney dominated the global distribution market of movies. Among the top 20 best-selling movies, there were also four Chinese movies. 2020 was the year when the COVID-19 pandemic started. China was hit hard by the pandemic from January until March and recovered because it managed to contain the virus. Western countries were from March 2020 onwards hit by the pandemic, which resulted in repeated phases of lockdown. The US-dominated movie industry suffered from the pandemic. As a consequence, Chinese movies were among the world's best-selling motion pictures. In 2020, six Chinese movies were among the top 20 best-selling movies, including the best-selling movie worldwide. Ten of the top 20 best-selling movies were distributed by US companies, which means that US corporations still dominated the global movie market, but their market power was weakened. In 2021, five of the 20 best-selling movies were produced in China and 14 in the USA. This means that the 2020 trend continued into 2021. In 2020, Walt Disney made losses of US$ –2.4 billion, whereas its profits were US$ 10.4 billion in 2019 (data source: Disney SEC-Filings Form 10-K, financial year 2020). Netflix, the dominant player in video streaming, increased its profits from US$ 2.6 billion in 2019 to US$ 4.6 billion in 2020 (data source: Disney SEC-Filings Form 10-K, financial year 2020). Netflix's global subscribers increased from 167.1 million in 2019 to 203.7 million in 2020 (ibid.). During the pandemic, many cineastes switched from watching movies in movie theatres to subscription-video-on-demand (SVOD). This also becomes evident from the fact that the global box sales of the top 20 movies decreased from US$ 18.6 in 2019 to US$ 4.8 billion in 2020 and stood at US$ 10.0 billion in 2021. This means that the global movie box office in 2020 decreased by 75% in one year due to the COVID-19 pandemic.

The data shows that crises of capitalism can strengthen non-Western corporations in the culture industry. However, this strengthening in the movie industry has become possible through an absolute shrinking of the Western market and a switch of movie watchers and their spending to SVOD.

It is not enough to describe the existence of media flows and "contra-flows"; one must look at the distribution of power between them. Days Thussu warns that talking about the existence of regional contra-media flows can create the false impression that there is a shift of financial power:

> Prominent "examples of 'subaltern' and 'geo-cultural' media flows may give a false impression that the world communication has become more diverse and democratic. [...] Despite the growing trend towards contra-flow [...], the revenues of non-Western media organizations, with the exception of Japanese animation, are relatively small and their global impact is restricted to geo-cultural markets or at best to small pockets of regional transnational consumers. None of the Latin *telenovelas* have had the international impact comparable with US soaps such as

Dallas or the cult following of *Friends* or *Sex and the City,* and, despite the growing presence of Indian films outside India, its share in the global film industry valued in 2004 at $200 billion was still less than 0.2 per cent".

(Thussu 2007, 25)

In the case of the transformations of the global movie industry, Chinese movies are playing a more important role not because of the increasing transnational financial power of Chinese companies but because of the shrinking global box office market in the light of the COVID-19 pandemic. China Film Group Corporation is a state-owned enterprise. The other Chinese media corporations involved in the distribution of films listed in the previous tables, such as CMC Pictures (China Media Capital), Universe Films Distribution, Wanda Pictures (Wanda Media), Huaxia, Emperor Motion Pictures, Beijing Enlight Pictures, Huayi Brothers, and Bona Film Group Entertainment, are privately owned for-profit corporations. Therefore, a relative shift of movie sales from the USA to China does not change the fact that capitalist culture dominates the global culture industry. This is what Schiller (1991) characterises as transnational corporate domination, where transnational capital controls the media and culture by the logic of capital accumulation. Oliver Boyd-Barrett argues in this context:

> the actual phenomenon of media imperialism, on the other hand, has never disappeared or ceased to be important. I shall propose that this field of study is sustainable, has evolved, and has never been more relevant than in the current, so-called digital age.

(Boyd-Barrett 2015, 8)

8.5 China, Global Capitalism, and Cultural Imperialism

8.5.1 China and the West

Yuezhi Zhao (2011) argues China is not simply opposed to Western cultural imperialism, but has a complex relationship with the West: it is neither completely different from Western capitalism, nor the same. The "challenge of China" is that China is "a poor country that has managed to rise up in the global capitalist order while dramatically increasing domestic class inequalities, and a nation with staggering ethnic, gender, urban-rural, and regional divides" (Zhao 2011, 563).

Zhao argues for a transnational Political Economy of Communication in China. Since the reform period started in 1978 (Deng Xiaoping), China has advanced ICTs, the commercialisation of the media, the rise of a Chinese form of neoliberalism that combines commodification with state control, incorporation of Western marketing and public relations. At the same time, there is a political and ideological legacy of Mao and socialism that cannot be done away with and that shapes Chinese identity, as well as a cultural form of nationalism. Chinese media celebrate the new urban middle class.

The Chinese "soft power" strategy is that China has "launched a multi-faceted effort to project China abroad through its media and cultural institutions" (Zhao 2011, 574), which includes CCTV International (now called CGTN), China Radio International, China Daily, Global Times, the export of Chinese movies, and the Confucius Institutes.

8.5.2 The Belt and Road Initiative

China has created new banks that provide loans to other countries as part of the Belt and Road Initiative (BRI), a large-scale Chinese project to build and network infrastructures in other countries, including airports, bridges, dams, ports, powerplants, railroads, skyscrapers, telecommunications cables and networks, and tunnels.

China advances finance capital and supports Chinese companies that create scientific and technological innovations, as well as investments abroad and loans to other countries as part of the Belt and Road Initiative. The Belt and Road Initiative is a large-scale Chinese investment project that exports capital from China to other countries where it is used for investing in the creation of infrastructures.

China's construction industry was threatened by overaccumulation of capital. It has lots of fixed capital such as steel, cement, and coal that it could not use domestically. China has tried to create a spatial fix to a looming crisis of its capital by exporting capital via the Belt and Road Initiative. "China experienced, in short, a predictable problem of overinvestment in the built environment" (Harvey 2016, 13). Based on David Harvey, Mehdi P. Amineh (2023, 17) argues that the Belt and Road Initiative "as a framework of China's capitalist expansion can be understood as specific spatial and geographical strategies to solve the overaccumulation and the limited space of accumulation at the national level". Africa is a key location for the export and transnationalisation of Chinese capital in the BRI.

China's political-economic activities are characterised by state monopoly capital, the fostering of finance capital, the export of capital, the transnationalisation of Chinese capital, and the creation of infrastructures that can be used in conflicts over territorial control.

The basic ideology underlying organisations such as the International Monetary Fund (IMF), the World Bank and the World Trade Organization (WTO) as well as China's international development strategy is that free trade, capital investments, fostering capitalist enterprise, and providing loans to poor countries and private companies in them are the best ways of advancing poor countries' development. The criticism of this strategy has been that it advances capitalist development that advances polarisation between the rich and the poor, as well as between capital and labour, creates financial dependency of poor countries on developed countries as well as debt-traps that these poor countries cannot escape so that they have to hand over ownership of key infrastructures and parts of the public sector to foreign investors and banks. Another point of criticism is that foreign capital investments and loans provide dependence on companies and infrastructures in poor countries on Western standards, software, hardware, and technologies, which means that constant payments for such resources have to be made, which means a transfer of value from poor countries to rich countries. There is also the criticism that foreign capital investments create profits for companies in rich countries by exploiting the labour in poor countries. With respect to free trade agreements and international trade between poor and rich countries, there is criticism that poor countries have lower levels of productivity, which makes it hard for them to compete on the world market, which results in them having to sell their commodities cheaply based on the prices and productivity levels set by companies in rich countries, which results in low wages and high exploitation of workers in poor countries.

Table 8.16 shows China's rise as an international creditor of poorer countries. From 2000 until 2020, the total money that poorer countries (middle- and low-income countries) owe to China increased by a multiplication factor of 28.5. Whereas the USA as a country has decreased the debt owed to it by poorer countries, China is today the world's largest creditor country with respect to middle- and low-income countries. The debt that is owed to it

Table 8.16 Development of external debt of low- and middle-income countries to China, the USA, The World Bank's International Development Association (IDA), the World Bank's International Bank for Reconstruction and Development (IBRD), and the International Monetary Fund (IMF), in billion US$

Year	China	USA	IMF	IBRD	IDA
2020	171	34	225	204	177
2015	104	52	110	153	131
2010	40	32	150	123	119
2005	8	33	70	95	121
2000	6	46	79	105	87
1995	3	74	58	100	72
1990	3	99	31	84	45
1985	2	106	35	43	24
1980	3	44	11	19	12
1975	1.5	26	4	8	5
1970	0.4	13	0.7	4	2

Data source: World Bank Data, World Bank International Debt Statistics, accessed on 19 August 2022.

is comparable to the one owed to the IMF, the World Bank's International Development Association or the World Bank's International Bank for Reconstruction and Development.

In 2020, poorer countries (middle- and low-income countries) owed 4.4% of their total debt to the World Bank, 2.6% to the IMF, 2.0% to China and 0.4% to the USA. In 1985, they owed 14% of their total debt, which was much smaller, to the USA and 0.3% to China. In 2020, bondholders controlled 27.8% of poorer countries' external debt, namely US$ 2.4 trillion. Bondholders were always important creditors. In 2000, they controlled 19% of poorer countries' external debt (source of all data in this paragraph: World Bank Data, International Debt Statistics). Bondholders are private financial and non-financial corporations and governments. There are statistics available for international debt securities issued as bonds (see Table 8.17).

In 2021, there were US$ 2.7 trillion in international debt securities. 84.0% of it was controlled by private corporations, primarily banks, and 8.7% by governments. British corporations were the world's largest holders of international debt bonds. China was the world's tenth largest location of international debt securities and held a value of international debt bonds that was larger than the one of Spain and Japan. The data shows that Chinese corporations and the Chinese government are among the world's largest creditors to nation-states. China, together with Western corporations, Western

Table 8.17 International debt securities in 2021, in billion US$

	Total	*Corporations*	*Government*	*Other*
Total	27,832	23,374	2,400	2,058
UK	3,405	3,383	22	0
Cayman Islands	2,660	2,660	0	0
USA	2,445	2,442	3	0
Netherlands	2,274	2,273	1	0
France	1,420	1,408	11	1
Germany	1,349	1,250	99	0
Ireland	1,061	1,042	18	1
Canada	1,058	894	164	0
Luxembourg	1,025	1,021	3	1
China (incl. Hong Kong and Macau)	650	602	48	0
Spain	590	581	8	1
Japan	544	537	7	0

Data source: Bank for International Settlements (BIS) Statistics, https://stats.bis.org/, accessed on 19 August 2021.

governments, and international institutions such as the World Bank and the IMF, where it plays an important role, is making up the system of financial imperialism that continues to indebt poor countries. While the external debt of middle- and low-income countries stood at a high of 36.1% of their combined GDP in 1995, this value decreased to 16.7% in 2010 but increased again to 29.1% in 2020. The international debt economy has enriched the corporations and governments of a few countries and has contributed to the impoverishment of poorer countries. China does not play a dominant, but an important role in finance capitalism. It has continuously increased its role and importance in global capitalism and has become an important power.

The balance between credits and debts of a country is called the International Investment Position (IIP). In 2022, China (including Hong Kong) followed by Japan and Germany had the world's largest IIP surplus, while the USA followed by the UK, Spain, and France had the world's largest IIP deficit (data source: Balance of Payments and International Investment Position Statistics, IMF, https://data.imf.org/, accessed on 20 August 2022). While the USA was the world's largest debtor, China was the world's largest creditor.

In 2020, China controlled 33% of Angola's external debt, which accounted for 125.9% of the country's Gross National Income. China controlled 55% of Tonga's debt, 52% of Djibouti's, 48% of the Republic of Congo's, 38% of the Maldives', 36% of Vanuatu's, 35% of Samoa's, 32% of Lao PDR's, 22% of Cambodia's, and 20% of Pakistan's and Kyrgyzstan's debts. Most of these countries have become more indebted since 2015. Comparing 2015 to 2020, the share of external debt in the GDP rose from 25.8% to 45.3% in Pakistan, from 44.7% to 125.9% in Angola, from 51.1% to 81.5% in Djibouti, from 26.6% to 96.9% in the Maldives, from 42.3% to 61.1% in the Republic of Congo, from 55.7% to 70.8% in Cambodia, from 84.5% to 94.8% in Lao PDR, and from 34.5% to 46.9% in Vanuatu (data source of all data in this paragraph: World Bank Data, International Debt Statistics, https://databank.worldbank.org/source/international-debt-statistics, accessed on 20 August 2022). There is a significant number of countries that are indebted and where a significant share of the debt is controlled by China.

8.5.3 Digital Silk Road

The Digital Silk Road is the digital dimension of global capitalism with Chinese characteristics, the creation and globalisation of digital technologies and communication networks that are under China's authoritarian state control.

The private Chinese Hengtong Group is the major investor in the construction of the PEACE Cable (Pakistan & East Africa Connecting Europe Cable), a 15,000 kilometre-long system of underwater 200G fibre-optic communications cables that wants to connect Asia, Africa, and Europe by linking China, the Maldives, Seychelles, Kenya, South Africa, Somalia, Djibouti, Pakistan, Egypt, Cyprus, Malta, and France (see http://www.peacecable.net/#about). Huawei is also an important investor. It is one of the major projects of what

China calls the Digital Silk Road (DSR), the digital dimension of the Belt and Road Initiative, its version of digital imperialism. Until 2019, as part of the DSR initiative, China had according to its own information signed Memorandums of Understanding for Chinese investments with 16 countries (Huang 2019). The Digital Silk Road promises to build fast phone and Internet communications infrastructure in poor countries.

The Chinese government and its state-owned media argue that the Digital Silk Road is "helping developing countries" by bringing investment and jobs and empowering

> them with the ability to embrace the digital age. [...] Infrastructure projects have helped the continent better embrace the digital age, and the small country of Djibouti, which now has seven submarine cables connecting it with the rest of the world, is a good demonstration of this. [...] China has so far built over 30 cross-border land communication cables and over a dozen international submarine communication cables with economies involved.
>
> (Ren 2019)

Through the DSR, Chinese digital corporations have found a way to try to make profits by capital export that can create dependency of phone and Internet communication in other countries on Chinese digital capital.

8.5.4 Colin Sparks: China and Imperialism

Colin Sparks (2020) argues that China's export of capital (channelled into projects such as the Belt and Road Initiative), its integration of state control and big capital, its dominant role in the BRICS association (Brazil, Russia, India, China, South Africa), and its military expansion are evidence that "China is evolving into an imperialist power" (278) and an "emerging cultural imperialist" (275). He situates China's international media and cultural activities that are often termed "soft power" in the context of this imperialist power, which means that for Sparks, China is also a cultural imperialist power. Graham Murdock (2020, 301) argues that China's Digital Silk Road initiative as part of the Belt and Road Initiative is an expression of its "networked imperialism".

In China, there is a large number of migrant workers that form a new urban proletariat and are a supply of cheap labour for exporting consumer goods and consumer electronics to the West. As a result, social struggles of Chinese workers have emerged. Chinese workers in their struggles make use of blogs, Weibo, online video, social networks, etc. Therefore, Jack Qiu (2009) speaks of the emergence of a working-class network society. China has "the largest exploited working class of the global information age" (Qiu 2009, x). These workers use the Internet for creating worker-generated content that is also utilised in social struggles (Qiu 2016, chapter 5).

8.5.5 *After Mobile Phones, What?*

When Dallas Smythe wrote about communication in China in the early 1970s in his article "After bicycles, what?" (Smythe 1994, 230–244), he wrote about communication in China. He was thinking about how the broadcasting system could be organised democratically. Smythe spoke of a "two-way system in which each receiver would have the capability to provide either a voice or voice-and-picture response. [...] a two-way TV system would be like an electronic tatzupao system" (Smythe 1994, 231–232). These considerations have parallels with Hans Magnus Enzensberger's (1974/1982) concept of emancipatory media use, Walter Benjamin's (1934) idea of the reader/author, and Bertolt Brecht's (1932/2000) notion of an alternative radio in his radio theory.

Yuezhi Zhao (2011) points out the relevance of Smythe's article and his ideas of an alternative non-capitalist communication system for contemporary China. Faced with a world dominated by the logic of capitalism in both the West and China, she emphasises, inspired by Smythe, the importance of creating communication and geo-systems based on a non-capitalist logic. Zhao (2007, 92) argues that Smythe posed the question "After bicycles, what?" in the "context of China's search for a socialist alternative to capitalist modernity, with the hope that China would avoid the capitalist path of development". Although Smythe misjudged the political situation in China in the 1970s in some respects, his contribution still "provides a useful starting point for analysing not only the use and development of ICTs in China during the reform era, but also the broad trajectory of China's post-Mao development strategy and its sustainability" (Zhao 2007, 96). The question to ask about Chinese media today, in the spirit of Dallas Smythe, would be: After mobile phones, what? (Zhao 2007). While Smythe's answer to the question "After bicycles, what?" was that China should create a media structure that would "provide public goods and services [...] against goods and services for individual, private use" (Smythe 1994, 243), ICTs today, according to Zhao, not only serve capitalist purposes, but are social "by their very nature" and therefore allow "alternative uses", including collective political practices (Zhao 2007, 96). ICTs in China are antagonistic technologies. They are both means of domination and means of protest.

8.6 Conclusion

This chapter asked: How does the Political Economy of global media look like? We can now summarise the main findings:

Finding 1: Global Capitalism

Since the 1970s, capitalism has been globalised in order to increase profits by outsourcing labour globally so that wage costs can be saved, searching for cheap resources, selling on international markets, and exporting capital internationally. The result has been an increase in the number and power of transnational corporations.

Finding 2: Global Media

The rise of digital technologies has been the medium and outcome of capitalism's globalisation since the 1970s. Transnational information corporations organise and dominate the media, cultural, and digital industry and play an important role in global capitalism.

Finding 3: Cultural and Media Imperialism

The theory of cultural and media imperialism has started as a theory of global US cultural domination that imposes the American Way of Life on the world. Facing various criticisms, the theory has been revised. Herbert Schiller conceives cultural imperialism as transnational corporations' global spread of capitalist logic and commodity culture.

Media and cultural imperialism should not only be understood as the spread of capitalism at the level of media and cultural content. Rather, global capitalism has a dimension of media and culture. Media, culture, and digital technologies play a role in the reorganisation and globalisation of global capitalism. The Political Economy of global capitalism combines global capital export, the dominance of finance capital, monopoly capital, and capital concentration, global geographical inequalities and global stratification, and political-economic conflicts over influence in the world, which includes warfare.

Finding 4: China and Global Capitalism

China has since the 1980s started to play an important role in capital import, capital export and commodity exports. It has become a major player in the world economy. It has become a global power that competes with the USA for world dominance. Both the USA and China utilise media, culture, and digital technologies as means of imperialism. China is a working-class network society with the world's largest working class that is highly exploited and uses new technologies in its social struggles.

Notes

1 https://www.telekom.com/de/investor-relations/unternehmen/aktionaersstruktur, accessed on 22 November 2021.
2 https://www-statista-com.uow.idm.oclc.org/statistics/778856/market-share-mobile-service-providers/, accessed on 22 November 2021.
3 Data source: Forbes 2000, years 2022, 2021 and 2020.

4 Data source: World Development Indicators (WDI), http://wdi.worldbank.org/, accessed on 15 December 2022.
5 Data source: https://www.kek-online.de/medienkonzentration/tv-sender/unter nehmenssteckbriefe/bertelsmann, accessed on 12 January 2022.
6 Data source: https://www.telekom.com/en/company/companyprofile/company-profile-625808, https://www.telekom.com/en/company/worldwide, accessed on 12 January 2022.
7 Translated from the German original: „Erst wenn wir die Macht in Händen haben, dann wird es vorbei sein mit Kriegen und mit Kasernen".

References

Amineh, Mehdi P. 2023. China's Capitalist Industrial Development and the Emergence of the Belt and Road Initiative. In *The China-Led Belt and Road Initiative and Its Reflections*, edited by Mehdi Parvizi Amineh, 11–35. Abingdon: Routledge.
Barber, Benjamin. 2003. *Jihad vs. McWorld*. London: Corgi Books.
Bauman, Zygmunt. 1998. *Globalization. The Human Consequences*. Cambridge: Polity.
Beck, Klaus. 2018. *Das Mediensystem Deutschlands. Strukturen, Märkte, Regulierung*. Wiesbaden: Springer VS. Second edition.
Beck, Ulrich. 1999. *World Risk Society*. Cambridge: Polity Press.
Benjamin, Walter. 1934. The Author as Producer. In *Walter Benjamin: Selected Writings Volume 2, Part 2, 1931–1934*, 768–782. Cambridge, MA: Belknap Press.
Boyd-Barrett, Oliver. 2015. *Media Imperialism*. London: SAGE.
Brecht, Bertolt. 1932/2000. The Radio as an Apparatus of Communications. In *Brecht on Film & Radio*, edited by Marc Silberman, 41–46. London: Methuen.
Enzensberger, Hans Magnus. 1974/1982. Constituents of a Theory of the Media. In *Critical Essays*, 46–76. New York: Continuum.
Flew, Terry. 2007. *Understanding Global Media*. Basingstoke: Palgrave Macmillan.
Fuchs, Christian. 2010. New Imperialism: Information and Media Imperialism? *Global Media* and *Communication* 6 (1): 33–60.
Golding, Peter and Phil Harris, eds. 1997. *Beyond Cultural Imperialism. Globalization, Communication & the New International Order*. London: SAGE.
Hafez, Kai. 2007. *The Myth of Media Globalization*. Cambridge: Polity.
Harvey, David. 2016. *The Ways of the World*. London: Profile Books.
Harvey, David. 2010. *The Enigma of Capital and the Crises of Capitalism*. Oxford: Oxford University Press.
Harvey, David. 2006. *Spaces of Global Capitalism. Towards a Theory of Uneven Geographical Development*. London: Verso.
Harvey, David. 2001. *Spaces of Capital. Towards a Critical Geography*. New York: Routledge.
Harvey, David. 2000. Contemporary Globalization. In *Spaces of Hope*, 53–72. Berkeley: University of California Press.
Herman, Edward S. and Robert W. McChesney. 1997. *The Global Media*. London: Cassell.
Huang, Yong. 2019. Construction of Digital Silk Road Lights Up BRI Cooperation. *People's Daily*, 24 April 2019. http://en.people.cn/n3/2019/0424/c90000-9571418.html
Jessop, Bob. 2002. *The Future of the Capitalist State*. Cambridge: Polity.

Luxemburg, Rosa. 1970. *Rosa Luxemburg Speaks*. New York: Pathfinder Press.
Luxemburg, Rosa. 1914. Militarismus Und Arbeiterklasse. In *Rosa Luxemburg Gesammelte Werke Band 7/2*, 845–850. Berlin: Dietz
Luxemburg, Rosa. 1913/2003. *The Accumulation of Capital*. London: Routledge.
Marx, Karl. 1885. *Capital. Volume 2*. London: Penguin.
Marx, Karl. 1867. *Capital. Volume 1*. London: Penguin.
Marx, Karl. 1857/1858. *Grundrisse*. London: Penguin.
McChesney, Robert. 1999. *Rich Media, Poor Democracy*. New York: New Press.
Mosco, Vincent. 2009. *The Political Economy of Communication*. London: SAGE. Second edition.
Murdock, Graham. 2020. The Empire's New Clothes: Political Priorities and Corporate Ambitions in China's Drive for Global Ascendency. In *Media Imperialism: Continuity and Change*, edited by Oliver Boyd-Barrett and Tanner Mirrlees, 291–303. Lanham, MD: Rowman & Littlefield.
Qiu, Jack L. 2016. *Goodbye iSlave: A Manifesto for Digital Abolition*. Urbana: University of Illinois Press.
Qiu, Jack L. 2009. *Working-Class Network Society: Communication Technology and the Information Have-Less in China*. Cambridge, MA: MIT Press.
Ren, Xiaojin. 2019. Digital Silk Road Helping Developing Countries. *China Daily*, 27 April 2019. https://www.chinadaily.com.cn/a/201904/27/WS5cc3a6e7a3104842260b8add.htm
Sassen, Saskia. 1995. *On Concentration and Centrality in the Global City*. In *World Cities in a World-System*, edited by Paul L. Know and Peter J. Taylor, 63–75. Cambridge: Cambridge University Press.
Sassen, Saskia. 1991. *The Global City*. Princeton, NJ: Princeton University Press.
Schiller, Herbert I. 1991. Not-Yet the Post-Imperialist Era. In *International Communication. A Reader*, edited by Daya Kishan Thussu, 247–260. Oxon: Routledge. Chapter 14.
Schiller, Herbert. 1969/1992. *Mass Communications and American Empire*. Boulder, CO: Westview Press. Updated second edition.
Schiller, Herbert. 1975/1976. Communication and Cultural Domination. *International Journal of Politics* 5 (4): 1–127.
Smythe, Dallas W. 1994. *Counterclockwise*. Boulder, CO: Westview Press.
Sparks, Colin. 2020. China: An Emerging Cultural Imperialist. In *Media Imperialism: Continuity and Change*, edited by Oliver Boyd-Barrett and Tanner Mirrlees, 275–289. Lanham, MD: Rowman & Littlefield.
Sparks, Colin. 2007. *Globalization, Development and the Mass Media*. London: SAGE.
Thussu, Daya Kishan. 2007. Mapping Global Media Flow and Contra-Flow. In *Media on the Move. Global Flow and Contra-Flow*, edited by Daya Kishan Thussu, 10–29. London: Routledge.
Zhao, Yuezhi. 2011. The Challenge of China. Contribution to a Transcultural Political Economy of Communication in the Twenty-First Century. In *The Handbook of the Political Economy of Communications*, edited by Janet Wasko, Graham Murdock, and Helena Sousa, 558–582. Chichester: Wiley-Blackwell.
Zhao, Yuezhi. 2007. After Mobile Phones, What? Re-embedding the Social in China's "Digital Revolution"? *International Journal of Communication* 1: 92–120.

Recommended Readings and Exercises

Readings

The following texts are recommended as accompanying readings to this chapter:

David Harvey. 2006. *Spaces of Global Capitalism*. London: Verso.
Chapter 2: Notes towards a Theory of Uneven Geographical Development.

David Harvey. 2000. Contemporary Globalization. In *Spaces of Hope*, 53–72. Berkeley: University of California Press.

Christian Fuchs. 2020. *Communication and Capitalism. A Critical Theory*. London: University of Westminster Press.
Chapter 11: Global Communication and Imperialism (pp. 259–290).
Open access: https://doi.org/10.16997/book45.k

Vincent Mosco. 2009. *The Political Economy of Communication*. London: SAGE. Second edition.
Chapter 8: Spatialization: Space, Time, and Communication.

Yuezhi Zhao. 2011. The Challenge of China. Contribution to a Transcultural Political Economy of Communication in the Twenty-First Century. In *The Handbook of the Political Economy of Communications*, edited by Janet Wasko, Graham Murdock and Helena Sousa, 558–582. Chichester: Wiley-Blackwell.

Exercise 8.2   Global Media Corporations

Discuss:

What global/transnational media companies do you know?
How do these transnational media companies make money/profit?
How much profit do they make?
What criticisms of these companies have you heard? Conduct a search for news articles that focus on such criticisms and present your findings.

Exercise 8.3   The Tax Free Tour

Watch the following documentary film about transnational corporations' tax avoidance.

Marije Meerman, dir. 2013. *The Tax Free Tour*. Vrijzinnig Protestantse Radio Omroep (VPRO). Information: https://www.imdb.com/title/tt4162994/
https://www.youtube.com/watch?v=d4o13isDdfY

Discuss:

How does corporate tax avoidance work?

What are the impacts of corporate tax avoidance on society?

Are there other examples of corporate misbehaviour and crimes that you know about? Which ones?

What could be done to avoid such negative impacts of global corporations?

Discuss the following statement: "Thinking that taxation policies can be reformed is unrealistic. Companies can simply move to a country with more favourable policies".

Inform yourself about attempts to better tax global capital (such as the G7 agreement to introduce a global minimum corporation tax rate of 15%; see https://en.wikipedia.org/wiki/Global_minimum_corporate_tax_rate as starting point). How do you assess such attempts? Are they sufficient or not? Why respectively why not?

Exercise 8.4   Global Corporations' Rate of Profit

The rate of profit measures companies' profits in comparison to their investment costs into labour-power and resources. It can be calculated in the following manner:

$$RP = \frac{p}{c+v}$$

RP ... rate of profit, p ... annual profit, c ... annual investments into resources/means of production (constant capital), v ... investment into labour-power (variable capital).

Transnational corporations have annual financial reports. All those listed on US stock markets have to publish an annual SEC Filing 10-K form, which is a financial report that can often be found on the company website in a section titled "Investor Relations", as well as under https://www.sec.gov/edgar/searchedgar/companysearch.html

Annual company financial reports specify the annual profits (net income) and revenues/sales, which allows to calculate the profit rate in the following manner:
RP (in %) = profit / investment costs = net income / (revenues − net income) * 100

Let us have a look at data for Google/Alphabet from its SEC Filing 10-K report:

in million US$	2016	2017	2018	2019	2020	2021	2022
Revenues	90,272	110,855	136,819	161,857	182,527	257,637	282,836
Net income	19,478	12,662	30,736	34,343	40,269	76,033	59,972

Let us calculate Google's rate of profit for 2020:
RP (2020) = 40,269 / (182,527 − 40,269) = 28.3%

We can also calculate Google's rate of profit for the other years:

in %	2016	2017	2018	2019	2020	2021	2022
Google's rate of profit	27.5%	12.9%	29.0%	26.9%	28.3%	41.9%	26.9%

Select a transnational media/cultural/digital corporation that has an annual financial report that allows you to obtain data on revenues and profits for the past ten to twenty years.

Search for the relevant data.

Calculate the rate of profit data for the respective years.

Visualise the development of the company's rate of profit by creating a visual line chart in a spreadsheet application.

9 Media Work

The Political Economy of Cultural Labour in the Media Industry

What You Will Learn in This Chapter

- You will learn what labour is and how to analyse working conditions;
- You will learn about how to theorise and analyse cultural labour;
- You will learn about the working conditions in the culture, media and digital industry, and cultural co-operatives as an alternative mode of organisation;
- You will read about transformations of labour in the context of COVID-19.

9.1 Introduction

Work is a key feature of society. In modern society, wage-labour has come to play an important role. Given that many societies have experienced an increasing importance of the culture and digital industry, cultural labour, and media labour have become important. Most students of Media and Communication Studies aim to work in the cultural and digital sector. It therefore makes sense that they acquire a critical understanding of what it is like to be a cultural or digital worker. This chapter provides an introduction to the analysis of cultural and media labour.

This chapter asks: How does the political economy of cultural labour look like? Section 9.2 deals with the issue of how to define cultural labour. Section 9.3 focuses on how to define cultural labour. Section 9.4 presents insights into work in the culture industry. Section 9.5 discusses changes of labour in the COVID-19 crisis. Conclusions are presented in Section 9.6.

9.2 What Is Labour?

To define cultural labour, we need to understand both culture and labour.

9.2.1 What Is Culture?

Culture is one of the most complex theoretical categories. "Culture is one of the two or three most complicated words in the English language" (Williams 1983, 87).

DOI: 10.4324/9781003391203-11

The word "culture" comes from the Latin word "colere", which means to inhabit, cultivate, protect, and honour with worship. There are three modern meanings of the term "culture":

i the "general process of intellectual, spiritual and aesthetic development, from C18";
ii "a particular way of life, whether of a people, a period, a group, or humanity in general";
iii "the works and practices of intellectual and especially artistic activity. This seems often now the most widespread use: culture is music, literature, painting and sculpture, theatre and film" (Williams 1983, 90).

(i) and (iii) have been closely related. Raymond Williams (1981, 13) defines culture as "the signifying system through which necessarily (though among other means) a social order is communicated, reproduced, experienced and explored". Signification appears as "language, [...] as a system of thought or of consciousness, or, to use that difficult alternative term, an ideology; and again as a body of specifically signifying works of art and thought" (Williams 1981, 208). Culture involves "signifying institutions, practices and works" (Williams 1981, 208). A "culture is also a pool of diverse resources, in which traffic passes between the literate and the oral, the superordinate and the subordinate, the village and the metropolis; it is an arena of conflictual elements" (Thompson 1991, 6). "[I]nformation processes [...] have become a qualitative part of economic organization" (Williams 1981, 231).

> Thus a major part of the whole modern labour process must be defined in terms which are not easily theoretically separable from the traditional 'cultural' activities. [...] so many more workers are involved in the direct operations and activations of these systems that there are quite new social and social-class complexities.
> (Williams 1981, 232)

Culture has to do with the processes in which humans produce meaning as part of their everyday life, their ways of life. This understanding also underlies the definition of culture provided by the Cultural Studies scholars John Clarke, Stuart Hall, Tony Jefferson, and Brian Roberts:

> The 'culture' of a group or class is the peculiar and distinctive 'way of life' of the group or class, the meanings, values and ideas embodied in institutions, in social relations, in systems of beliefs, in *mores* and customs, in the uses of objects and material life.
> (Clarke, Hall, Jefferson and Roberts 1975/2006, 4)

Information is a central aspect of economic production in information societies. Therefore, the culture concept cannot be confined to popular culture, entertainment, works of art, and the production of meaning in the consumption of goods, but has to be extended into the realm of economic production and value creation in the form of the concept of cultural labour.

Williams calls his approach Cultural Materialism. He argues that ideas are not immaterial and individual, but material and social. There "is a real danger of separating human thought, imagination and concepts from 'men's material life-process'" (Williams 1989, 203). Marx's focus was on the "totality of human activity" (Williams 1989, 203). We "have to emphasise cultural practice as from the beginning social and material" (Williams 1989, 206). The "productive forces of 'mental labour' have, in themselves, an inescapable material and thus social history" (Williams 1989, 211).

9.2.2 What Is Work?

Adam Smith (1776, 10) starts the *Wealth of Nations* with the following sentence:

> THE annual labour of every nation is the fund which originally supplies it with all the necessaries and conveniences of life which it annually consumes, and which consist always, either in the immediate produce of that labour, or in what is purchased with that produce from other nations.

He speaks of value in use as "the utility of some particular object" (Smith 1776, 44) and argues that the value of a produced good is determined by labour time: "The real price of every thing, what every thing really costs to the man who wants to acquire it, is the toil and trouble of acquiring it" (Smith 1776, 47).

David Ricardo writes that produced things are useful because they "contribute to our gratification" (Ricardo 1824, 2). "By far the greatest part of those goods which are the objects of desire, are procured by labour" (Ricardo 1824, 3). Smith and Ricardo did not provide definitions of work and labour. We have to resort to Karl Marx's works for such definitions. Marx writes:

> The coat is a use-value that satisfies a particular need. A specific kind of productive activity is required to bring it into existence. This activity is determined by its aim, mode of operation, object, means and result. We use the abbreviated expression 'useful labour' for labour whose utility is represented by the use-value of its product, or by the fact that its product is a use-value. In this connection we consider only its useful effect.
>
> (Marx 1867, 132)

For Marx, work is the activity of production that creates goods and services that satisfy human needs. He considers work as an aspect of all societies:

> Labour, then, as the creator, of use-values, as useful labour, is a condition of human existence which is independent of all forms of society: it is an eternal natural necessity which mediates the metabolism between man and nature, and therefore human life itself.
>
> (Marx 1867, 133)

Labour

> is an appropriation of what exists in nature for the requirements of man. It is the universal condition for the metabolic interaction [Stoffwechsel] between man and nature, the everlasting nature-imposed condition of human existence, and it is therefore independent of every form of that existence, or rather it is common to all forms of society in which human beings live.
>
> (Marx 1867, 290)

In the essay *The Meanings of Work*, Raymond Williams (2022, 76) defines work in general as "the process of giving human energy to a desired end". In work, we use our hands and brains to produce something that helps us achieve defined goals. Williams points out that in contemporary society, there are many forms of work, such as housework, that are often not recognised as work because they are unpaid. The reason is that such individuals "are not, though working, engaged in wage-labour for another" (85). Williams argues that contemporary society defines labour as wage-labour to legitimate and privilege the capital/labour difference, where capital employs labour and thereby yields profit.

All work utilises and combines the activities of the brain and the rest of the body:

> Tailoring and weaving, although they are qualitatively different productive activities, are both a productive expenditure of human brains, muscles, nerves, hands etc., and in this sense both human labour. They are merely two different forms of the expenditure of human labour-power.
>
> (Marx 1867, 134)

All types of work are "functions of the human organism, and that each such function, whatever may be its nature or its form, is essentially the expenditure of human brain, nerves, muscles and sense organs" (Marx 1867, 164).

An author writing a book utilises the brain for creating ideas, reading other books, etc. They also use their hands for recording these ideas on paper or in a digital document. A builder uses their hands and entire body for laying bricks. They must think constantly about the correctness of their brickwork, what comes next, etc. All workers utilise their body and their brain, which means all work is mental and physical. But the products they create are different, some are more physical (a house), and some are more mental (a book), which allows us to distinguish between physical work on the one hand and mental/knowledge/information work on the other hand.

Work is a transformative process whereby humans bring about something new in society. In work, humans take matter from their environment that they transform so that something new emerges:

> Labour is, first of all, a process between man and nature, a process by which man, through his own actions, mediates, regulates and controls the metabolism between himself and nature. He confronts the materials of nature as a force of nature. He sets in motion the natural forces which belong to his own body, his arms, legs, head and hands, in order to appropriate the materials of nature in a form adapted to his own needs. Through this movement he acts upon external nature and changes it, and in this way he simultaneously changes his own nature.
>
> (Marx 1867, 283)

It sounds like Marx here primarily has agricultural and manufacturing work in mind. But also the creation of ideas is part of nature because nature is the largest system that exists in the world. Nature encompasses all forms of matter, including humans and their ideas. In cultural work, humans change not just nature, but also a specific part of nature and society, namely culture, the world of ideas.

Creative thinking is a crucial aspect of human existence and distinguishes humans from animals:

> A spider conducts operations which resemble those of the weaver, and a bee would put many a human architect to shame by the construction of its honeycomb cells. But what distinguishes the worst architect from the best of bees is that the architect builds the cell in his mind before he constructs it in wax. At the end of every labour process, a result emerges which had already been conceived by the worker at the beginning, hence already existed ideally. Man not only effects a change of form in the materials of nature; he also realizes [verwirklicht] his own purpose in those materials. And this is a purpose he is conscious of, it determines the mode of his activity with the rigidity of a law, and he must subordinate his will to it.
>
> (Marx 1867, 284)

> Yet, it is reasonable to assume that there is something that distinguishes humans from other animals, in addition to the opposable thumb, that is, purposeful work made possible by imagination, creative labour.
>
> (McGuigan 2010, 325)

Figure 9.1 visualises the work process based on Marx's works.

Marx identifies three key aspects of the work process: "The simple elements of the labour process are (1) purposeful activity, that is work itself, (2) the object on which that work is performed, and (3) the instruments of that work" (Marx 1867, 284).

The worker is the work process's subject and has certain characteristics such as acquired skills, knowledge, work experience. Workers stand in relations of production to other subjects. In class societies, these are class relations between the working class and the dominant class. In capitalism, class relations are relations of production between the working class and the capitalist class. The means of production consist of the instruments of labour, chiefly technologies, and the object of labour, the object on which changes take place. "An instrument of labour is a thing, or a complex of things, which the worker interposes between himself and the object of his labour and which serves as a conductor, directing his activity onto that object" (Marx 1867, 285). The workers utilise the instruments to change the nature of the object so that a new product emerges, the result of the work process. The subject (worker) uses objects (means of production) to create a subject-object (the product).

In the case of an author, the means of production consist of previous ideas generated by themselves and others (objects), their brain and writing technologies (instruments). The product is new ideas that take on the form of a novel, an academic book, a film script, a comic book, etc.

Man is a "tool-making animal" (Marx 1867, 286). It "is not what is made but how, and by what instruments of labour, that distinguishes different

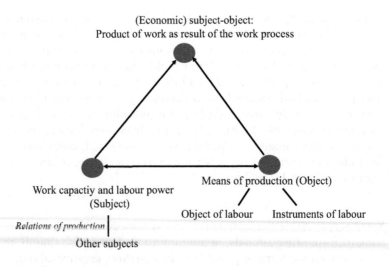

Figure 9.1 The work process.

economic epochs" (Marx 1867, 286). Marx characterises cultural work as the general intellect:

> The development of fixed capital indicates to what degree general social knowledge has become a direct force of production, and to what degree, hence, the conditions of the process of social life itself have come under the control of the general intellect and been transformed in accordance with it. To what degree the powers of social production have been produced, not only in the form of knowledge, but also as immediate organs of social practice, of the real life process.
>
> (Marx 1857/1858, 706)

9.2.3 The Valorisation Process

Capitalist production is (a) a labour process and (b) a valorisation process: Commodities are produced that have use-value, value, and exchange-value.

> Our capitalist has two objectives: in the first place, he wants to produce a use-value which has exchange-value, i.e. an article destined to be sold, a commodity; and secondly he wants to produce a commodity greater in value than the sum of the values of the commodities used to produce it, namely the means of production and the labour-power he purchased with his good money on the open market. His aim is to produce not only a use-value, but a commodity; not only use-value, but value; and not just value, but also surplus-value.
>
> (Marx 1867, 293)

An example: A media company invests 100,000 Euro per year in wages (v) and 100,000 Euro in infrastructure and technology (c). It wants not only to get back the 200,000 Euro, but to make a surplus/profit beyond this invested capital. In capitalist production, the monetary value of the sold commodities must be larger than the value of the invested capital. They contain a surplus value created by labour. The media content or the advertisements sold contain a surplus created by the employees in the case of media content and the audience in the case of advertising.

> The cotton originally bought for £100 is for example re-sold at £100 + £10, i.e. £110. The complete form of this process is therefore M-C-M', where $M' = M + \Delta M$, i.e. the original sum advanced plus an increment. This increment or excess over the original value I call 'surplus-value'.
>
> (Marx 1867, 251)

In the capital accumulation process $M - C .. P - C' - M'$ (see Chapter 8, Section 8.2), labour-power is present in the form of one of the commodities C that the capitalist buys. Workers play the key role in the production process P where they create the new commodity C' that contains a surplus product that is turned into monetary surplus value (profit) when the commodity C' is sold successfully. For Marx, there are two sides of labour in class societies:

1 the production of use-value: the qualitative side of a good, the way it satisfies human needs;
2 the production of value and exchange-value: the quantitative side of a good in commodity-producing societies; value: the number of hours needed for producing the good; exchange-value: a relationship of exchange between two goods: x commodity A = y commodity B.

Economic value has to do with the question of how much value a good has on the market. How much do you get for it or how much do you have to pay for it? Why, for example, is a car much more expensive than a toothbrush?

The Labour Theory of Value says that the price and value of a good are not random, but that the value of a good is determined by the average labour time needed to produce it. The production of a car takes much longer and is much more labour-intensive than the production of a toothbrush.

In the production of media content, there are specific characteristics of value production. Very high costs and a lot of labour time must be spent to produce the first copy. Once the content is created, it can be recycled with relatively little labour.

The marketing and valorisation of successful TV series, cinema films, music albums, etc. is cheap and requires relatively little labour time compared to the initial production. Media content production requires a lot of investment capital, involves great risks and generates income through the sale of rights. Valorisation only works for "hits".

For Marx, value and exchange-value exist only in class societies. What is specific about labour in capitalism, that is the modern form of the economy?

1 "First, the worker works under the control of the capitalist to whom his labour belongs" (Marx 1867, 291);
2 "Secondly, the product is the property of the capitalist and not that of the worker, its immediate producer. The labour process is a process between things the capitalist has purchased, things which belong to him. Thus the product of this process belongs to him" (Marx 1867, 292).

Marx speaks in this context also of "double free" labour:

> Free workers, in the double sense that they neither form part of the means of production themselves, as would be the case with salves, serfs, etc., nor do they own the means of production, as would be the case with self-employed peasant proprietors.
>
> (Marx 1867, 874)

Other than slaves, workers employed under capitalist conditions are not the physical property of someone. They sell their labour-power via a contract to an

employer. This means that they are free from their bodies being owned by someone. At the same time, they are also free from the products they produce, which
means they do not own these products. Workers in capitalism are structurally co-
erced by the market and the dominance of commodity logic to sell their labour-
power. There is a "silent compulsion of economic relations" (Marx 1867, 899).

9.2.4 Economic Alienation

Class has to do with the question of who owns the means of production and
surplus value. Class means a relation of power and exploitation between a
dominant class and dominated/exploited class. Marx (1867, 742) argues in
Capital that in capitalism, workers are "merely a machine for the production
of surplus-value" and capitalists are "a machine for the transformation of this
surplus-value into surplus capital". Class position is determined by a group's
role in the production process and its relation to the means of production.

Marx speaks of a dialectic of poverty and wealth in capitalism. Capital's
wealth is derived from the working class's lack of property:

> Labour as *absolute poverty*: poverty not as shortage, but as total exclu-
> sion of objective wealth. [...] labour is *absolute poverty as object*, on
> one side, and is, on the other side, the *general possibility* of wealth as
> subject and as activity.
>
> (Marx 1857/58, 296)

Building on the work of Georg Lukács, the German philosopher Axel Honneth conceives of alienation as reification. He characterises alienation as
"forgetfulness of recognition" (Honneth 2008, 59). It is forgotten and not
recognised that people should participate in social production processes that
affect them. The result is asymmetrical economic, political and cultural power
so that some groups have a lot of power and others have little or none. This
leads to the unequal distribution of wealth, political decision-making power
and reputation. Forgetfulness of recognition means "the process by which
we lose the consciousness of the degree to which we owe our knowledge and
cognition of other persons to an antecedent stance of empathetic engagement
and recognition" (Honneth 2008, 56).

Economic alienation means that in capitalism, workers are not in control
of their labour-power (as it has to be sold for them to be able to survive), the
means of production, and the products they create. Figure 9.2 visualises the
process of economic alienation.

Marx summarises the economic alienation process as follows:

> Therefore the worker himself constantly produces objective wealth, in
> the form of capital, an alien power that dominates and exploits him; and
> the capitalist just as constantly produces labour-power, in the form of a
> subjective source of wealth which is abstract, exists merely in the physical
> body of the worker, and is separated from its own means of objectification

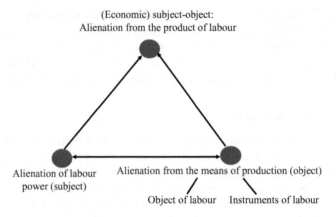

Figure 9.2 The process of economic alienation.

and realization; in short, the capitalist produces the worker as a wage-
labourer. This incessant reproduction, this perpetuation of the worker, is
the absolutely necessary condition for capitalist production.

(Marx 1867, 716)

9.2.5 The Working Class

Classes are groups in the economy characterised by different, opposing interests, different positions and roles in the production process and the economy,
and different levels of ownership.

In capitalist society, the relations of production are relations between
capital on the one side and dependent workers on the other hand, including
wage workers, houseworkers, freelancers, racialised workers who are paid
low wages and are compelled to take on, unfree workers such as slaves, etc.
They are dependent workers because they depend on conducting labour to
survive. And they are dependent because they do not own companies that
hire workers, money capital for investments, a large amount of resources,
etc. They form the working class. The sociologist Erik Olin Wright (1997,
10; 2005, 23) argues that there are three characteristics of the working class:

1 Exclusion:
    The working class does not own society's central means of production
    that allow the production of wealth;

2 Inverse interdependent welfare:
    The welfare of the dominant class is connected to the deprivation of the
    working class;

3 Appropriation:
    The dominant class has the power to appropriate and own the fruits of the
    working class's labour, that is that what workers produce but do not own.

Wright (1997) presents a class scheme that identifies 12 class positions. The basic distinction is between those who own means of production and capital and those who don't. Owners of capital are subdivided according to the number of employees in their companies. Employees are further subdivided according to the level of authority and the level of education and skills they have. Table 9.1 presents a further development of Wright's class scheme.

How large is the working class? How large is the capitalist class?

Wright (1997) analysed how the class structure of the labour force in the USA changed in the years from 1960 until 1990. The results are shown in Table 9.2.

Table 9.1 A class scheme

Owners of Means of Production		*Non-owners: Employees*			
Many employees	Large capital		Skills: Low (Unskilled)	Skills: Medium (Skilled workers)	Skills: High (Experts)
Few or some employees	Small- and medium-sized capital	Authority: High (Managers)	Non-skilled managers	Skilled managers	Expert managers
No employees	Freelancers	Authority: Medium (Supervisors)	Non-skilled supervisors	Skilled supervisors	Expert supervisors
		Authority: Low (Non-management)	Non-skilled workers	Skilled workers	Expert workers

Source: Based on Wright (1997, 25).

Table 9.2 Changes in the USA's class structure from 1960 until 1990 (based on Wright 1997, 99), data in percentage of the total labour force

	1960 (%)	1970 (%)	1980 (%)	1990 (%)
Managers (non-skilled and skilled)	7.5	7.6	8.0	8.3
Supervisors (non-skilled and skilled)	13.7	14.9	15.2	14.8
Expert managers	3.9	4.4	5.1	6.0
Experts (expert workers and expert supervisors)	3.5	4.5	5.5	6.9
Skilled workers	13.5	14.1	12.9	12.8
Unskilled workers	44.6	45.1	44.1	41.4
Freelancers	5.5	4.1	4.5	5.2
Small, medium, and large capitalists	7.9	5.3	4.8	4.7

Table 9.3 Aspects of the global working class, data in million

	1991	2020
Total labour force	2,395.1	3,409.2
Total employment	2,260.1	3,189
Wage workers	995	1,701.2
Own account workers	739.9	1,103.7
Contributing family workers	466.5	300.1
Unemployment	134.9	220.3
Employers	60.6	84.0
Persons not in the labour force (excluding those aged below 15)	1,247.9	2,400.2

Data source: ILO World Employment and Social Outlook, accessed on 26 November 2021.

The share of capitalists in the total economically active population de-creased somewhat in the USA between 1960 and 1990, which is an indication of increasing capital concentration. Among employees, the most significant change was an increase in experts, which is an indication of the increasing importance of higher education in the economy (see Table 9.3).

In 2020, there were more than 3.4 billion workers in the world. Workers and employers together make up 3.5 billion individuals active in the econ-omy. The share of workers active in the economy was 97.6%, and the share of employers was 2.4%.

There were 2.4 billion individuals not active in the labour force. If we assume that the poor are part of the working class and retired people have the same class status as those who are economically active, then it is a good estimate that at least 2.3 billion individuals (97.6% of those active in the economy) not in the labour force were part of the working class in 2020 because they were either poor or retired, which brings the estimation of the total size of the global working class to 5.8 billion in 2020. Employers made up 2.4% of those active in the economy. Their number was 84 million. If we add an estimation of retired employers (2.4% of 2.4 billion individuals who were not economically active), then the number increases from 84 to 141 mil-lion. The world's 2 billion children were left out of this calculation.

The working class is the largest subgroup of humanity. It was with 5.8 bil-lion people in 2020 larger than all other subgroups. The class of employers was with 141 million members in 2020 comparatively small, but very power-ful because of the capital it controls. The world population was around 7.75 billion in 2020 (data source: World Bank Data). We can therefore calculate that in 2020, the working class made up 74.2% of the world population and the capitalist class 1.8%. The working class is larger than all other subgroups of humanity.

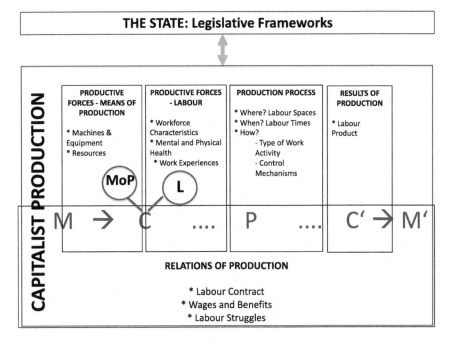

Figure 9.3 Aspects of working conditions in the capitalist economy.

Source: Sandoval (2013), reproduced with permission.

9.2.6 The Analysis of Working Conditions

Figure 9.3 visualises aspects of working conditions in the capitalist economy. Table 9.4 specifies questions one can ask when analysing specific working conditions. These questions are also important for the analysis of cultural labour.

Having dealt with some foundations of the concepts of work and labour, let us next take a closer look at the phenomenon of cultural labour.

9.3 What is Cultural Labour?

9.3.1 Three Types of Defining Cultural Labour

There are three ways one can define cultural workers: a narrow definition, an intermediate one and a broad one:

1 Narrow definitions:
     Cultural labour is labour "that is directly creative", "those jobs that directly manipulate symbols to create an original knowledge product, or add obvious value to an existing one" (Mosco and McKercher 2009, 24). The work of a writer falls under this definition, but not the one of a librarian;

Table 9.4 Dimensions of working conditions

Productive forces – Means of production	Machines and equipment	Which technology is being used during the production process?
	Resources	What resources are used during the production process?
Productive forces – Labour	Workforce characteristics	What are important characteristics of the workforce, for example, in terms of age, gender, ethnic background, etc.?
	Mental and physical health	How do the employed means of production and the labour process impact the mental and physical health of workers?
	Work experiences	How do workers experience their working conditions?
Relations of production, class relations and power relations	Labour contracts	Which type of contracts do workers receive, and what do they regulate?
	Wages and benefits	How high/low are wage levels and what are other material benefits for workers?
	Labour struggles	How do workers organise and engage in negotiations with capital and what is the role of worker protests?
	Discrimination and disadvantages	Are there differences in the workforce in terms of gender, origin, and skin colour? If so, do such differences play a role in the organisation? If so, to what extent? Are there disadvantaged groups? In what ways?
Production process	Labour spaces	Where does the production process take place?
	Labour times	How many working hours are common within a certain sector, how are they enforced and how is the relationship between work and free time?
	Work activity	What types of mental and/or physical activity are workers performing?
	Control mechanism	What types of mechanisms are in place that are used for the control and monitoring of workers' behaviour?
Results of production	Labour product	What kinds of products or services are being produced?
The state	Labour law	What regulations regarding minimum wages, maximum working hours, safety, social security, etc. are in place and how are they enforced?

Source: Sandoval (2013), reproduced with permission.

2 Intermediate definitions:
    Cultural labour is "the labor of those who handle, distribute, and convey information and knowledge" (Mosco and McKercher 2009, 24). The labour of both a writer and a librarian falls under this definition;

3 Broad definitions:
    Cultural labour is conducted by "anyone in the chain of producing and distributing knowledge products" (Mosco and McKercher 2009, 25). In the case of books, the writer, the librarian, and the printer are based on this definition of cultural workers.

9.3.2 Industry- and Occupation-Based Definitions

Whereas the first and the second definition are based on occupation, the third one is focused on the industry. There are occupation- and industry-based definitions of cultural labour.
    Examples of industry-based definitions of cultural workers:

- "A chemical engineer employed in the food industry, a designer in the shoe industry, an accountant or a lawyer in the chemical industry, all are engaged in the production of knowledge according to their *occupation*, but not according to the *industry* in which they work" (Machlup 1962, 45);
- A "cultural worker could be defined as someone who works in a cultural industry, whether the work that person does is 'cultural' (producing cultural output such as writing poetry or acting) or 'non-cultural' (such as selling tickets for a theatre company)" (Throsby 2010, 217);
- Knowledge workers are all

    the people whose work consists of conferring, negotiating, planning, directing, reading, note-taking, writing, drawing, blueprinting, calculating, dictating, telephoning, card-punching, typing, multigraphing, recording, checking, and many others, are engaged in the production of knowledge in the sense in which we understand these words;

    (Machlup 1962, 41)

- A knowledge or cultural worker is

    anyone in the chain of producing and distributing knowledge products. In this view, the low-wage women workers in Silicon Valley and abroad who manufacture and assemble cables and electronic components are knowledge workers because they are an integral part of the value chain that results in the manufacturing of the central engine of knowledge production: the computer. [...] Similarly, call-center workers, who sell communication products and services, would also fall within this broad definition of knowledge work because they are central to marketing information and because they make use of the products of communication technology to carry out their work.

(Mosco and McKercher 2009, 25)

Examples of occupation-based definitions of cultural workers:

- "a janitor in a school building, a charwoman in a research laboratory, a mechanic in a television studio, all are engaged in the production of knowledge according to the *industry* in which they work, but not according to their *occupation*. If the phrase 'knowledge industry' were to be given an unambiguous meaning, would it be a collection of industries producing knowledge in whatever industries they are employed? Would it thus include all people employed, and factor cost paid, in education, research and development, book publishing, magazines and newspapers, telephone and telegraph, radio and television? or rather all people employed, and factor cost paid to them, as accountants, actors, architects, artists, auditors, authors" (Machlup 1962, 45–46);
- Cultural occupation means that there is a "cultural nature of the work" that has a "recognizable input (creativity)" rather than culture as output (Throsby 2010, 217). Cultural work provides "direct input to the production of cultural content" (Throsby 2010, 27);
- Cultural labour involves activities that "produce and disseminate symbols in the form of cultural goods and services, generally, although not exclusively, as commodities" (Garnham 1990, 156);
- Cultural labour "involves the production of symbols for primarily expressive, aesthetic or informational purposes, and for experience by distant others (or support for those who carry out such work)" (Hesmondhalgh and Baker 2008, 103). Creative labour means "jobs, centred on the activity of symbol-making, which are to be found in large numbers in the cultural industries" (Hesmondhalgh and Baker 2011, 9). Cultural labour deals "primarily with the industrial production and circulation of texts" (Hesmondhalgh 2013, 17). Texts provide meaning and "are created with communicative goals primarily in mind" (Hesmondhalgh 2013, 16). The products are "symbolic, aesthetic, expressive, and/or informational" (Hesmondhalgh 2013, 60). Cultural work is "the work of symbol creators" (Hesmondhalgh 2013, 20). For Hesmondhalgh, it includes work in broadcasting, film, music, publishing, video and computer games, advertising, marketing, public relations and web design;

- Immaterial labour is "labor that produces the informational and cultural content of the commodity" (Lazzarato 1996, 133), labour "that creates immaterial products, such as knowledge, information, communication, a relationship, or an emotional response" (Hardt and Negri 2004, 108).

Hesmondhalgh's definition of cultural workers excludes hardware production, software engineering, and work in telecommunications and the Internet industry. He opposes broad definitions of cultural work because "such a broad conception risks eliminating the specific importance of *culture*, of *mediated communication*, and of the *content* of communication products" (Hesmondhalgh and Baker 2011, 60).

The opposition to industry definitions of cultural work faces several problems:

- Idealism: It does not see the materiality of culture;
- Dualism: The focus on content and ideas neglects the connectedness of technology and content;
- Digital blindness: The approach is blind for large parts of digital media that are crucial in contemporary economies. It privileges work in music, broadcasting, film, publishing, advertising, and games as more important than software engineering, hardware production and Internet work. It implies that digital media production is not creative and that digital media are not part of culture;
- Politics: Workers are facing the globalisation and convergence of capital, which makes it difficult for them to act if they are separated as a class. Therefore, various unions have united different information workers. "A more heterogeneous vision of the knowledge-work category points to another type of politics, one predicated on questions about whether knowledge workers can unite across occupational or national boundaries, whether they can maintain their new-found solidarity, and what they should do with it." (Mosco and McKercher 2009, 26.) One "big union is better" for "workers to come together across the knowledge industry" (Mosco and McKercher 2009, 42). It strengthens them in resisting the commodification and privatisation of public services.

Mosco and McKercher argue that for workers to be successful in making demands on employers, they need to be organised based on entire industries so that the workforce in one company, independent of their occupation, makes demands together. An example of a cross-occupation union is the Communications Workers of America. It represents, among others, flight attendants, telecommunications workers, electronic, electrical, salaried, machine and furniture workers, journalists and other news workers, broadcasting employees and technicians.[1] ver.di is Germany's largest union. It represents workers in services, education, research, public services, financial services, local communities, health and social care, trade, media, the arts, the postal service, logistics, social security, telecommunications, information technology, transport, utilities, and the disposal of waste.[2]

Cultural labour takes place under specific conditions, which we will look at in more detail in the next section.

9.4 Labour in the Culture Industry

9.4.1 Cultural Labour and Cultural Commodities

Labour that is conducted in capitalist relations of production creates commodities. There is a variety of models of cultural commodity production that involve different forms of cultural labour. Table 9.5 gives an overview of these models and associated forms of labour.

9.4.2 Precarious Labour

Guy Standing is an economist who has analysed the changes in working conditions. In his book *The Precariat*, Standing (2011) analyses the rise and features of precarious labour.

Neoliberalism led to the rise of flexible labour markets, including the loss of economic security in one or several of the seven different categories that characterise workplaces. Typical features of precarious labour are temporary jobs, part-time employment, dependent contract work, call centre workers, interns, long working hours, the blurring of work time and leisure time, as well as workplace, the home and public spaces, high levels of stress and overwork, multiple jobs, unhealthy lifestyles, a lack of work-life balance, falling wages, and a lack of time.

Standing (2011, 10) defines seven forms of labour security:

- Labour market security: the security that everyone can find decent work;
- Employment security: the security that one can keep a job and does not face arbitrary dismissal;
- Job security: the security that one can improve one's role and position at the workplace in terms of status, income, etc.;
- Work security: secure and social working conditions (workplace safety, working time limits, protection of workers' health, work-life balance, etc.);
- Skill reproduction security: opportunities for workers to develop their skills;

Table 9.5 Models of cultural commodity production and relevant forms of labour

Cultural Commodity Type	Example Commodities	Example Workers
Access to cultural events	Theatre performances, exhibitions, talks, lectures, readings, discussions, concerts, live performances, movie screenings in the cinema, pay-per-view access to live television events, etc.	Actors, dancers, musicians, museum workers, performance artists, theatre and cinema employees, event technicians, sound engineers, advertising and public relations workers, etc.
Cultural content	Books, newspapers, magazines, audio recordings (e.g. vinyl records), recorded audiovisual content (e.g. movies distributed on DVDs, Blu-ray discs, computer hard disks, or downloaded on the Internet) purchased artworks, posters or prints	Writers, novelists, journalists, musicians, recording engineers, advertising and public relations workers, visual artists, filmmakers, etc.
Advertising space	Outdoor and transit ads, direct mail, newspaper and magazine ads, radio ads, television ads, digital and online ads	Audiences produce attention for advertisements, advertising workers, advertising technology engineers, etc.
Subscriptions for regular access to cultural content	Newspaper and magazine subscriptions, theatre subscriptions, museum subscriptions, cinema subscriptions, pay television	subscription sales and management personnel; PR and advertising workers responsible for marketing subscriptions
Technologies for the production, distribution and consumption of information	Record player, stereo, television set, computer, mobile phone, laptop, camera, audio recorder	Miners extracting minerals used for the production of components, scientists and engineers, sales, advertising and public relations workers who brand and market technologies, etc.
Mixed models of cultural commodities	Newspaper and magazine models that combine the sale of advertising, printed copies and subscriptions, one-time digital access and digital subscriptions; cultural corporations that sell technologies and access to content	Combination of various workers creating different cultural commodities

- Income security: security that one gains a decent income in the form of minimum wage regulations, welfare state mechanisms, progressive and re-distributive taxation that reduces inequalities, etc.;
- Representation security: freedom that workers organise collectively (trade unions, the right to strike, etc.).

Since the middle of the 1970s, neoliberalism has in many countries led to the rise of flexible labour markets and the loss of economic security in one or several of the seven dimensions of labour security. "The number of people in insecure forms of labour multiplied" (Standing 2011, 6).

The motivation for cultural work is "some expectation of favourable op-portunity for connecting conception and execution, the accomplishment of something like non-alienated work" (McGuigan 2010, 326). Humans have a desire for self-determined work, in which they can express their creativity. One form of work security that Standing's dimensions are missing is work satisfac-tion. Humans have the desire to conduct work that they find self-fulfilling. Work satisfaction not only has to do with the subjective assessment of the existence or non-existence of Standing's dimensions but also has to do with the assessment of the content of work, work activities and social relations at work.

9.4.3 Wage Repression

The basic cause of the deterioration of working conditions has been the ne-oliberal structuration of society, which includes wage repression, the com-modification of everything, including social security and welfare, the individualisation of social risks, privatisation, deregulation of employment laws, liberalisation of markets, the globalisation of capitalism accompanied by the offshoring of employment and competitive nation-states, tax reliefs for companies, the weakening of unions, the financialisation of the econ-omy, economic crisis, austerity politics after states bailed out banks, etc.

> The neoliberal switch to 'post-Fordism' is characterised by the disaggre-gation of vertically integrated major corporations, outsourcing, reduction in the social wage and faster response to consumer trends facilitated by computerized information systems. The balance of power in the labour bargain between capital and labour shifted inexorably from the latter to the former and working life became much less secure and more precarious.
>
> (McGuigan 2010, 328)

Table 9.6 shows the development of the wage share for a variety of countries. The wage share is the share of the sum-total of wages in the gross domestic product. The data shows that there has been a significant decrease in the wage share in recent decades. The decreasing wage share has been the conse-quence of neoliberal wage repression, that is the politics to reduce wages in relation to profits.

Table 9.6 Adjusted wage share as a percentage of GDP at current market prices

Country	2022	2019	2013	2007	2000	1990	1980	1970	1960
European Union (15 countries)	55.7	56.3	56.1	56.6	55	56.3	58.2	63.6	61.4
Belgium	58.4	59.1	59	62	59	60.5	60.8	66.2	55.4
Bulgaria	58.6	58.4	59.4	54	43.8	49.4	-	-	-
Czechia	48.7	51.8	51.6	49.5	47.2	45.9	-	-	-
Denmark	52.6	54.2	54.7	55.1	55.6	53.9	57.9	61.3	60.9
Germany	58.2	58.9	58.2	57.5	54.2	59	58.8	63.7	61.1
Ireland	30	33	33.8	47.1	48.7	47.5	57.1	67.3	64.6
Greece	53.4	51.9	51.8	52.3	51.3	49.5	54.8	53	56.9
Spain	53	53.2	52.7	54.1	55.2	58.8	60.3	66.3	63.7
France	56.9	57.3	58.3	58.4	55.4	55.9	58.3	65.9	62.6
Italy	53.2	52.6	52.4	53.1	51.9	50.9	58.4	63.4	62
Netherlands	56.7	57.4	57.3	58.9	55.6	59.3	62.3	68.7	65.8
Austria	54.3	55.1	54.6	55	52.4	56	59.1	63.9	60.6
Poland	49.5	49.3	49.3	47.8	48.2	56.7	-	-	-
Portugal	53.4	52.1	52.1	53.6	56.1	60.2	55.5	67.3	73.2
Finland	50.9	52.5	52.4	55.9	51.8	52.9	62.2	63.1	62.2
Sweden	48.7	49.7	49.8	50.5	47.6	47.8	51.3	54.8	52.7
UK	57.8	58.6	57.6	57.9	58.7	55.8	56	60	61.1
Turkey	46.9	48.9	46.9	43.3	42.3	55	72.6	-	-
USA	56.3	56.6	56.5	56.2	58.6	61.3	60.8	61.7	63.2
Japan	58.7	57.7	57.2	57.2	58.2	61.5	62.7	71	-
Canada	-	55.7	55.3	55.6	54.9	55.9	59	58.6	59.9
Norway	50.9	51.4	48.8	47.9	45	45.8	53.1	54.6	58
Mexico	-	38.5	37.1	40.3	38.4	39.5	-	-	-
Korea	-	61.6	61.1	61	64.2	-	-	-	-
Australia	-	53.1	52.1	53.4	54.7	57.1	59.1	63.6	59.8
New Zealand	-	53.5	52.6	50.2	51.5	47.9	52.4	-	-

Data source: AMECO, accessed on 9 November 2021.

9.4.4 Ten Features of Labour in the Capitalist Cultural and Digital Industry

Rosalind Gill (2002, 2011) analysed labour in the new media industry. She conducted interviews with programmers, interaction designers, editors, copywriters, business managers, artists, illustrators, researchers, content managers, concept makers, software document writers, consultants, project managers, Web developers, etc. in Austria, Finland, Ireland, the Netherlands, Spain, and the UK.

She identified ten key features of work in the digital and cultural industry:

1 Love of the work:
   "It's like being paid for a hobby" (Gill 2011, 253);
2 Entrepreneurialism:
   Cultural and digital workers often have the aspiration to innovate, create something and be pioneers;
3 Short-term, precarious, insecure labour:
   One respondent said: "It's insecure. Maybe I will look for jobs two days a week to pay the rent. But really I'm too busy for that" (Gill 2011, 253). There is a "lack of access to benefits, insurance, and pension schemes and attendant worries about becoming ill, having an accident, or having to work into old age" (Gill 2011, 253). Another respondent reported:

   > It's very intensive and I don't have enough time to rest. Because it's always going on. And if you don't plan something for yourself, some-one will call and say you have to be there, and there. You can't say no to a job. Because you don't know when the next job is going to be;
   > (Gill 2011, 254)

4 Low pay:
   In the digital and cultural industry, we find heavy competition and "competitive pressures on prices" (Gill 2011, 254);
5 Long-hours culture:
   Freelancers in this industry regularly often work 60–80 hours per week.

   > Many projects had extremely tight deadlines (which workers had to agree to meet in order to get the contract) and these necessitated intense round-the-clock working for a short period, which might then be followed by several weeks with no (new media) work at all. This pattern was the norm for workers in this study and has been described elsewhere as the 'bulimic career';
   > (Gill 2002, 83–84)

6 Keeping up:
   Knowledge, standards and technology constantly change, and one needs to constantly keep up with these changes and educate oneself about them, which is time-consuming;
7 DIY learning:
   The learning of new skills mostly takes on the form of self-taught knowledge;

8 Informality:
   Work in these industries has a play ethos. Finding work and getting clients
   is based on friends and personal networks, "people you meet at conferences, parties, drinks evenings, friends of friends, ex-colleagues, and so
   on" (Gill 2011, 257). The interview partners reported that people in the
   digital and cultural industry feel networking is an obligation, a compul-
   sory sociality;

9 Exclusions and inequality:
   There are inequalities related to gender, age, class, race, ethnicity, and dis-
   ability. For example, one respondent argued:

   > We are trying to have a baby, so then we will see. I definitely want to
   > keep on working and have my own income. I hope it won't get less.
   > So I think I'll bring the baby to the creche. But frankly I have no idea.
   > I am a bit afraid and I think nothing is arranged to women like me
   > who have their own companies.
   >
   > (Gill 2011, 258)

   It is "extremely difficult for a woman to combine child-rearing with the
   bulimic patterns of the portfolio new media career" (Gill 2002, 84). Another respondent said:

   > I have a relationship with somebody. She is also involved in this
   > work. I don't know if we are going to have kids. It scares the living
   > hell out of me, the whole idea. Because overwork is just the reality of
   > what I am doing, like all people in new media. Horrifying overwork
   > is the reality. Like how many hours a week? Oh man, the amount
   > of hours I have to put in in a week or this job – it amounts to 2 full-
   > time jobs easily. And I mean I am working with a very good planner
   > and I'm having a hell of a time keeping the hours. That is what I'm
   > most scared of in my personal life. The impact of having no time for
   > a kid or... that is what I'm most scared of. If I had some kids, boy it
   > would be a tough life;
   >
   > (Gill 2011, 258)

10 No future:
    Workers in the digital industry often cannot think about how life will
    look like in five years because they are so engaged in their work in the
    present:

    > In new media work there is a great deal to take care of – particularly,
    > but not exclusively – for those freelancing or setting up micro-
    > businesses. You are required to train yourself, keep up-to-date, find
    > or create your own work, monitor your progress, compare yourself
    > with others, anticipate what will come next, maintain your distinct

reputation, meet deadlines whatever costs they exert on your body or relationships, prepare for contingencies such as illness, injury or old age, make contacts, network and socialise, and to do all of this in an atmosphere in which your success or failure is understood in entirely individualistic terms. There is no time when you can switch off, because all of life has become a 'social factory' (Tronti 2019), an opportunity for work. Whoever you meet, wherever you go – a friend's wedding, a high-school reunion, a cycling holiday with friends – represents a possible opportunity. There is no 'outside' to work, as one of our interviewees put it: 'life itself is a pitch'.

(Gill 2011, 260)

Hesmondhalgh and Baker (2011) confirmed the results of Rosalind Gill's work in interviews with 63 creative workers in TV, music recording and magazine publishing that show the ambivalence of much creative industry work as precarious, but cherished because of the fun, contacts, reputation, creativity, and self-determination that it often involves.

Boltanski and Esquerre (2020, chapter 14) analysed data for cultural workers in France. They included visual artists, performance artists, journalists, publishers, writers, translators, architects, documentation workers, archivists, and arts teachers. There are many freelancers in the cultural, media, and digital sectors. The analysis shows that these workers have an average income that is 12% lower than that of people with a comparable level of education (e.g. engineers). Boltanski and Esquerre emphasise that many cultural workers manage with some effort to achieve a standard of living "that is not very different from the one they would have had if they had opted for classic careers" (317). Among other things, this means that in addition to creative content production, they also need management skills to manage and market themselves, which is time-consuming.

These activities are indispensable for remaining informed about new trends and new projects, negotiating contracts, mastering the intricacies of funding arrangements, making oneself known (in particular via social networks), and *making oneself stand out*, in a highly competitive situation, in dealings with very diverse agencies and persons.

(318)

It is difficult for freelancers to organise themselves in trade unions because their work is individualised and they are both entrepreneurs and workers, so it is not immediately clear to whom wage demands can be made. Answers to these problems are, for example, the foundation of trade union suborganisations for freelancers, the demand for a guaranteed basic income for cultural workers, and the founding of cultural co-operatives.

9.4.5 EA Spouse and Labour in the Video Game Industry

Nick Dyer-Witheford and Greig de Peuter (2006) present a case study of labour in video game production. Electronic Arts is one of the world's largest and most profitable video game–producing companies. It publishes games such as Tetris, The Sims, SimCity, FIFA Soccer, Command & Conquer, Medal of Honor, Star Wars.

In 2004, an anonymous open letter from the spouse of a software developer working for Electronic Arts was published. "EA Spouse" wrote:

> The current mandatory hours are 9am to 10pm – seven days a week – with the occasional Saturday evening off for good behavior (at 6:30pm). This averages out to an eighty-five hour work week. [...] The stress is taking its toll. After a certain number of hours spent working the eyes start to lose focus; after a certain number of weeks with only one day off fatigue starts to accrue and accumulate exponentially. [...] And the kicker: for the honor of this treatment EA salaried employees receive a) no overtime; b) no compensation time! ('comp' time is the equalization of time off for overtime -- any hours spent during a crunch accrue into days off after the product has shipped); c) no additional sick or vacation leave. [...] Never should it be an option to punish one's workforce with ninety hour weeks; in any other industry the company in question would find itself sued out of business so fast its stock wouldn't even have time to tank. [...] EA's annual revenue is approximately $2.5 billion. This company is not strapped for cash; their labor practices are inexcusable. [...] If I could get EA CEO Larry Probst on the phone, there are a few things I would ask him. 'What's your salary?' would be merely a point of curiosity. The main thing I want to know is, Larry: you do realize what you're doing to your people, right? And you do realize that they ARE people, with physical limits, emotional lives, and families, right? Voices and talents and senses of humor and all that? That when you keep our husbands and wives and children in the office for ninety hours a week, sending them home exhausted and numb and frustrated with their lives, it's not just them you're hurting, but everyone around them, everyone who loves them? When you make your profit calculations and your cost analyses, you know that a great measure of that cost is being paid in raw human dignity, right?[3]

Based on interviews with video game workers, Dyer-Witheford and de Peuter (2006) identify four features of such labour: enjoyment, exclusion, exploitation, and exodus:

1 Enjoyment:
   Digital labour involves "[c]reativity, co-operativeness and coolness" (Dyer-Witheford and de Peuter 2006, 603). Interviewees said: "We have

very little hierarchy" (604); "There is a lot of teamwork. You make really good friends" (604); "None of our people would ever attend a meeting in a suit" (604); "If I'm at a bar, and someone cares about it, and I say I'm working [in the game industry], they go, 'Whooo, that's cool'" (605). Workers describe labour in the video games industry as playful;

2 Exclusion:
Statistics and studies show that the video game industry is "an industry built around games made by males for males" (606);

3 Exploitation:
Most video game workers work for more than 40 hours a week. There are also times of "crunch time", where 65–80 or more hours are usual. The problems are hard deadlines and that the work is project-oriented. There are scheduled milestones in a software project. One interviewee said: "There's a lot of pressure when you're looking at a deadline and something just has to work and it doesn't, but you just have to make it work by next Tuesday. You end up working really long hours" (608). In the USA, where Electronic Arts has its headquarters, the Fair US Labor Standards Act (Section 13 (a) 17) provides an exemption from overpayment for computer systems analysts, software engineers or similar workers.

Other interview partners said: "they promote, you know, 'Hey, we have a couch here. You can sleep here all night … You're nineteen" (610); "Youthful enthusiasm, home-away-from-home workplaces, stock options, the risks of leaving, macho bravado, and a cool corporate culture – these are among the softly coercive elements of video game companies' culture of extreme work" (611). There is a "forced workaholism" (611);

4 Exodus:
A significant share of workers cannot stand the work pressure over time and therefore leave their job or the industry.

"EA Spouse" is Erin Hoffman, an American video game developer and blogger (https://en.wikipedia.org/wiki/Erin_Hoffman). Her fiancé Leander Hasty was part of a lawsuit against Electronic Arts, where software engineers successfully demanded compensation for unpaid overtime. Hoffman concluded that "the only thing that will get publishers to budge is unionization" (Dyer-Witheford and de Peuter 2006, 613).

The discussion shows that in cultural and digital labour, one can often observe a variety of forms of alienation. A significant share of cultural workers enjoys the content of their work and is facing precarious working conditions. They are simultaneously happy and unhappy. They conduct labour they love under conditions one should hate.

9.4.6 Cultural Co-operatives

What alternatives are there to precarious labour? Cultural workers can and should inform themselves about the changes and realities of the economy, observe closely what employers are doing, support campaigns for the strengthening of labour rights, support civil society groups that want to improve working conditions, and unionise themselves and struggle for better working conditions. Some cultural workers have found it feasible to form cultural co-operatives. "Co-operatives are member-owned and controlled democratic organisations" (Co-operatives UK 2019, 2). In a worker co-operative, the workers together own the company and make decisions together. Co-operatives are democratically owned and governed. They are also called self-managed companies. A cultural co-operative is a co-operative operating in the cultural sector (see Sandoval 2016a, 2016b, 2018).

Marisol Sandoval (2016a, 2016b, 2018) studied cultural co-operatives, that is worker co-operatives in the cultural sector. Cultural co-ops are on the one hand an alternative to capitalist organisation models that are "democratising ownership and decision power" (Sandoval 2016a, 62), and on the other hand, they operate in a high-risk, unpredictable industry so that workers in a co-op "might end up co-owning very little or nothing" (64). Sandoval, therefore, argues that co-operatives should act as parts of social movements for radical reforms that overcome precarious labour. In the cultural sector, this would have to mean making political demands such as "the stricter taxation of corporate profits to redistribute wealth, a guaranteed basic income, public grants for starting co-operatives and increases in public funding for the cultural sector" (68).

De Peuter, Dreyer, Sandoval, and Szaflarska (2020) conducted a cultural co-op survey where 106 co-ops in Canada, the UK, and the USA participated (De Peuter, Dreyer, Sandoval, and Szaflarska 2020; Dreyer, de Peuter, Sandoval, and Szaflarska 2020). They report:

> 55.5% of the co-ops surveyed reported that their pay 'meets' or 'exceeds' the average for their industry. Yet 43.6% of co-ops reported that competitive remuneration is a challenge for them. The top five selected benefits of working at a co-op were: supportive work relationships; a friendly work environment; opportunities for creative self-expression; a work culture that encourages teamwork and co-operation; and low hierarchy at work. Over 90% of the co-ops surveyed agreed that democratic decision-making is a priority in their co-op. [...] Our respondents agreed that increasing the number of new co-ops requires, above all, educating the public about co-ops and improving access to funding.
> (Dreyer, de Peuter, Sandoval, and Szaflarska 2020, 8)

9.5 Labour and the COVID-19 Crisis

9.5.1 Spatio-Temporal Aspects of Labour in the Context of COVID-19

Based on the French philosopher Henri Lefebvre's (1974/1991) theory of space, the critical theorist David Harvey (2005) provides a typology of social space (see Table 9.7). Using Lefebvre's distinction between perceived, conceived, and lived spaces as three dimensions of space, Harvey distinguishes between physical space, representations of space, and spaces of representation. He adds to Lefebvre's theory the distinction between absolute, relative, and relational space. Spaces are absolute in that they are locales that have certain physical boundaries. They are relative because objects are placed in them that have certain distances from each other. And they are relational because these objects stand in relations to each other. In society, humans produce and reproduce social space by a dialectic of social practices and social structures. The cells in Table 9.7 describe particular aspects of social space.

Table 9.8 shows how social spaces were changing and were organised during the coronavirus crisis.

In the coronavirus crisis, humans are largely confined to the physical space of the home, for which certain organisational strategies are needed so that everyday life can be organised from the home. Humans experience, conceptualise, live and thereby also produce social space-time in manners that make social spaces converge in the supra-time-space of the home. Communication technologies play a decisive role in organising everyday life from the locale of the home in the coronavirus crisis.

Everyday life refers to social practices within the totality of society (Lefebvre 2002, 31). Everyday life is an "intermediate and mediating *level*" of society (45). Lefebvre identifies three dimensions of everyday life: natural forms of necessity, the economic realm of the appropriation of objects and goods, and the realm of culture (62). So Lefebvre sees nature, the economy, and culture as the three important realms of everyday life. What is missing is the realm of politics, where humans take collective decisions that are binding

Table 9.7 David Harvey's (2005) typology of social space

	Physical Space (Experienced Space)	Representations of Space (Conceptualised Space)	Spaces of Representation (Lived Space)
Absolute space	Physical locale	Symbols, maps, and plans of physical locales	Locales as social spaces where humans live, work, and communicate
Relative space (time)	Humans in a physical locale	Symbols used and meanings created by humans in physical locales	Humans as social actors acting in social roles
Relational space (time)	Social relations of humans in a physical locale	Language as social and societal structure	Communicative practices that produce and reproduce social relations, sociality, and social spaces

Table 9.8 Social space in the coronavirus crisis

	Physical Space (Experienced Space)	*Representations of Space (Conceptualised Space)*	*Spaces of Representation (Lived Space)*
Absolute space	The home as the supra-locale	Plans and strategies of how to use the supra-locale of the home for the organisation of everyday life	The home as the dominant social space and supra-social space where humans simultaneously organise multiple aspects of their life and work, the convergence of absolute spaces in the home
Relative space (time)	Humans stay predominantly in one locale, their homes	Symbols used and meanings created by humans in the supra-locale of the home	Convergence of humans' social roles in the supra-space of the home
Relational space (time)	Social relations at a physical distance organised via communication technologies between home locales	Language as social structure	The convergence of humans' communicative practices in the convergent space and under conditions of the convergent time of the home, mediation of the convergence of space-time by communication technologies

Table 9.9 Lefebvre's distinction between the lived and the living

The Lived (le vécu)	*The Living (le vivre)*
Individual	Group
Experience, knowledge, doing	Context, horizon
Practices	Structures
Present	Presence

Source: Lefebvre (2002, 166, 216–218).

for all and take on the forms of rules. The critique of everyday life analyses how humans live, "how badly they live, or how they do not live at all" (18). Lefebvre argues that in phases of fundamental societal change, "*everyday life is suspended, shattered or changed*" (109). The coronavirus crisis has suspended, shattered and necessitated the reorganisation of the practices, structures, and routines of everyday life.

Lefebvre distinguishes between the lived (le vécu) and the living (le vivre) as two levels of everyday life (see Table 9.9).

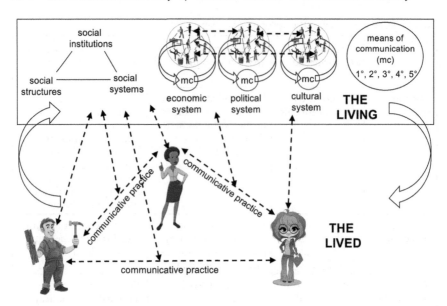

Figure 9.4 Everyday life and everyday communication.

Figure 9.4 shows a model of everyday life. At the level of lived reality, humans produce social objects through communicative practices. They do so under the conditions of the living, that is structural conditions that enable and constrain human practices, production, and communication. The level of living life consists of an interaction of social structures, social systems, and social institutions. All structures, systems and institutions have economic, political, and cultural dimensions. In many social systems, one of these dimensions is dominant so that we can differentiate between economic, political, and cultural structures/systems/institutions. At the level of lived life, humans relate to each other through communicative practices. These communicative practices are the foundations of the production, reproduction, and differentiation of economic, political, and cultural structures/systems/institutions that condition human practices. There is a dialectic of the living and the lived in any society. This is a dialectic of human subjects and social objects.

Means of communication mediate the dialectic of objects and subjects and the relations between humans.

Figure 9.5 visualises the transformation of everyday life and everyday communication at the time of the coronavirus crisis. Humans isolate themselves and therefore avoid direct communicative relations. This circumstance is visualised at the level of the lived by enclosed individuals and small enclosed groups. Dense networks of direct communication and direct social relations are suspended. At the structural level of the lived, the economic, political, and cultural dimensions are not organised as separate locales but tend to converge in the social system of the home that takes on the form of

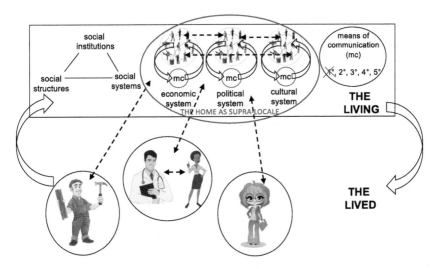

Figure 9.5 Everyday life and everyday communication in the coronavirus crisis.

a supra-locale from where economic, political, and cultural life is organised and structured from a distance. Humans spend the vast majority of their time in physical isolation in their homes, from where they access and organise social structures, systems, and institutions at a distance by making use of secondary, tertiary, quaternary, and quinary means of communication. The use of the primary means of communication, namely face-to-face communication, is avoided. Whereas under regular conditions humans organise the economy, politics, and culture in the form of separate social systems that they access in everyday life by commuting to different specialised physical locales, in the coronavirus crisis specialised physical locales are suspended. These systems' structural social roles are preserved: A multitude of humans who are located in the physical locales of their homes organises these systems at a distance with the help of mediated communication. Humans hardly communicate with each other face-to-face but through mediating communication technologies.

In the coronavirus crisis, most people traverse only smaller physical distances and fewer goods are transported so that everyday life is decelerated and comes to a relative standstill. There are fewer people who spend overall less time on the streets, in public and intermediate spaces. At the same time, the number of social activities and communicative practices taking place at home and conducted from there at a distance massively increases. As a consequence, communication networks such as the Internet and mobile phone networks are used at a maximum capacity. The thinning out of social activity in public spaces corresponds to the thickening and multiplication of social activities taking place in the home and locally. The coronavirus crisis de-globalises and therefore localises everyday life.

9.5.2 Empirical Studies

There are some factors that shaped work during the COVID-19 pandemic, in which the home office played a significant role:

- In the home office, the spatial separation of labour and leisure is eliminated;
- Labour time, free time and social roles become more easily blurred;
- One saves travel times and meeting times;
- When children are at home, as during the COVID lockdowns, it can be difficult to organise labour and child-rearing;
- There is a danger that superiors expect you to be available in the home office at all times;
- Technologies at home are often not up to the standard of the workplace, and it can be unclear who pays for the technology costs;
- There is a need for clear regulation of working time and resource issues for working from home;
- Feelings of isolation can be stronger than with traditional work;
- A lot of time in front of the screen can be exhausting.

A study of working conditions during the COVID-19 pandemic conducted an online survey with 5,748 participants from 29 countries in Europe. Table 9.10 shows the statements that achieved the highest agreement. These

Table 9.10 Advantages and disadvantages of the home office in the COVID-19 pandemic, mean scores on a Likert scale (1: "I strongly disagree", 5: "I strongly agree")

Statement	Mean Agreement
Advantages	
I contribute to lowering the risk of spreading COVID-19	4.60
I do not expose myself to the risk of getting a disease	4.38
I save on the normal commute time to my workplace	4.37
I can take a break when I want to	3.66
I get time to focus on my work without interruptions from other people	3.48
Disadvantages	
I do not get to see my colleagues or other people as much as I would like to	3.83
I miss getting out of my home	3.67
The physical conditions in my home do not afford a good working environment (adjustable table and chair, enough light, quietness, good monitor, etc.)	3.06

Source: Ipsen, van Vaeldhoven Kirchner, and Hansen (2021, table 2).

are pros and cons. The values are averages, using a Likert scale where 1 means strongly disagree and 5 means strongly agree.

A study by Eurofound (2021) where 1,276 managers participated in a survey found that only 20% of companies reimbursed their homeworkers' telecommunications and utility costs during the COVID-19 pandemic. If companies do not cover such costs, they are outsourcing constant capital costs for infrastructure to workers who have to cover these costs from their salaries, which means a reduction of their wage income. Legal and company policies should take this problem into account and make sure employers cover homeworkers' infrastructure costs.

The study identified both advantages and disadvantages, with the advantages rated as greater.

> In addition to lowering the risk of contracting and spreading the disease, the saving of commuting time and greater flexibility (regarding food and breaks) were rated as the most important advantages. The biggest disadvantages were missing colleagues, missing getting out of the home and poor physical work conditions in the home office.
>
> (Ipsen, van Vaeldhoven Kirchner and Hansen 2021, 12)

Comparing the answers of people with and without children, there are differences in terms of undisturbed concentration on work and work efficiency: "the people without children scored higher than the people with children at home" (9). Home office technologies were also often considered inadequate: "Our analysis indicated that 'Inadequate tools' [...] was one of the factors hindering the current way of working" (13).

Hofmann, Piele, and Piele (2021) surveyed 215 companies in October 2021. 81.2% of the companies surveyed stated that office employees will be able to work off-site from any location within the country in the future. Eurofound (2021) surveyed European managers about business transformations during the COVID-19 pandemic (N = 1,276). Fourteen per cent of the managers who responded said they think the amount of telework will after the COVID pandemic increase, 57% said it will remain the same, and 29% said it will decrease. This shows that companies acknowledge the importance of homework and telework in post-COVID societies.

6,309 working people took part in an online survey conducted by the Hans Böckler Foundation in June 2020 (Hans-Böckler-Stiftung 2020). A relative majority of 48% said that they would like to work from home as often after the crisis as during the crisis. Thirty-three per cent of 6309 employed respondents said they work exclusively, mainly or partly from home. 60% said that the boundaries between work and leisure are blurred in the home office. Seventy-seven per cent said the home office made it easier to reconcile family and work. Two factors play a role here: On the one hand, the time saved on travel and meetings, and on the other hand, the physical proximity to the children. Overall, parents tend to rate the home office positively.

Ahlers, Mierich, and Zucco (2021) surveyed over 6,000 workers aged 16 and over in each of four survey waves (maximum of 7,677). According to the survey, in April 2020, at the beginning of the pandemic, 82% of the employed in the media, information, communication, and arts sectors worked from home. Before Corona, the figure was 29%. Forty-nine per cent said they would like to work from home as often after the crisis as during the crisis. This desire is significantly greater among employees of companies that have company rules on working from home. "Company policies facilitate the implementation of the home office. Where agreements exist and are already lived practice, procedures can be implemented more easily in the Corona pandemic" (16).

> Unpaid overtime can be counteracted by recording working time. If working time is permanently exceeded, work processes and quantities must be adjusted if necessary. The duration, location and distribution of work in the home office are defined on the basis of company agreements. In this way, the connection to the company is guaranteed and the availability of employees remains transparent through the definition of specific times. Concrete availability times can have a relieving effect on all concerned.
>
> (18)

People with a double workload (wage-labour, child-rearing) find working in a home office significantly more stressful than working without, which makes it clear that adequate childcare is necessary for the home office to work.

In a study by Eurofound (2020), a survey of 91,753 participants was conducted on work during the COVID-19 crisis. The majority were satisfied with working from home and would like to maintain a certain level of working remotely even after the end of the crisis. The

> experience of working from home during the COVID crisis appears to have been a positive one for the majority of employees who did so [...] with 70% 'overall [...] satisfied with the experience of working from home'. A much lower share of teleworking employees (47%) indicated that their employer had provided the equipment needed to work from home. [...] Overall, 78% of employees in the July round of the e-survey indicated a preference for working from home at least occasionally if there were no COVID-19 restrictions. The main teleworking preference cited was several times a week (32%) with only 13% indicating that they would like to telework daily. The preferred teleworking arrangement for most respondents, therefore, still involves a significant continuing presence at the workplace.
>
> (Eurofound 2020, 34)

Overall, such studies show that from the perspective of workers and companies, the home office will and should be an important part of the post-COVID economy. There are potential disadvantages in terms of social contacts, childcare, technology use and working hours. However, many workers believe the advantages outweigh the disadvantages. Crucially, legal and workplace regulations and welfare state mechanisms help to make the home office, if used, socially viable.

The COVID-19 pandemic has advanced the digitalisation of labour and the blurring of the boundaries between the home and the office, private and public life, and leisure and labour time. These are tendencies that have shaped the world of labour for some time. They have been accelerated, deepened, and extended during the pandemic.

9.6 Conclusion

This chapter introduced the Political Economy of cultural labour. Let us now summarise the main findings.

Finding 1: Work and Labour

Work is a process where humans with the help of means of production produce something new that satisfies certain human needs. In capitalism, work is to a significant degree organised as labour that produces commodities that have not just use-value but also exchange-value and value. In class societies, workers are economically alienated, which means that they do not own the means of production and the products they create. They do not determine the conditions of their labour.

Finding 2: Cultural Labour

There are narrow, intermediate, and broad, as well as industry-based and occupation-based, definitions of cultural workers. The advantage of industry-based and broad definitions is that they imply that such workers organise themselves collectively based on the experiences they make in the same company and industry. When a larger number of workers make demands, they have more power to achieve their goals.

Finding 3: Working in the Cultural Industry

Neoliberalism has brought about precarious labour conditions in general to maximise corporations' profits. In the cultural industry, the consequence has been that cultural workers often love their work activities but face precarious working conditions.

Finding 4: Cultural Co-operatives

Cultural worker co-operatives are worker-owned and worker-governed companies in the cultural sector. They are potential alternatives to the capitalist organisational model in the cultural and digital sector.

Finding 5: Work and COVID-19

Labour has changed significantly in the context of the COVID-19 pandemic. More work is taking place from home. This has created new opportunities and risks. It is crucial that the home office and the digitalisation of work are regulated in a socially viable way.

Notes

1 Data source: https://cwa-union.org/about, accessed on 29 November 2021.
2 Data source: https://www.verdi.de/wegweiser/++co++ee809444-cfd3–11e0–5780-0019b9e321cd, accessed on 29 November 2021.
3 https://boards.fool.com/letter-from-an-ea-spouse-long-21588406.aspx?sort=recommendations, accessed on 30 November 2021.

References

Ahlers, Elke, Sandra Mierich, and Aline Zucco. 2021. *Homeoffice: Was wir aus der Zeit der Pandemie für die zukünftige Gestaltung von Homeoffice lernen können.* WSI Report 65, April 2021. Düsseldorf: Wirtschafts- und Sozialwissenschaftliches Institut der Hans-Böckler-Stiftung.
Boltanski, Luc and Arnaud Esquerre. 2020. *Enrichment. A Critique of Commodities.* Cambridge: Polity.
Clarke, John, Stuart Hall, Tony Jefferson, and Brian Roberts. 1975/2006. Subcultures, Cultures and Class. In *Resistance through Rituals: Youth Subcultures in Post-War Britain*, edited by Stuart Hall and Tony Jefferson, 3–59. Abingdon: Routledge. Second edition.
Co-operatives UK. 2019. *Co-operative Corporate Governance Code.* Manchester: Co-operatives UK.
de Peuter, Greig, Bianca C. Dreyer, Marisol Sandoval, and Aleksandra Szaflarska. 2020. *Sharing Like We Mean It: Working Co-operatively in the Cultural and Tech Sectors.* Cultural Workers Organize. https://culturalworkersorganize.org/wp-content/uploads/2021/01/Sharing-Like-We-Mean-It-Web.pdf
Dreyer, Bianca C., Greig de Peuter, Marisol Sandoval, and Aleksandra Szaflarska. 2020. *The Co-operative Alternative and the Creative Industries. A Technical Report on a Survey of Co-operatives in the Cultural and Technology Sectors in Canada, the United Kingdom, and the United States.* Cultural Workers Organize. https://culturalworkersorganize.org/wp-content/uploads/2020/12/The-Cooperative-Alternative-Technical-Report-Web.pdf
Dyer-Witheford, Nick and Greig de Peuter. 2006. "EA Spouse" and the Crisis of Video Game Labour: Enjoyment, Exclusion, Exploitation, Exodus. *Canadian Journal of Communication* 31 (3): 599–617.
Eurofound. 2021. *Business Not as Usual: How EU Companies Adapted to the COVID-19 Pandemic.* Luxembourg: Publications Office of the European Union.
Eurofound. 2020. *Living, Working and COVID-19.* Luxembourg: Publications Office of the European Union.
Garnham, Nicholas. 1990. *Capitalism and Communication. Global Culture and the Economics of Information.* London: SAGE.
Gill, Rosalind. 2011. "Life Is a Pitch": Managing the Self in New Media Work. In *Managing Media Work*, edited by Mark Deuze, 249–262. London: SAGE.

Gill, Rosalind. 2002. Cool, Creative and Egalitarian? Exploring Gender in Project-Based New Media Work in Europe. *Information, Communication & Society* 5 (1): 70–89.

Hans-Böckler-Stiftung. 2020. Homeoffice: Besser klar geregelt. *Böckler Impuls* 2020 (15). https://www.boeckler.de/de/boeckler-impuls-homeoffice-besser-klar-geregelt-27643.htm

Hardt, Michael and Antonio Negri. 2004. *Multitude*. New York: Penguin Press.

Harvey, David. 2005. Space as Keyword. In *Spaces of Neoliberalization*, 93–115. Stuttgart: Franz Steiner Verlag.

Hesmondhalgh, David. 2013. *The Cultural Industries*. London: SAGE. Third edition.

Hesmondhalgh, David and Sarah Baker. 2011. *Creative Labour. Media Work in Three Cultural Industries*. London: Routledge.

Hesmondhalgh, David and Sarah Baker. 2008. Creative Work and Emotional Labour in the Television Industry. *Theory, Culture & Society* 25 (7–8): 97–118.

Hofmann, Josephine, Alexander Piele, and Christian Piele. 2021. *Arbeiten in der Corona-Pandemie. Folgeergebnisse. Ausgestaltung des „New Normal"*. Stuttgart: Fraunhofer-Institut für Arbeitswirtschaft und Organisastion IAO.

Honneth, Axel. 2008. *Reification. A New Look at an Old Idea*. Oxford: Oxford University Press.

Ipsen, Christine, Marc van Veldhoven, Kathrin Kirchner, and John Paulin Hansen. 2021. Six Key Advantages and Disadvantages of Working from Home in Europe during COVID-19. *International Journal of Environmental Research and Public Health* 18 (4): 1826. DOI: https://doi.org/10.3390/ijerph18041826

Lazzarato, Maurizio. 1996. Immaterial Labour. In *Radical Thought in Italy*, edited by Michael Hardt and Paolo Virno, 133–147. Minneapolis: University of Minnesota Press.

Lefebvre, Henri. 2002. *Critique of Everyday Life. Volume II: Foundations for a Sociology of the Everyday*. London: Verso.

Lefebvre, Henri. 1974/1991. *The Production of Space*. Malden, MA: Wiley-Blackwell.

Machlup, Fritz. 1962. *The Production and Distribution of Knowledge in the United States*. Princeton, NJ: Princeton University Press.

Marx, Karl. 1867. *Capital. Volume 1*. London: Penguin.

Marx, Karl. 1857/1858. *Grundrisse*. London: Penguin.

McGuigan, Jim. 2010. Creative Labour, Cultural Work and Individualisation. *International Journal of Cultural Policy* 16 (3): 323–335.

Mosco, Vincent and Catherine McKercher. 2009. *The Laboring of Communication. Will Knowledge Workers of the World Unite?* Lanham, MD: Lexington Books.

Ricardo, David. 1824. *On the Principles of Political Economy and Taxation*. London: John Murray. Third edition.

Sandoval, Marisol. 2018. From Passionate Labour to Compassionate Work: Cultural Co-ops, Do What You Love and Social Change. *European Journal of Cultural Studies* 21 (2): 113–129. DOI: https://doi.org/10.1177/1367549417719011

Sandoval, Marisol. 2016a. Fighting Precarity with Co-operation? Worker Co-operatives in the Cultural Sector. *New Formations* 88: 51–68. DOI: http://doi.org/10.3898/newF.88.04.2016

Sandoval, Marisol. 2016b. What Would Rosa Do? Co-operatives and Radical Politics. *Soundings: A Journal of Politics and Culture* 63: 98–111.

Sandoval, Marisol. 2013. Foxconned Labour as the Dark Side of the Information Age: Working Conditions at Apple's Contract Manufacturers in China. *tripleC: Communication, Capitalism & Critique* 11 (2): 318–347. DOI: https://doi.org/10.31269/triplec.v11i2.481

Smith, Adam. 1776. *The Wealth of Nations*. 2 Volumes. Indianapolis, IN: Liberty Fund.

Standing, Guy. 2011. *The Precariat. The New Dangerous Class*. London: Bloomsbury.

Thompson, Edward P. 1991. *Customs in Common*. Pontypool: Merlin Press.

Throsby, David. 2010. *The Economics of Cultural Policy*. Cambridge: Cambridge University Press.

Tronti, Mario. 2019. *Workers and Capital*. London: Verso.

Williams, Raymond. 2022. *Culture and Politics*. London: Verso.

Williams, Raymond. 1989. *What I Came to Say*. London: Hutchinson Radius.

Williams, Raymond. 1983. *Keywords. A Vocabulary of Culture and Society*. New York: Oxford University Press. Revised edition.

Williams, Raymond. 1981. *The Sociology of Culture*. Chicago, IL: University of Chicago Press.

Wright, Erik Olin, ed. 2005. *Approaches to Class Analysis*. Cambridge: Cambridge University Press.

Wright, Erik Olin. 1997. *Class Counts*. Cambridge: Cambridge University Press.

Recommended Readings and Exercises

Readings

The following texts are recommended as accompanying readings to this chapter:

Karl Marx. 1867. Chapter 7: The Labour Process and the Valorization Process: I. The Labour Process. In *Capital. Volume 1*, 282–292. London: Penguin.

Christian Fuchs. 2020. *Marxism: Karl Marx's Fifteen Key Concepts for Cultural and Communication Studies*. New York: Routledge.
Chapter 5: Labour and Surplus-Value (pp. 77–104).
Chapter 6: The Working Class (pp. 105–126).

Rosalind Gill. 2011. "Life is a Pitch": Managing the Self in New Media Work. In *Managing Media Work*, edited by Mark Deuze, 249–262. London: Sage.

Nick Dyer-Witheford and Greig de Peuter. 2006. "EA Spouse" and the Crisis of Video Game Labour: Enjoyment, Exclusion, Exploitation, Exodus. *Canadian Journal of Communication* 31 (3): 599–617. http://www.cjc-online.ca/index.php/journal/article/view/1771/2052

Marisol Sandoval. 2016. Fighting Precarity with Co-operation? Worker Co-operatives in the Cultural Sector. *New Formations* 88: 51–68. DOI: http://doi.org/10.3898/newF.88.04.2016

Christian Fuchs. 2020. Everyday Life and Everyday Communication in Coronavirus Capitalism. *tripleC: Communication, Capitalism & Critique* 18 (1): 375–399. DOI: https://doi.org/10.31269/triplec.v18i1.1167

Exercise 9.1   Work Experiences in the Cultural Sector

Discuss in groups:

How many of you have done an internship before? What have been your internship experiences?

Why are unpaid internships such a big thing today? What are the structural causes of this phenomenon in society and the economy?

How many of you have had a full-time or part-time job before? What have been your work experiences in these jobs?

What was your worst internship or other work experience? Why?

What does a good internship/job in the media and cultural industry look like? What characteristics does a good internship/job in this industry have?

Exercise 9.2   Cultural Co-operatives

Read the following texts:

Marisol Sandoval. 2016. Fighting Precarity with Co-operation? Worker Co-operatives in the Cultural Sector. *New Formations* 88: 51–68. DOI: http://doi.org/10.3898/newF.88.04.2016

Marisol Sandoval. 2016. What Would Rosa Do? Co-operatives and Radical Politics. *Soundings: A Journal of Politics and Culture* 63: 98–111.

Greig de Peuter, Bianca C. Dreyer, Marisol Sandoval, and Aleksandra Szaflarska. 2020. *Sharing Like We Mean It: Working Co-operatively in the Cultural and Tech Sectors.* Cultural Workers Organize. https://culturalworkersorganize.org/wp-content/uploads/2021/01/Sharing-Like-We-Mean-It-Web.pdf

Bianca C. Dreyer, Greig de Peuter, Marisol Sandoval, and Aleksandra Szaflarska. 2020. *The Co-operative Alternative and the Creative Industries. A Technical Report on a Survey of Co-operatives in the Cultural and Technology Sectors in Canada, the United Kingdom, and the United States*. Cultural Workers Organize. https://culturalworkersorganize.org/wp-content/uploads/2020/12/The-Cooperative-Alternative-Technical-Report-Web.pdf

Discuss:

What is a cultural co-operative?

What makes working in a cultural co-operative different from a capitalist company?

In your view, what are the advantages and disadvantages of cultural co-operatives? How do you assess this organisational model?

Do you prefer to work in a regular company or in a cultural co-operative? Why?

Exercise 9.3   Labour and the COVID-19 Pandemic

Work in groups:
Search for empirical studies of how labour has changed in the COVID-19 pandemic and post-COVID societies. Present and compare the findings of these analyses.

Discuss:

What are the major changes labour has been facing in post-COVID societies?

What changes of life and work have you experienced during the COVID-19 pandemic?

What opportunities and problems are there concerning the changes of labour in post-COVID societies?

How should labour in post-COVID societies best be regulated? What are the most important policies and legal regulations that you think are needed?

10 The Political Economy of the Internet and Digital Media

What You Will Learn in This Chapter

- You will learn about social media's Political Economy;
- You will better understand digital labour and digital surveillance;
- You will learn about alternatives to the capitalist Political Economy of the Internet and digital media.

10.1 Introduction

The Internet has become the central information and communication technology of many contemporary societies. It plays a role in all aspects of everyday life. We learn online, entertain us, communicate with others, conduct parts of work online, etc. The Internet has both economic and political aspects. Think, for example, of Instagram, Facebook and TikTok that are owned by large transnational corporations – Meta Platforms in the case of Instagram and Facebook, ByteDance in the case of TikTok. These Internet platforms are also involved in controversies over fake news, censorship, surveillance, etc. In this chapter, we will look at how political and economic aspects of the Internet look like and interact.

In this chapter, we deal with the following question: How does the Political Economy of the Internet and digital media look like?

Section 10.2 deals with the Political Economy of social media. Section 10.3 discusses digital labour. Section 10.4 focuses on the Political Economy of digital surveillance. Section 10.5 asks if there are alternatives to the capitalist Political Economy of the Internet and digital media. Section 10.6 presents the chapter's main findings.

10.2 Social Media's Political Economy

In Chapter 7, Dallas Smythe's Political Economy of advertising, which uses the notions of the audience commodity and audience labour, was introduced. These notions remain of key importance in the analysis of the Internet's Political Economy, but need an update that reflects the realities of 21st-century capitalism.

DOI: 10.4324/9781003391203-12

Targeted digital advertising is a major capital accumulation model of the world's leading social media platforms and apps such as Google, You-Tube, Facebook, Instagram, TikTok, Twitter, Blogspot/Blogger, Weibo, LinkedIn, VK, Tumblr, Pinterest. In targeted advertising, not all users of an ad-based medium see the same ads. Rather, ads are targeted and personalised based on specific criteria and collected data. For example, adverts for children's clothes will only be targeted at those who have children. To identify such users, users' profiles are monitored for child-related information.

10.2.1 *Targeted Advertising and Internet Platforms' Policies*

Targeted advertising as a capital accumulation model requires a legal foundation. In their terms of use and privacy policies, platforms and apps define what data they collect and use for advertising. Let us have a look at some examples:

- Facebook's Data Policy (v 21/8/2020):
  "To create personalized Products that are unique and relevant to you, we use your connections, preferences, interests and activities based on the data we collect and learn from you and others";
- Twitter's Privacy Policy (v 19/8/2021):
  "We use information you provide to us and data we receive, including Log Data and data from third parties, to make inferences like what topics you may be interested in, how old you are, and what languages you speak. This helps us better promote and design our services for you and personalize the content we show you, including ads";
- Google's Privacy Policy (v 1/7/2021):
  "We use the information we collect to customize our services for you, including providing recommendations, personalized content, and customized search results. [...] Depending on your settings, we may also show you personalized ads based on your interests";
- TikTok's Privacy Policy (v 2 June 2021):
  "We will use the information we collect about you in the following ways: [...] provide you with personalised advertising; [...] We share information with advertisers and third-party measurement companies to show how many and which users of the Platform have viewed or clicked on an advertisement. We share your device ID with measurement companies so that we can link your activity on the Platform with your activity on other websites; we then use this information to show you adverts which may be of interest to you;
- Weibo's Privacy Policy (v 22/11/2021)":
  "When you use Weibo, we will use your device information, IP address and location information to deliver personalised ads to you".[1]

These example policy excerpts show that apps and Internet platforms use all data they can get hold of in order to personalise adverts. They are conducting massive user surveillance in order to accumulate capital by selling advertisements.

10.2.2 Google and Targeted Advertising

Google is the dominant actor in the business of targeted ads (see Fuchs 2021, chapter 5). Figure 10.1 visualises the development of its profits. Google was founded by Larry Page and Sergey Brin in 1998. The company's profits first exceeded US$ 1 billion in 2005 and first had profits of over US$ 10 billion in 2012.

Targeted advertising has proven to be very profitable for Google. The corporation has become one of the world's largest transnational corporations (see Table 10.1). At the same time, its founders Larry Page and Sergey Brin, as well as its former CEO (2001–2011) and Executive Chairman (2011–2017) Eric Schmidt, became very rich (see Table 10.2).

Figure 10.2 shows the traditional capital accumulation cycle as explained in Chapter 8. M – C .. P – C' – M' is the formula of the capitalist economy's accumulation process. Capitalist companies invest money capital M into the purchase of the commodities C, labour-power and means of production. In the production process P, labour uses the means of production for creating new commodities C' that the workers do not own. The company offers these commodities C' for sale on the market. If the sale is successful, a sum of money capital M' that is larger than the invested money capital M is generated. M' contains a profit. Parts of M' and the profit are reinvested to try to accumulate even more capital.

Figure 10.3 shows the cycle of capital accumulation in the case of targeted advertising–based Internet platforms such as Google.

As we saw in Chapter 7, for Dallas Smythe (1994, 266–291) the material aspect of communications is that audiences work, are exploited and are sold as a commodity to advertisers. Smythe's approach is also valid in the context of Internet platforms. Such an updated analysis needs to take the affordances and specificities of the Internet's Political Economy into account. Conducting a Google search is no commodity; it is offered as a free service. It is, as Smythe (1977, 5) says, "an inducement (gift, bribe or 'Free lunch') to recruit potential members of the audience and to maintain their loyal attention" (Smythe 1977, 5). On ad-funded social media, the "gift" and inducement are the "free" use of the platform. Google's users create attention for advertisements, as well as a massive amount of data on various platforms (not just Google) that Google and others monitor, that is store, analyse and never delete. Google identifies interest groups and uses predictive algorithms for identifying potential interests that group members might have. User surveillance is used for targeting ads. Google's commodities are the users and their attention. Google users are workers who produce a data commodity and an online attention commodity.

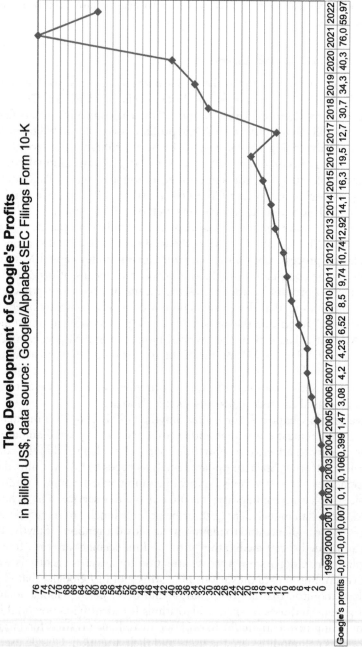

	1999	2000	2001	2002	2003	2004	2005	2006	2007	2008	2009	2010	2011	2012	2013	2014	2015	2016	2017	2018	2019	2020	2021	2022
Google's profits	-0,01	-0,01	0,007	0,1	0,106	0,399	1,47	3,08	4,2	4,23	6,52	8,5	9,74	10,74	12,92	14,1	16,3	19,5	12,7	30,7	34,3	40,3	76,0	59,97

The Development of Google's Profits
in billion US$, data source: Google/Alphabet SEC Filings Form 10-K

Figure 10.1 The development of Google's profits.

Table 10.1 Google's ranking in the list of the largest public companies in the world

Year	Rank
2004	904
2005	439
2006	289
2007	213
2008	155
2009	120
2010	120
2011	120
2012	103
2013	68
2014	52
2015	39
2016	27
2017	24
2018	23
2019	17
2020	13
2021	13
2022	11

Data source: Forbes 2000 list for various years.

10.2.3 Differences Between Classical and Digital, Targeted Advertising

There are several features of the audience commodity on the Internet, where advertising is digital, targeted and personalised, that make it distinct from classical print and broadcasting advertising:

- **Creativity, prosumption, social relations:**
  Audiences produce attention and make meanings of content; Internet users also produce data, content and social relations. They are prosumers, productive consumers who produce commodities;
- **Surveillance:**
  The measurement of audiences has in broadcasting and print traditionally been based on studies with small samples of audience members. Measuring user behaviour on social media is constant, total and algorithmic. Audience commodification on social media is based on the constant real-time surveillance of users;

Table 10.2 Development of the ranking of Google's three richest
directors in the list of the 400 richest Americans

Year	Larry Page	Sergey Brin	Eric Schmidt
2004	43	43	165
2005	16	16	52
2006	13	12	51
2007	5	5	48
2008	14	13	59
2009	11	11	40
2010	11	11	48
2011	15	15	50
2012	13	13	45
2013	13	14	49
2014	13	14	49
2015	10	11	48
2016	9	10	36
2017	9	10	35
2018	6	9	33
2019	6	7	33
2020	8	9	33
2021	5	6	30
2022	6	7	34

Data source: Forbes 400 list of the Richest Americans, various years.

- **Targeted and personalised advertising:**
  Digital advertising is often targeted and personalised;
- **Predictive algorithms:**
  User measurement uses predictive algorithms (if you like A, you may also like B because 100 000 people who like A also like B);
- **Algorithmic auctions:**
  Ad prices are often set based on algorithmic auctions (pay-per-view, pay-per-click).

Facebook and Google are not communications companies. They do not sell digital services. Rather, they sell ads. They are the world's largest advertising agencies.

Users' digital labour on advertising-funded platforms such as Instagram, YouTube, Facebook, TikTok or Snapchat is fully unpaid but produces

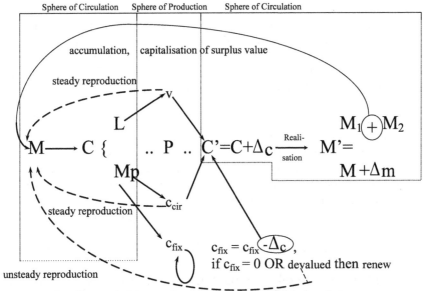

c_{cir}: raw- and auxiliary-materials, operating supply items, semi-finished products,
c_{fix}: machines, buildings, equipment; circulating capital: c_{cir}, v; fixed capital: c_{fix}

Figure 10.2 The cycle of capital accumulation.

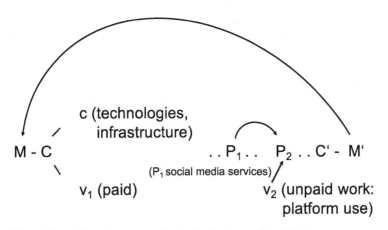

C' = Internet prosumers' **big data commodity**
(user-generated content, transaction data, virtual
advertising space and attention time);
Most social media services are free to use, they are no
commodities. User data and attention is the social media
commodity.

Figure 10.3 Targeted advertising's capital accumulation cycle.

commodities. There is a long history of unpaid labour in capitalism. House-work includes unpaid labour such as care, cleaning, shopping, cooking, do-ing the laundry. Such labour reproduces labour-power. Without housework, there would be no labour-power that is sold as a commodity on the labour market. Federici (1975) emphasises the importance of housework in the economy. Housework helps capital make profits. It is unpaid.

> the unwaged condition of housework has been the most powerful weapon in reinforcing the common assumption that housework is not work, thus preventing women from struggling against it, [...] the wage at least recognizes that you are a worker, and you can bargain and struggle around and against the terms and the quantity of that wage, the terms and the quantity of that work.
>
> (Federici 1975, 77, 76)

The Wages for Housework Campaign based on these insights demands a wage for housework.

Unpaid labour also takes on the form of consumer labour where parts of the production process are outsourced to consumers so that companies save labour costs and make more profit. Examples are IKEA self-assemblage furniture, fast food restaurants where customers are their own waiters, self-check-in kiosks at airports, check-out kiosks in supermarkets, self-ser-vice petrol stations. Such labour is also referred to as prosumption, since consumers also become producers of goods.

Instagram and YouTube users are like houseworkers unpaid, commodity-producing workers. Kylie Jarrett, therefore, speaks of them as digital house-workers. The labour involved in both housework and user-labour "is physi-cal, but features significant cognitive, affective and communicative elements [...] Moreover, consumer labour occupies a similar position in relation to the generation of surplus-value as domestic work" (Jarrett 2015, 210–211).

> Consumer labour is akin to domestic labour not only because it is un-paid and occurs outside of formal factory walls in what is ostensibly free time. It is also akin to it because it is a site of social reproduction.
>
> (Jarrett 2016, 71)

The artist Laurel Ptak has created the online artwork Wages for Facebook. She has replaced the word "housework" in the Wages for Housework Mani-festo (Federici 1975) with "Facebook" (see http://wagesforfacebook.com/). The artwork illustrates the parallels between housework and the use of ad-vertising-funded Internet platforms.

Dal Yong Jin (2013) speaks of "platform imperialism" because "the cur-rent state of platform development implies a technological domination of U.S.-based companies that have greatly influenced the majority of people and countries" (Jin 2013, 154). Imperialism does not mean US domination of the world. Capitalism, not geography is the decisive aspect of imperialism. Jin misconceives imperialism and platform imperialism as geographical domination. The Internet does not become non-imperialist when it is no longer dominated by US capital, but by other capital. It makes no difference if the Internet is dominated by US, Chinese, Brazilian, Korean, French, etc. capital. Imperialism is a type of capitalism where finance capital, monopoly capital, capital export, war and global capitalist domination play a role (Fuchs 2010).

The Internet is not just a realm of capital accumulation but also one of ideology.

10.2.4 Internet Ideologies

There are ideologies of and on the Internet (see Fuchs 2021). We will here focus on one example of ideology in the context of the Internet, namely how social media platforms present themselves. Instagram says it gives "people the power to build community and bring the world closer together"; Facebook "helps you connect and share with the people in your life"; TikTok's "mission is to inspire creativity and bring joy"; Snapchat says it enables users to "be creative, shine in the spotlight, get rewarded".[2] YouTube describes its goal as follows:

> Our mission is to give everyone a voice and show them the world. We believe that everyone deserves to have a voice, and that the world is a better place when we listen, share and build community through our stories.[3]

Social media companies advance an engaging/connecting/creating/sharing-ideology. They argue their primary aim is to create a better and more social world, where users engage with each other, connect to each other and create appealing content that they share with others. They promise to advance sociality. At the same time, they do not talk about their profit interests.

Commodity fetishism means that in capitalism, we are confronted with the economic in the form of commodities and money that hide their social nature, namely the relations of production, and the class relations where workers produce commodities (see Chapter 7 in this book, Section 7.6). On social media, there is a kind of inverted commodity fetishism: The commodity character of Facebook and other capitalist platforms' data is hidden behind the social use-value of Facebook, that is the social relations and functions enabled by platform use. The object status of users, that is the fact that they serve the profit interests of Facebook, is hidden behind the social networking enabled by Facebook. The social benefit, the social relations and the obtained visibility are at the heart of the commercial and corporate side of Facebook, its exchange-value and commodity dimension. Exchange-value gets hidden in use-value. The object side of Facebook hides itself in social relations.

Next, we will focus on another important aspect of the Political Economy of the digital, namely digital labour.

10.3 Digital Labour

Digital labour is labour that is involved in the production of digital commodities. It involves labour such as the extraction of minerals that are the physical foundation of computing hardware, the assemblage of computing and communication hardware, software engineering, the use of software and Internet platforms for the creation of digital services and goods.

10.3.1 The International Division of Digital Labour

There is an international division of digital labour where we encounter the exploitation of slaves in mines, Taylorist assemblage workers in Chinese factories, play workers in the Googleplex, e-waste workers who disassemble hardware in developing countries, highly paid and highly stressed software engineers, precarious platform workers and crowdworkers, unpaid user labour, etc. (Fuchs 2014, 2015).

Figure 10.4 visualises the international division of digital labour. The various labour processes are visualised as dialectical triangles where workers (subjects) use objects in order to create products. In this international division, various products created by digital workers enter other production processes. Minerals extracted under partly slave-like conditions in Africa are an object in the production and assemblage of components and hardware. Computing hardware is used by digital content workers as technology for the production of software and other digital content and services. Digital labour is internationally connected via class relations where digital capital,

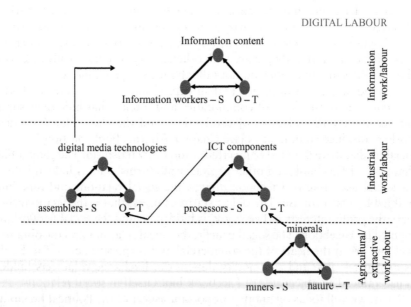

Figure 10.4 The international division of digital labour.

the capital invested in the digital industry (where digital commodities are produced), exploits digital labour in various manners.

Marx speaks in this context of the existence of a collective labourer:

> In order to work productively, it is no longer necessary for the individual himself to put his hand to the object; it is sufficient for him to be an organ of the collective labourer, and to perform any one of its subordinate functions.
>
> (Marx 1867, 644)

Digital workers together form a collective digital labourer that is exploited by collective digital capital.

The international division of digital labour is an expression of the new international division of labour that emerged in the context of the globalisation of capitalism in the 1970s and 1980s (see Chapter 8 in this book):

> commodity production is being increasingly subdivided into fragments which can be assigned to whichever part of the world can provide the most profitable combination of capital and labour [...] The development of the world economy has increasingly created conditions (forcing the development of the new international division of labour) in which the survival of more and more companies can only be assured through the relocation of production to new industrial sites, where labour power is cheap to buy, abundant and well-disciplined; in short, through the transnational reorganization of production. [...].
>
> (Fröbel, Heinrichs and Kreye 1981, 14, 15)

Marx and Engels (1845/1846) argue that the division of labour is an expression of class relations. "Division of labour and private property are, after all, identical expressions" (Marx and Engels 1845/1846, 46). They write that the gender division of labour is the oldest division of labour and class relations. There are also divisions of labour between mental and manual work, urban and rural labour, capitalism's centres, semi-periphery and periphery, etc. The colonial system advanced the international division of labour: "The colonial system and the extension of the world market, both of which form part of the general conditions for the existence of the manufacturing period, furnish us with rich materials for displaying the division of labour in society" (Marx 1867, 474).

Labour produces commodities, which is why when discussing digital labour, we also have to take a look at what kind of digital commodities digital labour produces. We will do so next.

10.3.2 Digital Commodities and Digital Labour

Table 10.3 identifies several models of capital accumulation in the digital industry, as well as digital workers involved in the production of the

Table 10.3 A typology of digital workers and capital accumulation models
in the digital culture economy

Model	Workers	Example Corporations
The digital content as a commodity model	Software engineers, designers, digital content marketers, etc.	Microsoft, Adobe, Oracle, SAP, Electronic Arts (computer games)
Digital finance model	Software engineers, designers, digital service marketers, etc.	eBanking, PayPal, Google Checkout, Amazon Payments, cryptocurrency and digital currency exchanges (e.g. Bitstamp, Coinbase, Coinmama, Kraken)
Hardware model	Miners in developing countries extracting minerals (known as "conflict minerals") out of which digital technologies are produced, hardware assemblage workers working for companies such as Foxconn, hardware engineers, scientists, advertising and public relations workers who brand and market hardware, sales workers, e-waste workers, etc.	Apple, HP, Dell, Fujitsu, Lenovo
Network model	Telecommunications technicians, network engineers, sales workers, telecommunications marketing workers, etc.	Telecommunications and Internet service providers: AT&T, Verizon, China Mobile, Deutsche Telecom, Orange, BT
The online advertising model	Users as workers, software engineers, advertising workers, etc.	Google, Facebook, Twitter
The online retail model	Warehouse workers, transport workers, advertising workers, etc.	Amazon, Alibaba, Apple iTunes, eBay,
The sharing economy-pay-per-service model	Uber and Deliveroo drivers, Upwork/Guru/Fiverr freelancers	Uber, Deliveroo, Upwork, Guru, Fiverr, Freelancer, PeoplePerHour, Amazon MTurk
The sharing economy-rent-on-rent model	Waged workers employed by the platforms mediating the rental process, no productive labour is conducted by the owners of the leased property and the leasers	Airbnb, Hiyacar, Drivy

(Continued)

Table 10.3 (Continued)

Model	Workers	Example Corporations
Digital subscription model	Engineers, salespersons, subscription managers and other waged employees	Netflix, Spotify, Amazon Prime, Apple Music
Mixed models	Various workers producing different commodities	Spotify, online newspapers, Apple

commodities that define these models. Digital labour is best understood based on a broad definition and an industry-based understanding (see Chapter 9, Section 9.3).

Next, we will discuss a case study of digital labour: the hardware manufacturers at Foxconn.

10.3.3 Apple-iPhone's Political Economy: The Exploitation of Labour at Foxconn

Hon Hai Precision (Foxconn) is a Taiwanese manufacturing company. In the 2021 Forbes List of the World's 2,000 Biggest Public Companies, Foxconn was the 94th largest corporation.[4] In the 2022 Forbes list, it held rank number 124.[5] Foxconn has assembled, for example, the iPad, iMac, iPhone, Kindle and various consoles (by Sony, Nintendo, Microsoft). Its customers are Western companies such as Apple, Dell, HP, Motorola, Nokia, Sony, Sony Ericsson. A large share of Foxconn's workers is located in Chinese factories, such as in Chengdu, Chongqing, Guanlan and Longhua, Hangzhou, Kunshan, Langfang, Nanhai (in the city of Foshan), Taiyuan, Tianjin or Zhengzhou.

In 2021, Apple was the world's sixth-largest company and in 2022 the seventh-largest.[6] In the financial year 2021, Apple made profits of US\$ 94.7 billion, up from US\$ 57.4 billion in 2020 and US\$ 55.3 billion in 2019.[7] In 2022, Apple's profit increased further to US\$ 99.8 billion.[8] In 2021, 52.5% of Apple's sales came from the iPhone.[9] In the period between January and August 2010, 17 workers at Foxconn, where many iPhones were manufactured at the time, attempted to commit suicide because they could no longer stand the terrible working conditions. Studies of working conditions at Foxconn showed a problematic picture (SACOM 2010, 2011, 2012):

- Unpaid work assemblies;
- Long hours (12 hours a day, 6 days a week);
- Unpaid overtime;
- Yellow unions;
- Disgusting food in the canteen;
- Military drill;

- Punishments;
- Lack of breaks;
- Health and safety threats;
- Forced student interns;
- Crowded dorms.

"In order to maximize productivity, workers at Foxconn are made to work like machines" (SACOM 2010, 10). In 19th-century Britain, Marx described fabric inspectors' reports on the working conditions in a wallpaper factory that sound like contemporary descriptions from SACOM's reports:

> I have seen when the children could none of them keep their eyes open for the work; indeed, none of us could. [...] J. Lightbourne: 'Am 13 [...] We worked last winter till 9 (evening), and the winter before till 10. I used to cry with sore feet every night last winter.
>
> (Marx 1867, 357)

Scholars have assessed the exploitation of workers at Foxconn:

> Foxconn as a form of monopoly capital generates a global 'race to the bottom' production strategy and repressive mode of management that weighs heavily on the rural migrant workers who form its work force, depriving them of their hopes, their dreams, and their future.
>
> (Pun and Chan 2012, 405)

Apple

> is more than a 'bad apple'. It is an example of structures of inequality and exploitation that characterize global capitalism.
>
> (Sandoval 2013, 344)

> There is a planetary network whose central nexus is the Apple-Foxconn alliance – or Appconn – the 'master', so to speak, who owns, manipulates, and exploits untold numbers of iSlaves. Almost all brands and contract manufacturers of the digital media sector have their share in sustaining this highly problematic world system I call Appconn.
>
> (Qiu 2016, 6)

> Apple and other international companies are responsible for rights violations at Foxconn and other supplier factories. Leading American and European firms, having actively shed domestic employment through outsourcing and other forms of subcontracting, have failed to honor labor rights in the companies that now produce and assemble their prod ucts, whatever their company codes state.
>
> (Chan, Selden and Pun 2020, 197)

What did the situation at Foxconn look like ten years after the Foxconn suicides? In 2019, investigative researchers conducted research at the Zhengzhou Foxconn factory:

> Chinese labor law mandates that workers must not work more than 36 overtime hours a month. However, during the peak production seasons, workers at Zhengzhou Foxconn put in at least 100 overtime hours a month. There have been periods where workers have one rest day for every 13 days worked or even have only one rest day for a month. [...] If work is not completed by the time the shift ends, workers must work overtime and workers are not paid for this. [...] The factory does not provide workers with adequate personal protective equipment and workers do not receive any occupational health and safety training. [...] The factory does not report work injuries. [...] Verbal abuse is common at the factory.
>
> (China Labor Watch 2019, 4–5)

China dealt with the COVID-19 pandemic by implementing a zero-COVID strategy that involved large-scale lockdowns with curfews. In late autumn 2022, a COVID wave spread in China, including in Foxconn factories. Many workers left because they feared "being forced into quarantine with insufficient necessities" (China Labor Watch 2022). Reports stressed that Foxconn workers who caught the virus were treated like things and cattle:

> Zhengzhou is Foxconn's main base for the production of iPhones. [...] production is going on, regardless of cross-infection and accumulating sick workers. [...] no pause of production was suggested by the management. This led to the subsequent outbreak of the epidemic in the factory. On October 14, the factory began to implement 'closed-loop production'; movement of workers is strictly controlled between the production line and the dormitory, and mobility between the factory and the outside area is minimized. [...] many manufacturers across the country choose closed-loop production, confining workers within the factory, asking them to commute only between the assembly line and their dormitory [...] the closed loop is only a means for maintaining production; the health of workers and the safety of patients' lives are placed in a secondary position [...] workers who were taken away from the dormitory to the quarantine sites were left unattended and therefore had to ask for help on social media. [...] After all the roommates showed symptoms such as fever, cold, and breath difficulty, they did not receive any medicines or medical treatment. [...] The so-called 'quarantine' involved only a spatial transfer of workers from one place to another; the new location not only does not provide conditions for solo quarantine, but also lacks subsequent medical care and food distribution. [...] Meanwhile, workers who remain in the factory are coerced

to continue to work in the midst of the Covid-19 outbreak. [...] sanitation at the dormitory area cannot keep up to the pace of the accumulating trash, causing worrisome sanitary conditions that only make it even more unsafe for workers to live [...] Many workers, however, no longer want to continue to work amid the chaos and just want to stay safe. Unfortunately, there is no way to leave Foxconn; the 'closed loop' management means that employees cannot leave the port area where Foxconn is located without special authorization. Some employees eventually gave up their wages and chose to flee the factory. [...] The message earlier also showed that part of the pressure on Foxconn to rush work 'came from Apple'. The Zhengzhou plant has more than 90 production lines and about 350,000 workers. It is also Foxconn's main manufacturing base for Apple's iPhones, which account for half of global iPhone sales. Right now is the peak production season when Foxconn is rushing to work on Apple's latest product, the iPhone 14.

(China Labor Watch 2022)

Hardware assemblers, miners who extract minerals that are used for ICT components, or e-waste workers are cultural and digital workers too, just like online journalists, software programmers or online freelancers. Marisol Sandoval argues for the conceptual and political unification of digital workers:

what unites them is not only that they all, in different ways, deal with new information and communication technologies, but also that they are all subject to exploitation, high work pressure and often precariousness. Rather than using concepts such as 'immaterial labour' (Hardt and Negri 2004) that reinforce the separation of manual and mental work it seems more useful to extend concepts such as knowledge work or digital labour to include the manual work of those who are producing computer technologies, electronic equipment and media technologies. [...] Such extended notions can provide a conceptual framework for analyzing the international division of digital labour. Broad understandings of digital labour can furthermore be a starting point for building connections and moments of solidarity along the global value chain of computer technologies from mineral miners and production workers to call centre agents, software engineers, and the labour of unpaid prosumers, back to waste workers in electronics dumping grounds.

(Sandoval 2013, 345)

Nick Dyer-Witheford (2014, 166) characterises what he terms the global worker:

Today's global worker is collective labour that is:
  i trans-nationalized by the movement of industrial capital beyond
     its traditional heartlands,

    ii variegated by an increasingly complex division of labour, with the fastest growth neither in industry nor agriculture but in the circulation and social reproduction (aka 'the service sector');

    iii feminized by the inclusion of women who both work for a wage and perform the unpaid domestic labour that is the basis of the formal economy;

    iv mobile and migrant both within and across borders;

    v precarious, rendered chronically insecure by a vast reserve army of the un- or under-employed

    vi earth-changing in the effects of labours that, while historically cumulative, are only now becoming visible in an anthropogenic crisis of the natural environment; and finally – the focus of this essay –

    vii connected by 2 billion Internet accounts and 6 billion cell phones.

Dyer-Witheford points out that the globalisation of labour in capitalism has come along with lots of precarious labour and the digitalisation of the economy and society. Workers around the world use the Internet and the mobile phone, which enables them to also put these tools to use when they demand better working conditions, go on strike and protest. Using broad notions of digital and global labour also has political implications: "To name the global worker is to make a map; and a map is also a weapon" in struggles for a better society (Dyer-Witheford 2014, 175).

Another important phenomenon of the Internet's Political Economy is digital surveillance.

10.4 Digital Surveillance

Surveillance is the collection, assessment and use of data about humans for advancing domination (see Fuchs 2011, 2012). Digital surveillance is the use of digital technologies for surveillance. Economic surveillance advances the surveillance of consumers and workers for economic ends such as capital accumulation. Political surveillance advances the surveillance of citizens in order for political ends such as the defence and extension of power.

Digital surveillance is part of today's political economy of the Internet. We have already seen that social media collect, store and economically valorise big data for advertising purposes. Surveillance is part of their business model. This is why Shoshana Zuboff (2019) speaks of surveillance capitalism. She defines surveillance capitalism in the following manner:

1. A new economic order that claims human experience as free raw material for hidden commercial practices of extraction, prediction, and sales; 2. A parasitic economic logic in which the production of goods and services is subordinated to a new global architecture of behavioral modification; 3. A rogue mutation of capitalism marked by concentrations of wealth, knowledge, and power unprecedented in human history.

(Zuboff 2019, v)

Besides the economic forms of digital surveillance that Zuboff talks about, there is also digital surveillance where private Internet platforms collect data that state institutions' access. Politics and economics play together in this form of digital surveillance: There are an economic interest of the platform companies in data collection and a state interest in accessing this data.

We can therefore speak of a Political Economy of digital surveillance. We will look at some examples of the Political Economy of digital surveillance.

Internet surveillance takes place in many parts of the world, both in non-Western and in Western countries. We will discuss two examples, namely Internet surveillance in China and on Facebook.

10.4.1 *Internet Surveillance in China*

In 2014, the Cyberspace Administration of China was created as a new state institution in charge of Internet regulation. It is the central agency in charge of the regulation, monitoring, control and censorship of the Internet in China. It also operates the Great Firewall of China, a technical Internet blockage, surveillance and filtering technology. It restricts access to certain foreign websites by users in China, monitors, filters, censors and blocks Internet usage in China and access to Internet sites based on lists of forbidden keywords (see, e.g., Hoang et al. 2021, Rambert et al. 2021). The Great Firewall

> eavesdrops on traffic between China and the rest of the world, and terminates requests for banned content for example, upon seeing a request for 'http://www.google.com/?falun', regardless of actual destination server) by injecting a series of forged TCP Reset (RST) packets that tell both the requester and the destination to stop communicating.
>
> (Marczak et al. 2015, 3)

In 2022, foreign platforms blocked in China included, among others, Google, YouTube, Facebook, Wikipedia, Instagram, WhatsApp, Twitter, LinkedIn, BBC, the New York Times, the Guardian, the Washington Post and the Internet Archive.[10]

In 2017, the Chinese Cybersecurity Law came into effect. It is a unified Internet regulation framework. Its provisions include that users are not allowed to "conduct any activity that endangers national security, honor and interest", incite "undermine national unity", or create or disseminate "false information to disrupt the economic and social order" (Article 12).[11] Article 21 obliges Internet platforms and service providers to monitor their users. Article 28 obliges these operators to provide access to public and national security organs in investigations of criminal activities and for "safeguarding national security".[12] Article 37 requires all Internet operators in China to store the data of Chinese users in Mainland China to make access of Chinese authorities to the data easier.

Yang (2019) argues that the Chinese Internet has been the site of online protests, cyber-nationalism, surveillance and censorship. He says that softer forms of Internet control in China have in the Xi era included national campaigns against certain Internet developments, the presence of official party and state accounts on popular Internet platforms such as Weibo, WeChat, Toutiao and Douyin, to make Internet platforms commit to the self-control of content, support and encourage Party-loyal Internet influencers and the creation of a 50 Cent Army consisting of individuals who are paid for spreading Party-propaganda. Hard measures of Internet control include the Great Firewall of China and trials of China's social credit system (Yang 2019). "The general trend in recent decades is the gradual curtailing of citizens' power in using the internet to challenge the party-state. Nevertheless, internet politics in China must be understood as a dynamically unfolding story of contention and control" (Yang 2019, 451).

10.4.2 Facebook and the Cambridge Analytica Scandal

The Cambridge Analytica scandal shows how the political economy of digital surveillance works and how economic surveillance and political surveillance interact (see Fuchs 2021, chapter 6). The company Cambridge Analytica paid Global Science Research (GSR) for conducting fake online personality tests on Facebook to obtain personal Facebook data of almost 90 million users. The obtained data were used for targeting political ads, including in the 2016 US presidential election where the goal was to support Trump's campaign.

Cambridge Analytica is a story about how the combination of digital capitalism/neoliberal politics/far-right ideology threatens democracy. The far-right fosters the use of dubious and manipulative information and communication strategies in politics. Far-right ideologues will do everything necessary to win elections and gain power. Social media corporations turn data into profit and are supported by neoliberal governments. As a consequence, there has been lax regulation of data and privacy protection. Tolerating manipulative and democracy-threatening ads makes money. Facebook did not do anything against the Cambridge Analytica/GLS data breach. Lax data protection regulations played an important role. Not humans, but algorithms control ads. Social media corporations have no interest in human control because such control costs money and means fewer profits. Facebook aims at capital accumulation by advertising, and far-right demagogues at manipulating politics.

Also, Edward Snowden's revelations displayed the interaction of economic and political surveillance. Snowden leaked documents that showed that police and secret services had direct access to personal user data stored by AOL, Apple, Facebook, Google, Microsoft, Paltalk, Skype, Yahoo! and YouTube.

The examples show that in digital surveillance, there is an inherent interconnection of economic and political processes and interests. C. Wright Mills argued in 1956 that there is a power elite that connects economic, political and military power:

> There is no longer, on the one hand, an economy, and, on the other hand, a political order containing a military establishment unimportant to politics and to money-making. There is a political economy linked, in a thousand ways, with military institutions and decisions. [...] there is an ever-increasing interlocking of economic, military, and political structures.
>
> (Mills 2000, 7–8)

In the surveillance-industrial complex, user data is first externalised and made public or semi-public on the Internet to enable users' communication processes. Second, data is privatised as private property by Internet platforms to accumulate capital. Third, data is particularised by secret services that bring massive amounts of data under their control that is made accessible and analysed worldwide with the help of profit-making security companies such as Booz Allen Hamilton.

Given that the dominant Internet platforms and companies exploit digital labour and engage in surveillance, the question arises of what alternatives there are.

10.5 Towards an Alternative Political Economy of the Internet

How can alternatives to the capitalist political economy of the Internet look like and be achieved?

A first argument one encounters is that Apple, Facebook, Google, etc. are great companies that enrich the world and that therefore no change is needed. The problem with this argument is that digital capital exploits digital labour and there are ideologies on and of the Internet, as well as digital domination such as digital surveillance (see Fuchs 2021).

A second approach is an attempt to improve the regulation of Internet corporations through data protection legislation, privacy laws, anti-monopoly regulations, the taxation of digital capital, etc. This is the approach that the European Union has taken in recent years.

A third approach is the attempt to advance civil society alternatives to capitalist Internet corporations. An example is platform co-operatives. These are Internet platforms that are owned, governed and run by workers and users (see Scholz and Schneider 2016, Scholz 2016). A general problem of alternative media that are organised by civil society (e.g. as community media) is that often they lack resources and cannot compete with the capitalist media giants, which is why within capitalism they tend to remain rather unknown and based on voluntary, self-exploitative labour.

A fourth approach is the creation of a Public Service Internet and of Public Service Internet platforms. The Public Service Media and Public Service

Internet Manifesto (Fuchs and Unterberger 2021) demands the safeguarding of the existence, independence and funding of PSM such as the BBC, ARD and ZDF, as well as the development of a Public Service Internet and the resourcing of PSM to provide online platforms. The Manifesto can be signed by visiting http://bit.ly/signPSManifesto

Public Service Internet platforms are provided by Public Service Media organisations with a not-for-profit imperative and the digital remit to advance information, news, debate, democracy, education, entertainment, participation and creativity with the help of the Internet. The Manifesto demands:

> We need to rebuild the Internet. While the contemporary Internet is dominated by monopolies and commerce, the Public Service Internet is dominated by democracy. While the contemporary Internet is dominated by surveillance, the Public Service Internet is privacy-friendly and transparent. While the contemporary Internet misinforms and separates the public, the Public Service Internet engages, informs and supports the public. Although the contemporary Internet is driven by and drives the profit principle, the Public Service Internet puts social needs first.
>
> (Fuchs and Unterberger 2021, 13)

Vincent Mosco (2017) argues that in many countries, the postal service is a public utility service and that the Internet should be organised based on the same principle. "All that is keeping us from using the postal service public utility model for the Next Internet is the failure of our public imagination and the pressures of business to make communication serve profit over people" (Mosco 2017, 187). The Internet as a public utility is "a universal system of communication that" is "public, open and accessible" (Mosco 2017, 208–209). Mosco describes the Internet as a public communication system in the following manner:

> Building public information utilities offers an alternative to the singular dominance of the Big Five and their equally singular commitment to commodifying and militarizing the entire production, distribution and use of data, information, knowledge and entertainment. Public information utilities would be driven by the commitment to universal and equal access to open networks. They would support public control over platforms for social media to create a genuine electronic commons. They would also promote analog alternatives to the digital world. Moreover, public information utilities would provide an essential space for addressing the environmental, privacy and workplace issues that bedevil the post-Internet world. We now have the technical capacity to achieve these goals. It remains to be seen whether we can build the social movements essential to bringing about a more democratic and egalitarian post-Internet world.
>
> (Mosco 2017, 212)

10.6 Conclusion

This chapter focused on the Political Economy of the Internet and digital media. We can now summarise the main findings.

Finding 1: The Political Economy of Social Media

Targeted advertising is an important capital accumulation model of social media companies. It is based on unpaid digital labour that produces attention, data, content and social relations.

Finding 2: The Political Economy of Digital Labour

Digital labour is labour that is involved in the production of digital commodities. There are different forms of digital labour that are exploited in an international division of digital labour from which digital capital profits. Examples such as the exploitation of Foxconn workers who produce the iPhone show how digital labour works.

Finding 3: The Political Economy of Digital Surveillance

Surveillance is the collection, assessment and use of data about humans for advancing domination. Digital surveillance is the use of digital technologies for surveillance. Examples such as Internet surveillance in China, the Cambridge Analytica scandal and Edward Snowden's revelations show how economic interests and political interests interact in digital surveillance.

Finding 4: Towards an Alternative Political Economy of the Internet and Digital Media

Alternatives to the capitalist Internet and capitalist digital media include political regulation, platform co-operatives and Public Service Internet platforms.

Notes

1 Translated from the Mandarin original: 在您使用微博时，我们会根据您的设备信息、IP地址和位置信息向您推送个性化广告。
2 Data sources: http://www.instagram.com, http://www.facebook.com, https://www.tiktok.com/, https://www.snapchat.com/, accessed on 25 November 2021.
3 Data source: https://about.youtube, accessed on 16 January 2022.
4 Data source: https://www.forbes.com/lists/global2000, accessed on 4 December 2021.
5 Data source: https://www.forbes.com/lists/global2000, accessed on 3 November 2022.
6 Data source: https://www.forbes.com/lists/global2000, accessed on 4 December 2021 and 3 November 2022.
7 Data source: Apple SEC-Filings Form 10-K, financial year 2021.
8 Data source: Apple SEC-Filings Form 10-K, financial year 2022.

9 Data source: Own calculation based on Apple SEC-Filings Form 10-K, financial year 2021 (pdf version), page 24: Total net sales 2021: US$ 365.817 billion, iPhone sales: US$ 191.973 billion.
10 https://en.wikipedia.org/wiki/List_of_websites_blocked_in_mainland_China, accessed on 3 November 2022.
11 https://digichina.stanford.edu/work/translation-cybersecurity-law-of-the-peoples-republic-of-china-effective-june-1–2017/, accessed on 3 November 2022.
12 https://digichina.stanford.edu/work/translation-cybersecurity-law-of-the-peoples-republic-of-china-effective-june-1–2017/, accessed on 3 November 2022.

References

Chan, Jenny, Mark Selden, and Ngai Pun. 2020. *Dying for an iPhone: Apple, Foxconn, and the Lives of China's Workers*. Chicago, IL: Haymarket Books.
China Labor Watch. 2022. Zhengzhou Foxconn Coerces Employees to Work on iPhone 14 Production Amid COVID-19 Outbreak, While Hiding the Number of Sick Workers. *China Labor Watch*. 28 October 2022. https://chinalaborwatch.org/zhengzhou-foxconn-coerces-employees-to-work-on-iphone-14-production-amid-covid-19-outbreak-while-hiding-the-number-of-sick-workers/, accessed on 26 November 2022.
China Labor Watch. 2019. *iPhone 11 Illegally Produced in China. Apple Allows Supplier Factory Foxconn to Violate Labor Laws*. New York: China Labor Watch. https://3on4k646b3jq16ewqw1ikcel-wpengine.netdna-ssl.com/wp-content/uploads/2021/06/Zhengzhou-Foxconn-English-09.06.pdf
Dyer-Witheford, Nick. 2014. The Global Worker and the Digital Front. In *Critique, Social Media and the Information Society*, edited by Christian Fuchs and Marisol Sandoval, 165–178. New York: Routledge.
Federici, Silvia. 1975. *Wages against Housework*. Bristol: Falling Wall Press and the Power of Women Collective.
Fröbel, Folker, Jürgen Heinrichs, and Otto Kreye. 1981. *The New International Division of Labour*. Cambridge: Cambridge University Press.
Fuchs, Christian. 2021. *Social Media: A Critical Introduction*. London: SAGE. Third edition.
Fuchs, Christian. 2015. *Culture and Economy in the Age of Social Media*. New York: Routledge.
Fuchs, Christian. 2014. *Digital Labour and Karl Marx*. New York: Routledge.
Fuchs, Christian. 2012. Political Economy and Surveillance Theory. *Critical Sociology* 39 (5): 671–687. DOI: https://doi.org/10.1177%2F0896920511435710
Fuchs, Christian. 2011. How to Define Surveillance? *MATRIZes* 5 (1): 109–133. DOI: https://doi.org/10.11606/issn.1982-8160.v5i1p109-136
Fuchs, Christian. 2010. New Imperialism: Information and Media Imperialism? *Global Media and Communication* 6 (1): 33–60. DOI: https://doi.org/10.1177/1742766510362018
Fuchs, Christian and Klaus Unterberger, eds. 2021. *The Public Service Media and Public Service Internet Manifesto*. London: University of Westminster Press. DOI: https://doi.org/10.16997/book60
Hardt, Michael and Antonio Negri. 2004. *Multitude*. New York: Penguin Press.
Hoang, Nguyen Phong et al. 2021. How Great Is the Great Firewall? Measuring China's DNS Censorship. In Proceedings of the 30th USENIX Security Symposium. https://www.usenix.org/system/files/sec21-hoang.pdf

Jarrett, Kylie. 2015. Devaluing Binaries: Marxist Feminism and the Value of Consumer Labour. In *Reconsidering Value and Labour in the Digital Age*, edited by Eran Fisher and Christian Fuchs, 207–223. Basingstoke: Palgrave Macmillan.

Jarrett, Kylie. 2016. *Feminism, Labour and Digital Media: The Digital Housewife*. New York: Routledge.

Jin, Dal Yong. 2013. The Construction of Platform Imperialism in the Globalization Era. *tripleC: Communication, Capitalism & Critique* 11 (1): 145–172. DOI: https://doi.org/10.31269/triplec.v11i1.458

Marczak, Bill et al. 2015. *China's Great Cannon. Research Brief*. https://citizenlab.ca/wp-content/uploads/2009/10/ChinasGreatCannon.pdf, accessed on 3 November 2022.

Marx, Karl. 1867. *Capital. Volume 1*. London: Penguin.

Marx, Karl and Friedrich Engels. 1845/1846. The German Ideology. Critique of Modern German Philosophy According to Its Representatives Feuerbach, B. Bauer and Stirner, and of German Socialism According to Its Various Prophets. In *Marx & Engels Collected Works (MECW) Volume 5*, 15–539. London: Lawrence & Wishart.

Mills, Charles Wright. 2000. *The Power Elite*. Oxford: Oxford University Press.

Mosco, Vincent. 2017. *Becoming Digital: Towards a Post-Internet Society*. SocietyNow Series. Bingley: Emerald.

Pun, Ngai and Jenny Chan. 2012. Global Capital, the State and Chinese Workers: The Foxconn Experience. *Modern China* 38 (4): 383–410.

Qiu, Jack. 2016. *Goodbye iSlave. A Manifesto for Digital Abolition*. Urbana: University of Illinois Press.

Rambert, Raymond, Weinberg Zachary, Diogo Barradas, and Nicolas Christin. 2021. Chinese Wall of Swiss Cheese? Keyword Filtering in the Great Firewall of China. In *Proceedings of the Web Conference 2021 (WWW '21), April 19–23, 2021, Ljubljana, Slovenia*. New York: ACM. DOI: https://doi.org/10.1145/3442381.3450076

Sandoval, Marisol. 2013. Foxconned Labour as the Dark Side of the Information Age. Working Conditions at Apple's Contract Manufacturers in China. *tripleC: Communication, Capitalism & Critique* 11 (2): 318–347. DOI: https://doi.org/10.3269/triplec.v11i2.481

Scholz, Trebor. 2016. *Platform Cooperativism: Challenging the Corporate Economy*. New York: Rosa Luxemburg Stiftung New York Office.

Scholz, Trebor and Nathan Schneider, eds. 2016. *Ours to Hack and to Own: The Rise of Platform Cooperativism, a New Vision for the Future of Work and a Fairer Internet*. New York: OR Books.

Smythe, Dallas W. 1994. *Counterclockwise*. Boulder, CO: Westview Press.

Smythe, Dallas W. 1977. Communications: Blindspot of Western Marxism. *Canadian Journal of Political and Social Theory* 1 (3): 1–27.

Students & Scholars against Corporate Misbehaviour (SACOM). 2012. *New iPhone, Old Abuses. Have Working Conditions at Foxconn in China Improved?* http://sacom.hk/wp-content/uploads/2018/10/2012-New-iPhone-Old-Abuses-Have-working-conditions-at-Foxconn-in-China-improved.pdf, accessed on 8 December 2022.

Students & Scholars against Corporate Misbehaviour (SACOM). 2011. *Foxconn and Apple Fail to Fulfil Promises: Predicaments of Suicides*. http://sacom.hk/wp-content/

uploads/2018/10/2011-Foxconn-and-Apple-Fail-to-Fulfill-Promises-Predicaments-of-Workers-after-the-Suicides.pdf, accessed on 8 December 2022.

Students & Scholars against Corporate Misbehaviour (SACOM). 2010. *Workers as Machines. Military Management in Foxconn.* https://www.somo.nl/wp-content/uploads/2010/08/military-management-in-Foxconn.pdf, accessed on 8 December 2022.

Yang, Guobin. 2019. Policy Case Study: Internet Politics. In *Politics in China: An Introduction*, edited by William A. Joseph, 440–454. Oxford: Oxford University Press. Third edition.

Zuboff, Shoshana. 2019. *The Age of Surveillance Capitalism: The Fight for a Human Future at the New Frontier of Power.* London: Profile Books.

Recommended Readings and Exercises

Readings

The following texts are recommended as accompanying readings to this chapter:

Christian Fuchs. 2014. *Digital Labour and Karl Marx*. New York: Routledge. Chapter 4: Dallas Smythe and Audience Labour Today.

Christian Fuchs. 2015. *Culture and Economy in the Age of Social Media.* New York: Routledge.
Chapter 6: Social Media's International Division of Digital Labour.

Marisol Sandoval. 2013. Foxconned Labour as the Dark Side of the Information Age. Working Conditions at Apple's Contract Manufacturers in China. *tripleC: Communication, Capitalism & Critique* 11 (2): 318–347. DOI: https://doi.org/10.3269/triplec.v11i2.481

Jack L. Qiu. 2015. Reflections on Big Data. "Just because It's Accessible Does Not Make It Ethical". *Media, Culture & Society* 37 (7): 1089–1094. DOI: https://doi.org/10.1177/0163443715594104

Exercise 10.1   Social Media

Discuss:

What do you see as the main advantages of social media?

What do you see as the main disadvantages of social media?

Exercise 10.2   Digital Labour

Choose one type of digital labour you are particularly interested in. Search for at least two academic articles or reports that analyse this form of digital labour. Discuss:

What do the working conditions of the analysed digital labour look like? What problems do such workers face?

What role do or can unionisation, strikes and protests play in the context of the exploitation of the analysed form of digital labour?

How could the problems that digital workers face best be overcome?

Exercise 10.3   Digital Surveillance

First, read the following two texts:
Christian Fuchs. 2012. Political Economy and Surveillance Theory. *Critical Sociology* 39 (5): 671–687. DOI: https://doi.org/10.1177%2F0896920511435710
Christian Fuchs. 2011. How to Define Surveillance? *MATRIZes* 5 (1): 109–133. DOI: https://doi.org/10.11606/issn.1982-8160.v5i1p 109-136

Second, search for an important example of digital surveillance. Ask yourself and discuss: What is surveillance? What is the role of surveillance in capitalism? What is digital surveillance? What is the role of digital surveillance in capitalism? Analyse your example from a Political Economy perspective and prepare a short presentation of this analysis.

Exercise 10.4   Alternative Political Economy of the Internet and Digital Media

Search for at least three news articles about non-commercial alternatives to the capitalist organisation of the Internet and digital media. You can, for example, focus on a particular type of platform (e.g. user-generated video, social network, search engine) or digital technology.

Discuss:

How do the non-commercial technologies/platforms you read about work? What is their Political Economy like?

How do they differ from the dominant model of the Internet and digital media?

In an ideal world, what would the Internet and digital media look like?

Exercise 10.5   Digital Social Credit Systems

Find out on the Internet (through documentaries, newspaper articles and academic papers) what the Chinese social credit system is, how it works and in what form it is used today.

Watch the episode "Nosedive" of the science fiction series Black Mirror (season 3, episode 1).

Discuss:

What is the impact on society of a social credit system where people are permanently assessed and judged?

How do you assess China's social credit system?

11 The Political Economy of the Information Society and Digital Capitalism

What You Will Learn in This Chapter

- You will understand concepts such as the information society, the post-industrial society, and the network society;
- You will learn about criticisms of information society theory;
- You will engage with concepts such as information capitalism, cognitive capitalism in the society of singularities, data capitalism, platform capitalism, surveillance capitalism, and digital capitalism.

11.1 Introduction

Since the 1960s, the notion of the information society and related terms such as knowledge society, post-industrial society, and network society has become very popular for characterising contemporary societies where the media, culture, communication, information, knowledge labour, computers, and the Internet play an important role. In this chapter, we will discuss whether such notions are meaningful or not. Do we really live in an information society? Or are such claims mere ideology?

This chapter focuses on the following questions: What kind of society do we live in? Do we live in an information society or a capitalist society? What is digital capitalism?

Section 11.2 discusses the foundations of information society theory. Section 11.3 presents sceptic views on information society theory. Section 11.4 asks whether we live in a capitalist society or an information society. Section 11.5 presents conclusions.

DOI: 10.4324/9781003391203-13

11.2 Information Society Theory

Exercise 11.1 What Kind of Society Do We Live in?

Discuss in groups:

What kind of society do we live in? Why? What concept fits best to describe contemporary society? Why?

A global society
A capitalist society
An information society
A network society
A modern society

11.2.1 Information Society Theory: Fritz Machlup

The economist Fritz Machlup (1962) advanced an early version of information society theory. He created a grouping of occupations that he used for analysing the development of the US economy (see Table 11.1):

A White-collar workers:
    A1. professional, technical, and kindred workers;
    A2. managers, officials, and proprietors, except farm;
    A3. clerical and kindred workers;
    A4. sales workers;
B Manual and service workers:
    B1. craftsmen, foremen, and kindred workers;
    B2. operatives and kindred workers;
    B3. private household workers;
    B4. service workers, except private household;
    B5. labourers, except farm and mine;
C Farm workers:
    C1. farmers and farm managers;
    C2. farm labourers and foremen.

Machlup formulated information society's central assumption that many societies have developed first from agricultural societies into industrial societies and then into information/knowledge societies:

> If all manual workers, industrial and agricultural, are taken together, their combined share in the labor force decreased from 82.4 per cent in 1900 to 57.9 per cent in 1959. White-collar workers, conversely, increased from 17.6 per cent of the labor force in 1900 to 42.1 per cent in 1959. This trend, uninterrupted for 60 years and probably longer, is most impressive.
> (Machlup 1962, 382)

Table 11.1 The development of the occupational structure in the USA

Category	1900 (%)	1910 (%)	1920 (%)	1930 (%)	1940 (%)	1950 (%)	1959 (%)
White-collar labour	17.6	21.3	24.9	29.4	31.1	36.6	42.1
Manual and service labour	44.9	47.7	48.1	49.4	51.5	51.6	48.0
Farm labour	37.5	30.9	27.0	21.2	17.4	11.8	9.9

Data source: Machlup (1962, 381).

In agricultural societies, agriculture dominates occupations and value pro-duction, in industrial societies, manufacturing is dominant, and in informa-tion societies, information work is dominant.

11.2.2 Information Society Theory: Daniel Bell

In his book *The Coming of Post-Industrial Society*, Daniel Bell (1974) intro-duced the concept of the post-industrial society, which is another term for "information society". He argues that a post-industrial society has five key dimensions:

1. Economic sector: the change from a goods-producing to a service economy;
2. Occupational distribution: the pre-eminence of the professional and technical class;
3. Axial principle: the centrality of theoretical knowledge as the source of innovation and of policy formulation for the society;
4. Future orientation: the control of technology and technological assessment;
5. Decision-making: the creation of a new 'intellectual technology' (Bell 1974, 14).

Bell argues that in a post-industrial society, services dominate production. Services are a difficult category that includes a wide range of different occupations, including professional services (teachers, lawyers, doctors, engineers, architects) just like care services, personal services (hairdresser, masseur, cosmeticians, etc.), retail services, management and consulting, media work, transport services. The service sector is difficult to define. It is a residual category that includes all work that is not part of agricul-ture and manufacturing. Bell argues that professional workers and tech-nicians play a key role in post-industrial society. Furthermore, he speaks of the rise of a new "intellectual technology", which is a reference to the computer.

11.2.3 Information Society Theory: Manuel Castells

In the 1990s, Manuel Castells published the trilogy *The Information Age*, in which he characterises contemporary societies as network societies:

> A new world is taking shape at this turn of the millennium. It originated in the historical coincidence, around the late 1960s and mid-1970s, of three *independent* processes: the information technology revolution; the economic crisis of both capitalism and statism, and their subsequent restructuring; and the blooming of cultural social movements, such as libertarianism, human rights, feminism, and environmentalism. The interaction between these processes, and the reactions they triggered, brought into being a new dominant social structure, the network society; a new economy, the informational /global economy; and a new culture, the culture of real virtuality.
>
> (Castells 2010, 372)

For Castells, the two central changes in society since the 1970s have been the rise of the Internet and the globalisation of society in the economy, politics, and culture. Technological networks (the Internet) would interact with global social networks of humans, commodities, money, power, and ideas. For Castells, the network society consists of networked organisations that communicate globally via the Internet.

Other representatives of information society theory include James R. Beniger (1986), Frances Cairncross (1997), Peter Drucker (1969), Yoneji Masuda (1980) Nicholas Negroponte (1995), Marc Porat (1977), Radovan Richta (1969), Nico Stehr (1994), Alain Touraine (1974), and Alvin Toffler (1980).

11.3 Information Society Scepticism

11.3.1 Is the Information Society a New Society?

A key feature of information society theories is the claim that the information/knowledge/network society is a radically novel society. Here are some examples:

> The post-industrial society is "a new type of society".
>
> (Touraine 1974, 4)

> The "post-industrial society" means "the emergence of a new kind of society [that] brings into question the distributions of wealth, power, and status that are central to any society".
>
> (Bell 1974, 43)

> The third-wave society (the information society) is a "wholly new society".
>
> (Toffler 1980, 261)

The knowledge society means "an Age of Discontinuity in world economy and technology".

(Drucker 1969, 10)

The knowledge society means that "the age of labor and property is at an end" (Stehr 1994, iix) and the "emergence of knowledge societies signals first and foremost a radical transformation in the *structure of the economy*".

(Stehr 1994, 10)

The "information technology revolution induced the emergence of informationalism, as the material foundation of a new society".

(Castells 2010, 372)

11.3.2 Criticisms of Information Society Theory

The claim of radical novelty has resulted in criticism. Nicholas Garnham argues that "the shift from energy to brainpower does not necessarily change the subordination of labour to capital" (Garnham 1998/2004, 178). "The 'information society' is a concept with no objective co-relative in the real world. Used as an ideological mantra it merely and dangerously distracts – as is often intended – from the real issues" (Garnham 2000, 151).

The sociologist Frank Webster formulates two main criticisms of information society theory. First, he argues that this kind of social theory fetishises quantification: "If there is just more information then it is hard to understand why anyone should suggest that we have before us something radically new" (Webster 2002, 26). Second, he argues that information society theories are versions of technological determinism:

A connected and familiar criticism of technological conceptions of an information society is that they are determinist [...]. First, they assume that technology is the major force in social change – hence arguments which refer to the 'world the steam engine made', 'the atomic age', the 'computer society'. [...] Second, technological determinists work with a model which holds to a clear separation of technology and society, the former being in some way apart from social influence yet destined to have the most profound social effects.

(Webster 2002, 28)

The most fundamental criticism of information society theory is that notions such as "the information society", "the network society", "the post-industrial society", and "the knowledge society" sound very positive and distract attention from the actual problems of contemporary societies such as socio economic inequality, power asymmetries, the global environmental crisis, economic crises of capitalism, war and terror. The argument of information society critics is that information society theory is an ideology that denies the existence of capitalism and class by claiming that society has fundamentally changed.

When one agrees that lots of information society theory is ideological in character, it is a false inference to conclude that nothing has changed in society and that it suffices to stress that we have been living in capitalist societies for a long time.

For example, Walter Runciman (1993) argues that British capitalism has not changed since the First World War. Great Britain is, according to Runciman, a "capitalist-liberal-democratic" society with a "capitalist mode of production" and a "liberal mode of persuasion" (Runciman 1993, 65). Runciman rejects notions such as "managerial" capitalism, or late capitalism, or finance capitalism, or corporatist capitalism as they have, according to him, "generated more confusion than illumination" (Runciman 1993, 54). Jonathan Friedman (2002) argues that capitalism's fundamental features are commodification, fictitious capital, financialisation, and exploitation.

> All these processes are abetted by the new high technology, but they are certainly not its cause, and if anything, they are the symptoms of a capitalism in dire straits, a situation quite predictable from the logic of the system.
> (Friedman 2002, 302)

The only new thing would be the ideology that we live in a new (information) society, "the strange air of radical identity or self-identity among those intellectuals who are both representatives of the privileged classes and translators of ordinary liberalism into the language of radicalism" (Friedman 2002, 302).

Capitalism is a dynamic system that remains the same system of commodification, class structuration, and exploitation at its most fundamental level by changing at lower levels of the organisation. Crises of capitalism play an important role in this context and have triggered the emergence of new phases of capitalist development (see, e.g., the contributions in Westra and Zuege 2001). Capitalism needs to change to remain the same. There is a dialectic of continuity and change that manifests itself in economic, political, and cultural crises of capitalism.

11.4 Capitalism or Information Society?

11.4.1 What Is Capitalism?

In social theory, there is disagreement on the question if capitalism is a type of economy or a type of society (see Fuchs 2022, chapter 1). Wolfgang Streeck (2016) takes the second approach:

> How to study contemporary capitalism, then? My first answer is: not as an economy but as a society – as a system of social action – and a set of social institutions. [...] A capitalist society, or a society that is inhabited by a capitalist economy, is one that has on a current basis to work out

how its *economic social relations,* its specific relations of production and exchange, are, to connect to and interact with its *non-economic social relations.* [...] For this reason alone, capitalism must be studied, not as a static and timeless ideal type of an economic system that exists outside of or apart from society, but as a *historical social order* that is precisely about the relationship between the social and the economic.

(Streeck 2016, 201, 203)

Streeck (2016, chapter 9) argues that analysing capitalism as society means analysing it as an economic system, historical social order, culture, polity, and way of life.

A formation of society (*Gesellschaftsformation*) is the totality of all dialectics of practices and structures and all dialectics of objects and subjects that humans *produce and reproduce* and through which *humans produce and reproduce* their life and relations in a routinised manner in space-time. A formation of society is a fundamental unity and totality of humans' social production processes (see Fuchs 2020, chapter 5). That such a totality of human life is routinised in space-time means that a formation of society's dialectics of practices and structures is not just produced once, but is again and again recreated (reproduction) based on routines and social roles.

Capitalism as a particular formation of society includes economic relations such as commodity production, markets, capital, and labour, as well as social, political, legal and cultural relations. Capitalism is a formation of society (*Gesellschaftsformation*) that is shaped by the logic of accumulation, where the economic production of commodities for the sake of accumulating capital and creating profit plays an important role, and the logic of accumulation takes on specific non-economic forms in politics where we find the accumulation of decision-power and influence, as well as in culture where we find the accumulation of reputation and distinction.

Table 11.2 shows how we can make sense of accumulation as a general process and as a process in capitalist society. In capitalism, alienation takes

Table 11.2 Accumulation as a general process in capitalist society

Realm of Society	Central Process in General	Central Process in Capitalist Society	Underlying Antagonism in Capitalist Society
Economy	Production of use-values	Capital accumulation	Capital vs. labour
Politics	Production of collective decisions	Accumulation of decision-power and influence	Bureaucrats vs. citizens
Culture	Production of meanings	Accumulation of reputation, attention, respect	Ideologues/celebrities/influencers vs. everyday people

on the form of accumulation processes that create classes and inequalities. Capitalism is based on capitalists' accumulation of capital in the economy, bureaucrats' accumulation of decision-power and influence in the political system, and ideologues', influencers' and celebrities' accumulation of reputation, attention, and respect in the cultural system. Capitalism is an antagonistic system. Its antagonisms (see Table 11.2) drive its development and accumulation. Accumulation is an antagonistic relation that not just constitutes dominant classes and groups but also subordinated, dominated, and exploited groups such as the working class in the capitalist economy, dominated citizens in the capitalist political system, and ideologically targeted everyday people in capitalism's cultural system.

Capitalist society's antagonistic relations that drive accumulation are the source of inequalities and crises, which means that capitalism is an inherently negative dialectical system. Capitalism is also an ideological system where dominant groups use the logic of scapegoating for blaming certain groups for society's ills and problems. Scapegoating entails the logic of the friend/enemy-scheme. And the friend/enemy-scheme can lead to violence, fascism, racism, anti-Semitism, and nationalism. Crises of capitalism can be fascism-producing crises that turn barbarism from a potentiality of capitalism into an actuality.

In capitalist society, powerful actors control natural resources, economic property, political decision-making, and cultural meaning-making, which has resulted in the accumulation of power, inequalities, and global problems, including environmental pollution, as well as the degradation and depletion of natural resources in the nature-society relation, socio-economic inequality in the economic system, dictatorships and war in the political system, ideology and malrecognition in the cultural system.

11.4.2 Information Capitalism

The present author's approach to theorising capitalism and the information society is to argue based on a dialectic of continuity and change. Capitalism is an antagonistic system that sooner or later results in phases of economic, political, and cultural crisis. The outcome of a crisis of capitalism is undetermined. The results of crises depend on human agency and praxis, that is class and social struggles. In this context, Immanuel Wallerstein speaks of capitalism as a historical system:

> Such historical systems, like all systems, are partially open, partially closed; that is, they have rules by which they operate (they are systemic), and everevolving contours and contradictions (they are historical). [...] In a crisis, the fluctuations become wilder, and we have a bifurcation, with an indeterminate outcome.
>
> (Wallerstein 2004a)

In systemic crises, the future is open and humans therefore have to make collective choices about the direction the system should develop. The

> system encounters problems it can no longer resolve, and this causes what we may call systemic crisis. [...] the system is faced with [...] alternative solutions for its crisis, [...] which are intrinsically possible. [...] the members of the system collectively are called upon to make a historical choice about which of the alternative paths will be followed, that is, what kind of new system will be constructed.
>
> (Wallerstein 2004b, 76)

The rise of the importance of computing technology and knowledge labour in capitalism – the process we can term "informatisation" – has arisen from capitalism's need to develop the productive forces, that is to increase its productivity to accumulate ever more capital. Science and technology are means of relative surplus value production in capitalism, methods of creating more commodities, surplus value and profit in the same time period than before. Capitalism is an economy of time that is driven by the need to produce ever more commodities, value, and profit in ever-less time. In *Grundrisse*, Marx anticipated the emergence of capitalism that is based on information; information capitalism:

> Nature builds no machines, no locomotives, railways, electric telegraphs, self-acting mules, etc. These are products of human industry; natural material transformed into organs of the human will over nature, or of human participation in nature. They are organs of the human brain, created by the human hand; the power of knowledge, objectified. The development of fixed capital indicates to what degree general social knowledge has become a direct force of production, and to what degree, hence, the conditions of the process of social life itself have come under the control of the general intellect and been transformed in accordance with it. To what degree the powers of social production have been produced, not only in the form of knowledge, but also as immediate organs of social practice, of the real life process.
>
> (Marx 1857/1858, 706)

Marx in this passage argues that technologies are the result of human labour, namely labour that reflects the knowledge and scientific insights of society. They are objectified scientific knowledge. Technologies are part of fixed capital, that part of capital that is fixed in the production process for a longer time. Marx foresees a point of development of the economy where the general intellect – knowledge labour and information technologies – has become a "direct force of production". This means that the development of the productive forces at some point in time calls forth the creation of an economy where information technologies and knowledge work play a key role. Marx furthermore points out that knowledge is not just a matter of objects and structures (technologies) but also one of "social practice". Information operates in society both as knowledge work and as information technologies.

11.4.3 A Typology of Information Society Theories

Figure 11.1 shows a typology of information society theories. It has two axes. The x-axis shows the analysed theories' primary dimension. Subjective theories are focused on the human subject and their activities such as thought and work. Objective theories are focused on objects such as technologies. The y-axis is focused on society's differentiation. Radical change on the one end indicates the assumption that society has been undergoing radical changes. Continuity on the other end of the axis stands for the assumption that structures and practices have remained relatively undifferentiated over time. The combination of the x- and the y-axis results in four types of information society theories.

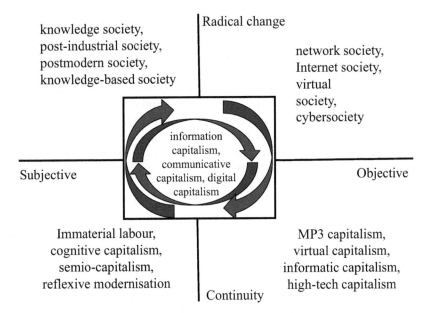

knowledge society, post-industrial society, postmodern society, knowledge-based society

Radical change

network society, Internet society, virtual society, cybersociety

information capitalism, communicative capitalism, digital capitalism

Subjective

Objective

Immaterial labour, cognitive capitalism, semio-capitalism, reflexive modernisation

MP3 capitalism, virtual capitalism, informatic capitalism, high-tech capitalism

Continuity

Figure 11.1 A typology of information society theories.

Subjective radical change theories assume that knowledge or knowledge work has become the key feature of society and that this change constitutes a new society. Example concepts are the concepts of the knowledge society, the knowledge-based society, the post-industrial society, and the postmodern society. They tend to stress the roles of knowledge, knowledge work and truth claims in society and assume that radical changes have been occurring.

Objective radical change theories argue that computer technologies, computer networks such as the Internet, or knowledge or network structures dominate in an information society and have created a new society. Examples are the notions of the network society, the Internet society, the virtual society or cybersociety. Continuous information society theories stress that the primary feature of society is that it is a capitalist society or modern society, and that although there are certain changes, the primary feature has not changed. They more stress continuity than discontinuity but ascertain that there are certain changes at lower levels of society's organisation. There are both subjective and objective continuous theories. Subjective continuous theories stress the role of knowledge and knowledge work in capitalism or modern society. They include notions such as immaterial labour, cognitive capitalism, semio-capitalism, and reflexive modernisation. Objective continuous theories emphasise the role of computer technologies or network structures (both social and technological ones) in society. Examples are concepts such as MP3 capitalism, virtual capitalism, informatic capitalism or high-tech capitalism.

A dialectical approach to information society theory as advanced by the present author holds that the four different information society theories are neither right nor wrong; they are incomplete. Subjective theories tend to ignore objective aspects of society. Objective theories tend to ignore subjective aspects. Continuous theories are too focused on what does not change; discontinuous theories are too focused on what changes.

A dialectical critical theory of society argues that we live in a capitalist (world) society that is changing in order to maintain its structures of economic, political and ideological accumulation of capital, power, and reputation. Some of these changes of capitalist society stand in the context of knowledge, knowledge work, information and computer technologies, technological networks, and social networks. There is a dialectic of continuity and discontinuity in capitalism (and society in general). And there is a dialectic of objective and subjective dimensions of information. Knowledge production results in the creation of information structures, including technologies and networks that store and process information. These structures enable, condition, and constrain further knowledge practices. In what we can term information capitalism or communicative capitalism, the dialectic of information production and information structures plays an important role in the accumulation of money capital, political decision-power, and reputation. Digital capitalism is an aspect and subdomain of information capitalism and communicative capitalism that describes all processes in capitalist society where accumulation takes place based on a dialectic of digital practices and digital structures, where information is produced and communicated in digital forms.

11.4.4 Capitalism or Information Society?

In 1968, six years before the publishing of Daniel Bell's book *The Coming of Post-Industrial Society*, which was pathbreaking for the information society discourse, in a time before the high rise of the information society hypothesis, Theodor W. Adorno (1968/2003) gave an introductory keynote talk on the topic of "Late Capitalism or Industrial Society?" at the annual meeting of the German Sociological Association (DGS).

Adorno said that the "fundamental question of the present structure of society" is "about the alternatives: late capitalism or industrial society". It is about

> whether the capitalist system still predominates according to its model, however, modified, or whether the development of industry has rendered the concept of capitalism obsolete, together with the distinction between capitalist and noncapitalist states and even the critique of capitalism. In other words, the question is whether it is true that Marx is out of date.
>
> (Adorno 1968/2003, 111)

Adorno writes that dichotomous answers to this question (either/or) "are themselves predicaments modelled on dilemmas taken from an unfree society" (113). And he gives an answer that considered the importance and relation of the productive forces and the relations of production in the capitalist mode of production:

> In terms of critical, dialectical theory, I would like to propose as an initial, necessarily abstract answer that contemporary society undoubtedly is an industrial society according to the state of its *forces* of production. Industrial labor has everywhere become the model of society as such, regardless of the frontiers separating differing political systems.
>
> It has developed into a totality because methods modeled on those of industry are necessarily extended by the laws of economics to other realms of material production, administration, the sphere of distribution, and those that call themselves culture.
>
> In contrast, however, society is capitalist in its *relations* of production. People are still what they were in Marx's analysis in the middle of the nineteenth century [...] Production takes place today, as then, for the sake of profit.
>
> (Adorno 1968/2003, 117)

We can build on Adorno's insights concerning information society theory. A fundamental question of the present structure of society is about the alternatives: capitalism or information society.

Contemporary society is an information society according to the state of its *forces* of production. In contrast, however, society is capitalist in its *relations* of production. Production takes place today, as then, for the sake of profit. For achieving this end, it to a certain extent makes use of knowledge and information technology in production. Productive forces and relations of production are interlocking phenomena; they contain each other.

The informational forces of production (just like the non-informational ones) are mediated by class relations, which means that the establishment of information technologies (as part of the instruments of production) and knowledge work (which is characterised by a composition of labour, where mental and communicative features dominate over manual features) as features of economic production are strategies for advancing the production and appropriation profit. Capital thereby hopes to achieve higher profit rates. Society cannot be explained by the informational forces of production. In capitalist society, information technologies and knowledge work play important roles not only in the accumulation of capital but also in the accumulation of political decision-power and the accumulation of ideologically defined reputation.

The counter-claim that nothing has changed because we still live in a society dominated by capitalist class relations is a reaction to overdrawn claims about the information society and information technology. A dialectical analysis cannot leave out that there are certain changes taking place that are intended to support the deepening of the class structure.

11.4.5 Manuel Castells: Informational Capitalism

For Manuel Castells, informational capitalism is the economic subdomain of the network society. He argues that

> the most decisive historical factor accelerating, channeling and shaping the in formation technology paradigm, and inducing its associated social forms, was/is the process of capitalist restructuring undertaken since the 1980s, so that the new techno-economic system can be adequately characterized as *informational capitalism*.
>
> (Castells 2000, 18)

Castells speaks of informationalism as a new mode of development. "Each mode of development is defined by the element that is fundamental in fostering productivity in the production process" (Castells 2000, 16).

> In the new, informational mode of development the source of productivity lies in the technology of knowledge generation, information processing, and symbol communication. [...] what is specific to the informational mode of development is the action of knowledge upon knowledge itself as the main source of productivity [...]. Information processing is focused on improving the technology of information processing as a source of productivity, in a virtuous circle of interaction between the knowledge sources of technology and the application of technology to improve knowledge generation and information processing: this is why, rejoining popular fashion, I call this new mode of development informational, constituted by the emergence of a new technological paradigm based on information technology.
>
> (Castells 2000, 17)

For Castells, capitalism is a techno-economic system. In contrast for Marx, it is a formation of society (*Gesellschaftsformation*) that extends beyond the economy into politics and culture. Castells, therefore, limits the notion of informational capitalism to the economy and sees it as a subdomain of the network society. What he terms the mode of development is in Marxist theory often characterised as the technology aspect of the productive forces. But the productive forces also contain labour-power that humans utilise in the production process in order to create new products with the help of the instruments and objects of labour. Castells does not justify why he uses the term "mode of development". Given his focus on technology when talking about this mode, the term creates the impression that technology determines the development of society.

Figure 11.2 visualises what Marx terms the mode of production.

The mode of production is the dialectic of the relations of production, the social relations that humans enter when they produce, and the productive forces. The productive forces are a system where human subjects use objects (means of production) in order to create new products in the work process. The relations of production and the productive forces interact. In class societies, the economic relations of production are class relations.

Table 11.3 identifies three modes of the productive forces, and Table 11.4, five modes of production defined by the relations of production.

There are agricultural, industrial and informational productive forces that result, respectively, in basic products, manufactured (industrial) products and informational products. The distinction between agricultural, industrial and information society refers to the three dimensions of the productive forces. They constitute just one aspect of society, which means that theories

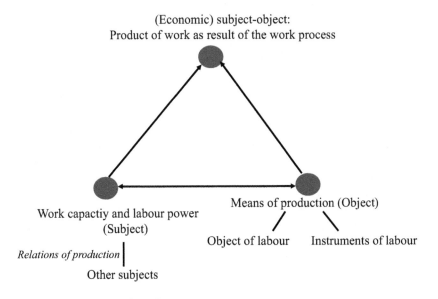

Figure 11.2 The mode of production.

Table 11.3 Three modes of the organisation of the productive forces

Mode	Instruments of Work	Objects of Work	Products of Work
Agricultural productive forces	Body, brain, tools, machines	Nature	Basic products
Industrial productive forces	Body, brain, tools, machines	Basic products, industrial products	Industrial products
Informational productive forces	Body, brain, tools, machines	Experiences, ideas	Informational products

Table 11.4 Five modes of production defined by their class relations

	Owner of Labour-power	Owner of the Means of Production	Owner of the Products of Work
Patriarchy	Patriarch	Patriarch	Family
Slavery	Slavemaster	Slavemaster	Slavemaster
Feudalism	Partly self-control, partly lord	Partly self-control, partly lord	Partly self-control, partly lord
Capitalist society	Worker	Capitalist	Capitalist
Socialist society	Self	All	Partly all, partly individual

using this distinction often disregard society's relations of production. The importance of informational productive forces today does not eliminate the existence of agricultural and industrial productive forces. Rather, there are dialectics of different productive forces in contemporary society.

Class relations are of key importance in capitalist and other class societies. Theories that argue that capitalist society has not changed since the 19th century are focused on the analysis of class relations. For Marx, there is a dialectic of productive forces and relations of production, which implies that capitalist society changes by developing new productive forces. Marx says that there is a capitalist antagonism between productive forces and the (class) relations of production. In information capitalism, this antagonism means that information labour and information technologies help to advance potentials of overcoming the commodity form and toil, but under class relations, they aggravate commodification, domination, and ideologisation, as well as the asymmetric distribution of labour time.

The term "informational productive forces" does not characterise entirely new productive forces, but depending on a specific indicator the degree to which a certain aspect of the productive forces is informational and the composite degree to which it is non-informational.

It is unlikely that all aspects of contemporary society or contemporary capitalist economies are suddenly informational. Therefore, the notion of informational capitalism does not make sense as a category of totality. There are multiple interacting dimensions of capitalism such as finance capitalism, hyper-industrial capitalism, mobility capitalism, and information capitalism.

11.4.6 Radovan Richta's Approach

Radovan Richta was a Czech philosopher who at the time of the Prague Spring studied together with a research group the potential of informatisation for the creation of a democratic socialist society. This work resulted in the Richta Report (Richta 1969), which is a rather forgotten information society theory (see, e.g., Webster 2014, where the discussion of Richta's work is missing).

For Richta, the scientific and technological revolution is an expression of the contradiction between the development of the productive forces and the relations of production:

> In the light of these realities, capital itself appears as a persisting contradiction – on the one hand, it extends work on all sides; on the other, it endeavours to reduce necessary work to a minimum. It mobilizes the forces of science, social combinations, etc., in order to 'make the creation of wealth independent of the labour time', while 'it wants to measure the enormous social forces so created in terms of labour time'.
>
> (Richta 1969, 82)

Marx formulated the antagonism between productive forces and relations of production in the following manner:

> Capital itself is the moving contradiction, [in] that it presses to reduce labour time to a minimum, while it posits labour time, on the other side, as sole measure and source of wealth. Hence it diminishes labour time in the necessary form so as to increase it in the superfluous form; hence posits the superfluous in growing measure as a condition – question of life or death – for the necessary.
>
> (Marx 1857/1858, 706)

Richta argued for the democratic and socialist shaping of technology: Socialism requires "a new, technical basis in the shape of the fully implemented automatic principle" (Richta 1969, 52).

11.4.7 The Development of Agricultural, Industrial and Information Labour

Tables 11.5 11.6, 11.7, and –11.8 show the development of agricultural, industrial and information labour in the world and specific regions.

Table 11.5 Global agricultural employment, in million

	1991	2019
Total:	998.7	883.5
Northern, Southern, and Western Europe	13.3	6.6
USA	2.3	2.2
China	392.6	194.4

Data source: ILO World Employment and Social Outlook, accessed on 23 January 2022.

Table 11.6 Global manufacturing employment, in million

	1991	2010	2019
Total:	497.9	672.7	7411.4
Northern, Southern, and Western Europe	56.0	46.1	46.4
USA	31.3	27.8	32.1
China	140.7	217.5	210.4

Data source: ILO World Employment and Social Outlook, accessed on 23 January 2022.

Table 11.7 Global service employment, in million

	1991	2019
Total:	781.1	1670.2
Northern, Southern, and Western Europe	106.3	155.2
USA	87.0	127.2
China:	124.3	362.4

Data source: ILO World Employment and Social Outlook, accessed on 23 January 2022.

Table 11.8 The development of employment in agriculture, manufacturing, and services, in millions and %

	1991	%	2019	%	2020	%
Employment in agriculture	998.8	43.8	883.5	26.4	873.8	27.4
Employment in manufacturing	497.9	21.9	749.4	22.7	693	21.7
Service employment	781.1	34.3	1,670.2	50.6	1,622.2	50.9
	2277.8		3348.1		3189.8	

Data source: http://www.ilo.org/wesodata, accessed on 23 January 2022.

At the global level, society has in the past decades seen a decrease in agricultural employment, an increase in manufacturing employment, and a massive increase in service employment. The Western World experiences simultaneous deindustrialisation and informatisation. China had a different development model that saw simultaneous industrialisation and informatisation.

Table 11.9 Global Labour Income Share

Year	Share (%)
2004	54.1
2005	53.6
2006	53.1
2007	52.7
2008	53.1
2009	53.9
2010	52.6
2011	52.1
2012	52.2
2013	52.2
2014	52.5
2015	52.5
2016	52.6
2017	52.5
2018	52.5
2019	52.6

Data source: ILOSTAT, accessed on 16 December 2022.

Tables 11.5–11.8 present data that operate at the level of the productive forces. Information society theories should, however, also look at the level of the relations of production. Table 11.9 gives an example of data that operates at the level of the relations of production, namely the Global Labour Income Share.

The Global Labour Income Share is the share of wages, salaries, and benefits in the global gross domestic product (GDP). The data shows that the global dominance of neoliberal capitalism has been based on wage repression, that is the decrease in the wage share that benefits capital. At the same time, societies have become more global, more networked, and more based on the use of the Internet and mobile phones. This means that the "network" and "information" society is an information capitalism with deep class divisions.

11.4.8 How Information Society Theorists Respond to Their Critics

Information society theorists have responded to their critics. Here are two examples: Nico Stehr claims that "the radical critique is long on constant, static and fixed ills and somewhat short on dynamic and evolving configurations of socioeconomic and political realities in modern society" (Stehr 1994,

55). In a comparable manner, Castells writes: "After all, if nothing is new under the sun, why bother to try to investigate, think, write, and read about it?" (Castells 2010, 372).

Stehr and Castells simply posit the notion that there is a radical break against the very critique of this notion. They do not answer the criticism that assuming a radical break obscures the continuity of capital accumulation, inequality, and stratification.

The term "information capitalism" should be used as a term that characterises all those parts of the mode of production where capital accumulation is based on information, which includes knowledge labour (that produces knowledge), the production of information technologies, and the combination of both.

Contemporary global society is simultaneously an agricultural, industrial and information society at the level of the productive forces and a class and capitalist society at the level of the relations of production. This can be seen by the interaction of the labour of mineral workers (agricultural labour), hardware assemblers and e-waste workers (industrial labour), and software engineering, prosumption, and ICT use that shape the production and use of digital media.

11.4.9 *Cognitive Capitalism in the Society of Singularities*

The German social theorist Andreas Reckwitz characterises contemporary society as the society of singularities.

> Late-modern society – that is, the form of modernity that has been developing since the 1970s or 1980s – is a *society of singularities* to the extent that its predominant logic is the social logic of the particular. It is also – and this cannot be stressed enough – the first society in which this is true in a comprehensive sense. In fact, the social logic of the particular governs *all* dimensions of the social: things and objects as well as subjects, collectives, spaces, and temporalities. 'Singularity' and 'singularization' are cross-sectional concepts, and they designate a cross-sectional phenomenon that pervades all of society.
>
> (Reckwitz 2020, 4–5)

Typical for the society of singularities are characterised by struggles for visibility and markets governed by attractiveness (Reckwitz 2020, 3). Individualisation has certainly been an important feature of capitalist society in the past decades. Think, for example, of the creation of the massive amount of freelancers (single-person companies), which has individualised economic risk, the demise of traditional economic, political, and cultural collectives such as trade unions, political parties, or churches, flexible accumulation that has allowed the production of commodities that are personalised, individualised and are presented as being special and speaking to the lifestyles of particular groups and individuals. Individualisation has been part of the restructuration of capitalist society through neoliberalism, an economic, political, and ideological model that combines commodification, privatisation, marketisation, and individualisation and has shaped many realms of society. The goal of both neoliberalism and individualisation is the strengthening of the power of the few at the expense of the many, that is the accumulation of economic capital, political power, and cultural distinction. Singularisation is an aspect of neoliberal capitalism, so there is no need to speak of a "society of singularities". Rather, capitalism has been undergoing transformations that have given more importance to information and communication, and culture.

For the present author, individualisation and singularisation are phenomena subsumed under the logic of capitalism. For Reckwitz, singularisation is the primary process in contemporary society under which capitalism is subsumed as a (purely) economic system. Reckwitz (2021, chapter 3) argues that a cognitive-cultural capitalism has replaced classical industrial capitalism. This type of capitalism is characterised by automation, global networks of production, knowledge labour, permanent innovations, and polarisation between precarious, simple, unskilled services and complex, highly skilled well-paid knowledge work. Reckwitz (2021, 85) therefore speaks of a "polarized post-industrialism". Reckwitz tends to present an economic and cultural antagonism between precarious service and industrial workers on the one side and highly skilled and well-paid middle-class professionals on the other side as cultural capitalism's main antagonism. The problem is that he leaves out the antagonism between capital and labour as capitalism's main antagonism. This antagonism has been transformed and culturalised: Wealth has become ever-more concentrated in transnational corporations, where cultural and digital corporations play an important role. Labour has been squeezed concerning its share in global wealth. The share of wages and salaries in the GDP has significantly decreased (see Table 11.9 in this chapter and Table 9.6 in Chapter 9). At the same time, the share of capital in the global GDP has significantly increased. This means that in the past decades, the class polarisation between capital and labour has increased. Also, many cultural and digital workers have faced various forms of precarity (see Discussion in Chapters 9 and 10). Big capital has strongly grown, while the globalisation and informatisation of capitalism have brought about lots of precarious labour among new and old forms of labour. Contemporary capitalism's central antagonism is not one between a new middle class and an old working class, but between transnational capital and the global working class.

Reckwitz (2020, 2021) characterises contemporary capitalism as cognitive-cultural capitalism. He restricts the notion of capitalism to the capitalist economy. Reckwitz (2021, chapter 3) argues that the key aspect of cognitive capitalism is a shift from physical commodities towards an increased importance of cultural commodities such as services, events, and media formats. "Ideas, knowledge and social relationships" have increasingly been turned into capital (Reckwitz 2021, 94). Knowledge work would play a key role in the production of "immaterial capital" (94). Knowledge work and culture would also play an important role in the realm of traditional, industrial products such as sneakers, cars, household products. Marketing and branding play an important role in this context as they create an aura of the commodity's authenticity, singularity, and individuality (see Discussion of lifestyle marketing and branding in Chapter 5 of this book). "In short, large portions of the economy have become 'cognitive' in late modernity" (Reckwitz 2021, 95). Cultural and cultural commodities are, according to Reckwitz, not simply functional but are bought by consumers because of their aesthetics, the narratives associated with them, their playfulness, or their creative or ethical appeal (Reckwitz 2021, 95–96).

> What is characteristic of cultural capitalism, as it has expanded since the 1980s, is that its cultural goods typically claim to be *unique* (*singular*) and that consumers expect them to be so. In other words, cultural capitalism is *singularity capitalism*, with an extremely diversified form of consumption that revolves around *singularity goods* and their qualitative differences. Singularity is not an objective feature of a good – rather, it depends on the perspective of the consumer and on authoritative evaluations, which certify its aesthetic, ethical, narrative, or ludic uniqueness.
>
> (Reckwitz 2021, 97)

Reckwitz argues that cognitive-cultural capitalism has in processes of economisation shaped many parts of society, including education, cities, love relations, and the Internet:

> the communicative space of the *internet* as a whole can be interpreted as a sphere in which a (cultural) economization of the social has taken place that affects the daily life of nearly every individual. Although there are also online social networks and communities that are not necessarily market-structured, the internet overall fundamentally has – even independent of its commercial use – the structure of an attractiveness market in which individuals, with their profiles, compete for the attention of other users (a scarce resource) and for their positive evaluation. Here, too, it is the case that only those people who seem to be singular – different, surprising, special – can potentially have success. Individuals attempt to be influential and to attract 'followers' in this way; everyone is constantly a consumer – and, at the same time, at least potentially also a producer who is presenting himself or herself as a cultural singularity good. Within the context of the digital attention economy, the winner-take-all constellations are drastic. The few phenomenally successful user profiles – for instance, on YouTube or Twitter or as a blog – stand in contrast to the many that are unsuccessful: extreme visibility on the one hand, social invisibility on the other.
>
> (Reckwitz 2021, 108)

Reckwitz analyses important aspects of the transformation of capitalism. These transformations do not justify speaking of a "society of singularities", but singularisation is an important economic, political, and cultural process in information capitalism and capitalism in general that is based on the logic of accumulation. Splitting up humans from groups into individuals who are individually addressed as singular entrepreneurs, citizens, and consumers weakens the power of collectives and thereby potentials for resistance to the logic of accumulation that shapes capitalist society.

11.4.10 Cognitive Capitalism

Reckwitz's analysis partly resonates with Autonomous Marxism. He explicitly refers to Moulier-Boutang's (2011) analysis of cognitive capitalism:

> Whereas industrial capitalism can be characterised by the fact that accumulation was based mainly on machinery and on the organisation of manual labour, understood here as the organisation of production and the allocation of workers to fixed jobs, cognitive capitalism is a different system of accumulation, in which the accumulation is based on knowledge and creativity, in other words on forms of immaterial investment. In cognitive capitalism, the capture of gains arising from knowledge and innovation is the central issue for accumulation, and it plays a determining role in generating profits.
>
> (Moulier-Boutang 2011, 56–57)

The Autonomist Marxists Michael Hardt and Antonio Negri have popularised the notion of immaterial labour that was first introduced by Maurizio Lazzarato (1996) and that, according to authors such as Boutang and Reckwitz, is at the heart of cognitive capitalism:

> The passage toward an informational economy necessarily involves a change in the quality and nature of labor. [...] Most services indeed are based on the continual exchange of information and knowledges. Since the production of services results in no material and durable good, we define the labor involved in this production as *immaterial labor* – that is, labor that produces an immaterial good, such as a service, a cultural product, knowledge, or communication. [...] In short, we can distinguish three types of immaterial labor that drive the service sector at the top of the informational economy. The first is involved in an industrial production that has been informationalized and has incorporated communication technologies in a way that transforms the production process itself. Manufacturing is regarded as a service, and the material labor of the production of durable goods mixes with and tends toward immaterial labor. Second is the immaterial labor of analytical and symbolic tasks, which itself breaks down into creative and intelligent manipulation on the one hand and routine symbolic tasks on the other.

Finally, a third type of immaterial labor involves the production and manipulation of affect and requires (virtual or actual) human contact, labor in the bodily mode. These are the three types of labor that drive the postmodernization of the global economy.

(Hardt and Negri 2000, 289, 290, 293)

The increasing importance of knowledge labour and cultural commodities is an important and undeniabl feature of contemporary capitalism and the transformations it has been undergoing in the past decades. The theoretical question is if the terms "immaterial labour" and "immaterial capital" are suited. They imply that culture, knowledge, and communication are not material, which results in a separation of matter from the mind and of the economy from culture. The present author takes a different approach influenced by Raymond Williams' approach of Cultural Materialism where "modes of consciousness are material" (Williams 1977, 190). Matter and consciousness are "disjoined" in "idealism or in mechanical materialism" (Williams 1977, 190). Ideas and consciousness are material because humans produce and reproduce them in social relations. They are the results of social production.

The implication of such concepts [of immateriality] is that either the mind is considered to be the world's substance and phenomena are reduced to the mind or that matter and mind are postulated as the world's two substances. [...] If something existed outside of matter, then the world would in the first and the last instance not have a sufficient ground. [...] The mind is an organisational level of matter that emerged in and in the context of the emergence of the human being and society. [...] The human brain produces the mental world of ideas. [...] That the mind is material means that cognition emerges from the brain's dynamic, networked activities of production.

(Fuchs 2020, 35–36)

11.4.11 *Data Capitalism, Platform Capitalism, Surveillance Capitalism*

Terms that have been used as alternatives to the notions of information capitalism, communicative capitalism and digital capitalism are, for example, data capitalism, platform capitalism, and surveillance capitalism.

Myers West (2019) defines data capitalism as follows: "Data capitalism is a system in which the commoditization of our data enables an asymmetric redistribution of power that is weighted toward the actors who have access and the capability to make sense of information" (Myers West 2019, 20). This definition does not include aspects of labour and class.

Nick Srnicek (2017) introduces the notion of platform capitalism. He argues that "in the twenty first century advanced capitalism came to be centred upon extracting and using a particular kind of raw material: data" (Srnicek 2017, 39). "Just like oil, data are a material to be extracted, refined, and used in a variety of ways" (40). Platforms "became an efficient way to monopolise, extract, analyse, and use the increasingly large amounts of data that were being recorded" (42–43). Platforms "extract data from natural processes (weather conditions, crop cycles, etc.), from production processes (assembly lines, continuous flow manufacturing, etc.), and from other businesses and users (web tracking, usage data, etc.). They are an extractive apparatus for data" (48).

Platform capitalism has to do with commodities produced on the Internet by digital labour. It is a subtype of digital capitalism. It is not an autonomous type of capitalism.

Shoshana Zuboff has coined the notion of surveillance capitalism

> Surveillance capitalism unilaterally claims human experience as free raw material for translation into behavioral data. [...] Surveillance capitalists know everything *about us*, whereas their operations are designed to be unknowable *to us*. They accumulate vast domains of new knowledge *from us*, but not *for us*. They predict our futures for the sake of others' gain, not ours.
>
> (Zuboff 2019, 8, 11)

For her, surveillance capitalism is a "new economic order that claims human experience as free raw material for hidden commercial practices of extraction, prediction, and sales" and a "parasitic economic logic in which the production of goods and services is subordinated to a new global architecture of behavioral modification" (7). "[S]urveillance capitalism is a new actor in history" (14). "Instead of labor, surveillance capitalism feeds on every aspect of human experience" (9). "Surveillance capitalism's products and services are not the objects of a value exchange" (10).

Zuboff speaks of "behavioural surplus" that is independent of labour. However, lots of data collection stands in the context of digital labour. Surveillance is an aspect of the capitalist economy, contemporary states, and the interaction of the two. It is not the main feature of capitalism today.

Zuboff leaves out

- the exploitation of information labour and digital labour;
- the political control of (digital) information;
- ideology of and on the Internet.

Surveillance is not new: The overseeing of slaves, Taylorist time and motion studies, etc., were methods of surveillance used in the exploitation and control of workers. Labour and surveillance are not independent, but connected on the Internet, not detached: digital labour produces data, content, and social relations on Internet platforms so that commodities are produced whose sale results in profit. Zuboff's book

> is helpful for better understanding digital surveillance, but does not acknowledge the importance of labour, including the digital labour of

users who produce data, content, and social relations online that Facebook and the likes of Cambridge Analytica monitor and instrumentalise for economic, political, and ideological purposes.

(Fuchs 2021, 169)

Digital/informational/communicative capitalism is a more suited term than surveillance capitalism. Surveillance is one of the means to advance exploitation, control/domination, and manipulation/ideology in capitalism.

11.4.12 Digital Capitalism

The notion of digital capitalism originated in the context of the eulogisation of finance capitalism: The earliest mention of the term "digital capitalism" that I was able to trace was in a 1993 article in *Forbes* magazine, where *Forbes* then-senior editor Robert Lenzner and *Forbes* reporter William Heuslein wrote the issue's cover story titled "The Age of Digital Capitalism" (Lenzner and Heuslein 1993). The article describes "computerized financial instruments" (Lenzner and Heuslein 1993, 63), derivatives such as options, futures, currency forwards, interest-rates swaps, options on futures and swaps. "Computers make all this magic [of derivatives] possible. [...] Think of all this as an adult Nintendo game with big dollar signs attached" (Lenzner and Heuslein 1993, 63).

Dan Schiller (1999) published the first book that contained the term "digital capitalism" in its title: *Digital Capitalism. Networking the Global Market System*. He sees the Internet as a means of the globalisation of capitalism

> Networks are directly generalizing the social and cultural range of the capitalist economy as never before. That is why I refer to this new epoch as one of *digital capitalism*. The arrival of digital capitalism has involved radical social, as well as technological, changes. [...] As it comes under the sway of an expansionary market logic, the Internet is catalyzing an epochal political-economic transition toward what I call digital capitalism – and toward changes that, for much of the population, are unpropitious.

(Schiller 1999, xiv, xvii)

Marx (1867, 103, 134, 667, 797, 875, 1063; 1894, 953) sees capitalism as a society, a formation of society (*Gesellschaftsformation*). "But capital is not a thing, it is a definite social relation of production pertaining to a particular historical soci[et]al formation, which simply takes the form of a thing and gives this thing a specific social character" (Marx 1894, 953). At the level of society in general, the economy plays an important role in the form of the production of use-values and social relations.

Capitalism is a type of society where the mass of humans is alienated from the conditions of economic, political, and cultural production, which means that they do not control the conditions that shape their lives, which enables

Table 11.10 Levels and structures of capitalist society

	Micro-level	Meso-level	Macro-level
Economic structures	Commodity, money	Companies, markets	Capitalist economy
Political structures	Laws	Parties, government	The capitalist state
Cultural structures	Ideology	Ideology-producing organisations	The capitalist ideological system

privileged groups' accumulation of capital in the economy, decision-power in politics, and reputation, attention and respect in culture. Alienation in the economy means the dominant class exploitation of the working-class labour. Alienation in non-economic systems means domination; that is, one group benefits at the expense of other groups via means of control such as state power, ideology and violence. In capitalism, we find the accumulation of capital in the economy, the accumulation of decision-power and influence in politics, and the accumulation of reputation, attention, and respect in culture. The key aspect is not that there is growth, but that there is the attempt of the dominant class and dominant groups to accumulate power at the expense of others who as a consequence have disadvantages. Capitalist society is therefore based on an economic antagonism of exploitation between classes and social antagonisms of domination. Table 11.10 shows the levels and structures of capitalist society.

David Harvey (2014, 7) defines capitalism as capitalist society, namely as "any social formation in which processes of capital circulation and accumulation are hegemonic and dominant in providing and shaping the material, social and intellectual bases for social life. Capitalism is rife with innumerable contradictions". For Harvey, capital accumulation is the central feature of capitalist society that shapes all aspects of this society.

Digital capitalism is the dimension of capitalist society where processes of the accumulation of capital, decision-power and reputation are mediated by and organised with the help of digital technologies and where economic, political, and cultural processes result in digital goods and digital structures. Digital labour, digital capital, political online communication, digital aspects of protests and social struggles, ideology online, and influencer-dominated digital culture are some of the features of digital capitalism. In digital capitalism, digital technologies mediate the accumulation of capital and power.

Information capitalism also includes economic, political, and cultural accumulation processes where non-digital technologies and non-digital forms of information production play a role (e.g. capital accumulation based on theatre and live entertainment).

Tables 11.11 and 11.12 show the antagonisms of capitalism in general and digital capitalism in particular. Table 11.13 gives an overview of accumulation processes in digital capitalism.

Table 11.11 Accumulation as a general process in capitalist society

Realm of Society	Central Process in General	Central Process in Capitalist Society	Underlying Antagonism in Capitalist Society
Economy	Production of use-values	Capital accumulation	Capital vs. labour
Politics	Production of collective decisions	Accumulation of decision-power and influence	Bureaucrats vs. citizens
Culture	Production of meanings	Accumulation of reputation, attention, respect	Ideologues/celebrities/influencers vs. everyday people

Table 11.12 The antagonisms of digital capitalism

Realm of Society	Underlying Antagonism in Capitalist Society	Antagonisms in Digital Capitalism	Examples
Economy	Capital vs. labour	Digital capital vs. digital labour, digital commodity vs. digital commons	The monopoly power of Google, Facebook, Apple, Amazon, Microsoft, etc.
Politics	Bureaucrats vs. citizens	Digital dictators vs. digital citizens, digital authoritarianism/fascism vs. digital democracy	Donald Trump's use of Twitter and other social media
Culture	Ideologues and celebrities vs. everyday people	Digital ideologues vs. digital humans, digital hatred/division/ideology vs. digital friendship in culture.	Asymmetrical attention economy in popular culture on social media: the cultural power of online influencers such as PewDiePie (> 100 million followers)

Table 11.13 The role of accumulation in digital capitalism

Realm of Society	Accumulation in Digital Capitalism
Economy	Accumulation of digital capital based on digital commodities
Politics	Accumulation of decision-power concerning the control of digital knowledge and digital networks
Culture	Accumulation of reputation, attention, and respect by the spread of ideologies on and of the Internet

Digital capitalism is a still relatively novel dimension of capitalism and capitalist accumulation processes. It is an important topic of research that requires an interdisciplinary critical approach to social research.

11.5 Conclusion

This chapter asked: What kind of society do we live in? Do we live in an information society or a capitalist society?

We can now summarise the main findings:

Finding 1: Information Society Theory

Information society theory deals with the question: In what kind of society do we live? What is the role of information in contemporary society? Many information society theories argue that knowledge labour and/or computer technologies have resulted in a new society, the information society (also referred to as knowledge society or network society).

Finding 2: Information Society Theory as Ideology

Critics and sceptics of information society theory argue that the latter is an ideology that distracts attention from the realities, problems and inequalities of capitalism. Some conclude that capitalism has not changed.

Finding 3: The Dialectic of Capitalism and the Information Society

Information capitalism, communicative capitalism, and digital capitalism are specific dimensions and aspects of capitalist society. These terms are better suited for describing the changes and continuities of capitalism than notions such as surveillance capitalism, data capitalism or platform capitalism. Information capitalism is based on dialectics of continuity and discontinuity, subjective and objective information, and the productive forces and the relations of production.

References

Adorno, Theodor W. 1968/2003. Late Capitalism or Industrial Society? The Fundamental Question of the Present Structure of Society. In *Can One Live after Auschwitz?*, edited by Rolf Tiedemann, 111–125. Stanford, CA: Stanford University Press.

Bell, Daniel. 1974. *The Coming of Post-Industrial Society*. London: Heinemann.

Beniger, James R. 1986. *The Control Revolution. Technological and Economic Origins of the Information Society*. Cambridge, MA: Harvard University Press.

Cairncross, Frances. 1997. *The Death of Distance. How the Communications Revolution Will Change Our Lives*. Cambridge, MA: Harvard Business School Press.

Castells, Manuel. 2010. *End of Millennium. The Information Age: Economy, Society and Culture. Volume 3*. Malden, MA: Wiley-Blackwell. Second edition with a new preface.

Castells, Manuel. 2000. *The Rise of the Network Society. The Information Age: Economy, Society and Culture. Volume 1*. Malden, MA: Blackwell. Second edition.

Drucker, Peter. 1969. *The Age of Discontinuity*. London: Heinemann.

Friedman, Jonathan. 2002. Modernity and Other Traditions. In *Critically Modern*, edited by Bruce M. Knauft, 287–313. Bloomington: Indiana University Press.

Fuchs, Christian. 2022. *Digital Capitalism: Media, Communication and Society Volume Three*. London: Routledge.

Fuchs, Christian. 2021. *Social Media: A Critical Introduction*. London: SAGE. Third edition.

Fuchs, Christian. 2020. *Communication and Capitalism. A Critical Theory*. London: University of Westminster Press. DOI: https://doi.org/10.16997/book45

Garnham, Nicholas. 1998/2004. Information Society Theory as Ideology. In *The Information Society Reader*, edited by Frank Webster, 165–183. New York: Routledge.

Garnham, Nicholas. 2000. "Information Society" as Theory or Ideology. *Information, Communication & Society* 3 (2): 139–152.

Hardt, Michael and Antonio Negri. 2000. *Empire*. Cambridge, MA: Harvard University Press.

Harvey, David. 2014. *Seventeen Contradictions and the End of Capitalism*. Oxford: Oxford University Press.

Lazzarato, Maurizio. 1996. Immaterial Labor. In *Radical Thought in Italy*, edited by Paolo Virno and Michael Hardt, 133–147. Minneapolis: University of Minnesota Press.

Lenzner, Robert and William Heuslein, 1993. The Age of Digital Capitalism. *Forbes* 151 (7): 62–72.

Machlup, Fritz. 1962. *The Production and Diffusion of Knowledge in the United States*. Princeton, NJ: Princeton University Press.

Marx, Karl. 1894. *Capital. Volume 3*. London: Penguin.

Marx, Karl. 1867. *Capital. Volume 1*. London: Penguin.

Marx, Karl. 1857/1858. *Grundrisse*. London: Penguin.

Masuda, Yoneji. 1980. *The Information Society as Post-Industrial Society*. Bethesda, MD: World Future Society.

Moulier-Boutang, Yann. 2011. *Cognitive Capitalism*. Cambridge: Polity.

Myers West, Sarah. 2019. Data Capitalism: Redefining the Logics of Surveillance and Privacy. *Business & Society* 58 (1): 20–41.

Negroponte, Nicholas. 1995. *Being Digital*. New York: Alfred A. Knopf.

Porat, Marc. 1977. *The Information Economy*. Washington, DC: US Department of Commerce.

Reckwitz, Andreas. 2021. *The End of Illusions. Politics, Economy, and Culture in Late Modernity*. Cambridge: Polity.

Reckwitz, Andreas. 2020. *The Society of Singularities*. Cambridge: Polity.

Richta, Radovan. 1969. *Civilization at the Crossroads. Social and Human Implications of the Scientific and Technological Revolution*. White Plains, NY: International Arts and Sciences Press Inc.

Runciman, Walter G. 1993. Has British Capitalism Changed Since the First World War? *British Journal of Sociology* 44 (1): 53–67.

Schiller, Dan. 1999. *Digital Capitalism. Networking the Global Market System.* Cambridge, MA: The MIT Press.

Srnicek, Nick. 2017. *Platform Capitalism.* Cambridge: Polity Press.

Stehr, Nico. 1994. *Knowledge Societies.* London: SAGE.

Streeck, Wolfgang. 2016. *How Will Capitalism End? Essays on a Failing System.* London: Verso.

Toffler, Alvin. 1980. *The Third Wave.* New York: Bantam.

Touraine, Alaine. 1974. *The Post-Industrial Society. Tomorrow's Social History: Classes, Conflicts and Culture in the Programmed Society.* London: Wildwood House.

Wallerstein, Immanuel M. 2004a. *The Uncertainties of Knowledge.* Philadelphia, PA: Temple University Press. Ebook version.

Wallerstein, Immanuel M. 2004b. *World-Systems Analysis.* Durham, NC: Duke University Press.

Webster, Frank. 2014. *Theories of the Information Society.* London: Routledge. Fourth edition.

Webster, Frank. 2002. The Information Society Revisited. In *Handbook of New Media,* edited by Sonia Livingstone and Leah Lievrouw, 22–33. London: Sage.

Westra, Richard and Alan Zuege, eds. 2001. *Phases of Capitalist Development. Booms, Crises and Globalizations.* Basingstoke: Palgrave.

Williams, Raymond. 1977. *Marxism and Literature.* Oxford: Oxford University Press.

Zuboff, Shoshana. 2019. *The Age of Surveillance Capitalism: The Fight for a Human Future at the New Frontier of Power.* London: Profile Books.

Recommended Readings and Exercises

Readings

The following texts are recommended as accompanying readings to this chapter:

Radovan Richta. 1969. *Civilization at the Crossroads. Social and Human Implications of the Scientific and Technological Revolution.* White Plains, NY: International Arts and Sciences Press Inc.
Chapter 1: The Nature of the Scientific and Technological Revolution (pp. 1–103).
Chapter 2: Radical Changes in Work, Skills and Education (pp. 104–154).

Christian Fuchs. 2013. Capitalism or Information Society? The Fundamental Question of the Present Structure of Society. *European Journal of Social Theory* 16 (4): 413–434.

Christian Fuchs. 2022. *Digital Capitalism: Media, Communication and Society Volume Three.* London: Routledge.
Chapter 1: Introduction: What Is Digital Capitalism? (S. 3–37).

Frank Webster. 2002. The Information Society Revisited. In *Handbook of New Media*, edited by Sonia Livingstone and Leah Lievrouw, 22–33. London: SAGE. Chapter 22.

Christian Fuchs. 2020. *Marxism: Karl Marx's Fifteen Key Concepts for Cultural and Communication Studies*. New York: Routledge.
Chapter 11: Class Struggles (pp. 247–279).

Andreas Reckwitz. 2021. *The End of Illusions. Politics, Economy, and Culture in Late Modernity*. Cambridge: Polity.
Chapter 3: Beyond Industrial Society: Polarized Post-Industrialism and Cognitive-Cultural Capitalism (pp. 73–110).

Yann Moulier-Boutang. 2011. *Cognitive Capitalism*. Cambridge: Polity.
Chapter 3: What Is Cognitive Capitalism? (pp. 47–91).

Michael Hardt and Antonio Negri. 2000. *Empire*. Cambridge, MA: Harvard University Press.
Chapter 3.4: Postmodernization, or the Informatization of Production (pp. 280–303).

Christian Fuchs. 2020. *Communication and Capitalism. A Critical Theory*. London: University of Westminster Press. DOI: https://doi.org/10.16997/book45
Chapter 2: Materialism (pp. 27–39).
Chapter 3: Materialism and Society (pp. 41–67).
Chapter 4: Communication and Society (pp. 70–107).
Chapter 5: Capitalism and Communication (pp. 111–152).
Chapter 7: Communication Society (pp. 173–195).

Exercise 11.2   Information Society Theory

Search for a book or article that theorises the "information society".

Discuss. If you work in a group or class, present your results to each other.

What are the main insights of the chosen approach?
What kind of information society theory is it?
How do you assess the approach?

Exercise 11.3 Cognitive Capitalism

Read at least one and best all three of the following texts:

Andreas Reckwitz. 2021. *The End of Illusions. Politics, Economy, and Culture in Late Modernity*. Cambridge: Polity.
Chapter 3: Beyond Industrial Society: Polarized Post-Industrialism and Cognitive-Cultural Capitalism (pp. 73–110).

Yann Moulier-Boutang. 2011. *Cognitive Capitalism*. Cambridge: Polity.
Chapter 3: What Is Cognitive Capitalism? (pp. 47–91).

Michael Hardt and Antonio Negri. 2000. *Empire*. Cambridge, MA: Harvard University Press.
Chapter 3.4: Postmodernization, or the Informatization of Production (pp. 280–303).

If you work in a group or class, present summaries of these chapters. Discuss:

How do Reckwitz, Moulier-Boutang and Hardt/Negri characterise contemporary capitalism?
What do they understand by "immaterial labour" and "immaterial capital"?
What are the commonalities and differences of the three approaches?
How do you assess the analyses of capitalism by Reckwitz, Moulier-Boutang and Hardt/Negri?

Exercise 11.4 A Cultural-Materialist Analysis of Capitalism and Communication

Read the following chapters:

Christian Fuchs. 2020. *Communication and Capitalism. A Critical Theory*. London: University of Westminster Press. DOI: https://doi.org/10.16997/book45
Chapter 2: Materialism (pp. 27–39).
Chapter 3: Materialism and Society (pp. 41–67).
Chapter 4: Communication and Society (pp. 70–107).
Chapter 5: Capitalism and Communication (pp. 111–152).
Chapter 7: Communication Society (pp. 173–195).

Discuss:
What is matter? What is materialism?
What are the features of a materialist analysis of society?
What are features of a materialist analysis of communication in society?
What commonalities and differences are there between the approach of
Cultural Materialism outlined in these chapters and the three texts by
Andreas Reckwitz, Yann Moulier-Boutang and Michael Hardt/Antonio
Negri that were used in Exercise 11.3?

Exercise 11.5   Digital Capitalism

Read the following text:

Christian Fuchs. 2022. *Digital Capitalism: Media, Communication and
Society Volume Three*. London: Routledge.
Chapter 1: Introduction: What is Digital Capitalism? (S. 3–37).

Discuss:

What are the main features of Christian Fuchs' concept of digital
capitalism?
Give a definition of capitalism.
What are the main features of digitalisation?
Think about your definition of capitalism and the main features of digi-
talisation, and create and write down your own definition of digital
capitalism.
If you work in a learning group, compare your definitions.

12 The Political Economy of the Public Sphere and the Digital Public Sphere

What You Will Learn in This Chapter

- You will learn about the foundations of public sphere theory;
- You will learn about the role of the media in the public sphere;
- You will learn what the digital public sphere is all about.

12.1 Introduction

We all together form and are the public. Where humans come together and communicate in public, a public sphere is formed. The media are publishing systems; they help humans make information public. The public sphere is about the question who can make certain topics visible in society. It therefore has to do with the question how (un)democratic societies are. The political economy of the media plays an important role in this context.

This chapter asks: What does the political economy of the public sphere and the digital public sphere look like? Section 12.2 discusses the notion of the public sphere. Section 12.3 is focused on the digital public sphere. Section 12.4 presents some conclusions.

12.2 The Political Economy of the Public Sphere

12.2.1 Jürgen Habermas' the Structural Transformation of the Public Sphere

Jürgen Habermas' (1989) book *The Structural Transformation of the Public Sphere*[1] has been the most influential work on the public sphere, a key concept in critical theories of society. "We call events and occasions 'public' when they are open to all, in contrast to close or exclusive affairs" (Habermas 1989, 1). The public sphere has in essence the task of engaging citizens in "critical public debate" (54). The public sphere needs communication systems for political debate. The logic of the public sphere is independent of economic and political power: "[l]aws of the market [...] [are] suspended" as are the "laws of the state" (36). Habermas argues that the public sphere is not just a sphere of public political communication, but also a sphere that

DOI: 10.4324/9781003391203-14

is free from state censorship and from private ownership. It is free from particularism and instrumental reason.

Habermas (1989, 122–129, 136) discusses key characteristics of the public sphere:

- The public sphere is a realm for the formation of public opinion;
- In a true public sphere, all citizens have access;
- The public sphere enables political debate in an unrestricted fashion (freedom of assembly, freedom of association, freedom of expression, and publication of opinions) about matters of general interest;
- The public sphere enables political debates about the general rules governing social relations;
- Private property, influence and skills enable individuals to be heard in the bourgeois public sphere. Workers have been excluded from these resources. This circumstance becomes, for example, evident in the lower rates of access of working-class children to higher education and lower completion rates;
- The bourgeois class only serves and advances its own particular interests which are profit interests and not the common interest;
- Marx saw socialism as the public sphere and as an alternative to the bourgeois state that serves class interests. This became evident in his analysis of the Paris Commune (March-May 1871) as a specific kind of public sphere.

The public sphere is a sphere of society that interacts with politics, the economy, and culture. It is a kind of interface between the other spheres of society, the realm of public communication. Whenever humans talk and gather in public, they act in the public sphere. Examples are public debates, the mass media, demonstrations, and protest campaigns.

12.2.2 The Public Sphere as a Communication System

Following Habermas, Gerhards, and Neidhardt, we conceive of the public sphere as a communication system that is in principle universally accessible and open for participation by everyone, provides public access to information and enables public voice, communication and debate about topics that matter for and in society. Neidhardt argues that the public sphere includes speakers, media of communication, and audiences. "There must exist: speakers. who say something; an audience, that listens; and mediators who relate speakers and the audience if they are not in immediate contact with one another-that is, journalists and the mass media" (Neidhardt 1993, 340).

There are different types of publics: Micropublics are small publics where humans directly encounter each speech to each other, mainly face-to-face, in everyday situations and spaces such as "pubs, coffee houses, and salons" (Gerhards and Neidhardt 1990, 20). Mesopublics are medium-sized publics that take on the form of public events. An example is a rock concert or an evening-filling book presentation with accompanying audience discussion.

Macro-publics are large-scale publics at the level of society where many humans access information or communicate. Mass media often play an important role in macro-publics. The public sphere is an interface of society that interacts with the economic system, the political system, and the cultural system (Fuchs 2008, 2014). Figure 12.1 presents a model of the public sphere.

We distinguish between micro-, meso-, and macro-publics as three types of publics that together constitute the public sphere. Economic, political, and cultural actors interact with the public sphere in that they are the subject of news, information, and entertainment. Furthermore, economic, political, and cultural groups often try to lobby in the public sphere to gain visibility and support for their views and positions. Financial resources from the economy provide funding for media organisations operating in the public sphere (e.g. in the form of ad revenue, subscription fees, licence fees). Policies and laws regulate the media. Norms, moral values, worldviews, and ideologies as cultural structures influence public opinion, public debates, and the public sphere at large. At the level of human practices, human beings cognise, which means that they perceive, experience, and interpret the world; they communicate with each other about what is happening in their social environment and society; and they co-operate and socially produce new realities and social relations. Processes of cognition, communication, and co-operation are the practices that form the foundation of the public sphere where opinions,

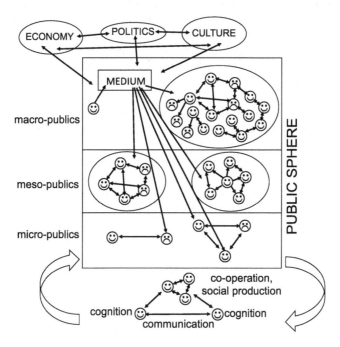

Figure 12.1 A model of the public sphere.

content, and knowledge are produced. Opinions, content, and knowledge produced in the public sphere influence the way humans think, communicate, and produce.

12.2.3 Slavko Splichal: Publicness and the Public Sphere

Slavko Splichal argues that the translation of Habermas' concept of Öffentlichkeit as public sphere is misleading. The public sphere is an "infrastructure" that is nothing without human members ("the public") who "act, form, express opinion, and share the feeling of belonging" (Splichal 2012, 67). Therefore, Splichal prefers the term publicness as the translation of Öffentlichkeit, which refers to "discursive actions of opening issues to public scrutiny and discussion and often presupposes the existence of a critical public" (Splichal 2012, 66). Publicness means a dialectic of system and actor, structures and agency, space and practices, object and subject, public sphere and the public. "There is no public without a public sphere and no public sphere without a public" (Splichal 2012, 79). Splichal argues that the public sphere is sometimes incorrectly presented as an actor, which denies the agency of humans and groups in them. "Clearly, perceiving and thematising social problems are tasks that can only be performed by people (communicatively) *acting in* the public sphere, that is, by *the public* and *in* the public sphere but not *by* the public sphere" (Splichal 2022a, 68).

Therefore, in Figure 12.1 there is both a level of human practices and a structural level. At the level of practices, humans communicate in public, engage with public information, and engage in public social action, forms of social production that bring about changes. These are interacting processes of cognition, communication, and co-operation. Humans encounter other humans with whom they form the public mediated through systems, spaces, and structures that condition, enable, and constrain their public practices.

Splichal (2022a, 72–73) argues that the public sphere as infrastructure requires communication technologies, democratic institutions, and a public culture of democratic practices, values, and norms. He also says that publicness has to do with humans' visibility of social access, and access to information and communication channels, reflexive communicative action (reflexive publicity), the mediation of social relations and of the relationship between civil society and the state, and the formation of public opinion that influences decisions and legitimates power. Splichal (2022a, 133–143; 2022b) characterises the components of publicness as "VARMIL": visibility, access, reflexive publicity, mediation, influencing decisions, legitimation of power and specific collective decisions.

Visibility means that public-worthy developments in society should be made visible to the public. The public should have *access* to the means of communication, which requires "freedom of thought, expression, assembly and association" (Splichal 2022a, 133–134). *Reflexive and deliberative publicity* means that there is "*rationally guided* discussion" (134). *Mediation* means that there are channels such as the media system that mediate between the state and civil society (134). *Influencing decision-making* is about public opinion influencing political decision-making in the form of democratic procedures (134). *Legitimation* is about a system of trust and distrust so that political decisions are debated and criticised by the public that holds politicians and governments accountable and political decisions are not arbitrary but based on democratic will (134). The next table shows Splichal's model that combines public sphere infrastructures and publicness (see Table 12.1).

Habermas' concept of the public sphere has often been misunderstood as either an idealisation of communication in capitalist society or an idealisation that does not and cannot exist in actual society. These are, however, misunderstandings. Habermas' concept of the public sphere is a critical theory concept. It defines democracy and democratic communication as the ideal organisational models of society. And it allows criticising processes that distort or destroy democracy and democratic communication.

Habermas argues that in feudal societies, political and economic power was controlled by monarchs and the aristocracy. Feudalist societies were agricultural economies in which households acted as economic units. There was a family-based economic structure.

The "Church, the prince, and the nobility" were "the carriers of the representative publicness" (Habermas 1989, 11). They represented what the public stood for and took decisions in an authoritarian manner that were binding for all. The public sphere consisted of the representation of monarchical, religious, and aristocratic power.

The French Revolution was a revolution against monarchical power. Politics became disembedded from the economy and organised in a separate system, the modern state, that dialectically interacts with the capitalist economy. Habermas argues that bourgeois society is based on the rebellion against monarchical power and the rule of churches, but has established new centres of power, namely capitalist corporations and political bureaucracies, that dominate the public sphere and marginalise other voices.

The Enlightenment, the French Revolution, industrialisation and the rise of capitalism led to the transformation of the structure of society, namely the disembedding of the economy from the state, the rise of wage labour, the factory, the working class, the class of private owners, commodity production and modern industry.

The public sphere was thereby a sphere of questioning monarchical and ecclesiastical rule, of the struggle for democracy and against the monarchy. Newspapers and magazines debated and challenged public authority. There were two main parts of the political public sphere:

1 Newspapers and media;
2 Town life.

The public played an important role in the French Revolution (1789–1799) and the revolutions of 1848. It was outside the direct control of the church and state. Newspapers were political. They were, according to Karl Bücher, a

Table 12.1 Splichal's model of publicness and the public sphere

Components of Publicness →	Structural Conditions of the Public Sphere		Communicative Actions Constitutive of the Public/ Public Sphere		Roles of Public Opinion	
	Visibility	Access	Reflexive Publicity	Mediation	Influencing Decisions	Legitimising Power
Infrastructural Pillars of the Public Sphere ↓						
Communication Technology: maturity and availability, democratic affordances, availability and control						
Democratic Institutional Structures: political structures, economic structures, media						
Public Culture: norms, values, practices						

Source: Based on Splichal (2022a, 139).

German economist and co-founder of the newspaper economy, "bearers and leaders of public opinion – weapons of party politics" (Habermas 1989, 140).

Movable-type printing originated in China in the 9th century, where wooden tablet printing used movable type. Characters were cut into wooden blocks that were arranged to form book pages. Johannes Gutenberg founded printing around 1450 with the printing press with movable type, which enabled the rise of publishing. The first modern newspaper was published in Germany in 1605. It bore the title "Relation aller Fürnemmen und gedenckwürdigen Historien" (= Collection of All Excellent and Meritorious News) and appeared until 1659.

Town life was the centre of life for the public and the location of coffee houses, salons, table societies, and pubs, which were spaces of literary and political criticism.

12.2.4 The Re-Feudalisation of the Public Sphere

Habermas' notion of the public sphere is critical because it is inherently tied to the notion of the re-feudalisation of the public sphere. The bourgeois public sphere negates its own foundations. In capitalism,

> the social preconditions for the equality of opportunity were obviously lacking, namely: that any person with skill and 'luck' could attain the status of property owner and thus the qualifications of a private person granted access to the public sphere, property and education. The public sphere [...] contradicted its own principle of universal accessibility.
> (Habermas 1989, 124)

"Under the conditions of a class society, bourgeois democracy thus from its very inception contradicted essential premises of its self-understanding" (Habermas 1989, 428). The bourgeois public sphere faces a negative dialectic: It promises freedom and democracy that are undermined by the power of large corporations and bureaucracies.

Habermas is in this context especially critical of the use of advertising and marketing in the economy and politics, which he says undermine rational debate and aim at manipulating the public into following the suggestions of powerful organisations to buy certain commodities, follow particular leaders, adopt specific lifestyles, etc.

> The public sphere assumes advertising functions. The more it can be deployed as a vehicle for political and economic propaganda, the more it becomes unpolitical as a whole and pseudo-privatized.
> (Habermas 1989, 175)

> The public sphere has become a "platform for advertising".
> (Habermas 1989, 181)

The history of the big daily papers in the second half of the nineteenth
century proves that the press itself became manipulable to the extent that
it became commercialized. [...] Ever since the marketing of the editorial
section became interdependent with that of the advertising section, the
press (until then an institution of private people insofar as they constituted a public) became an institution of certain participants in the public
sphere in their capacity as private individuals; that is, it became the gate
through which privileged private interests invaded the public sphere.

(Habermas 1989, 185)

[W]ithin the framework of the manufactured public sphere the mass
media are useful only as vehicles of advertising.

(Habermas 1989, 217)

In the *Theory of Communicative Action*, Habermas (1984, 1987) reformulated the notion of the feudalisation of the public sphere as the colonisation
of the lifeworld: "The thesis of internal colonization states that the subsystems of the economy and state become more and more complex as a consequence of capitalist growth, and penetrate ever deeper into the symbolic
reproduction of the lifeworld" (Habermas 1987, 367). The "colonization of
the lifeworld by system imperatives [...] drive[s] moral-practical elements out
of private and political public spheres of life" (Habermas 1987, 325). The
"imperatives of autonomous subsystems make their way into the lifeworld
from the outside – like colonial masters coming into a tribal society – and
force a process of assimilation upon it" (Habermas 1987, 355).

The colonisation of the lifeworld (Habermas 1984, 1987) results in the
centralisation of economic power (companies, market concentration, monopolies) and political power (state, bureaucracy). *Bureaucratisation* is
a transformation through which "the state was infused into [civil] society
(bureaucracy) and, in the opposite direction, through which [civil] society
was infused into the state (special-interest associations and political parties)"
(Habermas 1989, 197). Bureaucratisation has to do with rational calculation, administration by specialised officials, formalisation, and the institutional form (Habermas 1987, 306). *Monetarisation* and commodification
transmogrify the public sphere into "a sphere of culture consumption" that is
only a "pseudo-public sphere" (Habermas 1989, 162) and a "manufactured
public sphere" (Habermas 1989, 217). Monetarisation means that the logic
of commodities and money is introduced as organising principles into specific
social relations.

In *The Structural Transformation of the Public Sphere* and *The Theory of
Communicative Action*, there is hardly any discussion of ideology. The basic
reason is probably that Habermas wanted to go beyond the ideology critique
of Horkheimer, Adorno, and Marcuse. The consequence is, however, that ideology is a blindspot in his works. It is not seen as a process of re-feudalisation
and the colonisation of the lifeworld. One work where Habermas explicitly
focuses on ideology is *Technology and Science as "Ideology"*, a reflection

on Herbert Marcuse's works (Habermas 1968/1987). In it, Habermas does not provide a definition of ideology, but argues that ideology is about "the legitimation of domination" (83) and arises just like domination "under conditions of distorted communication" (112).

12.2.5 Administrative Research

George Gallup was the founder of what is today Gallup Inc., one of the world's largest opinion polling companies, and a professor of journalism and advertising. He pioneered opinion polling methods. Based on the British politician and academic James Bryce, Gallup understands public opinion as the "aggregate of the views men hold regarding matters that affect or interest the community" (Gallup 1957, 23).

Gallup's understanding of public opinion and the public is methodologically individualistic. It views the public as an aggregate of individual thoughts that like a heap of sand can be technologically dissected. Methodological individualism ignores that the public and public opinions arise from social processes, public communication and debates, public conflicts, society's conflicts of interest and struggles, etc. The proper analysis of public opinion, therefore, requires the combination of theories of society and empirical social research.

The problem with opinion polling is that it views and treats the public as an aggregate of individuals that it sees passively and deprives of agency. The public is seen as what the majority of independently living and acting individuals think and that can be quantified by opinion polls. The public is thereby treated in an individualistic and purely quantified manner. What is left out is the focus on the social and societal communication processes, debates, the nature and quality of arguments, social and societal conflicts and contradictions that result in public opinion.

Theodor W. Adorno (2005) criticises the view that public opinion polls are mechanisms constituting publicness, as expressed by Gallup and others, as administrative research that is an "ideology" (123) and a "machinery of public opinion" that turns citizens "into an appendage" (121). "Men's right to publicness turned into their allotted supply of publicness; while they should be its subjects, they turned into its objects" (121). Adorno argues that publicness is not simply "given", but emerges from democratic processes that involve "citizens who are responsible and well informed" (Adorno 2005, 121). Adorno does not deny the importance of empirical research and argues for the integration of the critical theory of society and empirical social research so that subjective opinions can be compared to society's objective conditions (Adorno 1972, 538–546).

12.2.6 Alienation and the Public Sphere

We can extend Habermas' notions of re-feudalisation and colonisation by combining them with Marx's notion of alienation and its application to the societal realms of the economy, politics, and culture.

Table 12.2 Antagonisms in three types of alienation

Type of Alienation	Alienating Subjects	Alienated Subjects
Economic alienation: exploitation	The ruling class, exploiters	Exploited class
Political alienation: domination	Dictator, dictatorial groups	Excluded individuals and groups
Cultural alienation: ideology that results in disrespect	Ideologues	Disrespected individuals and groups

Table 12.3 The main actors in alienated society and humanist society

	Alienated Society	Humanism
Economy	The exploited	The socialist/commoner
Politics	The dictator	The democrat
Culture	The ideologue/demagogue	The friend

Source: Based on Fuchs (2020, 103, table 4.4).

Alienation means that people are confronted with structures and conditions that they cannot control and influence themselves. Individuals do not control the economic, political, and cultural products that influence their lives and everyday life. Alienation means the "*loss* of the object, his product" (Marx 1844, 273). Alienation means "vitality as a sacrifice of life, production of the object as loss of the object to an alien power, to an *alien* person" (Marx 1844, 281). Use-values, collectively binding decisions and collective meanings are social products resulting from human practices. In capitalist society, however, they are controlled by only a few, resulting in objectively alienated conditions (Table 12.2).

Table 12.3 illustrates the antagonism between alienated and humanist societies along the three social dimensions of economy, politics, and culture. In an alienated society, the main actors are the exploiter in the economy, the dictator in politics, and the ideologue/demagogue in culture. Humanism is the alternative to the alienated society. In a humanist society, the main actors are the socialist and the commoner in the economy, the democrat in politics, and the solidary friend in culture.

Combining Marx and Habermas, we can distinguish between the economic, political, and ideological colonisation and re-feudalisation of the public sphere:

- Economic alienation of the public sphere:
  Through *capitalisation, commodification,* and *class structuration,* the logic of money, capital and the commodity form penetrate people's everyday lives and lifeworlds;

- Political alienation of the public sphere:
  Through *domination*, society is organised in such a way that particular interests prevail and some people or groups or individuals gain advantages at the expense of others;
- Cultural alienation of the public sphere:
  Ideologisation presents partial interests, exploitation and domination as natural and necessary by presenting reality in a distorted or manipulated way.

Economic, political, and cultural alienation of the public sphere undermine freedom:

- They limit the freedom of speech and public opinion:
  If individuals do not have the same formal education and material resources available, then this can pose limits to participation in the public sphere (Habermas 1989, 227);
- They limit the freedom of association and assembly:
  Big political and economic organisations "enjoy an oligopoly of the publicistically effective and politically relevant formation of assemblies and associations" (Habermas 1989, 228).

The concept of the public sphere and the associated notion of re-feudalisation together do not simply describe the reality or ideal of society and political communication but are normative-critical concepts that allow measuring how society is against a democratic standard of critique. Slavko Splichal summarises the critical potential of the concept of publicness (Öffentlichkeit) in the following manner:

> Personal freedom and public use of reason and the right of the public to control political authorities are hardly compatible with the media owned by private capital or the political state, which pursue as their main goal maximization of commercial profit or political power rather than 'maximization of publicness'.
>
> (Splichal 2012, 91)

Marx himself was a critical journalist who worked as an editor and writer. In Germany, the democratic press faced repression by the Prussian state, which is why Marx had to leave Germany when *the Rheinische Zeitung* that he edited was banned in 1843. In this context, Marx wrote texts on the freedom of the press. He opposed both political and economic censorship of the press. He argued that political censorship does not guarantee equality of people before the law and must therefore be abolished: "The real, *radical cure for the censorship* would be its *abolition;* for the institution itself is a bad one" (Marx 1843, 131). He also argued that capitalist media monopolies and concentration are forms of censorship: "*The primary freedom of the press lies in not being a trade*" (Marx 1842, 175). "Press freedom in England up to now has been the exclusive privilege of capital" (Marx 1855, 121).

12.2.7 *Criticisms of Public Sphere Theory*

Critics of the theory of the public sphere have argued, among other points, that Habermas' notion is too universalistic and disregards that new social movements have developed their multiple counter-public spheres (e.g. Benhabib 1992, Eley 1992, Fraser 1992, Mouffe 1999, Roberts and Crossley 2004) and that Habermas' concept is too much focused on European nation-states and disregards transnational and non-Western aspects (e.g. McGuigan 1998, Sparks 1998). Habermas has taken these concerns seriously and has stressed the importance of pluralising and transnationalising public spheres (e.g. Habermas 1992). In the meantime, concepts such as counter-publics (e.g. Asen 2000, Warner 2002), the black public sphere (e.g. Gilroy 1997, Squires 2002), feminist publics (e.g. Zackodnik 2011, Zobl and Drüeke 2012), the proletarian public sphere (Negt and Kluge 1993), networked counter-publics (Renninger 2015), the global public sphere (e.g. Buck-Morss 2002, Volkmer 2014), and the transnational public sphere (e.g. Fraser et al. 2014; Guidry, Kennedy and Zald 2000; Wessler et al. 2008) have emerged. There have also been advances in the empirical analysis of the public sphere (e.g. Cammaerts and Van Audenhove 2005; Dahlberg 2004; Gerhards 1997; Gerhards and Schäfer 2010; Koopmans 2007; Machill, Beiler and Fischer 2006; Trenz 2004). Sixty years after the publication of Habermas' book, public sphere theory and analysis is of high academic, social, and political importance (Seeliger and Sevignani 2021).

It is important to stress that there are different experiences and contexts of domination in society. But groups who suffer in a different context but within the same world system also have something in common and joint interests. The danger of creating ever-more micro-counter-public spheres is that social struggles and public communication become isolated. Today, lots of echo chambers exist online and offline, where humans only talk to and engage with like-minded individuals. Counter-publics can advance this tendency of the fragmentation of the public sphere. Therefore, it is important that the common aspects of humans in society as humans, workers, consumers, and citizens are kept in mind and that humans organise across existing divides around the common interests of humanity.

James Curran (1991) argues that before the 1850s, there was a rich history of radical newspapers in the UK and that it was easy and cheap to create such newspapers. Examples of the radical 19th-century UK press are as follows: *Liberator, London Dispatch, Northern Star* (a Chartist newspaper that existed from 1837 until 1852 and had a circulation of around 50 000), *Political Register, Poor Man's Guardian, Reynolds News, Trades Newspaper, Twopenny Trash, Voice of the People, Voice of West Riding, Weekly Police Gazette* (Curran and Seaton 2010, chapter 2). The radical press had an important role in radical politics and was associated with civil society groups such as the National Union of the Working Classes, the Chartist Movement, and the Society for Promoting the Employment of Women. Later, advertising rose and it became ever-more expensive to run a newspaper so that the press shifted towards the right and the labour press came to an end in the 20th century. Curran argues that the 19th-century press had "a radical and innovatory analysis of society" and "challenged the legitimacy of the capitalist order" (Curran 1991, 40). Habermas would dismiss the role of the radical press, whereas 19th-century London press consisted of "conflicting public spheres" (Curran 1991, 42). Curran's position can be characterised as being close to Negt and Kluge's (1993) stress on a proletarian public sphere.

Public spaces and public spheres cannot only be found in the West. The claim that the public sphere is a Western-centric concept is therefore short-circuited. It also faces the danger of justifying undemocratic regimes that are opposed to the West and in the name of challenging Western-centrism and Euro-centrism advance authoritarianism. The public teahouse is an old cultural practice and space in many parts of the world, such as in China, Japan, Iran, Turkey, UK. Di Wang compares the early 20th-century Chinese teahouse to the British public houses. It is a common space, where people from all walks of life go for different purposes. The Chinese word for tea-house is 茶馆 (*cháguǎn*). Chengdu (成都) is the capital of the Southwestern Chinese province of Sichuan (四川). "Teahouses in Chengdu, however, were renowned for their multiclass orientation. One of the 'virtues' of Chengdu teahouses was their relatively equality" (Wang 2008, 421). Women were first excluded, but by 1930 fully accepted. These teahouses were not just cultural spaces, but also political meeting points, where political debates took place and political theatre pieces were performed, which attracted not only citizens, but also government spies. Wang discusses the role of the Chengdu teahouses during the 1911 Railroad Protection Movement. Public meeting places are spheres of civic engagement that can turn into political spaces of communication and protest.

The various Occupy movements that emerged after the 2008 world economic crisis were movements where protest and the occupation of spaces converged. They created public spheres of political communication that they controlled in a self-managed manner. This creation of public spheres did not just take place in the West, but in many parts of the world in times of global capitalism and social crises. A common aspect of these protests was that many of them used the tactic of making space public and political and that these protests took place in a common crisis of society. Resistance is as old as class societies, so public spheres have been formed as resisting publics throughout the history of class societies. The public sphere exists wherever humans gather to collectively organise and voice their anger and discontent with exploitation and domination.

12.3 The Digital Public Sphere

The rise of the World Wide Web (WWW), Internet platforms and social media has brought up the question of how the public sphere was transformed. We refer to this issue as the digital transformation of the public sphere, which is a contemporary manifestation of the structural transformation of the public sphere. Fundamental questions that have in the context of the digital transformation of the public sphere been discussed in the literature (for overview discussions of key issues, see, e.g., Dahlberg 1998, Fuchs 2014, Gripsrud and Moe 2010, Schäfer 2015) include the following: To what extent are there or are there not novel features of the public sphere in the digital age? What positive and/or negative features has the digital transformation of the public sphere brought about?

Jürgen Habermas has been sceptical concerning the question of whether or not, how, and to what degree the Internet and social media advance a public sphere. He argues that the Internet is democratic only in that it "can undermine the censorship of authoritarian regimes" but that it also fragments the public into "a huge number of issue publics" (Habermas 2006, 423). Institutional form Habermas (2022, 2021) interprets studies of the public sphere as confirmation of his view that the Internet and social media have resulted in "a mode of semi-public, fragmented and self-enclosed communication" that is due to the "commercial use of the digital network" (Habermas 2022, 146) and "the global spread of the neoliberal economic programme" (167). Habermas (2019, volume 2: 799, translated from German) argues that containing the "dangers of the oligopolistically dominated and for the time being destructively rampant Internet communication"[2] requires transnational political regulation, which shows the importance of communication policies in the context of the (digital) public sphere.

The traditional public sphere in modern society has been shaped by mass communication and mass media, where there is a small group of information producers using mass media for spreading information that is received and interpreted by audience members in various ways. Figure 12.2 visualises the **digital transformation of the public sphere** that has two main features (see Fuchs 2021a):

- **Prosumption:**
  On the Internet, consumers of information become potential producers of information, so-called prosumers (productive consumers) who engage in the production of user-generated content.
- **Convergence:**
  On the Internet, the boundaries between different social practices, social roles, social systems, and different publics converge so that humans on Internet platforms with the help of single profiles act in a variety of roles with a variety of practices and in a variety of different publics.

The patterned blue boxes in Figure 12.2 indicate that in the digital public sphere, human practices, micro-, meso-, and macro-publics, economy, politics, and culture are mediated by digital platforms. The red dotted lines indicate that on digital platforms, individuals' practices, cognition processes,

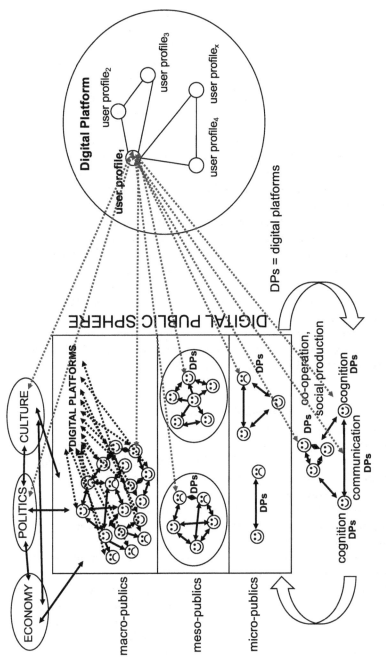

Figure 12.2 A model of the digital public sphere.

communication processes, co-operation processes, their activities in various publics, and their social roles in the economy (e.g. as worker or manager), politics (e.g. as citizen or politician), and culture (e.g. as member of a certain religion or community) converge on digital platforms' user profiles. This convergence includes the convergence of the private and the public sphere, of privateness and publicness. The Internet "links publicness and privateness together directly, inside a single technological platform" so that we see the "liquefaction of the boundary between publicness and privateness and the emergence of "hybrid public-private forms of communicative actions" (Splichal 2018, 3).

The information and communication processes organised with the help of digital platforms are different from traditional mass media in that all users are enabled to produce content and communicate with others through the platforms. A digital platform is an online software environment that organises human information, activities, and communication via mobile phone apps, the Internet, and the World Wide Web. Platforms are also social systems, which means they have a political-economic organisation and specific cultures. In the platform economy, we find organisational models that determine specific forms of ownership, work, economic activities, and relations of production. Platform governance involves laws and policies that determine what the actors involved in platforms are allowed to do, not to do, and are expected to do.

Digital communication and digitally mediated society face many problems that are an expression of the economic, political and ideological alienation/ colonisation of the Internet and digital media. These problems include the following:

1 **Corporate media and digital monopolies:**
   The turnover of the largest six digital corporations Apple, Microsoft, Alphabet/Google, Amazon, Alibaba, and Facebook (US$ 857.5 billion in 2019) is as large as the GDP of the world's 22 least developed countries (US$ 858.3 billion).[3] Such companies hardly pay taxes;
2 **Digital individualism:**
   Digital individualism consists of users accumulating attention with and approval of individual profiles and postings on social media;
3 **Digital surveillance:**
   State institutions and companies carry out digital surveillance of users;
4 **Anti-social social media:**
   "Social media" are anti-social. There is digital authoritarianism in the form of hatred, racism, nationalism, far-right ideology, and authoritarianism online. Edward Snowden's revelations and the Cambridge Analytica scandal have shown that capitalist social media are a danger to democracy. Right-wing ideologues and demagogues spread digital authoritarianism on social media and attack Public Service Media, independently

acting media and quality media. Populists characterise such media as "metropolitan elite media". They wish there were no independently acting media, which poses a danger to democracy;

5 **Algorithmic politics:**
Social media are characterised by automated, algorithmic politics. Automated computer programmes ("bots") replace human activity, post information and generate "likes". This has made it more difficult to distinguish what online activities and digital information are produced by humans or machine-generated;

6 **Echo chambers and filter bubbles:**
Fragmented online publics are organised as filter bubbles and echo chambers in which opinions are homogeneous and disagreements either do not exist or are avoided;

7 **Digital tabloids:**
The digital culture industry has organised social media as digital tabloids controlled by digital corporations. Online advertising and tabloid entertainment dominate the Internet, displacing engagement with political and educational content.

8 **Influencer-capitalism:**
On social media, so-called influencers shape public opinion, creating power asymmetries in terms of online attention and visibility. They advance a commodified online culture that presents the world as an endless shopping mile. The Internet is predominantly a huge shopping mall;

9 **Digital acceleration:**
Due to digital acceleration, our attention capacity is strained by superficial information that hits us at a very high speed. There is too little time and too little space for conversations and debates on social media;

10 **Fake news and post-truth culture:**
Post-truth politics and fake news are spreading globally through social media. In the age of new nationalisms and new authoritarianism, a culture has emerged in which false online news is spreading, many people distrust facts and experts, and there is an emotionalisation of politics through which people do not rationally examine what is real and what is fiction, but assume something is true if it suits their state of mind, emotions and ideology.

Table 12.4 maps the ten discussed problems to three forms of digital alienation.

The 21st century has thus far been a century of multiple crises. It started with the political crisis of 9/11 in 2001. Next, a new world economic crisis emerged in 2008. In the years following the world economic crisis, new authoritarianisms emerged, and a crisis of democracy unfolded. In 2020, the COVID-19 pandemic was accompanied by a health crisis, an economic crisis, a political crisis, a cultural crisis, a moral crisis, and a global crisis.

Table 12.4 Ten manifestations of digital alienation

Form of Digital Alienation	Manifestations of Digital Alienation
Economic digital alienation: digital exploitation	1 Digital capital/digital labour, digital monopolies, 2 Digital accumulation/individualism/competition
Political digital alienation: digital domination	3 Digital surveillance, 4 Anti-social social media/digital authoritarianism, 5 Algorithmic politics
Cultural digital alienation: digital ideology, digital disrespect	6 Fragmented online publics, echo chambers 7 Digital culture industry/digital tabloids, 8 Influencer capitalism, 9 Digital acceleration, 10 False news/algorithmic politics

In 2022, Vladimir Putin's army invaded Ukraine and Putin threatened to use nuclear weapons. The world is faced with the threat of a new World War and the threat of the nuclear extinction of humanity and life on Earth. These crises have advanced the polarisation of politics and the crisis of the public sphere.

12.4 Conclusion

This chapter focused on the Political Economy of the public sphere and the digital public sphere. It asked: What does the Political Economy of the public sphere and the digital public sphere look like?

Finding 1: Public Sphere Theory as Critical Theory

Jürgen Habermas' theory of the public sphere is a critical theory that assesses the reality of politics and society against normative standards of democracy and democratic communication. It is inherently connected to the notions of the re-feudalisation of the public sphere and the colonisation of the lifeworld. A revised model of the public sphere that combines Marx and Habermas is based on the economic, political, and cultural alienation of the public sphere, which refers to processes of commodification and exploitation (economic alienation), domination (political alienation), and ideologisation (cultural alienation).

Finding 2: The Digital Public Sphere

The contemporary Internet is not a (digital) public sphere. A critical theory of the public sphere helps us to critically analyse how economic, political, and ideological forces have colonised the Internet in capitalist society. The digital public sphere is a vision of a democratic Internet.

Notes

1 Slavko Splichal (2012) reminds us that besides Habermas, there have been other thinkers who have advanced important ideas about the public and public opinion, including Karl Marx, Gabriel Tarde, Karl Bücher, Ferdinand Tönnies, John Dewey or C. Wright Mills.
2 „Auch zur Bewältigung der längst diskutierten Gefahren der oligopolistisch beherrschten und einstweilen destruktiv ausufernden Internetkommunikation sind politische Regelungen nötig, die nur auf globaler Ebene möglich wären".
3 Data sources: https://www.forbes.com/global2000/list, http://hdr.undp.org/en/indicators, accessed on 17 April 2020.

References

Adorno, Theodor W. 2005. Opinion Research and Publicness. *Sociological Theory* 23 (1): 116–123.
Adorno, Theodor W. 1972. *Soziologische Schriften I. Adorno Gesammelte Schriften Band 8*. Frankfurt am Main: Suhrkamp.
Asen, Robert. 2000. Seeking the "Counter" in Counterpublics. *Communication Theory* 10 (4): 424–446.
Benhabib, Seyla. 1992. Models of Public Space: Hannah Arendt, the Liberal Tradition, and Jürgen Habermas. In *Habermas and the Public Sphere*, edited by Craig Calhoun, 73–98. Cambridge, MA: MIT Press.
Buck-Morss, Susan. 2002. A Global Public Sphere? *Situation Analysis* 1: 10–19.
Cammaerts, Bart and Leo Van Audenhove. 2005. Online Political Debate, Unbounded Citizenship, and the Problematic Nature of a Transnational Public Sphere. *Political Communication* 22 (2): 179–196.
Curran, James. 1991. Rethinking the Media as a Public Sphere. In *Communication and Citizenship. Journalism and the Public Sphere*, edited by Peter Dahlgren and Colin Sparks, 27–57. London: Routledge.
Curran, James and Jean Seaton. 2010. *Power without Responsibility. Press, Broadcasting and the Internet in Britain*. London: Routledge. Seventh edition.
Dahlberg, Lincoln. 2004. Net Public Sphere Research: Beyond the "First Phase". *Javnost – The Public* 11 (1): 27–43.
Dahlberg, Lincoln. 1998. Cyberspace and the Public Sphere. Exploring the Democratic Potential of the Net. *Convergence: The International Journal into New Media Technologies* 4 (1): 70–84.
Eley, Geoff. 1992. Nations, Public and Political Cultures. Placing Habermas in the Nineteenth Century. In *Habermas and the Public Sphere*, edited by Craig Calhoun, 289–339. Cambridge, MA: MIT Press.
Fraser, Nancy. 1992. Rethinking the Public Sphere. In *Habermas and the Public Sphere*, edited by Craig Calhoun, 109–142. Cambridge, MA: MIT Press.
Fraser, Nancy et al. 2014. *Transnationalizing the Public Sphere*. Cambridge: Polity.
Fuchs, Christian. 2021a. *Social Media: A Critical Introduction*. London: SAGE. Third edition.
Fuchs, Christian. 2021b. The Public Service Media and Public Service Internet Utopias Survey Report. In *The Public Service Media and Public Service Internet Manifesto*, edited by Christian Fuchs and Klaus Unterberger, 19–68. London: University of Westminster Press. DOI: https://doi.org/10.16997 /book60.c

Fuchs, Christian. 2020. *Communication and Capitalism. A Critical Theory.* London: University of Westminster Press. DOI: https://doi.org/10.16997/book45

Fuchs, Christian. 2014. Social Media and the Public Sphere. *tripleC* 12 (1): 57–101. DOI: https://doi.org/10.31269/triplec.v12i1.552

Fuchs, Christian. 2008. *Internet and Society. Social Theory in the Information Age.* New York: Routledge.

Gallup, George. 1957. The Changing Climate for Public Opinion Research. *The Public Opinion Quarterly* 21 (1): 23–27.

Gerhards, Jürgen. 1997. Diskursive versus liberale Öffentlichkeit: Eine empirische Auseinandersetzung mit Jürgen Habermas. *Kölner Zeitschrift für Soziologie und Sozialpsychologie* 49 (1): 1–39.

Gerhards, Jürgen and Friedhelm Neidhardt. 1990. *Strukturen und Funktionen moderner Öffentlichkeit: Fragestellungen und Ansätze.* WZB Discussion Paper, No. FS III 90–101. Berlin: Wissenschaftszentrum Berlin für Sozialforschung (WZB).

Gerhards, Jürgen and Mike S. Schäfer. 2010. Is the Internet a Better Public Sphere? Comparing Old and New Media in the USA and Germany. *New Media & Society* 12 (1): 143–160.

Gilroy, Paul. 1997. Exer(or)cising Power: Black Bodies in the Black Public Sphere. In *Dance in the City*, edited by Helen Thomas, 21–34. London: Palgrave Macmillan.

Gripsrud, Jostein and Hallvard Moe, eds. 2010. *The Digital Public Sphere.* Göteborg: Nordicom.

Guidry, John A., Michael D. Kennedy, and Mayer N. Zald, eds. 2000. *Globalizations and Social Movements: Culture, Power, and the Transnational Public Sphere.* Ann Arbor: The University of Michigan Press.

Habermas, Jürgen. 2022. Reflections and Hypotheses on a Further Structural Transformation of the Political Public Sphere. *Theory, Culture & Society* 39 (4): 145–171.

Habermas, Jürgen. 2021. Überlegungen und Hypothesen zu einem erneuten Strukturwandel der politischen Öffentlichkeit. In *Ein neuer Strukturwandel der Öffentlichkeit? Sonderband Leviathan 37*, edited by Martin Seeliger and Sebastian Sevignani, 470–500. Baden-Baden: Nomos.

Habermas, Jürgen. 2019. *Auch eine Geschichte der Philosophie.* Two volumes. Frankfurt am Main: Suhrkamp.

Habermas, Jürgen. 2008. Hat die Demokratie noch eine epistemische Dimension? Empirische Forschung und normative Theorie. In *Ach, Europa*, 138–191. Frankfurt am Main: Suhrkamp.

Habermas, Jürgen. 2006. Political Communication in Media Society: Does Democracy Still Enjoy an Epistemic Dimension? The Impact of Normative Theory on Empirical Research. *Communication Theory* 16 (4): 411–426.

Habermas, Jürgen. 1992. Further Reflections on the Public Sphere and Concluding Remarks. In *Habermas and the Public Sphere*, edited by Craig Calhoun, 421–479. Cambridge, MA: MIT Press.

Habermas, Jürgen. 1989. *The Structural Transformation of the Public Sphere.* Cambridge, MA: MIT Press.

Habermas, Jürgen. 1987. *The Theory of Communicative Action.* Volume 2. Boston, MA: Beacon Press.

Habermas, Jürgen. 1984. *The Theory of Communicative action.* Volume 1. Boston, MA: Beacon Press.

Habermas, Jürgen. 1968/1987. Technology and Science as "Ideology". In *Jürgen Habermas: Toward a Rational Society*, 81–122. Cambridge: Polity.

Koopmans, Ruud. 2007. Who Inhabits the European Public Sphere? Winners and Losers, Supporters and Opponents in Europeanised Political Debates. *European Journal of Political Research* 46 (2): 183–210.

Machill, Marcel, Markus Beiler, and Corinna Fischer. 2006. Europe-Topics in Europe's Media. The Debate about the European Public Sphere: A Meta-Analysis of Media Content Analyses. *European Journal of Communication* 21 (1): 57–88.

Marx, Karl. 1855. Napoleon and Barbès – The Newspaper Stamp. In *Marx & Engels Collected Works (MECW) Volume 14*, 121–123. London: Lawrence & Wishart.

Marx, Karl. 1844. Economic and Philosophic Manuscripts of 1844. In *Marx & Engels Collected Works (MECW) Volume 3*, 229–346. London: Lawrence & Wishart.

Marx, Karl. 1843. Comments on the Latest Prussian Censorship Instruction. In *Marx & Engels Collected Works (MECW) Volume 1*, 109–131. London: Lawrence & Wishart.

Marx, Karl. 1842. Proceedings of the Sixth Rhine Province Assembly. First Article. Debates on Freedom of the Press and Publication of the Proceedings of the Assembly of the Estates. In *Marx & Engels Collected Works (MECW) Volume 1*, 133–181. London: Lawrence & Wishart.

McGuigan, Jim. 1998. What Price the Public Sphere? In *Electronic Empires. Global Media and Local Resistances*, edited by Daya Kishan Thussu, 108–124. London: Hodder Arnold.

Midrand Call to Action. 2013. *The Midrand Call to Action Document: Media Freedom and Public Broadcasting in Africa*. https://soscoalition.org.za/wp-content/uploads/2015/01/AfriMAP_-_Midrand_Call_to_Action_Final.pdf

Mouffe, Chantal. 1999. Deliberative Democracy or Agonistic Pluralism? *Social Research* 66 (3): 745–758.

Negt, Oskar and Alexander Kluge. 1993. *Public Sphere and Experience. Toward an Analysis of the Bourgeois and Proletarian Public Sphere*. Minneapolis: University of Minnesota Press.

Neidhardt, Friedhelm. 1993. The Public as a Communication System. *Public Understanding of Science* 2 (4): 339–350.

Renninger, Bryce J. 2015. "Where Can I Be Myself … Where Can I Speak My Mind": Networked Counterpublics in a Polymedia Environment. *New Media & Society* 17 (9): 1513–1529.

Roberts, John Michael and Nick Crossley. 2004. Introduction. In *After Habermas: New Perspectives on the Public Sphere*, edited by Nick Crossley and John Michael Roberts, 1–27. Malden, MA: Blackwell.

Schäfer, Mike S. 2015. Digital Public Sphere. In *The International Encyclopedia of Political Communication*, edited by Gianpietro Mazzoleni, 322–328. London: Wiley Blackwell.

Seeliger, Martin and Sebastian Sevignani, eds. 2021. Ein neuer Strukturwandel der Öffentlichkeit? *Sonderband Leviathan* 37. Baden-Baden: Nomos.

Sparks, Colin. 1998. Is There a Global Public Sphere? In *Electronic Empires. Global Media and Local Resistances*, edited by Daya Kishan Thussu, 91–107. London: Hodder Arnold.

Splichal, Slavko. 2022a. *Datafication of Public Opinion and the Public Sphere: How Extraction Replaced Opinion and Why It Matters.* London: Anthem Press.

Splichal, Slavko. 2022b. The Public Sphere in the Twilight Zone of Publicness. *European Journal of Communication* 37 (2): 198–215. DOI: http://doi.org/10.1177/02673231211061490

Splichal, Slavko. 2018. Publicness-Privateness: The Liquefaction of "The Great Dichotomy". *Javnost – The Public* 25 (1–2): 1–10. DOI: https://doi.org/10.1080/13183222.2018.1424004

Splichal, Slavko. 2012. *Transnationalization of the Public Sphere and the Fate of the Public.* New York: Hampton Press.

Squires, Catherine R. 2002. Rethinking the Black Public Sphere: An Alternative Vocabulary for Multiple Public Spheres. *Communication Theory* 12 (4): 446–468.

Syvertsen, Trine. 2003. Challenges to Public Television in the Era of Convergence and Commercialization. *Television & New Media* 4 (2): 155–175.

Trenz, Hans-Jörg. 2004. Media Coverage on European Governance: Exploring the European Public Sphere in National Quality Newspapers. *European Journal of Communication* 19 (3): 291–319.

Volkmer, Ingrid. 2014. *The Global Public Sphere: Public Communication in the Age of Reflective Interdependence.* Cambridge: Polity.

Wang, Di. 2008. The Idle and the Busy. Teahouses and Public Life in Early Twentieth-Century Chengdu. *Journal of Urban History* 26 (4): 411–437.

Warner, Michael. 2002. *Publics and Counterpublics.* Cambridge, MA: The MIT Press.

Wessler, Hartmut et al. 2008. *Transnationalization of Public Spheres.* Basingstoke: Palgrave Macmillan.

Zackodnik, Teresa. 2011. *Press, Platform, Pulpit: Black Feminist Publics in the Era of Reform.* Knoxville: The University of Tennessee Press.

Zobl, Elke and Ricarda Drüeke, eds. 2012. *Feminist Media. Participatory Spaces, Networks and Cultural Citizenship.* Bielefeld: transcript.

Recommended Readings and Exercises

Readings

The following texts are recommended as accompanying readings to this chapter:

Jürgen Habermas. 1989. The Public Sphere: An Encyclopedia Article. In *Critical Theory and Society. A Reader,* edited by Stephen E. Bronner and Douglas Kellner, 136–142. New York: Routledge.

Slavko Splichal. 2012. *Transnationalization of the Public Sphere and the Fate of the Public.* New York: Hampton Press.

Chapter 4: Civil Society, the Public, and the Public Sphere (pp. 65–141).

Slavko Splichal. 2022. The Public Sphere in the Twilight Zone of Publicness. *European Journal of Communication* 37 (2): 198–215. DOI: http://doi.org/10.1177/02673231211061490

Exercise 12.1   The Public Sphere

Read the following texts:

Jürgen Habermas. 1989. The Public Sphere: An Encyclopedia Article. In *Critical Theory and Society. A Reader*, edited by Stephen E. Bronner and Douglas Kellner, 136–142. New York: Routledge.

Slavko Splichal. 2012. *Transnationalization of the Public Sphere and the Fate of the Public*. New York: Hampton Press.
Chapter 4: Civil Society, the Public, and the Public Sphere (pp. 65–141).

Slavko Splichal. 2022. The Public Sphere in the Twilight Zone of Publicness. *European Journal of Communication* 37 (2): 198–215. DOI: http://doi.org/10.1177/02673231211061490

Discuss:

What is the public sphere?
How has the public sphere been structurally transformed?
How relevant is the theory of the public sphere today for understanding the role of the Internet and digitalisation in society?

13 The Political Economy of Public Service Media and the Public Service Internet

What You Will Learn in This Chapter

- You will understand what Public Service Media are, how they differ from capitalist media, and what roles they have in the public sphere;
- You will engage with foundations of the Public Service Internet.

13.1 Introduction

Public Service Media such as the BBC in the UK, ARD in Germany or PBS in the USA are important media organisations. They have an economy in the form of a not-for-profit imperative, a democratic role, and help to advance culture. The Internet is largely controlled by private, for-profit companies. The question therefore arises if a Public Service Internet could be created as an alternative. In this chapter, we are dealing with the questions of what Public Service Media and a Public Service Internet are and what their political-economic aspects are.

This chapter asks: How does the Political Economy of Public Service Media and the Public Service Internet look like? Section 13.2 is focused on Public Service Media's Political Economy, and Section 13.3 is on the foundations of a Public Service Internet. Section 13.4 presents some conclusions.

13.2 Public Service Media

13.2.1 The Media and the Public Sphere

The media system is part of the public sphere in modern society. Figure 13.1 illustrates a model of the role of the media in the modern public sphere. Media organisations produce publicly accessible information in the media system. Such information usually serves to inform about news, to educate and to entertain. Through public news, members of the political system inform themselves about important events in society and politics. News is a trigger of political communication. People talk about what is based in politics and ideally participate in the decision-making process themselves. In a capitalist society, different interest organisations such as employers'

DOI: 10.4324/9781003391203-15

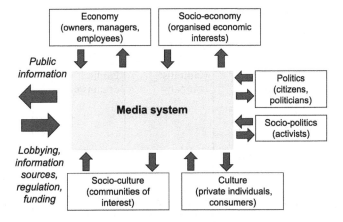

Figure 13.1 The media system as part of the public sphere. Further development based on Habermas 2008, diagrams 1 and 2.

associations, workers' associations such as trade unions, lobby organisations, political parties, NGOs, private individuals, social movements try to influence the media companies' reporting. This happens, among other things, through interviews, press releases, lobbying, advertising, public relations, the interweaving of organisations, etc. The media system interacts with the economy, politics, and culture. Citizens (purchase, broadcasting fee, subscriptions, etc.), the state (e.g. media funding) and business organisations (advertising) enable an economic resource base for the media to operate with. Politics regulates the framework conditions under which the media operate. Culture is a context of worldviews and ideologies that shape the climate of society and thus also have an influence on the media system and its organisations.

13.2.2 Four Political Economies of the Media

Table 13.1 illustrates the difference between four political economies of the media.

Authoritarian media are either controlled or owned by authoritarian states or other authoritarian organisations that strictly control, monitor, manipulate, and censor the mediated content. Public Service Media and citizen media are alternatives to the capitalist, profit-oriented organisation of the media. Citizen media often have the problem that although they are independent, they are based on unpaid or low-paid labour, and have few resources and only a small audience (Sandoval and Fuchs 2010).

The four types of Political Economy of the Media are related to Raymond Williams's (1976, 130–137) distinction between authoritarian, paternal, commercial, and democratic communications. Williams distinguishes between state control of the media (authoritarian) and cultural control of the media

Table 13.1 Four political economies of the media

	Authoritarian Media	Capitalist Media	Public Service Media	Citizen Media
Organisation	State-owned or state-controlled, owned and controlled by a politically or ideologically motivated organisation	Capitalist company	Public organisation	Civil society organisation
Goal	Political propaganda	Surplus value, profit, capital accumulation	Public service remit; Public value: information, education, entertainment; advancement of democratic understanding, arts, culture, science, diversity	Participation
Main actors	State-controlled or ideologically controlled and censored journalists	Professional journalists	Professional journalists	Citizen journalists, prosumers (consumers as producers)
Main funding source	State funding or state funding combined with another funding source or funding provided by an authoritarian organisation	Advertising, subscriptions, sale of single copies	Licence and media fee	Donations, membership fees, public subsidies
Property	State property, or private ownership under state control, or ownership by an authoritarian organisation	Private property	Public property	Non-profit association/organisation, co-operatives/self-managed companies

Source: Based on Fuchs (2020, chapters 8, 12 and 14); Murdock (2011).

(paternal). A newspaper that is ideologically controlled by its owner is also authoritarian in character. In my typology, Williams's two types of authoritarian and paternal communication are merged into authoritarian media. The four models are not strictly separate; there can be mixed forms. Public Service Media are always democratic forms of the media; authoritarian media are never democratic. Democratic media are committed to the advancement of democracy in society, which requires the support of opportunities for citizens to form opinions in an unbiased manner and debate society's key issues. Citizen media can be democratic media, but there are also fascist types of citizen media that advance racism, nationalism, authoritarianism, etc.

There has been a tradition of Public Service Broadcasting in Europe and other parts of the world that has been a crucial dimension of the modern media system in the 20th and 21st centuries.

13.2.3 Definitions of Public Service Media

Slavko Splichal (2007, 255; see also Splichal 2012, 102) gives the following definition of Public Service Media (PSM):

> In normative terms, public service media must be a service *of* the public, *by* the public, and *for* the public. It is a service *of* the public because it is financed by it and should be owned by it. It ought to be a service *by* the public – not only financed and controlled, but also produced by it. It must be a service *for* the public – but also for the government and other powers acting in the public sphere. In sum, public service media ought to become 'a cornerstone of democracy'.

Barbara Thomaß (2013, 83) defines Public Service Media as follows:

> A Public Service Media organisation is a media organisation "which seeks to reconcile the distance from the market and the state in order to provide independent information, educational and cultural services for social communication. It is supported by appropriate legislation which grants it a certain degree of protection from market forces and, in return, requires it to fulfil certain obligations in the service of the public".

Trine Syvertsen (2003, 157–158) gives the following definition of Public Service Broadcasting:

> The first key feature of the public broadcasting form of governance is that certain companies or institutions are entrusted with a set of privileges to insulate them to some degree from the market forces. The privileges may be of an economic or technical nature; in the case of broadcasting, a monopoly on advertising revenue, license fee funding, and the privilege to broadcast over the air to the general public have

been among the most valuable. [...] The second characteristic of the public broadcasting model, which follows structurally from the first, is that broadcasters are obliged to fulfill certain obligations in return for the privileges. These go beyond satisfying the needs of the consumers and are linked instead to more profound cultural and social purposes. The duties may vary, but in the case of the European public broadcasters, they have historically been of three kinds. The first is universal coverage: that the services should be accessible to the whole population. Second, there is a set of content requirements, most typically that programming should be diverse and of high quality, that minorities and smaller 'taste groups' also be served, and that news and political issues should be covered in an impartial manner. The third includes the obligation to protect and strengthen national culture and identity. [...] Common to these obligations is that they are related more to the public's role as citizens than as consumers. A key purpose of this form of governance from the beginning was to support a cultural and democratic sphere that would foster rational debate and enlighten the population on political, social, and cultural issues. [...] The third defining characteristic is the presence of a control structure, that is, certain bodies set up to assess the performance of the privileged institutions and ensure that the obligations are interpreted in line with the general consensus.

UNESCO has provided the following understanding of Public Service Broadcasting:

> Public Service Broadcasting (PSB) is broadcasting made, financed and controlled by the public, for the public. It is neither commercial nor state-owned, free from political interference and pressure from commercial forces. Through PSB, citizens are informed, educated and also entertained. When guaranteed with pluralism, programming diversity, editorial independence, appropriate funding, accountability and transparency, public service broadcasting can serve as a cornerstone of democracy.
>
> (UNESCO 2008, 54)

Neither commercial nor State-controlled, public broadcasting's only raison d'etre is public service. It is the public's broadcasting organization; it speaks to everyone as a citizen. Public broadcasters encourage access to and participation in public life. They develop knowledge, broaden horizons and enable people to better understand themselves by better understanding the world and others. Public broadcasting is defined as a meeting place where all citizens are welcome and considered equals. It is an information and education tool, accessible to all and meant for all, whatever their social or economic status. Its mandate is not restricted to information and cultural development-public broadcasting must also appeal to the imagination, and entertain. But it does so with a concern for quality that distinguishes it from commercial broadcasting. Because it is not subject to the dictates of profitability, public broadcasting must be daring and innovative, and take risks.

(UNESCO 2001, 7)

Cañedo, Rodríguez-Castro, and López-Cepeda (2022) analysed legislation and documents of Public Service Media in 14 European countries in order to construct a model that shows the self-understanding of Public Service Media's mission and understanding of public value. The 12 elements that make up this model are displayed in Table 13.2.

Table 13.2 Dimensions of Public Service Media's self-understanding in 14 countries

Dimension	Description
Social engagement	PSM inform, educate, and entertain their audience and promote democracy.
Diversity	PSM have diverse programmes, sources, audiences, and support diverse identities and languages.
Innovation	PSM develop creativity, digital and interactive services, new technologies, and new forms of participation.
Independence	PSM are trustworthy, have political distance and neutral reporting.
Excellence	PSM produce and broadcast professionally created high-quality content.
Universality	PSM are universally available to everyone within a defined geographical space, want to provide a variety of content aimed at all groups in society, are accessible to citizens independent of class, education, capabilities, and other features, and are available in barrier-free manners.
Citizen participation	Citizens are involved in the creation and broadcasting of content, all social groups are represented in programmes and content, and there are innovations in active and participatory audience involvement and engagement.
Media literacy	PSM help advancing the knowledge and understanding of society and its essential issues.
Accountability	PSM should be transparent, use public money in a responsible and efficient manner, and be sustainable.
Territorial cohesion	PSM should advance the integration of a variety of social community and help creating a common understanding and cohesion of society (including minorities, citizens overseas, and in diasporas)
Social justice	PSM should respect and promote human rights, equality, privacy, and the presumption of innocence.
Co-operation	PSM should advance the co-operation of regional PSM units, international co-operation and partnerships that help advancing its goals.

Source: Based on Cañedo, Rodríguez-Castro, and López-Cepeda (2022).

13.2.4 A Model of Public Service Media

Table 13.3 introduces a model of Public Service Media that operates on three dimensions. There are economic, political, and cultural dimensions of Public Service Media: organisation, participation, and content. On each level, there is the production, circulation, and use of a specific good that is organised in line with the logic of public service. So, for example, public ownership of PSM is an economic aspect of the means of communicative production.

On the economic level, PSM are means of production, circulation, and consumption of public information. PSM's means of production are publicly owned. The circulation of information is based on a not-for-profit logic. Consumption is made available in principle to everyone by giving citizens easy access to PSM's technology and information. On the political level, PSM make available inclusive and diverse political information that can support political debate and the achievement of political understanding. On the cultural level, PSM provide educational content that has the potential to support cultural debate and the achievement of understanding in society. PSM are one type of media operating in the public sphere. Others include commercial, for-profit media and community media operated by civil society organisations.

Public Service Media are a manifestation of the principles of the public sphere in the realm of the media. Habermas's "conception of reasoned discourse is closer, in fact, to the practice of British public-service broadcasting, with its ideology of disinterested professionalism, its careful balancing of

Table 13.3 A model of Public Service Media

Sphere	Media	Production	Circulation	Use
Culture: social meaning	Content	Independence, unity in diversity, educational content	Cultural communication and debate	Cultural dialogue and understanding
Politics: collective decisions	Participation	Independence, unity in diversity (representation of minority interests and common affinity and reference points for society), political information	Political communication and debate	Political dialogue and understanding
Economy: property	Organisation and technology	Public ownership	Non-profit, non-market	Universal access, universal availability of technology

opposed points of view and umpired studio discussions" (Curran 1991, 42). "The core rationale for public service broadcasting lies in its commitment to providing the cultural resources required for full citizenship" (Murdock 2005, 214). Public Service Media matter because they "can most reliably serve citizens in a democracy" (Cushion 2012, 203).

Public Service Media that are non-commercial and non-profit on the *economic level* embody values and relations "opposed to economic values and [...] essential to an operating democracy" (Garnham 1990, 111). Its *cultural and political* role is that it enables communication within the public sphere: "the collection and dissemination of *information* and the provision of a forum for *debate*" (Garnham 1990, 111). It has universal access obligations that enable "equal access to a wide range of high-quality entertainment, information and education" and ensure that "the aim of the programme producer is the satisfaction of a range of audience tastes rather than only those tastes that show the largest profit" (Garnham 1990, 120).

13.2.5 PSM and Developing Countries

Concerning the world's poorest continent Africa, *The Midrand Call to Action Document: Media Freedom and Public Broadcasting in Africa* maintains that "most 'public' broadcasters in Africa are still government-controlled state broadcasters" and argues that the Pan-African Parliament should promote "the transformation of state broadcasters into public service broadcasters" (Midrand Call to Action 2013).

Dean, Docquir, Mano, Sabry and Sakr (2020) argue that advancing PSM in developing countries and challenging settings is not futile, but an important undertaking that can be achieved by taking holistic approaches that situate PSM in the democratic transformation of societies. It would also be important to take the cultural specificities into account.

> The principles of PSM, or media in the public interest, need to be unpacked as part of public consultations informed by local concepts and experience. As such, media initiatives should be designed *with* the public, not just for them and their relevance needs to be readily apparent to potential users.
>
> (Deane, Docquir, Mano, Sabry and Sakr 2020, 24)

13.2.6 The British Broadcasting Corporation (BBC)

The BBC is the world's oldest Public Service Media organisation. It was founded on 18 October 1922. Jean Seaton argues that the BBC has been based on

> the idea of broadcasting as a public service – catering for all sections of the community, reaching all parts of the country regardless of cost,

seeking to educate, inform and improve, and prepared to lead public opinion rather than follow it.

(Curran and Seaton 2010, 343)

The legislation that governs the BBC's operations is the BBC Charter, which is rewritten every ten years. The current BBC Charter is valid for the period from 2017 until the end of 2026. During that period, the BBC is licensed by the Home Secretary, which takes on the form of the BBC Agreement. The Office of Communications (Ofcom) is the regulator of broadcasting, telecommunications and postal service in the UK, which also makes it the regulator of the BBC.

The BBC Board is since 2017 the BBC's governing body. Previously, this institution's name was BBC Trust (2007–2017) and the Board of Governors (1927–2007). The Queen or King also appoints the BBC Board's Chair. The Queen or King also appoints four members of the BBC Board who represent England, Scotland, Wales, and Northern Ireland. The Secretary of State consults the BBC on the appointment process. The respective UK nation's government has to agree to the appointment. The Board appoints five more non-executive members who are proposed by the Nomination Board, which is a subcommittee of the Board. The Board also appoints four members who have an executive role, including the BBC's Director-General. The executive members are proposed by the Nomination Board.

The BBC's governance is strongly based on representative democracy, which means that elected governments influence the appointment of Board members. An alternative that is based on a more participatory understanding of democracy is that licence fee payers elect Board members, including the Director-General.

The BBC Charter also defines the BBC's Mission and Public Purposes. "The Mission of the BBC is to act in the public interest, serving all audiences through the provision of impartial, high-quality and distinctive output and services which inform, educate and entertain" (BBC Charter 2017–2026, §5). The BBC has five defined Public Purposes:

1 To provide impartial news and information to help people understand and engage with the world around them [...] so that all audiences can engage fully with major local, regional, national, United Kingdom and global issues and participate in the democratic process, at all levels, as active and informed citizens.
2 To support learning for people of all ages [...]
3 To show the most creative, highest quality and distinctive output and services [...]
4 To reflect, represent and serve the diverse communities of all of the United Kingdom's nations and regions and, in doing so, support the creative economy across the United Kingdom [...]
5 To reflect the United Kingdom, its culture and values to the world (BBC Charter 2017–2026, §6).

The BBC as such is not allowed to undertake commercial activities but can do so based on subsidiaries: "The BBC as a corporation must not directly undertake any commercial activities and they must be provided through one or more commercial subsidiaries" (BBC Agreement 2017–2026, §23 (4)). Commercial activities are defined as activities that advance the BBC's Public Purposes, are not funded by the licence fee revenue, and "are undertaken with a view to generating a profit" (BBC Agreement 2017–2026, §23 (2)).

The BBC is funded by the licence fee. Legally, the collection of the licence fee from all British households and its payment to the BBC is regulated in the Communications Act 2003, §365. The BBC can sell advertisements on its commercial services, but its core services are advertising- and sponsorship-free. The BBC Agreement rules out advertising:

> The BBC must not, without the prior approval of the appropriate Minister, include any sponsored material in any of its services. [...] 'sponsored material' means any material that has some or all of its relevant costs met by a person, other than the BBC or the producer of the material, with a view to promoting their own or another's name, trade mark, image, activities or products or any other direct or indirect interest.
> (BBC Agreement 2017–2016, §50 (2) (4))

13.2.7 Public Service Media in Germany

The creation of Public Service Broadcasting in Germany was part of the reconstruction of the country after the end of World War II and the Nazi regime. The Public Service Media landscape in Germany consists of ARD (Arbeitsgemeinschaft der öffentlich-rechtlichen Rundfunkanstalten der Bundesrepublik Deutschland), ZDF (Zweites Deutsches Fernsehen), nine federal state broadcasting corporations (Bayerischer Rundfunk BR, Hessischer Rundfunk HR, Mitteldeutscher Rundfunk MDR, Norddeutscher Rundfunk NDR, Radio Bremen, Rundfunk Berlin-Brandenburg RBB, Saarländischer Rundfunk SR, Südwestrundfunk SWR, and Westdeutscher Rundfunk WDR), and Deutschlandradio. ARD is an association of the federal state broadcasting corporations and Deutsche Welle.

The general principles of Public Service Media were regulated from 1991 to 2020 in the Interstate Treaty on Broadcasting and Telemedia (*Staatsvertrag für Rundfunk und Telemedien*). At the end of 2020, the Interstate Media Treaty (*Medienstaatsvertrag*, MStV) came into force. In addition, there are legal regulations for individual broadcasters, such as the ZDF State Treaty (*ZDF-Staatsvertrag*).

Article 5 of the German Basic Law (Grundgesetz) defines freedom of speech and the media as a basic right:

> Every person shall have the right freely to express and disseminate his opinions in speech, writing and pictures and to inform himself without hindrance from generally accessible sources. Freedom of the press and

freedom of reporting by means of broadcasts and films shall be guaranteed. There shall be no censorship.[1]

Acknowledging the importance of Public Service Media for providing communications as universal service and the lack of capacity of private, profit-oriented media to provide universal service, in Germany, the existence and purpose of Public Service Media are legally defined for realising the constitutionally defined right of the freedom of the media. The Federal Constitutional Court (*Bundesverfassungsgericht*) argued in its Fourth Broadcasting Decision (*4. Rundfunkentscheidung*) that only Public Service Media can provide universal service:

> In this order, the indispensable 'universal service' is the responsibility of the public broadcasters, which they are able to provide because their terrestrial programmes reach almost the entire population and because they are not dependent on high audience figures in the same way as private broadcasters and are therefore able to offer a comprehensive range of programmes. The task thus set encompasses the essential functions of broadcasting for the democratic order as well as for cultural life in the Federal Republic of Germany.[2]
>
> (BVerfGE 73, 118, 157)

In the UK, there is no written constitution. The BBC's existence and purpose are legally granted in the form of a Royal Charter for ten years by the Queen or King, which means by the UK government. The need for the BBC of having to legally redefine its existence and purpose all ten years gives the UK government more direct power to exert political pressure on Public Service Media. Public Service Media in Germany is because of constitutional guarantees more independent from governments than in the UK (Rook 2019). Nonetheless, in Germany, there are also indirect powers of how governments and federal governments can exert pressure on Public Service Broadcasting in the form of a certain number of members they can send to Public Service Media's governing bodies.

> Market mechanisms are distrusted in Germany and trusted in the UK. Therefore, in Germany, the [public service] broadcasters are the guarantors of functioning broadcasting, whereas in the UK it is competition between all broadcasters that is as unhindered as possible. [...] The different roles of the BBC and the [German public service] broadcasters find their constitutional cause in the universal service mandate existing in Germany and lacking in the United Kingdom. [...] In the UK, the state can exert more direct influence on the BBC, whereas in Germany the state can exert more indirect influence on the [public service] broadcasters.[3]
>
> (Rook 2019, 325–326)

In addition to the MStV, the ARD is regulated by its Statute. One of the ARD member broadcasters is elected as managing broadcaster for one year at a time (ARD Statute, §3), whereby the respective Director-General is appointed as ARD Chairperson. The Chairperson is assisted by a General Secretary, who is elected by the Director-Generals for a five-year term of office by a two-thirds majority (§ 3). The organisation of the member broadcasters is regulated by their own federal state laws, such as the WDR Act (*WDR-Gesetz*) and the Bavarian Broadcasting Act (*Bayerisches Rundfunkgesetz*).

The basic governance principle of ZDF and the regional broadcasters is that a Broadcasting Council (*Rundfunkrat*) elects the Director-General. The Broadcasting Council represents different groups in society, which is intended to achieve diversity in decision-making. The principle of delegation applies. The Supervisory Board (*Verwaltungsrat*) is elected by the Broadcasting Council on the one hand, and delegates are selected by the Staff Council (*Personalrat*) or the federal states on the other. The Supervisory Board advises and controls the work of the Director-General.

The German regulation of Public Service Media is, on the one hand, federalist and, on the other hand, characterised by the principle of representation of the interests of social groups. "The members of the Television Council and the Supervisory Board are trustees of the interests of the general public" (ZDF-Staatsvertrag, §19a). In contrast, the BBC is organised in a much more centralised way and has representatives of the four countries as a federal element in the BBC Board. Representatives of societal groups are not specifically elected or appointed to the BBC Board. The BBC's Audience Councils have a purely advisory function. In both countries, the election of decision-making councillors by the audience plays no role.

At ZDF, the Broadcasting Council is called the Television Council ("Fernsehrat"). The ZDF State Treaty stipulates that the Television Council consists of 60 members. These include one member delegated by each of the federal state governments, two members delegated by the German government, members delegated by churches, trade union confederations, business associations, newspaper publishers, the German Journalists' Association, sports associations, environmental protection associations, victims' associations as well as federal state representatives in various fields of interest (e.g. consumer protection, digital affairs, science and research, music, migration, media industry and film, art and culture, LGBTQI, homeland and customs, Muslims, civic engagement, senior citizens, family, women and youth, inclusive society, civil defence and disaster control, regional and minority languages) (ZDF State Treaty, §21). The principle of delegation applies. The Television Council has a period of four years. The Television Council advises the Director-General on programming issues, establishes broadcasting guidelines, monitors compliance with guidelines and adopts the statutes and approves the budget (ZDF State Treaty, §20). The ZDF Supervisory Board (Verwaltungsrat) supervises the activities of the Director-General (ZDF State Treaty, §23). It consists of twelve members, four of whom are appointed jointly by the federal state governments and eight of whom are elected by the Television Council (ZDF Interstate Treaty, §24). The ZDF Director-General is elected by the Television Council for a period of five years (ZDF Interstate Treaty, §26).

The Interstate Media Treaty (Medienstaatsvertrag, MStV) defines the general tasks of Public Service Media in Germany:

1 Under their remit, the public-service broadcasting corporations are to act as a medium and factor in the process of the formation of free individual and public opinion through the production and transmission of their offers, thereby serving the democratic, social and cultural needs of society. In their offers, the public-service broadcasting corporations must provide a comprehensive overview of international, European, national, and regional events in all major areas of life. In so doing, they shall further international understanding, European integration, and the social cohesion on the federal and state levels. Their offers shall serve education, information, advice, and entertainment. They must in particular provide contributions on culture. Entertainment should also be provided in line with a public-service profile of offers.

2 In fulfilling their remit, the public-service broadcasting corporations shall pay due respect to the principles of objectivity and impartiality in reporting, plurality of opinion and the balance of their offers (MStV, §26 (1) (2))

A commonality between the German Public Service Media and the BBC is that their purpose is to provide high-quality information, educational content and entertainment, as well as objective, impartial, balanced, and diverse reporting to promote democracy, culture and social cohesion.

One difference is that the BBC's core services are not advertising-financed, whereas Public Service Media in Germany are licence fee- and advertising-financed: "Public-service broadcasting shall be funded through licence fees, income from television and radio advertising and other sources of revenue. The main source of income shall be the licence fee" (MStV, §35). Advertising on German Public Service Media is limited by law. On average, it may not exceed 20 minutes per day on ARD and ZDF, is prohibited after 8 p.m. and on Sundays and public holidays, and may not exceed 20% of the programme time per hour (MStV, § 39). Advertising is not permitted in the programmes of the federal state Public Service Broadcasters (MStV, § 39). Table 13.4 shows the income of BBC, ARD, and ZDF.

The annual budgets of BBC and ARD have a quite similar size. The composition is different. The BBC has no advertising in its core service but overall relies more on commercial income from advertising, sponsorship, sale of rights, etc. than ARD and ZDF. ARD and ZDF feature advertising and sponsorship on their core services, but in comparison to the BBC rely more

Table 13.4 The budgets of BBC, ARD, and ZDF

	BBC 2021	*ARD 2020*	*ZDF 2019*	*Deutschlandradio 2020*
Licence fee	£3.750 billion (74.1%)	€ 5.511 billion (84.3%)	€1 917 548 633 (85.5%)	€228 624 378.75 (91.4%)
Advertising and sponsorship		€ 0.149 billion (2.3%)	€173 174 125 (7.7%)	
Other income	£1.314 billion (commercial income including advertising and sponsorship) (25.9%)	€ 0.875 billion (13.4%)	€153 236 048 (6.8%)	€21 468 013.92 (8.6%)
Total	£5.064 billion	€ 6.535 billion	€2 243 958 806	€250 092 392.67

Data sources: BBC Group Annual Report and Accounts 2020/21, ARD Report on the Economic and Financial Situation of the State Broadcasting Corporations 2020, ZDF Annual Financial Statements 2019, Deutschlandradio Statement of Income and Expenditure for the 2020 Financial Year.[4]

on the licence fee and less on commercial income. Despite these differences, the major revenue source for all three companies is the licence fee.

In the UK, BBC is the Public Service Broadcaster. In Germany, ARD, ZDF, and Deutschlandradio are the three Public Service Broadcasters. Therefore, one needs to compare the BBC's budget to the combined budget of the three German PSM. Whereas the BBC's annual budget at the start of the 2020s was around €6 billion, German Public Service Broadcasting's total annual budget was around €9 billion and therefore 50% higher than the BBC's budget. Both in the UK and in Germany, the licence fee is paid per household. In 2023, the UK licence fee was £159 and the German licence fee (*Rundfunkbeitrag*) was €220.32. This means that the German licence fee is around 20% higher than the British one. In addition, in Germany, all households have to pay the licence fee, whereas in the UK only those have to pay who have a television receiver. If you do not have a television set, but a tablet or a laptop where you do not have the BBC iPlayer installed and do not watch BBC, you do not have to pay the licence fee. In contrast, in Germany, every household needs to pay the licence fee.

13.3 The Public Service Internet

Traditionally, one has spoken of Public Service Broadcasting because the corresponding services were focused on radio and television. Digitalisation has led to the convergence of the media. Public Service Broadcasters offer text-, audio-, and video-based services on the internet, including streaming of their audiovisual content. Broadcasting has become a digital medium, and digital media includes broadcasting. It is therefore more appropriate to speak of Public Service Media (PSM) today than of Public Service Broadcasting (PSB). This also suggests that PSM organisations are suited to develop, organise, and offer Internet platforms.

The rise of the Internet has taken place in the context of neoliberal capitalism, where privatisation and the commodification of everything have dominated. It is therefore no surprise that Public Service Media have come under attack. "For the most part, PSB has been and remains a group of publicly owned corporations – precisely the sort of organisational form that neo-liberalism set out to get rid of, with considerable success" (Goodwin 2018, 33) and that "public service media (PSM) providers have been increasingly marginalised in the development of the networked society" (Goodwin 2018, 29).

Graham Murdock argues that the Internet should be organised as a common good and that "the institution best placed to address the current problems with the Internet [...], public broadcasting has a pivotal role to play in building this digital commons" (Murdock 2005, 227; see also Murdock 2018, 2021).

> The digital commons, as I have sketched it here, has the potential to create contemporary coffeehouses without walls and social exclusions, combining access to the full range of imaginative and information resources that support effective participation with new spaces of encounter and deliberation.
>
> (Murdock 2021, 86)

Splichal (2022) argues for the democratic use of algorithms and data. He suggests the development of public-worthiness algorithms that calculate how publicly relevant certain events in society are, and suggests the resulting news items to members of the public who then select what they read and view. The key aspect of public-worthiness is the consequences of events for society (125), public relevance and "*issues of common concern*" (126). Public-worthiness algorithms are an example of technologies that are "*society-friendly* rather than *user-friendly*" (130).

13.3.1 The Public Service Media and Public Service Internet Manifesto

During the COVID-19 lockdown in 2020 and 2021, a group of several dozen concerned citizens around the world co-operated online in order to write *The Public Service Media and Public Service Internet Manifesto* (PSMI Manifesto Collective 2021). The Manifesto demands the safeguarding of the existence, independence, and funding of PSM such as the BBC, ARD, ZDF, as well

as the development of a Public Service Internet and the resourcing of PSM
to provide online platforms to support this. Until December 2022, around
1,300 individuals and organisations had signed and endorsed the Manifesto.
Among the supporters are Jürgen Habermas, Noam Chomsky, the International Federation of Journalists, the European Federation of Journalists,
and many more. The Manifesto can be supported by visiting http://bit.ly/
signPSManifesto.

In an age of "fake news" and post-truth politics, the existence of high-
quality media organisations both in broadcasting and online is more critical
than ever. The media and Internet platforms should not serve private but
public interests. They should be media of the public, by the public, and for
the public – media of the public sphere. The Manifesto ascertains:

> We need to rebuild the Internet. While the contemporary Internet is
> dominated by monopolies and commerce, the Public Service Internet
> is dominated by democracy. While the contemporary Internet is domi-
> nated by surveillance, the Public Service Internet is privacy-friendly
> and transparent. While the contemporary Internet misinforms and
> separates the public, the Public Service Internet engages, informs and
> supports the public. Although the contemporary Internet is driven by
> and drives the profit principle, the Public Service Internet puts social
> needs first.
>
> (PSMI Manifesto Collective 2021, 13)

A public and commons-based Internet is possible – an Internet on which
people share, communicate, decide, discuss, play, create, criticise, network,
collaborate, find, maintain and build friendships, fall in love, entertain themselves and each other, educate themselves as common activity without corporate mediation.

Public service Internet platforms are provided by Public Service Media organisations with a **not-for-profit imperative** and the **digital remit** to advance
information, news, debate, democracy, education, entertainment, participation, and creativity with the help of the Internet. PSM should redefine their
remit as the **digital remit** to advance information, entertainment, education,
and democracy by utilising digital platforms.

13.3.2 *Four Political Economies of Digital Platforms*

Table 13.5 outlines some foundations of four political economies of digital
platforms. Public Service Internet platforms and civil society Internet platforms are the two types of digital platforms that operate on non-capitalist
and non-statist principles and thereby negate the Political Economy of digital
capitalism. They operate in the digital public sphere. In contrast, capitalist
digital platforms and authoritarian platforms colonise, feudalise, alienate,
and destroy the digital public sphere. There are also mixed forms of the

Table 13.5 Four political economies of digital platforms

Dimension	Authoritarian Internet Platforms	Capitalist Internet Platforms	Public Service Internet Platforms	Civil Society Internet Platforms, Digital Community Media
Economy	Ownership and control by an authoritarian state or another authoritarian organisation	Digital capital, private ownership of digital platforms that accumulate capital	Public service organisation	Community ownership, civil society organisation ownership, co-operatives
Politics	Authoritarian top-down governance	Governance by private owners, shareholders and managers	Governance by a democratically legitimated board	Governance by the community of members/ workers/users
Culture	Publicly available digital content that is controlled, censored and reflects the authoritarian controller's political ideas	Publicly available digital content that is prone to ideology and capitalist values	Digital content and digital services that realise the public service remits of democratic communication, education, culture and participation	Digital content and services that support user-generated content, citizen journalism, and digital participation

media. Public Service Internet platforms and civil society Internet platforms are excellent foundations for advancing the digital commons, that is digital environmental sustainability (natural digital commons), digital socialism (economic digital commons), participatory digital democracy (political digital commons), and digital friendships (cultural digital commons). Creating such non-capitalist digital platforms is not a sufficient condition for the advancement of the digital commons, but a good foundation that has a better likelihood and chances to advance digital democracy, digital equality, and digital justice than digital capitalism and capitalist digital platforms. It takes a conscious human effort, social struggle, and material foundations to advance all dimensions of the digital commons. For example, a digital platform can be democratically governed and owned (political and economic) but advance e-waste and climate change. The organisations and communities operating these platforms should therefore support the creation of non-capitalist green computing.

13.3.3 *The Public Service Media/Internet Utopias Survey*

As preparatory work for the PSMI Manifesto, I conducted an exploratory survey among PSM experts. The Public Service Media/Internet Utopias Survey was run from 10 November until 26 December 2019. There were 141 participants. The survey focused on three themes:

- communication, digital media and the Internet in an ideal world;
- progressive reforms of Public Service Media;
- Public Service Media and the Internet in 2030.

The results were published as a report (Fuchs 2021b). Using thematic analysis, 12 themes related to topic 1 (the ideal Internet of the future) were identified. The respondents identified 12 features of an ideal Internet of the future:

1. The Internet is run **not-for-profit** and is advertising-free, and there are no corporate Internet monopolies;
2. The Internet has a decentralised technological and social structure;
3. The Internet economy is an **economic democracy** built on worker- and user-owned infrastructure and platform co-ops, the digital commons, and democratic governance;
4. Parts of the Internet are run and owned as a **public utility** by Public Service Media in the form of Public Service Internet platforms;
5. **Platform co-operatives (Internet platforms run and owned by users and workers)** and Public Service Internet providers co-exist and co-operate in synergetic ways;
6. There is **gratis access** to the Internet, and digital technologies, free software and open content are the standards;
7. Digital technologies are **environmentally sustainable**;
8. There is **no authoritarian state control, state censorship, and surveillance** of the Internet; the Internet is privacy-friendly and based on the principle of data minimisation;
9. Education includes critical **digital media literacy**; on the Internet, there is lots of engaging, critical educational content;
10. Users are enabled and encouraged to **participate in the production of media content**; the Internet and face-to-face encounters support democratic debate and decision-making in the public sphere; the democratic public sphere advances internationalism and solidarity and weakens hatred, fascism, nationalism, and racism;
11. On the Internet, there is **fact-based, fact-checked news, and high-quality content**; critical online media report the truth and expose power;
12. On the Internet, there is a **diversity of media content**, platforms, audiences, opinions, and a representation of diverse groups from all social backgrounds and realms, regions, and parts of the world.

The survey respondents argued that parts of the Internet should be run and owned as a public utility by Public Service Media in the form of Public Service Internet platforms. Here are some example answers obtained in the Public Service Media/Internet Utopias Survey:

> Countries desirous of an informed citizenry should set up and fund public institutions run by independently appointed persons to commission content designed to meet social needs unmet by market providers and to arrange its distribution on whatever platforms they deem appropriate.
>
> (#28)

> Public service media services across all platforms. Universal service, free to all at the point of reception, content catering to a full range of communities and needs, driven by civic, not commercial imperatives. The internet would be operated as a public utility with universal accessibility, and net neutrality, with provisions for anonymity and user-control over personal data coupled with checks and balances to prevent abuses (e.g. attempts to manipulate elections through targeted fake news, proliferation of extreme/hate-based ideologies, mass surveillance).
>
> (#695)

> The "media would be usable on a public and freely available worldwide information network that was collectively governed and open to all"
>
> (#388).

> Public media environment. The ideal media environment would be much more local and not market-based. I would love to get all my information from PSM media – from radio to entertainment and culture and socializing! PSM could provide also the strictly necessary digital components.
>
> (#345)

> Public Service Streaming Services: Rather than selling products to private streaming platforms, I would encourage alliances with other PSMs to build a transcontinental streaming platform, where these contents would be exclusively shown. Laws would limit competition from private providers.
>
> (#202)

> Provide decentralized and alternative platforms to YouTube or Netflix and create citizen-relevant content and make it freely available on these

platforms. This could be an effort made at international level, where PSM from different countries could collaborate to implement this vision.
(#815)

13.3.4 Public Service YouTube

Two potential Public Service Internet Platforms are a Public Service YouTube and Club 2.0. A Public Service YouTube is ideally run by an international network of PSM and other public organisations.

- There is a focus on topics that are important for democracy;
- The possibility for user-generated videos is accompanying public service radio and TV broadcasts;
- There is filtering of discriminatory content;
- The upload of videos on a certain topic is possible at particular points in time;
- There is the collective production of videos in school classes, groups of pupils and students, council houses, adult learning groups, unions, religious and philosophical groups, civil society organisations, etc.;
- Digital creativity is supported by making archived PSM material that is published based on a Creative Commons CC-BY-NC licence that allows remixing the content for non-commercial purposes;
- A selection of user-generated content can be broadcast at particular times on radio/TV;
- There is a co-operation of Public Service Media to establish a global video platform;
- The limited availability of online content contradicts the medium's affordances (e.g. BBC iPlayer: 30 days). On the Public Service YouTube, content has unlimited availability;
- The use of content for commercial, for-profit purposes is not possible.

13.3.5 Club 2.0

Club 2 was a debate format broadcast by the Austrian Broadcasting Corporation (ORF) from 1976 until 1995. It featured live studio debate, was uncensored, was open-ended, focused on controversial topics, had a living room atmosphere, no studio audience, 4–8 diverse guests, and one moderator. Club 2 was a prototype of "slow media". It was a democratic public sphere. The format disappeared with the rise of reality TV.

Club 2.0 is the idea of the renewal of Club 2 as a Public Service Internet format. It features a controversial live studio debate that is broadcast on television and a Public Service Internet platform where a limited number of users (e.g. selected by chance) can debate and upload videos. At certain points in the discussion, user-generated videos are broadcast as inputs to the studio debate. Figure 13.2 visualises the principles of Club 2.0.

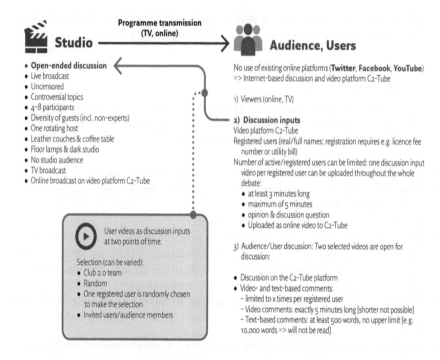

Figure 13.2 The concept of Club 2.0.

13.4 Conclusion

This chapter focused on the Political Economy of Public Service Media and the Public Service Internet. It asked: How does the Political Economy of Public Service Media and the Public Service Internet look like? Let us now summarise the main findings.

Finding 1: Public Service Media

Public Service Media are a manifestation and part of the public sphere. They are public sphere media and are very different from the logic of capitalist media and authoritarian media. Public Service Media are publicly owned, accountable to the public, and have a public service remit to create and provide access to high-quality information, news, education, and entertainment that help advance democracy, culture, learning, understanding, and debate.

Finding 2: Towards a Public Service Internet

The Internet is dominated by large transnational corporations that are focused on accumulating capital. The Public Service Media and Public Service

Internet Manifesto demands the safeguarding of the existence and funding of Public Service Media and the creation of a Public Service Internet, Internet platforms run by Public Service Media organisations. The Public Service Internet is a democratic alternative to the capitalist Internet.

Notes

1 https://www.gesetze-im-internet.de/englisch_gg/englisch_gg.html, accessed on 12 December 2021.
2 Translated from German:

> In dieser Ordnung ist die unerlässliche ‚Grundversorgung' Sache der öffentlich-rechtlichen Anstalten, zu der sie imstande sind, weil ihre terrestrischen Programme nahezu die gesamte Bevölkerung erreichen und weil sie nicht in gleicher Weise wie private Veranstalter auf hohe Einschaltquoten angewiesen, mithin zu einem inhaltlich umfassenden Programmangebot in der Lage sind. Die damit gestellte Aufgabe umfasst die essentiellen Funktionen des Rundfunks für die demokratische Ordnung ebenso wie für das kulturelle Leben in der Bundesrepublik.

3 Translated from German:

> In Deutschland wird den Marktmechanismen misstraut und im Vereinigten Königreich vertraut. Daher sind in Deutschland die [öffentlich-rechtlichen] Rundfunkanstalten die Garanten des funktionierenden Rundfunks, während es im Vereinigten Königreich ein möglichst ungehinderter Wettbewerb aller Rundfunkveranstalter ist. [...] Die unterschiedlichen Rollen der BBC und der [deutschen öffentlich-rechtlichen] Rundfunkanstalten finden ihre verfassungsrechtliche Ursache im in Deutschland bestehenden und im Vereinigten Königreich fehlenden Grundversorgungsauftrag. [...] Im Vereinigten Königreich kann der Staat mehr direkten Einfluss auf die BBC ausüben während in Deutschland der Staat mehr indirekten Einfluss auf die [öffentlich-rechtlichen] Rundfunkanstalten ausüben kann.
>
> (Rook 2019, 325–326)

4 German Original: ARD Bericht über die wirtschaftliche und finanzielle Lage der Landesrundfunkanstalten 2020, ZDF Jahresabschluss 2019, Deutschlandradio Ertrags- und Aufwandsrechnung für das Geschäftsjahr 2020

References

Cañedo, Azahara, Marza Rodríguez-Castro, and Ana Maria López-Cepeda. 2022. Distilling the Value of Public Service Media: Towards a Tenable Conceptualisation in the European Framework. *European Journal of Communication* 37 (6): 586–605. DOI: https://doi.org/10.1177/02673231221090777

Curran, James. 1991. Rethinking the Media as a Public Sphere. In *Communication and Citizenship. Journalism and the Public Sphere,* edited by Peter Dahlgren and Colin Sparks, 27–57. London: Routledge.

Curran, James and Jean Seaton. 2010. *Power without Responsibility. Press, Broadcasting and the Internet in Britain.* London: Routledge. Seventh edition.

Cushion, Stephen. 2012. *The Democratic Value of News. Why Public Service Media Matter.* Basingstoke: Palgrave Macmillan.

Deane, James, Pierre François Docquir, Winston Mano, Tarik Sabry, and Naomi Sakr. 2020. *Achieving Viability for Public Service Media in Challenging Settings: A Holistic Approach*. London: University of Westminster Press. DOI: https://doi.org/10.16997/book41

Fuchs, Christian. 2021a. *Social Media: A Critical Introduction*. London: SAGE. Third edition.

Fuchs, Christian. 2021b. The Public Service Media and Public Service Internet Utopias Survey Report. In *The Public Service Media and Public Service Internet Manifesto*, edited by Christian Fuchs and Klaus Unterberger, 19–68. London: University of Westminster Press. DOI: https://doi.org/10.16997 /book60.c

Fuchs, Christian. 2020. *Communication and Capitalism. A Critical Theory*. London: University of Westminster Press. DOI: https://doi.org/10.16997/book45

Fuchs, Christian. 2014. Social Media and the Public Sphere. *tripleC* 12 (1): 57–101. DOI: https://doi.org/10.31269/triplec.v12i1.552

Fuchs, Christian. 2008. *Internet and Society. Social Theory in the Information Age*. New York: Routledge.

Garnham, Nicholas. 1990. *Capitalism and Communication. Global Culture and the Economics of Information*. London: SAGE.

Goodwin, Peter. 2018. An Impossible Challenge for Public Service Media? The Intellectual Context of the Networked Society. In *Public Service Media in the Networked Society*, edited by Gregory Ferrell Lowe, Hilde Van den Bulck, and Karen Donders, 29–41. Gothenburg: Nordicom.

Habermas, Jürgen. 2008. Hat die Demokratie noch eine epistemische Dimension? Empirische Forschung und normative Theorie. In *Ach, Europa*, 138–191. Frankfurt am Main: Suhrkamp.

Murdock, Graham. 2021. Public Service Media for Critical Times: Connectivity, Climate, and Corona. In *The Public Service Media and Public Service Internet Manifesto*, edited by Christian Fuchs and Klaus Unterberger, 69–111. London: University of Westminster Press. DOI: https://doi.org/10.16997/book60.d

Murdock, Graham. 2018. Reclaiming Digital Space. From Commercial Enclosure to the Broadcast Commons. In *Public Service Media in the Networked Society*, edited by Gregory Ferrell Lowe, Hilde Van den Bulck, and Karen Donders, 43–58. Gothenburg: Nordicom.

Murdock, Graham. 2011. Political Economies as Moral Economies. Commodities, Gifts, and Public Goods. In *The Handbook of the Political Economy of Communications*, edited by Janet Wasko, Graham Murdock, and Helena Sousa, 13–40. Chichester: Wiley-Blackwell.

Murdock, Graham. 2005. Building the Digital Commons. Public Broadcasting in the Age of the Internet. In *Cultural Dilemmas in Public Service Broadcasting: RIPE@2005*, edited by Gregory Ferrell Lowe and Per Jauert, 213–230. Gothenburg: NORDICOM.

PSMI Manifesto Collective. 2021. The Public Service Media and Public Service Internet Manifesto. In *The Public Service Media and Public Service Internet Manifesto*, http://bit.ly/psmmanifesto also published in: edited by Christian Fuchs and Klaus Unterberger, 7–17. London: University of Westminster Press. DOI: https://doi.org/10.16997/book60

Rook, Robert. 2019. *Der Öffentlich-Rechtliche Rundfunk in Deutschland und im Vereinigten Königreich. Ein Rechtsvergleich*. Wiesbaden: Springer.

Sandoval, Marisol and Christian Fuchs. 2010. Towards a Critical Theory of Alternative Media. *Telematics and Informatics* 27 (2): 141–150.

Splichal, Slavko. 2022. *Datafication of Public Opinion and the Public Sphere. How Extraction Replaced Expression of Opinion.* London: Anthem Press.

Splichal, Slavko. 2012. *Transnationalization of the Public Sphere and the Fate of the Public.* New York: Hampton Press.

Splichal, Slavko. 2007. Does History Matter? Grasping the Idea of Public Service at Its Roots. In *From Public Service Broadcasting to Public Service Media. RIPE@2007*, edited by Gregory Ferrell Lowe and Jo Bardoel, 237–256. Gothenburg: Nordicom. S. 255.

Syvertsen, Trine. 2003. Challenges to Public Television in the Era of Convergence and Commercialization. *Television & New Media* 4 (2): 155–175.

Thomaß, Barbara. 2013. Public Service Broadcasting. In *Mediensysteme im Internationalen Vergleich*, edited by Barbara Thomaß, 81–98. Konstanz: UVK. Second Edition.

UNESCO. 2008. *Media Development Indicators: A Framework for Assessing Media Development.* Paris: UNESCO.

UNESCO. 2001. *Public Broadcasting. Why? How?* Montreal: World Radio and Television Council.

Volkmer, Ingrid. 2014. *The Global Public Sphere: Public Communication in the Age of Reflective Interdependence.* Cambridge: Polity.

Williams, Raymond. 1976. *Communications.* Harmondsworth: Penguin Books.

Recommended Readings and Exercises

Readings

The following texts are recommended as accompanying readings to this chapter:

Graham Murdock. 2005. Building the Digital Commons. Public Broadcasting in the Age of the Internet. In *Cultural Dilemmas in Public Service Broadcasting: RIPE@2005*, edited by Gregory Ferrell Lowe and Per Jauert, 213–230. Gothenburg: NORDICOM.

Christian Fuchs. 2021. The Public Service Media and Public Service Internet Utopias Survey Report. In *The Public Service Media and Public Service Internet Manifesto*, edited by Christian Fuchs and Klaus Unterberger, 19–68. London: University of Westminster Press. DOI: https://doi.org/10.16997/book60.c

PSMI Manifesto Collective. 2021. The Public Service Media and Public Service Internet Manifesto. In *The Public Service Media and Public Service Internet Manifesto*, http://bit.ly/psmmanifesto also published in: edited by Christian Fuchs and Klaus Unterberger, 7–17. London: University of Westminster Press. DOI: https://doi.org/10.16997/book60

Exercise 13.1   The British Broadcasting Corporation

Read the BBC Charter that regulates the BBC's organisation:

BBC Royal Charter 2017–2026:
https://www.bbc.com/aboutthebbc/governance/charter

Discuss:
What is the nature of a Public Service Medium?
What do you consider to be the most important characteristics of the BBC?
How does the BBC differ from capitalist media organisations? How do you assess its principles?
Inform yourself about recent debates and threats that Public Service Media have faced. How do you assess these developments?
How do you assess the use of the licence fee as the main funding mechanism of the BBC?
How does broadcasting work in other countries you are familiar with? What are the commonalities and differences between broadcasters in that country and the BBC?

Exercise 13.2   Public Service Media in Germany

Read the German Interstate Media Treaty (*Medienstaatsvertrag*) that regulates broadcasting, telemedia and Public Service Media in Germany. Give special attention to Section III (Special Provisions for Public Service Broadcasting):
German Interstate Media Treaty (*Medienstaatsvertrag*)

https://www.die-medienanstalten.de/fileadmin/user_upload/
Rechtsgrundlagen/Gesetze_Staatsvertraege/Interstate_Media_Treaty_
en.pdf

Discuss:
What do you consider to be the most important characteristics of Public Service Media in Germany?
How do Public Service Media in Germany differ from capitalist media organisations? How do you assess its principles?
What is the role of the licence fee and advertising in Germany's Public Service Media landscape? How do you assess the German organisational model of Public Service Media? How does it differ from the BBC?
What should Public Service Media look like in the future and what role should they play?

Exercise 13.3   Towards a Public Service Internet

Read The Public Service Media and Public Service Internet Manifesto:

PSMI Manifesto Collective. 2021. The Public Service Media and Public Service Internet Manifesto. In *The Public Service Media and Public Service Internet Manifesto*, http://bit.ly/psmmanifesto also published in: edited by Christian Fuchs and Klaus Unterberger, 7–17. London: University of Westminster Press. DOI: https://doi.org/10.16997/book60

Discuss:

What is the Public Service Internet?
How does the Public Service Internet differ from the capitalist Internet?
Do you rather agree or rather disagree that we need a Public Service Internet? Give reasons for your opinion.
Envision a new Public Service Internet platform and describe its core principles. How would it advance democracy in the public sphere?
Promote The Public Service Media and Public Service Internet Manifesto on the Internet. Work in groups. The goal is that each group gets at least 50 new users to sign the Manifesto here: http://bit.ly/signPSManifesto

14 The Political Economy of Media Management

What You Will Learn in This Chapter

- We will deal with the question: What is management?
- You will gain insights into the difference between Fordist-Taylorist and post-Fordist forms of management;
- We will look at the question of whether or not creativity and cultural work can be managed.

14.1 Introduction

The management of media organisations is a process that takes place at the microeconomic level. Management is influenced by society, so it is mediated by the political economy of society. This chapter is about political economy and the basics of media management. In order to understand how the media are managed, we need a basic understanding of what management is all about.

Section 14.2 asks the question: What is management? Section 14.3 clarifies the concept of media management. Section 14.4 explains the differences between Fordist and post-Fordist management. Section 14.5 deals with the management of culture, media, and creativity. Section 14.6 draws some conclusions.

14.2 What Is Management?

14.2.1 The Emergence of Management as Part of the Division of Labour

Let us first look at a classical definition of management. Henri Fayol (1841–1925) was a French engineer and entrepreneur who comparable to Frederick Winslow Taylor developed a theory of management.

Fayol gave one of the early definitions of management. He identifies five economic activities: technical activities (production), commercial activities (sales), security activities (the protection of property), accounting activities, and managerial activities (Fayol 1916/1949, 3). He defines management as

DOI: 10.4324/9781003391203-16

the activities "concerned with drawing up the broad plan of operations of the business, with assembling personnel, co-ordinating and harmonizing effort and activity" (5). To

> manage is to forecast and plan, to organize, to command, to co-ordinate and to control. To foresee and provide means examining the future and drawing up the plan of action. To organize means building up the dual structure, material and human, of the undertaking. To command means maintaining activity among the personnel. To co-ordinate means binding together, unifying and harmonizing all activity and effort. To control means seeing that everything occurs in conformity with established rule and expressed command.
>
> (Fayol 1916/1949, 6)

The rise of management occurred in the context of the transition from competitive capitalism to imperialist capitalism at the end of the 19th century. This resulted in the emergence of large corporations in which several companies were combined to eliminate competition. This transition has to do with the concentration and monopolisation tendencies inherent in the capitalist economy. Enterprises became so large and complex that the owners could no longer manage them and organise the work in them themselves. Therefore, they created a class of paid people to manage work groups, departments, and companies. The profession of the manager came into being. The idea of management is based on a division of labour between intellectual, planning, and organisational activities on the one hand and executing, applied and practical labour on the other.

Marx argues that the division of labour is characteristic of class societies (Marx and Engels 1845/1846, chapter I, 27–93). According to Marx, historical forms of the division of labour are the gender division of labour in the family; the division of labour between town and country; the division of labour between agriculture, industry, and commerce; the division of labour between mental and physical labour; the division of labour between different nations, etc. (ibid.). For Marx, the division of labour is an expression of alienation: "The *division of labour* is the economic expression of the *soci[et] al character of labour* within the estrangement" (Marx 1844, 317). Alienation means a state in which people have no control over the conditions and structures of their lives and the products of their labour. Marx sees the division of labour as "one of the chief forces of history up till now" (Marx and Engels 1845/1846, 59).

According to Marx, the division of labour in class society also includes the division between mental and physical labour: "Division of labour only becomes truly such from the moment when a division of material and mental labour appears" (Marx and Engels 1845/1846, 44–45). The critical theorist Alfred Sohn-Rethel argues that the division between physical and mental labour is as old as class societies and that it goes back to the division of labour in slave-holding societies, where slaves performed physical labour, while philosophers, politicians, and scientists focused on intellectual activities. "It is Greek philosophy which constitutes the first historical manifestations of the separation of head and hand in this particular mode" (Sohn-Rethel 1978, 66).

Marx also described a division of labour within the dominant class of capitalism as a division between intellectuals who produce ideology and the owners of capital:

> The division of labour, which we already saw above as one of the chief forces of history up till now, manifests itself also in the ruling class as the division of mental and material labour, so that inside this class one part appears as the thinkers of the class (its active, conceptive ideologists, who make the formation of the illusions of the class about itself their chief source of livelihood), while the others' attitude to these ideas and illusions is more passive and receptive, because they are in reality the active members of this class and have less time to make up illusions and ideas about themselves.
>
> (Marx and Engels 1845/1846, 59–60)

The division of labour between capital owners and managers is another division of labour within the ruling class of capitalism. The profession of the manager has to do with the division of labour in complex and highly productive class societies.

Karl Marx, in *Capital* and the related preparatory works, has given thought to the fundamentals of management. He argues that with the growth of the scope of the means of production, that is with the increasing size of enterprises, not only the co-operation of workers increases but also the necessity that capital exerts "effective control over the proper application of" the means of production (Marx 1867, 449), which requires "a plan drawn up by the capitalist" and "authority" that confront the workers by "the powerful will of a being outside them, who subjects their activity to his purpose" (450). Capitalist "direction" is "purely despotic. As co-operation extends its scale, this despotism develops the forms that are peculiar to it" (Marx 1867, 450). "The rise of management has institutionalized the lack of democratic control over the allocation of resources within, and by, work organization" (Alvesson and Willmott 1996, 12). Marx writes that the capitalist delegate

> the work of direct and constant supervision of the individual workers and groups of workers to a special kind of wage-labourer. An industrial army of workers under the command of a capitalist requires, like a real army, officers (managers) and N.C.O.s (foremen, overseers), who command during the labour process in the name of capital.
>
> (Marx 1867, 450)

The emergence of modern management meant that "the office of manager, the labour of superintendence" could "now be bought on the market" (Marx 1861–1863, 497) so that separation between capital and "industrial managers" emerged (497). Managers thus have a contradictory class position, since they are often highly paid by capital; that is, they are wage workers, and at the same time, they carry out labour that secures capital, namely the labour of controlling the workforce. We already find the concept of the manager in Marx.

The surveillance and control of the labour force are not specific to capitalism. In other class societies such as slave-holding societies, there are also controllers such as slave overseers. Where there are classes in the economy, there are also control and repressive mechanisms.

Erik Olin Wright argues that managers have a privileged, contradictory class position in that they organise the control of workers and are paid relatively high wages to do so:

> managers and supervisors can be viewed as exercising delegated capitalist class powers in so far as they engage in the practices of domination within production. In this sense they can be considered simultaneously in the capitalist class and the working class: they are like capitalists in that they dominate workers; they are like workers in that they are controlled by capitalists and exploited within production. They thus occupy what I have called contradictory locations within class relation [...] to see managers as occupying a privileged position with respect to the process of exploitation which enables them to appropriate part of the social surplus in the form of higher incomes. The specific mechanism through which this appropriation takes place can be referred to as a 'loyalty rent'. [...] [Managers] occupy what might be termed a privileged appropriation location within exploitation relations.
>
> (Wright 2000, 16, 17, 18)

Taylorism as a management method is also an expression of the development of the division of labour. Fredrick Winslow Taylor (1856–1915), the inventor of Taylorism, understood scientific management as the organisation, planning and development of the division of labour in the production process:

> The man in the planning room, whose specialty under scientific management is planning ahead, invariably finds that the work can be done better and more economically by a subdivision of the labor; [...] Perhaps the most prominent single element in modern scientific management is the task idea. The work of every workman is fully planned out by the management at least one day in advance, and each man receives in most cases complete written instructions, describing in detail the task which he is to accomplish, as well as the means to be used in doing the work.
>
> (Taylor 1911/1919, 38–39)

14.2.2 Management and Manager: Etymology and Definition

The word to "manage" goes back to the Latin term *manus*, which means "hand", as well as that something is handled. In Italian, the term *maneggiare* emerged that too means to handle something. Originally, this term meant the handling of horses. Raymond Williams writes that the terms "management", "to manage" and "manager" have been increasingly used in English for the control of economic affairs since the 18th century. Manager as a profession entered the English language and other languages in the 20th century.

> The increasingly general C20 [20th century] sense of management is related to two historical tendencies. First, there was the increasing employment of a body of paid agents to administer increasingly large business concerns. In English these became, with a new emphasis, the managers or the management, as distinct from public agents who were called (from residual reference to the monarchy) *civil servants* or, more generally, the bureaucracy [...] The polite term for semi-public institutions has been *the administration* (though this is also used as a political synonym for *government*). [...] The second historical tendency was in effect a mystification of capitalist economic relationships [...] [management] is an abstract term, and implies abstract and apparently disinterested criteria. [...] The description of negotiations between management and *men* often displaces the real character of negotiations between *employers* and *workers* and further displaces the character of negotiations about relative shares of the labour product to a sense of dispute between the general 'requirements' of a process (the abstract management) and the 'demands' of actual individuals (*men*). The internal laws of a particular capitalist institution or system can then be presented as general, abstract or technical laws, as against the merely selfish desires of individuals. This has powerful ideological effects.
>
> (Williams 1983, 140–141)

Williams thus emphasises that management is, on the one hand, an expression of the real division of labour and class structure of capitalism and, on the other hand, an ideological term that implies a profession that is neutral, attractive, and desirable and helps to mask class conflicts between labour and capital. In this ideology, management is associated with organisation and organising, which are not automatically negative terms.

Based on what has been said so far, we can define a manager as follows: A manager is a paid profession that is part of a company organised on the basis of a division of labour and classes, whose role is to organise, plan, coordinate and control the production process and the workforce so that the partial interests of the owners are enforced. There is a hierarchy and power imbalance between management and the managed/workers so that management as a group is separate from the workers and technocracy (expert group acting based on technological rationality and instrumental reason) makes the central decisions. In many capitalist enterprises, managers have a contradictory, multiple-class position, simultaneously performing wage labour and enforcing the interests of capital through the labour of controlling labour.

Management in capitalist organisations employs management methods that aim to make capital accumulation and commodity production more effective (accumulation of more capital and production of more commodities) and more efficient (increasing productivity so that more commodities, value and profit are produced in less time). Management treats workers as means to an end and reduces them to the status of things, which is why management often refers to humans as "human capital". Management is a form of instrumental action and instrumental reason that has a reifying effect. This means that people are turned into instruments by managers to achieve external ends that do not correspond to their interests. Managers receive higher wages than regular workers, a kind of extra wage that rewards their loyalty and important control function in the production process. This extra pay comes from deductions from the wages of regular workers. A typical phenomenon today is the bonus payments of top managers.

There are many approaches that define management and managers abstractly and independently of the division of labour and class relations. Such understandings are relatively common in management theory and advice literature. Here are some examples:

- "a manager is someone who gets things done with the aid of people and other resources. Management is the activity of getting things done with the aid of people and other resources" (Boddy 2017, 11);
- "Management is what 'managers' do, typically in a business or other organization, or it is a collective term for these managers, when contrasted with other employees ('labour' or 'workers') who don't have the same responsibilities. Managing, in this context, has strong connotations of being in control, of directing things, of designing and implementing systems and processes. [...] The word originates from a Latin term for handling or controlling a horse, and it was gradually extended from controlling horses to controlling weapons, boats, people, and, in Britain, affairs more generally" (Hendry 2013, 1–2). "The defining characteristic of management is responsibility for an organization or organizational unit and for the work of its members" (Hendry 2013, 12);
- "Management is defined as the efficient and effective pursuit of organizational goals" (Kinicki and Breaux Soignet 2022, 4). Management "is defined as (1) the pursuit of organizational goals efficiently and effectively by (2) integrating the work of people through (3) planning, organizing, leading, and controlling the organization's resources" (Kinicki and Breaux Soignet 2022, 5);
- "Managers get things done by coordinating and motivating other people" (Daft 2022, 7).[1]

In these definitions, managers and management have to do with getting things done, organisation, taking responsibility, directing things, and designing processes. Understood in such a broad way, we are all always constantly managing something in our lives, which means all humans in one way or another are managers. Inflating the meaning of the terms managers and management, however, makes them meaningless. By defining managers and management as an anthropological feature of humanity and society, management theorists create the impression that both are natural features of human existence. They also imply that management as we know it today (as part of class relations and capitalist organisations) and managerialist relations and organisations are essential and natural features of all societies. Such definitions therefore ideologically naturalise capitalism. They lack an understanding of the historical character of managers and management. There is a difference between organisers and organisation on the one hand and managers and management on the other hand.

Marx calls such ideological naturalisations of historical phenomena fetishism. Fetishism is an aesthetic and ideology in which social relations disappear behind things and certain social phenomena are reified, that is declared to be things or deemed to be things.

> These formulas, which bear the unmistakable stamp of belonging to a social formation in which the process of production has mastery over man, instead of the opposite, appear to the political economists' bourgeois consciousness to be as much a self-evident and nature-imposed necessity as productive labour itself.
>
> (Marx 1867, 174–175)

Marx criticises that some economists and philosophers define and analyse concepts like capital, commodity, exchange, division of labour as natural and eternal necessities. Management and managers are parts of these concepts that belong to class societies and capitalism as social formations, and are often fetishised. Management gurus, managers, neoliberals and management theorists often fetishise management. "[They] mystify, more or less consciously, the power relations that shape the formation and organization of management" (Alvesson and Willmott 1996, 38).

14.2.3 *CEOs in Transnational Digital Corporations*

It is a not infrequent practice in large shareholding companies that managers are partly rewarded with stock options and that founders who are current or former CEOs are major shareholders. The next table shows some examples from the digital technology industry (see Table 14.1).

Google and Facebook are examples of tech companies where the founders also act(ed) as CEOs and control the majority of the shares and voting rights. At Alphabet/Google, Sundar Pichai has been CEO since 2015.

Table 14.1 Top managers and founders of large digital corporations and their ownership power and voting power

Company	Founder	CEO in 2022	Largest Owners of Common Stock (% of the Stock Owned)	Voting Power Share (%)
Amazon	Jeff Bezos	Andrew Jassy (CEO), Jeff Bezos (Executive Chairman)	Bezos: 12.7% Vanguard Group: 6.6% BlackRock: 5.7%	Bezos: 12.7% Vanguard Group: 6.6% BlackRock: 5.7%
Apple	Steve Jobs, Steve Wozniak, Ronald Wayne	Tim Cook	Vanguard Group: 7.7% BlackRock: 6.5% Berkshire Hathaway/ Warren E. Buffet: 5.6% Cook: 0.02%	Vanguard Group: 7.7% BlackRock: 6.5% Berkshire Hathaway/ Warren E. Buffet: 5.6% Cook: 0.02%
Alphabet/ Google	Larry Page, Sergey Brin	Sundar Pichai	Class B stock: Page: 43.9%, Brin: 41.8%	Page: 26.2%, Brin: 24.9%
Microsoft	Bill Gates, Paul Allen	Satya Nadella	Vanguard Group: 8.2% BlackRock: 6.9%	Vanguard Group: 8.2% BlackRock: 6.9%
Alibaba	Jack Ma	Daniel Zhang	Softbank: 23.9%	Softbank: 23.9%
Meta Platforms/ Facebook	Mark Zuckerberg, Eduardo Saverin	Mark Zuckerberg	Class B stock: Zuckerberg: 88.7%	Zuckerberg: 56.9%

Data source: Company Proxy Statements 2022 [Alibaba: 2022 Annual Report].

Before that, Larry Page, who founded Google together with Sergey Brin, was
the company's CEO from 2011 to 2015. Pichai had little share ownership
and no voting rights at Alphabet/Google at least until 2022. His salary was
$6,322,599 in the fiscal year 2021. He is a classic highly paid top manager
who is not an owner but a wage earner responsible for controlling and organising the work. Mark Zuckerberg, on the contrary, is an example of a
company founder who is both the main owner and the top manager (CEO,
executive director), that is both a capitalist and a manager. In other companies such as Google or Microsoft, founders who acted as top managers have
given up the role of the CEO to other people. The examples in the table also

illustrate that investment firms such as Vanguard Group, BlackRock, and SoftBank have large ownership stakes in tech companies. This circumstance illustrates the coupling of financial capital and digital capital.

14.2.4 Self-managed Enterprises

Some companies are organised in a non-capitalist way, that is, do not make a profit. If they are workers' co-operatives, also known as co-operative enterprises, co-operatives, self-managed enterprises or workers' co-operatives, the means of production and the companies are collectively owned by the workers and there are democratic decision-making structures. The essential decisions are made collectively by all the workers. There is no management in self-managed enterprises, but self-organisation and self-management. "Self-management" indicates that in that the alienated, heteronomous control of the organisation in enterprises is removed and democratic decision-making structures are created in which the producers jointly determine how decisions are made. Self-management is not a profession like that of a manager; therefore, there is also no profession of a self-manager. Self-management is not a form of management because the division of labour and undemocratic decision-making are intrinsic parts of management.

When it comes to complex organisations, the delegation of organisational work often becomes necessary in self-managed workplaces, which necessitates the democratic selection and legitimisation of organisers. In such cases, it is crucial that workers collectively make democratic decisions about their own organisational structures. This is a good precondition for ensuring that decision-making power does not become independent from the workers as in capitalist enterprises.

However, there is always the danger that organisers become managers, that is people who have undemocratic decision-making power over what goes on in the company and act alone or as a small group to push through partial interests against the interests of the workforce.

Collective ownership of enterprises, such as in the form of public ownership or self-management, is not automatically a guarantee of democratic decision-making structures. Even within collective ownership structures, undemocratic management structures can be created, with highly asymmetric decision-making power and a strong unequal distribution of wages.

Marx (1894) argues that in the co-operative factory, "the antithetical character of the supervisory work disappears, since the manager is paid by the workers instead of representing capital in opposition to them" (512). In co-operatives, "the opposition between capital and labour is abolished [...], even if at first only in the form that the workers in association become their own capitalist, i.e. they use the means of production to valorize their own labour" (Marx 1894, 571). Marx considers the sublation of management as one of the advantages of co-operatives. He writes that the co-operative factories show that modern production can work without "a class of masters employing a class of hands" (Marx 1864, 11) and that "associated labour" shows that "to bear fruit, the means of labour need not be monopolised as a means of dominion over, and of extortion against, the labouring man himself" (Marx 1864, 11).

The economy does not determine politics. Democratic decision-making structures do not automatically derive from democratic property structures. Nevertheless, the democratisation of ownership also aids and makes easier the democratisation of the Political Economy, including decision-making power. However, there is no guarantee against sliding into managerialism.

In this section, we have learned some basics of management. It should have become clear what management is and how it came into being. In the next section, we will look at what media management is all about.

14.3 What Is Media Management?

Media management is not only a professional category in the media industry, which includes managers in media companies, but also an academic subfield of Media and Communication Studies, which includes degree programmes, modules, publications, conferences.

> In a media-saturated world where cultural production and consumption dominate everyday life, it is not surprising schools, departments, programs, and courses in information science, (tele-)communication, journalism, and (digital) media studies attract more students every year. [...] The vast majority of undergraduate and graduate students majoring in these disciplines want to either work in media industries, manage media companies, or study and understand how the industry and its creative process work.
>
> (Deuze and Steward 2011, 2)

Let's look at some characterisations of media management:

- "Media management means on the one hand the management of media as their conscious design and on the other hand the management of media companies. [...] Media are at the same time economic goods and cultural goods, media enterprises thus at the same time business units and cultural actors. The resulting areas of tension are art versus commerce, basic supply versus elite, information versus entertainment"[2] (Scholz 2006, 13);
- "Within the framework of Media Economics, two basic currents can currently be identified: On the one hand, the more Political Economy oriented Media Economics (sometimes also referred to as 'Media Economy' and 'Media Economy Studies'), and on the other hand, the more Business Studies-oriented Media Management"[3] (Scholz 2006, 33);

- "Media management encompasses all the goal-oriented activities of planning, organization, and control within the framework of the creation and distribution of information or entertainment content in media enterprises" (Wirtz 2020, 12);
- Media management must take into account the complex factors of the media. These include

> content, process, people, technology, and all other variables – not in the least including the implicit and unconscious aspects of organizational life such as beliefs, values, and emotions that can have a tremendous influence on planning and behavior. Managing media work is necessarily made up of both material and immaterial factors, which must be considered in conjunction. In other words, a key approach to media management is focusing on the many resources (both human and nonhuman) that combine to form the source of all media action.
>
> (Deuze and Steward 2011, 3)

Media management as a profession has two contexts of application. On the one hand, it has to do with the management of media organisations, that is companies in the media industry that organise the production, distribution, and consumption of information. On the other hand, it has to do with the management of media in companies in general. Managing a digital marketing department in a car company is just as much a part of the field of media management as managing a book publishing house or a film production company. Media management is therefore about organising, commanding, and controlling the media workers and the resources that exist in media companies and media departments. Media management is not only a job title in business, but also the name of a field of analysis that deals with the analysis of media management ("Media Management").

Scholz (2006, 36) argues that media management includes the management of media in companies and the management of media companies. In Media Management, one must be knowledgeable of Media Studies, Media History, Media Law, Media Policy, Media Technology, Media Economics, Media Ethics, Media Theory, and Media Psychology as contexts.

Deuze and Steward (2011, 5–9) write that while media managers operate at the micro-level of media companies, they also need to understand aspects of the meso- and macro-economy. They, therefore, identify three relevant levels of media management (Deuze and Steward 2011, 5–9). It should be noted that the meso-level is understood as the organisational level. In many approaches, however, organisations are part of the micro-level, that is business management. For Deuze and Steward, the institutional level of media markets is part of the macro-level.

1 **The micro-level of media management:**
   the level of individuals, interpersonal communication/workplace communication, social relationships at work, individual skills, professional identities, job satisfaction, work-life balance, new technologies and individual skills, etc.;

2 **The meso-level of media management:**
   the organisational level, organisational methods and techniques: Fordist management methods, participatory management, etc.; organisational culture: philosophy, organisational strategy, values/ethos, Corporate Social Responsibility, workplace culture, image/reputation/public relations (PR), organisational policy, management style, change of organisations through new technologies, etc.

3 **The macro-level of media management:**
   the economy as a totality, the world economy, global media organisations, the international division of labour, international markets for goods and labour, the industry level, competition structures, media concentration, political regulation of the economy, changes in the world economy due to new technologies.

Mierzejewska (2011) identifies some factors of media management:

- New technologies are often linked to changes in markets, skills, business models, audience and user needs and demands, media types, media organisation, etc.;
- Transnational media organisations;
- Cultural challenges: There are several cultures in an organisation that need to be reconciled;
- Leadership: Media work is creative labour and therefore requires a special leadership style.

Media organisations are both economic and cultural in nature. Media management is therefore always confronted with several aspects at the same time. These include technology/content, production/distribution/consumption (prosumption), human aspects/physical aspects, financial management/creativity management, conscious processes/unconscious processes, and individual/social aspects.

Charles Brown (2016) argues for critical media management, which means that those who study, work with and manage media should critically engage with the social, organisational, individual and technological aspects of media. He argues that Critical Management Studies, that is the critical analysis of management, should be combined with media management analysis to form

Critical Media Management. Such an analysis should focus on the activities of media managers and media workers, the technologies used, and media and organisational frameworks in the context of societal environmental factors (see Brown 2016, 95).

> Perhaps the primary focus of media management research is the respective and interdependent organisation and the managers and media workers within that organisation. A non-reductionist approach recognises that such organisations and workers are influenced by external environmental factors and also their own values and further that there are contradictions as well as overlapping interests. In the critical view, these are not fixed and immutable but rather develop over time through reflexive interaction (hence the porous boundaries delineating these entities in the diagram). These agents, in turn, use generic tools derived from management science and other tools and techniques that are specific to particular disciplines (e.g. sociology, anthropology, political science, audience studies, production studies, etc.).
>
> (Brown 2016, 96)

Media management, media work and media organisations, which are situated at the micro-level of the economy, can only be properly understood if they are situated in the context of the institutions of the economy and society, as well as the structures, dynamics, contradictions, practices, power relations and struggles of society, that is society as a totality. The Business Studies–oriented analysis of media management and media organisations often forgets political economy and is therefore often reductionist, affirmative and instrumental. The analysis of media management, media work and media organisations can only operate adequately if they are seen as aspects of the Political Economy of Media and Communication.

Having looked at the basics of media management, we will now look at different management methods and discuss what role they play in the information sector today.

14.4 Fordist-Taylorist and post-Fordist Management

14.4.1 Fordism and Taylorism

Taylorism is a management method that goes back to Fredrick Winslow Taylor (1856–1915) and was first used in the car factories of Henry Ford (1863–1947). Taylorism is an important aspect of the organisation of labour in the Fordist production model that is based on mass production and mass consumption.

Assembly line labour is a classic application of Taylorism. Carry out Exercise 14.1 (in the exercise section at the end of this chapter). You will watch a scene from Charlie Chaplin's film *Modern Times,* which is about assembly line labour and a critique of Taylorism. *Modern Times* is a satire of the Taylorist organisation of labour and its problems.

Taylorism was the dominant scientific-technical way of organising work in Fordism. Fordism as a regime of capital accumulation existed from the beginning of the 20th century until the 1970s. It has not ceased to exist today, but capitalism has been extended to include a flexible accumulation regime and new forms of management.

Fordism is characterised, among other things, by industrial mass production, semi-skilled labour, the standardisation of work on the assembly line, hierarchies, control, relatively high wages, strong trade unions, Taylorism, the rationalisation of production, large company complexes, the combination of mass production and mass consumption, consumer culture, consumer ideology, the culture industry, and the standardisation of products.

In Fordism, entrepreneurs expected increasing profits through a positive cycle of Fordism: Higher productivity through Taylorist methods → Rising wages → More demand → Higher profits → More investments → Higher productivity through Taylorist methods → Rising wages → More demand → Higher profits → ...

Fordism was coupled in many countries with the formation of Keynesian welfare states that featured state intervention in the economy, the strengthening of workers' rights and the introduction of welfare state services and insurance benefits.

From the mid-1960s, Fordism was confronted with problems. These included international competition, limits to the central planning of production, the rise in labour costs, and the slowdown in productivity growth.

Taylor was a mechanical engineer. He asked himself how industrial efficiency could be improved and developed the method of scientific management, which he documented in his book *The Principles of Scientific Management* (Taylor 1911/1919).

Taylorism sees itself as a science that collects, records, measures, and tabulates the knowledge of the workforce in order to identify the most efficient and rational way to organise production.

> The managers assume, for instance, the burden of gathering together all of the traditional knowledge which in the past has been possessed by the workmen and then of classifying, tabulating, and reducing this knowledge to rules, laws, and formulae which are immensely helpful to the workmen in doing their daily work.
>
> (Taylor 1911/1919, 36)

Taylorism is a management method, that is a specific way of dividing labour between management and workers and separating planning and executing activities:

> Thus all of the planning which under the old system was done by the workman, as a result of his personal experience, must of necessity under the new system be done by the management in accordance with the laws of the science; because even if the workman was well suited to the

development and use of scientific data, it would be physically impossible for him to work at his machine and at a desk at the same time. It is also clear that in most cases one type of man is needed to plan ahead and an entirely different type to execute the work.

(Taylor 1911/1919, 38)

In Taylorism as a method, there are five steps of scientific management: (1) Selection, (2) Analysis, (3) Comparison of the Sequence of Movements, (4) Elimination, and (5) Optimisation.

1 **Selection:**
"*First.* Find, say, 10 or 15 different men (preferably in as many separate establishments and different parts of the country) who are especially skilful in doing the particular work to be analysed" (Taylor 1911/1919, 117).
2 **Analysis:**
"*Second.* Study the exact series of elementary operations or motions which each of these men uses in doing the work which is being investigated, as well as the implements each man uses" (Taylor 1911/1919, 117).
3 **Comparison of the sequence of movements:**
"*Third.* Study with a stop-watch the time required to make each of these elementary movements and then select the quickest way of doing each element of the work" (Taylor 1911/1919, 117).
4 **Elimination:**
"*Fourth.* Eliminate all false movements, slow movements, and useless movements" (Taylor 1911/1919, 117).
5 **Optimisation:**

> *Fifth.* After doing away with all unnecessary movements, collect into one series the quickest and best movements as well as the best implements. This one new method, involving that series of motions which can be made quickest and best, is then substituted in place of the ten or fifteen inferior series which were formerly in use. This best method becomes standard, and remains standard, to be taught first to the teachers (or functional foremen) and by them to every workman in the establishment until it is superseded by a quicker and better series of movements. In this simple way one element after another of the science is developed.
>
> (Taylor 1911/1919, 117–118)

An example of Taylorism was the Bethlehem Steel Corporation, where the science of shovelling was applied. There were different sizes of shovels for different materials. It was measured how long it takes to shovel a certain amount of a certain material with different types of shovels. Workers were given tasks on a piece of paper instead of waiting for their supervisor/foreman to show them what to do on a given day. The work tasks were planned in advance. Frank B. Gilbreth was a construction entrepreneur and consultant who conducted time and motion studies in his business as part of the science of bricklaying. The number of steps required to lay a brick was reduced.

Marx analysed different methods that companies use to produce more value, commodities and profit. One is the method of relative surplus value production where we find

> an alteration in the labour process of such a kind as to shorten the labour-time socially necessary for the production of a commodity, and to endow a given quantity of labour with the power of producing a greater quantity of use-value.
>
> (Marx 1867, 431)

Taylorism is a management method used for the relative production of surplus value. By increasing the speed of work, more commodities are to be produced in less time; that is, the productivity of labour is to be increased.

The main criticism of Taylorism is that it promotes the alienation of labour and leads to monotony through the strenuous repetition of the same movements, as well as to the de-skilling of workers. This critique was formulated by Harry Braverman (1974), among others. Braverman created Labour Process Theory. He argues that Taylorism is inhuman, dehumanises production and de-qualifies people. Workers are treated like machines: "The physical processes of production are now carried out more or less blindly [...] The production units operate like a hand, watched, corrected and controlled by a distant brain" (Braverman 1974/1998, 125). Taylorism leads to the "*progressive alienation* of *the process* of *production* from the worker" (Braverman 1974, 58).

Taylorism was created for classic assembly line production in Fordism, but it still exists today in various forms. At McDonald's, burgers are produced as if on an assembly line. Assembly line labour is still relevant today, for example in the assembly of computer hardware in companies like Foxconn. In Chapter 10, the company was discussed as an example of digital labour. At Foxconn, Taylorist methods are used. Military drill, surveillance and punishment are used to try to get workers to work faster and faster, assembling more and more iPhones and other technologies per day. Workers are dehumanised and treated like machines.

> In order to maximize productivity, workers at Foxconn are made to work like machines. They have to work continuously for more than 10 hours a day. They cannot stop for a second. 'I think we are even faster than machines', a worker at the Longhua campus pointed out.
>
> (SACOM 2010, 10)

Taylorism is therefore not dead today, but very much alive. However, management, that is the control of workers, has been extended by new methods, which are also discussed under the term postmodern management.

14.4.2 Post-Fordist Management

Google's offices do not look like traditional workplaces. There are play-grounds, sports fields, restaurants, relaxation areas, entertainment options, lectures by intellectuals, etc. At Google, the boundaries between workplace and home, labour time and leisure time, labour and play (playbour: play and labour), production and consumption, etc. are blurred. Work at Google is characterised by a (pseudo) fun culture and freebies at work (food, sports, culture, education, socialisation, entertainment).

Conduct Exercise 14.2 (at the end of this chapter). It is about working at Google. The exercise illustrates that Google uses new management methods that differ from Taylorism. Employees' lives should be made pleasant so that they spend as much time as possible at the company. Management hopes that this will make people work more and more productively overall. Such strategies are also called post-Fordist management methods.

We have already learned about the method of relative surplus value production. Another method of surplus value production that Marx analyses is absolute surplus value production. "I call that surplus-value which is produced by the lengthening of the working day, *absolute surplus-value*" (Marx 1867, 432). Absolute surplus value production means the "prolongation of the working day beyond the point at which the worker would have produced an exact equivalent for the value of his labour-power" (Marx 1867, 645). The working day consists of the part in which workers produce the equivalent of their wages, necessary labour time, and surplus labour time, the part of the working day in which they work unpaid for capital and produce surplus value from which profit is made. The management strategy at Google is to create incentives for workers to spend as much time as possible in the company. Some of this time is then free time, but overall management hopes to increase surplus labour time by having employees spend more time on their actual work activity. Play labour (playbour) at Google is thus a strategy of absolute surplus value production, which aims to extend the working day and thus surplus labour time in absolute terms. If workers feel good in the company, their productivity may also increase by producing more in less time. Play labour can therefore also have the effect of relative surplus value production.

But how are the workers who are exposed to this management strategy of play labour as absolute surplus value production doing at Google? For the book *Social Media: A Critical Introduction*, I conducted an empirical analysis of posts by Google workers about their working conditions on Glassdoor.com and Reddit. I filtered out all posts that discussed working hours as a topic.

For the first English-language edition of the book, I was able to identify 76 such postings from 2008 to 2012 (Fuchs 2014, 141–146); for the third English-language edition, published as the second German-language edition, I found 46 relevant postings from 2019 (Fuchs 2021a, 120–124; 2021b, 197–202).

Complaints about a lack of work-life balance at Google were found in 58 out of 76 posts (76%) and 33 out of 46 posts (72%) respectively. Here are some sample statements (Fuchs 2021a, 121–122; 2021b, 197–198):

"Google is evil, long hours sometimes".

"Was very hard work that would sometimes take weekends".

"Lack of free time".

"no work-life balance".

"terrible work/life balance".

"Hours – you are expected to give everything to the company; little time for a personal life".

"Very stressing job and much overtime".

"Heavy workload. Staying at the office until the late hours just trying to get work done".

"Stop burying people in work and burning out engineers".

"Work/life balance is nearly non-existent and, as a result, there are increasing levels of burnout within the organization".

"Prepare to work all day and night long".

Between 2008 and 2019, working conditions at Google have not changed. Workers like the content of their work, and the perks like free food. They hate the long hours and the lack of work-life balance. In Fordism, labour was often perceived as alienating, but there was at least more separation of paid labour time and free time. If you work at Google, your whole life is Google: Google is labour. Google is leisure. Google is lifetime, labour time and leisure time. Google workers do not work to live, but they live to work for Google. They are mostly well-paid, some of them even rich, but at the same time, they are socially poor. Material wealth goes hand in hand with social poverty at Google. If the company where one works sucks up the lives of the employees, this is the end of the good life. Life as labour is a damaged life.

Next, conduct Exercise 14.3 (at the end of this chapter). In one of the articles you read as part of this exercise, a Google employee confirms the social poverty of working life at Google:

You do have free food available all the time, and many cafes, gyms, laundry rooms, etc. but over time as you start using all these perks (because it's just too convenient) you spend more and more of your time at the office. You start making the same choices day in and day out. You hang out more and more with the same people you work with.

(Edwards 2016)

The *New York Times* article you also read in Exercise 14.3 was written by the leaders of the Alphabet Workers Union (AWU), a union of Google workers (Koul and Shaw 2021). In the video you watch in the exercise, an AWU member talks about why a union was formed at Google.

For a long time, trade unions were hardly represented in the digital industry. This has to do with the fact that many software engineers have high salaries and often see themselves as entrepreneurs and inventors rather than workers. They thus form a kind of digital labour aristocracy. However, the real conditions in the tech sector have highlighted the power imbalance between digital capital and digital labour, which over time has led to greater unionisation in this industry. The new management methods that emphasise fun, participation, and co-operation are predominantly ideologies that do not change the real power of management and owners and lead to overwork for workers, which translates into a lack of work-life balance. Companies like Google present themselves as worker-friendly and progressive, but in reality, labour in these companies is characterised by a high degree of exploitation. So-called participative management, which also postulates the principle of "Do what you love", presents itself as humanisation and democratisation of (digital) labour, but is nothing more than an intensification and extensification of exploitation, that is an increase in unpaid labour time through absolute and relative surplus value production. A true humanisation and democratisation of companies like Google require their transformation into self-managed enterprises that are democratically administered by the employees and users and become their common property.

Management at Google is an expression of the post-Fordist organisation of work. Post-Fordist production is characterised by the following features, among others (Amin 1994; Harvey 1990):

- Post-Taylorist labour organisation: flexible, decentralised, global production;
- Use of information and communication technologies to organise production;
- Globalisation of production;
- Flexible specialisation: personalised and customised goods;
- Niche markets, niche tastes;
- Branding;
- Increase in the importance of knowledge work and services;
- Individualisation, pluralisation of lifestyles;
- Integration of leisure and labour, play and labour, fun and seriousness;
- Shaping of work and life by neoliberalism (privatisation, monetarisation, individual responsibility instead of collective responsibility, new management methods of extending working hours).

The term post-Fordism is unsatisfactory because it only implies that the organisation of labour and accumulation, as well as management methods, have changed; that is, there are forms that emerged chronologically after the Fordist-Taylorist organisation of labour (see Jessop 1992; Lipietz 1987, 2001), which does not mean the end of Taylorism but its transformation. David Harvey (1990) has aptly characterised post-Fordism as a flexible accumulation regime:

> *Flexible accumulation*, as I shall tentatively call it, is marked by a direct confrontation with the rigidities of Fordism. It rests on flexibility with respect to labour processes, labour markets, products, and patterns of consumption. It is characterized by the emergence of entirely new sectors of production, new ways of providing financial services, new markets, and, above all, greatly intensified rates of commercial, techno-logical, and organizational innovation. [...] It has also entailed a new round of what I shall call 'time-space compression' [...] in the capitalist world – the time horizons of both private and public decision-making have shrunk, while satellite communication and declining transport costs have made it increasingly possible to spread those decisions imme-diately over an ever wider and variegated space. These enhanced pow-ers of flexibility and mobility have allowed employers to exert stronger pressures of labour control.
>
> (Harvey 1990, 147)

In response to economic crises, companies and policymakers in many coun-tries have promoted innovation in digital technologies, as well as cultural labour and digital labour since the 1970s. Creativity and digital innovations are seen as a source of competitive advantage. The rise of the computer and the Internet in production and knowledge labour since the 1970s is thus the consequence of the transition to a flexible accumulation regime in the wake of the crisis of Fordism.

In their book *The New Spirit of Capitalism*, the two French sociologists Luc Boltanski and Ève Chiapello (2005) formulated a critique of postmodern management.

> In many respects, we are living today in a situation that is the reverse of the late 1960s and early 1970s. Then capitalism was experiencing a fall in growth and profitability bound up, at least according to Regulation-ist analyses, with a slowdown in productivity gains that was associated with a continuous increase in real wages proceeding at the same pace as before. Critique, for its part, was at its zenith, as demonstrated by the events of May 1968, which combined a social critique of a fairly classi-cal Marxist stamp with demands of a very different kind, appealing to creativity, pleasure, the power of the imagination, to a liberation affect-ing every dimension of existence, to the destruction of the 'consumer society', and so on.
>
> (Boltanski and Chiapello 2005, xxxv)

The 1968 student movement made "demands for autonomy and self-management, and the promise of an unbounded liberation of human creativity" (170). These moral values are realised in cultural labour today, but at the price of inequalities, lack of work-life balance, stress, insecurity, etc. Boltanski and Chiapello argue that the new management methods organise labour on a project basis:

> In the new world, anything is possible, since creativity, reactivity and flexibility are the new watchwords. Now no one is restricted by belonging to a department or wholly subject to the boss's authority, for all boundaries may be transgressed through the power of projects.
>
> (90)

The two authors criticise that while the new forms of management promote creativity and participation, misusing the language of the '68 movement, the real world of labour leads to overwork, precariousness, lack of work-life balance, inequalities, etc.

Boltanski and Chiapello distinguish between the artistic critique and the social critique. The first criticises a lack of autonomy, creativity, and authenticity and calls for liberation from alienation. Social critique is a critique of inequalities and individualism. It "denounces poverty and exploitation" (346). Management and companies have taken the artistic critique seriously and used it for their own purposes. There is now more autonomy and creativity of labour, but less justice in companies and in society.

Boltanski and Chiapello explain what is problematic about Taylorism on the one hand and post-Fordist management on the other:

> The Taylorization of work does indeed consist in treating human beings like machines. But precisely because they pertain to an automation of human beings, the rudimentary character of the methods employed does not allow the more human properties of human beings – their emotions, their moral sense, their honour, their inventive capacity – to be placed directly in the service of the pursuit of profit. Conversely, the new mechanisms, which demand greater commitment and rely on a more sophisticated ergonomics, integrating the contributions of post-behaviourist psychology and the cognitive sciences, precisely because they are more humane in a way, also penetrate more deeply into people's inner selves – people are expected to 'give' themselves to their work – and facilitate and instrumentalization of human beings in their most specifically human dimensions.
>
> (98)

Knowledge labour and social work are information labour and affective labour. They include a focus on emotions, morals, intellectual skills, etc. Such labour is about creating emotional responses in other people. Affective work plays a role in education, nursing, advertising/PR, psychotherapy, personal services with interpersonal contact, influencers on social media, social media managers, etc. Boltanski and Chiapello criticise that new management methods involve workers too much emotionally and socially in the work and thus overburden them.

Post-Fordist management promotes unstable and insecure labour and leads to a "truncated version of humanity – the freedom to align oneself with the organisational machine or to be punished" (Grey 2021, 91). The "post-bureaucratic variant of culture management" tries to "harness human agency without even offering stable employment in return" (Grey 2021, 91).

Based on the discussion of Fordism, Taylorism and post-Fordism, in the next section, we want to address the question of whether or not culture, media, and creativity can be managed.

14.5 The Management of Culture, Media, and Creativity

14.5.1 Creativity

The literature addresses the question of whether and how creative work can be managed (Bilton 2011; Bilton and Cummings 2014; Dwyer 2016; Rimscha and Siegert 2015, chapter 10). However, this first raises the question of what creativity is.

Let us look at some definitions of the concept of creativity:

- "I will use the word 'creativity' – and the phrase 'everyday creativity' [...] in relation to the activities of making which are rewarding to oneself and to others" (Gauntlett 2011, 13);
- "Creativity is understood as the genesis of the idea, innovation as the economic utilisation of the idea"[4] (von Rimscha and Siegert 2015, 161);
- For Richard Sennett, creativity has to do with craft and craftsmanship: The notion of craftsmanship refers to

> an enduring, basic human impulse, the desire to do a job well for its own sake. Craftsmanship cuts a far wider swath than skilled manual labor; it serves the computer programmer, the doctor, and the artist; parenting improves when it is practiced as a skilled craft, as does citizenship. In all these domains, craftsmanship focuses on objective standards, on the thing in itself. [...] Every good craftsman conducts a dialogue between concrete practices and thinking; this dialogue evolves into sustaining habits, and these habits establish a rhythm between problem solving and problem finding. The relation between hand and head appears in domains seemingly as different as brick-laying, cooking, designing a playground, or playing the cello – but all these practices can misfire or fail to ripen. There is nothing inevitable about becoming skilled, just as there is nothing mindlessly mechanical about technique itself;
>
> (Sennett 2008, 9)

- Creativity means "a set of loose and tight processes, personal qualities and product attributes which lead to new and valuable outcomes" (Bilton and Cummings 2014, 5).

Creativity produces something new. It is a person's reflective action that guides their practical action that produces something new. In public discourse, there is often reference to "creative labour" or the "creative industries". For example, Hesmondhalgh and Baker (2011) define creative labour in their book *Creative Labour* as "those jobs, centred on the activity of symbol-making, which are to be found in large numbers in the cultural industries" (9). By the cultural industries, the authors mean "'the arts' (painting, sculpture and literature and so on) but more prominently [...] the television, film, music and publishing businesses, [...] the various institutions known as 'the media'" (2). Essentially, then, this definition is about artistic activities. Hesmondhalgh and Baker's definition is comparable to that of Richard Florida. Florida defines creative workers in his book *The Rise of the Creative Class* as "people in science and engineering, architecture and design, education, arts, music, and entertainment whose economic function is to create new ideas, new technology, and new creative content" (Florida 2012, 8).

Both definitions are based on snobbery and elitism that sees artists as the better and more important workers and other work as uncreative and therefore simplistic and unimaginative.

In all work, symbols are produced through reflection and thereby ideas are generated. All work is based on a dialectic of mind and body. In all work, the human being must reflect on what result is to be produced. The result is therefore mentally anticipated and planned. Human beings' creativity thus consists of the fact that they mentally anticipate their own creations. Karl Marx already pointed this out when he explained the difference between humans and animals:

> A spider conducts operations which resemble those of the weaver, and a bee would put many a human architect to shame by the construction of its honeycomb cells. But what distinguishes the worst architect from the best of bees is that the architect builds the cell in his mind before he constructs it in wax. At the end of every labour process, a result emerges which had already been conceived by the worker at the beginning, hence already existed ideally.
>
> (Marx 1867, 284)

All work is creative in a certain sense because it produces something new. However, there is a difference between work that is primarily physically oriented and produces physical products and primarily intellectual work that produces ideas. One can therefore distinguish between physical work on the one hand and mental work on the other. Creativity is needed in both. Mental work is also called information work, knowledge work, intellectual work or cultural work.

14.5.2 *Cultural and Media Management as a Destructive Force:*
From Management to Self-Management

Mental activity is often spontaneous, open, unpredictable, uncontrollable, unplannable, and unpredictable. Management, on the contrary, is seen as more planning, closed, calculating, controlling and predictive. The question of whether knowledge work can and should be managed is therefore inevitably contradictory and linked to the question of whether management does not lead to the killing of initiative, spontaneity, and creative power. "Conventional management practices 'kill' creativity [...] because they inhibit employees' intrinsic motivation to work creatively" (Dwyer 2016, 348). Cultural activity "is tied to individuals whose input can and should be controlled and coordinated only to a limited extent, because a considerable amount of free space is necessary for the creative development of content"[5] (von Rimscha and Siegert 2015, 157).

Capitalism is ultimately always about the accumulation of capital and the generation of profit. In the culture industry, the openness, spontaneity and unpredictability of cultural activity must be subjugated to plans and instrumental rationality imposed by management. Managerialism and the attempt to control and plan cultural work, to manage it, however, inhibit the freedom of the activity and automatically mean a certain form of alienation. Cultural work, therefore, functions best when it is not subsumed under capital, but when cultural workers are active and free of capital constraints.

Managerialism is the control of an organisation and the work that takes place in it. Managerialism is centralistic and hierarchical. It restricts autonomy and freedom. It is an overmanagement of organisations and individuals.

> Managerialism combines management knowledge and ideology to establish itself systemically in organisations and society while depriving owners, employees (organisational-economical) and civil society (social-political) of all decision-making powers. Managerialism justifies the application of managerial techniques to all areas of society on the grounds of superior ideology, expert training, and the exclusive possession of managerial knowledge necessary to efficiently run corporations and societies.
>
> (Klikauer 2015, 1105)

Managerialism and ultimately all management stand in the Taylorist tradition.

The power-based nature inherent in management and the division of labour in which managers are not involved in the difficult everyday labour in the company destroy innovation potentials in knowledge-producing and other organisations. All it takes is one wrong person in a management position to destroy an entire organisation or suborganisation. Evaluitis, that is management's urge for permanent evaluations, detailed and strict plans, Key

Performance Indicators (KPIs), unrealistic targets, a bureaucratic, formalistic reporting culture, destroys knowledge-based organisations. Realistic goals that can be achieved motivate better than unrealistic and excessive goals that produce stress. Good organisers are themselves exemplary workers who are respected by others for their work, help others, and are involved in everyday work.

Good organisational work takes care of a good context in which knowledge workers can operate. A thriving garden in which many people garden together, grow new seeds and tend to existing plants is a good metaphor for good organisational work. Management, in contrast, is always a kind of steamroller that more or less subtly turns the garden into a concrete desert.

Through user-generated content, social media, and digitalisation, users and consumers have become potential and real cultural producers of content. This has made it more difficult to organise media work and thereby earn a living that ensures survival.

There is a classical separation between artists and management. Today, however, many artists and knowledge workers are freelancers, that is one-person businesses. Freelancers are workers and entrepreneurs, labourers, and managers at the same time. They are confronted with the contradiction that they want to realise themselves and at the same time must alienate themselves through management of the self. Management is now part of the work in the culture industry. This is expressed, for example, in the fact that cultural workers have profiles on social media to be in contact with consumers. They manage themselves.

Freelance cultural workers often work in a very self-determined way, but at the same time, they are often precarious workers. The risks of isolation of cultural workers can be minimised through trade union organisation and the organisation of cultural production in the form of self-managed enterprises and cultural co-operatives (see Discussion in Chapter 9). Here, management is replaced by self-management.

14.5 Conclusion

This chapter focused on the Political Economy and foundations of Media Management. We now want to summarise some key findings.

Finding 1: Definition of Managers and Management

Based on what has been said so far, we can define a manager as follows: A manager is a paid profession that is part of a company organised on the basis of a division of labour and classes, whose role is to organise, plan, co-ordinate and control the production process and the workforce so that the partial interests of the owners are enforced. There is a hierarchy and power imbalance between management and the managed/workers so that management as a group is separate from the workers and technocracy (expert group acting on the basis of technological rationality and instrumental reason) makes the central decisions. In many capitalist enterprises, managers have a contradictory multiple-class position, simultaneously performing wage labour and enforcing the interests of capital through the labour of controlling labour.

Management in capitalist organisations employs management methods that aim to make capital accumulation and commodity production more effective (accumulation of more capital and production of more commodities) and more efficient (increasing productivity so that more commodities, value and profit are produced in less time). Management treats workers as means to an end and reduces them to the status of things, which is why management often refers to humans as "human capital". Management is a form of instrumental action and instrumental reason that has a reifying effect. This means that people are turned into instruments by managers to achieve external ends that do not correspond to their interests. Managers receive higher wages than regular workers, a kind of extra wage that rewards their loyalty and important control function in the production process. This extra pay comes from deductions from the wages of regular workers. A typical phenomenon today is the bonus payments of top managers.

Finding 2: Media Management as a Profession and Field of Analysis

Media management as a profession has two contexts of application. On the one hand, it has to do with the management of media organisations, that is companies in the media industry that organise the production, distribution and consumption of information. On the other hand, it has to do with the management of media in companies in general. It is therefore about the organisation, command and control of media workers and the resources that exist in media companies and media departments. Media management is not only a job title in business, but also the name of a field of analysis that deals with the analysis of media management.

Finding 3: The Political Economy of Media Management

The analysis of media management, media work and media organisations can only operate adequately if they are considered as parts of the Political Economy of Media and Communication so that media management, media work and media organisations are analysed in the context of society as a totality, its structures, dynamics, contradictions, practices, power relations, and struggles.

Finding 4: Taylorist Management

Taylorism is a management method that attempts to increase productivity by analysing and reorganising the labour process. The speed of production is thereby to be increased.

Finding 5: Post-Fordist Management

Post-Fordist management methods have emerged in the wake of the advent of a flexible accumulation regime. They focus on activation and the integration of the whole worker, including his/her emotions and free time, into the labour process. Such methods work with the separation of workplace and home, labour time and free time, labour and fun (playbour: play and labour), production and consumption, etc.

Finding 6: The Management of Cultural Work

All work is creative because it produces something new and is based on a dialectic of mind and body and on the mental anticipation and planning of the product. However, a distinction can be made between primarily mental and primarily physical work.

Cultural work is the creation of ideas. It is also called mental work, knowledge work, intellectual work or information labour. The attempt to manage cultural work, including media work, and to subsume it under capital and the commodity form is a destructive force that inhibits and tends to destroy the innovative power of cultural activity and creates alienation.

Notes

1 Daft also gives a definition of management that admits that it is a process that is about control, instrumentality and hierarchy: "Management is defined as the attainment of organizational goals in an effective and efficient manner through planning, organizing, leading, and controlling organizational resources" (Daft 2022, 7).
2 Translated from German.
3 Translated from German.
4 Translated from German.
5 Translated from German.

References

Alvesson, Mats and Hugh Willmott. 1996. *Making Sense of Management. A Critical Introduction*. London: Sage.
Amin, Ash, ed. 1994. *Post-Fordism. A Reader*. Oxford: Blackwell.
Artero, Juan Pablo and Jean Luis Manfredi. 2016. Competencies of Media Managers: Are They Special? In *Managing Media Firms and Industries: What's So Special about Media Management?* edited by Gregory Ferrell Lowe and Charles Brown, 43–60. Cham: Springer.
Bilton, Chris. 2011. The Management of Creative Industries: From Content to Context. In *Managing Media Work*, edited by Mark Deuze, 31–42. Thousand Oaks, CA: SAGE.
Bilton, Chris and Stephen Cummings. 2014. A Framework for Creative Management and Managing Creativity. In *Handbook of Management and Creativity*, edited by Chris Bilton and Stephen Cummings, 1–12. Cheltenham: Edward Elgar.
Boddy, David. 2017. *Management: An Introduction*. Harlow. Pearson Education. Seventh edition.

Boltanski, Luc and Ève Chiapello. 2005. *The New Spirit of Capitalism*. London: Verso.

Braverman, Harry. 1974. *Labor and Monopoly Capital. The Degradation of Work in the Twentieth Century*. New York: Monthly Review Press.

Brown, Charles. 2016. Media Management: A Critical Discipline? In *Managing Media Firms and Industries: What's So Special about Media Management?* edited by Gregory Ferrell Lowe and Charles Brown, 83–100. Cham: Springer.

Daft, Richard L. 2022. *Management*. Boston, MA: Cengage. 14. Auflage.

Deuze, Mark and Brian Steward. 2011. Managing Media Work. In *Managing Media Work*, edited by Mark Deuze, 1–10. Thousand Oaks, CA: SAGE.

Dwyer, Paul. 2016. Managing Creativity in Media Organisations. In *Managing Media Firms and Industries: What's So Special about Media Management?* edited by Gregory Ferrell Lowe and Charles Brown, 343–365. Cham: Springer.

Edwards, Jim. 2016. Google Employees Confess all the Things They Hated Most about Working at Google. *Business Insider*, 12 December 2016. https://www.businessinsider.com/google-employees-worst-things-about-working-at-google-2016-12

Fayol, Henri. 1916/1949. *General and Industrial Management*. London: Sir Isaac Pitman & Sons.

Florida, Richard. 2012. *The Rise of the Creative Class, Revisited*. New York: Basic Books. Updated edition.

Fuchs, Christian. 2021a. *Social Media. A Critical Introduction*. London: SAGE. Third edition.

Fuchs, Christian. 2021b. *Soziale Medien und Kritische Theorie. Eine Einführung*. München: UVK/utb. Second German edition (Translation of the third English edition).

Fuchs, Christian. 2014. *Social Media. A Critical Introduction*. London: SAGE. First edition.

Gauntlett, David. 2011. *Making Is Connecting. The Social Meaning of Creativity, from DIY and Knitting to YouTube and Web 2.0*. Cambridge: Polity.

Grey, Chris. 2021. *A Very Short, Fairly Interesting and Reasonably Cheap Book about Studying Organizations*. Los Angeles, CA: SAGE. Fifth edition.

Harvey, David. 1990. *The Condition of Postmodernity*. Cambridge, MA: Blackwell.

Hendry, John. 2013. *Management: A Very Short Introduction*. Oxford: Oxford University Press.

Hesmondhalgh, David and Sarah Baker. 2011. *Creative Labor. Media Work in Three Cultural Industries*. London: Routledge.

Jessop, Bob. 1992. Fordism and post-Fordism: A Critical Reformulation. In *Pathways to Industrialization and Regional Development*, edited by Michael Storper and Allen J. Scott, 42–62. London: Routledge.

Kinicki, Angelo and Denise Breaux Soignet. 2022. *Management: A Practical Introduction*. New York: McGraw Hill. Tenth edition.

Klikauer, Thomas. 2015. What Is Managerialism? *Critical Sociology* 41 (7–8): 1103–1119.

Koul, Parul and Chewy Shaw. 2021. We Built Google. This Is Not the Company We Want to Work for. *The New York Times*, 4 January 2021. https://www.nytimes.com/2021/01/04/opinion/google-union.html

Lipietz, Alain. 2001. The Fortunes and Misfortunes of post-Fordism. In *Phases of Capitalist Development*, edited by Robert Albritton et al. 17–36. Basingstoke: Palgrave Macmillan.

Lipietz, Alain. 1987. *Mirages and Miracles. The Crises of Global Fordism*. London: Verso.

Marx, Karl. 1894. *Capital Volume III*. London: Penguin.

Marx, Karl. 1867. *Capital Volume I*. London: Penguin.

Marx, Karl. 1864. Inaugural Address of the Working Men's International Association. In *Marx & Engels Collected Works (MECW) Volume 20*, 5–13. London:
Lawrence & Wishart.

Marx, Karl. 1861–1863. *Economic Manuscript of 1861–63 (Continuation)*. *Marx
& Engels Collected Works (MECW) Volume 32*. London: Lawrence & Wishart.

Marx, Karl. 1844. Economic and Philosophic Manuscripts of 1844. In *Marx & Engels Collected Works (MECW) Volume 3*, 229–346. London: Lawrence & Wishart.

Marx, Karl and Friedrich Engels. 1845/1846. The German Ideology. In *Marx & Engels Collected Works (MECW) Volume 5*, 19–539. London: Lawrence & Wishart.

Mierzejewska, Bozena I. 2011. Media Management in Theory and Practice. In *Managing Media Work*, edited by Mark Deuze, 13–30. Thousand Oaks, CA: SAGE.

Scholz, Christian. 2006. Medienmanagement – Herausforderungen, Notwendigkeit
und ein Bezugsrahmen. In *Handbuch Medienmanagement*, edited by Christian
Scholz, 11–71. Berlin: Springer.

Sennett, Richard. 2008. *The Craftsman*. New Haven, CT: Yale University Press.

Sohn-Rethel, Alfred. 1978. *Intellectual and Manual Labour: A Critique of Epistemology*. London: Macmillan.

Students & Scholars against Corporate Misbehaviour (SACOM). 2010. *Workers as
Machines. Military Management in Foxconn*. https://www.somo.nl/wp-content/up-
loads/2010/08/military-management-in-Foxconn.pdf, accessed on 8 December 2022).

Taylor, Frederick Winslow. 1911/1919. *The Principles of Scientific Management*.
New York: Harper & Brothers.

von Rimscha, Bjørn and Gabriele Siegert. 2015. *Medienökonomie. Eine problemori-
entierte Einführung*. Wiesbaden: Springer VS.

Williams, Raymond. 1983. *Keywords. A Vocabulary of Culture and Society*. New
York: Oxford University Press.

Wirtz, Bernd W. 2020. *Media Management. Strategy, Business Models and Case Studies*. Cham: Springer. Second edition.

Wright, Erik Olin. 2000. *Class Counts*. Cambridge: Cambridge University Press.
Student edition.

Recommended Readings and Exercises

Readings

The following texts are recommended as accompanying readings to this chapter:

Raymond Williams. 1983. Management. In *Keywords. A Vocabulary of Culture and Society*, 139–141. New York: Oxford University Press.

Bob Jessop. 1992. Fordism and post-Fordism: A Critical Reformulation. In
Pathways to Industrialization and Regional Development, edited by Michael
Storper and Allen J. Scott, 42–62. London: Routledge.

Christian Fuchs. 2021. *Social Media. A Critical Introduction*. London:
SAGE. Third edition.
Chapter 5: Google: Good or Evil Search Engine? (pp. 109–137).

Luc Boltanski, Luc and Ève Chiapello. 2005. *The New Spirit of Capitalism.* London: Verso.
Chapter 1: Management Discourse in the 1990s (pp. 57–101).

Thomas Klikauer. 2015. What Is Managerialism? *Critical Sociology* 41 (7–8): 1103–1119.

Exercise 14.1   Taylorist-Fordist Labour Organisation

Watch the first scene in Charlie Chaplin's film *Modern Times* about the introduction of a food machine in a factory where people work on an assembly line. The idea is to semi-automate and speed up the lunch break and the meals in order to replace free time with labour time.

Charles Chaplin (director). 1936. *Modern Times.* United Artists. Film information: https://www.imdb.com/title/tt0027977/

Scene 1: Start: 00:00, End: 13:00

Discuss the following questions:

How do you assess Chaplin's film?

How do you assess the Taylorist way of management?

Are there aspects of Taylorism in the media, cultural and creative industries today?

What does the organisation of labour time look like in today's companies?

What forms of management do we need today? Why?

Exercise 14.2   The Post-Fordist Organisation of Labour at Google

Watch the following videos about work organisation at Google:

Life at Google (https://www.youtube.com/@LifeatGoogle): What's It like to Work at Google?
https://www.youtube.com/watch?v=n_Cn8eFo7u8

Life at Google (https://www.youtube.com/@LifeatGoogle): A Look inside Google's Culture
https://www.youtube.com/watch?v=1snG8ZmLOWE

Discuss:

What are the advantages and disadvantages of working (working conditions and workplace) at Google?

Exercise 14.3   Dissatisfaction and Unionisation at Google

Working at Google is not all fun. The long working hours and Google's political problems, such as its involvement in military projects, are perceived by employees as forms of alienation, against which resistance such as strikes and union organising has also arisen.

First read the following two articles and then watch the video.

Jim Edwards. 2016. Google Employees Confess all the Things They Hated Most about Working at Google. *Business Insider*, 12 December 2016. https://www.businessinsider.com/google-employees-worst-things-about-working-at-google-2016-12

Parul Koul und Chewy Shaw. 2021. We Built Google. This Is Not the Company We Want to Work for. *The New York Times*, 4 January 2021. https://www.nytimes.com/2021/01/04/opinion/google-union.html

Left Nite: Alex Gorowa. Interview mit Alex Gorowara, Sprecher der Alphabet Workers Union, einer Gewerkschaft von Google-Arbeiter:inne:n https://www.youtube.com/watch?v=Dwr3-rkgirI

Discuss:

How do you assess the management methods at Google?

Why did workers at Google form a trade union?

What do an ideal workplace and ideal company look like?

How can bad working conditions be avoided?

How should workers react to bad working conditions?

Index

Note: **Bold** page numbers refer to tables and *italic* page numbers refer to figures.

Chakravartty, Paula 111
Chaplin, Charlie 426
Chiapello, Ève 433–435
China/Chinese 256; construction
industry 253; Cybersecurity Law
322; export of capital 257; external
debt of low- and middle-income
countries to 254; foreign platforms
322; international creditor 254;
international development strategy
253; Internet surveillance in 322–323;
labor law 319; migrant workers 257;
political-economic activities 253;
social credit system 323; "soft power"
strategy 253
China Film Group Corporation 252
Chomsky, Noam 403; *Manufacturing
Consent. The Political Economy of
the Mass Media* 204–206
citizen media 389, 391
civil: servants 418; society 324, 376, 394
Clapp, Jennifer 38
Clarke, John 266
class 273–275; antagonism 29; relations
72, 89–90, 346; scheme 275,
275; societies 371, 415; structure/
structuration 72, 275, 275, 374;
struggles 89–90
classical: advertising 309–313;
economics 30; industrial capitalism
351
Classical Political Economy 22–25, 28
Club 2.0 407, *408*
cognition 354, 367, 368, 378
cognitive capitalism 342, 350–354;
analysis of 353; in society of
singularities 350–353
collective/collection: consumption
190; decision-making 10; labour
315, 320–321; ownership of
enterprises 422
The Coming of Post-Industrial Society
(Daniel Bell) 334, 342
commercial/commercialisation
229; activities 397; advertising/
advertisements 181, 183;
broadcasting 393; capital 178; media
63–64, 144, 195; services 397;
of telecommunications 229–230;
television 187, 189–190, 195
commodities/commodification 15, 16,
71, 84, 177, 337, 346, 350, 372, 374;
analysis 16; capital 175; circulation,
function of 70; culture 190, 191;

fetishism 203–204, 313; form of 313;
of labour 71; mass consumption and
production of 179; mass-produced
180; production 314; value 84
communication 64, 111, 367; analysis
of 72; approaches 67–69; capitalism
118, 342, 354, 356, 359; in
capitalist society 48, 369; channels
368; in China 258; critical moral
philosophy of 65; definitions of
61–67; description of 103; dimensions
of 75–83; economy 77, 81; industry
180; interaction of 65; and mass
media 378; means of 294; policies
378; principles of 70–71; process
48, 65; and production 10; services
142; studies 49, 111; systems 65;
technologies 72; work and means
of 48
concentration: capitalism 246;
journalistic 152; media *see* media
concentration; strategies of 135–136
conglomeration 136–137, 157
constant capital 75, 77, 84, 85, 225, 297
consumer: advocacy groups 207–208;
associations among 181–182;
goods 175; labour 312; movements
207–208; oriented capitalism
180; rights 208; society 433;
surveillance 149
consumer culture 70, 75, 141, 178–179,
188, 189, 427; development of 189;
globalisation of 141
consumption-oriented theory 146
contemporary capitalism 114, 118, 207,
337, 351, 354
contemporary society 268, 343, 346;
global 350; primary process in 351;
problems of 336; productive forces
in 345
content analysis 193; of television
programming **194**; type A
programming 194; type B
programming 194–195
convergence 49, 87, 281, 378, 402
co-operation 32, 50, 75, 112, 177,
245, 290–291, 367–368, 380, 416, 432
coronavirus crisis 292–295, *293*, 295
corporate media 148, 150, 201, 380, 403
corporate watchdogs 210, 212
corporations 208, **245**
COVID-19 241, 252, 291, 319;
digitalisation of labour 299; empirical
studies 296–299; home office in **296**;

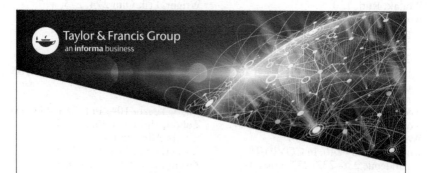